WEATHER DERIVATIVE VALUATION

Weather Derivative Valuation is the first book to cover all the meteorological, statistical, financial and mathematical issues that arise in the pricing and risk management of weather derivatives. There are chapters on meteorological data and data cleaning, the modelling and pricing of single weather derivatives, the modelling and valuation of portfolios, the use of weather and seasonal forecasts in the pricing of weather derivatives, arbitrage pricing for weather derivatives, risk management, and the modelling of temperature, wind and precipitation. Specific issues covered in detail include the analysis of uncertainty in weather derivative pricing, time series modelling of daily temperatures, the creation and use of probabilistic meteorological forecasts and the derivation of the weather derivative version of the Black–Scholes equation of mathematical finance. Written by consultants who work within the weather derivative industry, this book is packed with practical information and theoretical insight into the world of weather derivative pricing.

STEPHEN JEWSON works for a financial consultancy, where he manages a group that produces commercial software and meteorological data for the weather derivative industry. He has published a large number of articles in the fields of fundamental climate research, applied meteorology and weather derivatives.

ANDERS BRIX works for a financial software and consultancy company, where he runs a group with responsibility for researching and implementing stochastic models for natural catastrophes and weather risk. He has carried out research in probability and statistics, and has applied statistical modelling to a wide variety of fields including weather, insurance, weed science and medical research.

WEATHER DERIVATIVE VALUATION

The Meteorological, Statistical, Financial and Mathematical Foundations

STEPHEN JEWSON AND ANDERS BRIX

with contributions from Christine Ziehmann

CAMBRIDGE
UNIVERSITY PRESS

CAMBRIDGE UNIVERSITY PRESS
Cambridge, New York, Melbourne, Madrid, Cape Town, Singapore,
São Paulo, Delhi, Dubai, Tokyo

Cambridge University Press
The Edinburgh Building, Cambridge CB2 8RU, UK

Published in the United States of America by Cambridge University Press, New York

www.cambridge.org
Information on this title: www.cambridge.org/9780521142281

First published 2005
Reprinted 2007
This digitally printed version 2010

A catalogue record for this publication is available from the British Library

Library of Congress Cataloguing in Publication data

Weather derivative valuation: the meteorological, statistical, financial and mathematical
foundations / Stephen Jewson and Anders Brix, with contributions from Christine Ziehmann.
p.   cm.
Includes bibliographical references and index.
ISBN 0 521 84371 5 (hb : alk. paper)
1. Weather derivatives – Valuation   I. Brix, Anders.   II. Title.

HG6052.J49 2005
332.64'57 – dc22   2004054200

ISBN 978-0-521-84371-3 Hardback
ISBN 978-0-521-14228-1 Paperback

Contents

Figures

List of figures

Tables

Acknowledgements

There are many people to whom we are grateful for interesting discussions on topics related to weather derivatives pricing. In particular we would like to thank Ali al Ali, Andre de Vries, Anlong Li, Anna Maria Velioti, Arnaud Remy, Auguste Boissonnade, Barney Schauble, Bill Gebhardt, Cat Woolgar, Chris Michael, Claudio Baraldi, Dario Villani, Dave Pethick, Dave Whitehead, David Chen, Dorje Brody, Ed Kim, Fabien Dornier, Gearoid Lane, Guillaume Legal, James Dolby, Jas Badyal, Jay Ganz, Jeff Hamlin, Jeremy Penzer, Jeff Porter, Jerome Brochard, Joe Hrgovcic, Jo Syroka, Juerg Trueb, Lenny Smith, Lin Zhang, Marc Hannebert, Mark Lenssen, Mark Roulston, Martin Jones, Martin Malinow, Mark Nichols, Mark Tawney, Mihail Zervos, Neil Hohmann, Nick Ward, Olivier Luc, Pascal Mailier, Paul Vandermarck, Peter Brewer, Philipp Schönbucher, Richard Dixon, Rick Knabb, Rodrigo Caballero, Ross McIntyre, Sandeep Ramachandran, Sarah Lauridsen, Scott Lupien, Seth Padowitz, Sharad Agnihotri, Simon Mason, Stuart Jones, Tony Barnston and Vivek Kumar.

In addition we would like to thank the people who created and made available the various bits of free software that we have used (Tex, Latex and Miktek, Cygwin, Emacs, Ferret, OpenOffice and R), and to thank Earth Satellite Corporation for providing the data used to create some of the graphics.

Finally Stephen Jewson would like to thank Rie and Lynne for their patience and encouragement, without which it would not have been possible to write this book, and Anders Brix would like to thank Sarah for her support and patience throughout the project.

The authors' revenues from sales of this book will all be donated to Centrepoint, a charity for homeless and socially excluded young people in the United Kingdom (see http://www.centrepoint.org.uk).

1

Weather derivatives and the weather derivatives market

1.1 Introduction

This book is about the valuation of a certain class of financial contracts known as weather derivatives. The purpose of weather derivatives is to allow businesses and other organisations to insure themselves against fluctuations in the weather. For example, they allow natural gas companies to avoid the negative impact of a mild winter when no one turns on the heating, they allow construction companies to avoid the losses due to a period of rain when construction workers cannot work outside and they allow ski resorts to make up for the money they lose when there is no snow.

The weather derivatives market, in which contracts that provide this kind of insurance are traded, first appeared in the US energy industry in 1996 and 1997. Companies accustomed to trading contracts based on electricity and gas prices in order to hedge their electricity and gas price risk realised they could trade contracts based on the weather and hedge their weather risk in the same way. The market grew rapidly and soon expanded to other industries and to Europe and Japan. Volatility in the financial markets has meant that not all of the original participants are still trading, but the weather derivatives market has steadily grown and there are now a number of energy companies, insurance companies, reinsurance companies, banks and hedge funds that have groups dedicated purely to the business of buying and selling weather derivatives. The Weather Risk Management Association (WRMA), the industry body that represents the weather market, recently reported a total notional value of over $10 billion for weather derivative trades in the year 2002/2003.[1]

During the eight years since the first weather derivative trades took place the 'science' of weather derivative pricing has gradually developed. It now

---

[1] See http://wrma.org.

seems possible, and – hopefully – useful, to bring this information together
into one place, both for the benefit of those already involved in the market as
a point of reference and for those outside the market who are interested to
learn what weather derivative pricing is all about. Other than this chapter, which contains introductory material about weather derivatives and
the weather derivative market, the book focuses on the meteorological, statistical, mathematical and financial issues that determine the methods used
for the pricing, valuation and risk management of weather derivatives contracts and portfolios. We attempt to describe all the methods and models
currently in use in the weather market and give examples of how they can be
applied in practice. We cannot cover everything, however. There are many
ways of approaching the question of how to price a weather derivative, there
are strong financial incentives to invent (and keep secret!) new and more
accurate methods for such pricing, and there is undoubtedly much progress
still to be made.

The overall level of this book is such that a technical graduate with a
reasonable understanding of mathematics should be able to follow almost all
of it, and no particular background in meteorology, statistics, mathematics
or finance is required. We hope that, if you read this book, you will learn
something of each of these subjects.

This chapter proceeds with a brief introduction to the weather derivatives
market, a description of the various weather indices used by the market, a
description of how these weather indices are related to the pay-offs of weather
derivative contracts, and an overview of the methods used for the valuation
of weather contracts.

1.1.1 The impact of weather on business and the rationale for hedging

The types of impact of weather on businesses range from small reductions
in revenues, as might occur when a shop attracts fewer customers on a
rainy day, to total disaster, such as when a tornado destroys a factory. Tor-
nadoes are an example of what we will call *catastrophic* weather events.
Such weather events also include severe tropical cyclones, extra-tropical wind
storms, hail storms, ice storms and rain storms. They often cause extreme
damage to property and loss of life. Companies wishing to protect themselves against the financial impact of such disasters can buy insurance that
will pay them according to the losses they sustain. Weather derivatives,
however, are designed to help companies insure themselves against *non-
catastrophic* weather events. Non-catastrophic weather fluctuations include

warm or cold periods, rainy or dry periods, windy or calm periods, and so on. They are expected to occur reasonably frequently. Nevertheless, they can cause significant discomfort for (or bring significant benefits to) businesses with profits that depend in a sensitive way on the weather. Hedging with weather derivatives is desirable for such businesses because it significantly reduces the year-to-year volatility of their profits. This is beneficial for a number of reasons, including:

- low volatility in profits can often reduce the interest rate at which companies borrow money;
- in a publicly traded company low volatility in profits usually translates into low volatility in the share price, and less volatile shares are valued more highly;
- low volatility in profits reduces the risk of bankruptcy.

Although a company hedging its weather risk using weather derivatives will typically lose money, on average, on the hedge, it can still be very beneficial to hedge for these reasons.

Governmental and non-profit use of weather derivatives

Weather derivatives can also be used by non-business entities, such as local and national government organisations and charities. In these cases it would typically be weather-induced fluctuations in costs that would be hedged. Such hedging can reduce the variability of costs from season to season or year to year, and hence reduce the risk of unexpected budget overruns.

1.1.2 Examples of weather hedging

Weather variability affects different entities in different ways. In many businesses weather is related to the volume of sales transacted. Examples of this would include:

- a natural gas supply company, which would sell less gas in a warm winter;
- a ski resort, which would attract fewer skiers when there is little snow;
- a clothes retailing company, which would sell fewer clothes in a cold summer;
- an amusement park, which would attract fewer visitors when it rains.

But weather can also affect profits in ways other than through changes in the volume of sales. Examples include:

- a construction company, which experiences delays when it is cold or raining because labourers cannot work outside;
- a hydroelectric power generation company, which generates less electricity when rainfall is reduced;

- a vehicle breakdown rescue company, which has increased costs on icy days, when more traffic accidents occur;
- a fish farm, where fish grow less quickly when the sea temperature is lower.

All these risks could be hedged using weather derivatives.

1.1.3 The definition of a weather derivative

A standard weather derivative contract, as might be used to hedge the risks described above, is defined by the following attributes:

- the contract period: a start date and an end date;
- a measurement station;
- a weather variable, measured at the measurement station, over the contract period;
- an index, which aggregates the weather variable over the contract period in some way;
- a pay-off function, which converts the index into the cashflow that settles the derivative shortly after the end of the contract period;
- for some kinds of contract, a premium paid from the buyer to the seller at the start of the contract.

These basic attributes are supplemented by:

- a measurement agency, responsible for measuring the weather variable;
- a settlement agent, responsible for producing the final values of the index on the basis of the measured values; according to defined algorithms that (hopefully) cope with all eventualities, such as a failure of the measuring equipment;
- a back-up station, to be used in case the main station fails;
- a time period over which the settlement takes place.

It is not the purpose of this book to describe the legal and administrative aspects of weather derivatives, although these are, clearly, of vital importance for companies trading these contracts. Rather, we intend to investigate the methods that can be used to set reasonable prices for and assess the value of the various types of contracts available in the market today.

1.1.4 Insurance and derivatives

Weather derivatives have a pay-off that depends on a weather index that has been carefully chosen to represent the weather conditions against which protection is being sought. The economic effect of hedging using weather derivatives can also be achieved using an *insurance* contract that has a pay-off based on a weather index. Nevertheless, we will use the phrase weather *derivatives* throughout this book, although all the analysis presented applies equally well to both types of contract.

There are some differences between weather derivatives and index-based weather insurance that may mean that one is preferable to the other in certain circumstances. Some companies may not be happy with the idea of trading derivatives but comfortable with buying insurance, for instance.

Other ways in which insurance and derivatives differ include the following:

- it may be necessary to perform a frequent (daily, weekly or monthly) revaluation of derivative positions, known as mark to market or mark to model, but this is usually not necessary for insurance;
- tax liabilities may be different (most commonly, insurance incurs a tax but derivatives do not);
- the accounting treatment may be different;
- contractual details may be different.

All of these vary to a certain extent from country to country.

Indemnity-based weather insurance

There is also a kind of weather insurance in which the pay-off is related to financial loss rather than to a weather index. Such contracts are less suitable for the hedging of weather-related fluctuations in profits, because a lack of profit cannot necessarily be classified as a weather-induced loss. The modelling and pricing of these contracts are rather more complicated than those of weather derivatives, since they involve understanding the relationships between weather and loss, and the likelihood that the insured entity will make a claim. Such pricing is more akin to the pricing of catastrophe-related weather insurance (Woo, 1999) and is not covered in this book, although the analysis we present does form a good first step towards the pricing of such contracts in some cases.

1.1.5 Liquidity and basis risk

Because the pay-off of a weather derivative depends on a weather index, not on the actual amount of money lost due to weather, it is unlikely that the pay-off will compensate exactly for the money lost. The potential for such a difference is known as *basis risk*. In general, basis risk is smallest when the financial loss is highly correlated with the weather, and when contracts of the optimum size and structure, based on the optimum location, are used for hedging.

For a company deciding how to hedge its risk there is often a trade-off between basis risk and the price of the weather hedge. Weather contracts on standard indices on London, Chicago and New York temperatures are traded frequently, and consequently it is usually easy to trade such contracts at a good price. However, except in lucky cases, it is unlikely that such contracts will minimise basis risk for the hedging company. Hedgers then have a choice between, on the one hand, getting the best price but trading a contract that may not hedge their business particularly well and, on the other hand, hedging their business as well as possible but not necessarily getting such a good price.

1.1.6 Hedgers and speculators, primary and secondary markets

Every weather derivative is a transaction between two parties. We will classify all such parties as being either *hedgers*, who have weather risk they want to reduce or eliminate, or *speculators*, who are making a business by writing weather contracts. This separation of all traders of weather derivatives into hedgers and speculators is useful, but is also a simplification of reality. For instance, many hedgers also trade speculatively, partly in order to ensure that they understand the market before they buy a hedge, partly to disguise their hedging intentions to other traders and partly just to try and make money. Similarly, speculators may become hedgers if they decide that their speculative trading has led them to a position where they hold too much risk.

Transactions between hedgers and speculators are referred to as the primary market, while transactions between speculators and other speculators are known as the secondary market. The speculators trade contracts with each other either because they want to reduce the weather risk they have that arises from holding previously traded weather derivatives (in which case, they are also becoming hedgers), or simply because they think they can make money by doing so.

Very occasionally contracts are exchanged directly between two hedgers, who, by doing so, can hedge each other's risks simultaneously. However, this is extremely uncommon, since it is rare for two companies to have exactly equal and opposite weather risks.

From the point of view of the speculator, who may be a bank, insurance company, reinsurance company, energy company or hedge fund, trading weather derivatives forms an attractive proposition for two reasons. First, weather derivative pay-offs are generally uncorrelated with other forms of insurance or investment. As a result of this an insurance company can issue weather derivatives cheaply relative to other forms of insurance because the overall company risk will increase less. Similarly, a hedge fund can invest in weather derivatives knowing that their return is uncorrelated with the return on the other financial assets it may hold, such as equities and bonds.

Second, a portfolio of weather derivatives can, in itself, be very low risk because of the potentially offsetting nature of weather contracts. An ideal weather market would be driven by businesses that are, in aggregate, seeking to hedge against equal and opposite amounts of each weather risk. In principle this could lead to a situation in which the speculators hold very little risk because they would simply be middlemen passing weather risk from one hedger to another. The risk would be exchanged almost at cost price, with little or no risk premium.

1.1.7 Over-the-counter and exchange trading

There are a number of ways in which a weather derivative trade can take place. Primary market trades are usually 'over the counter' (OTC), meaning that they are traded privately between the two counterparties. Much of the secondary market is traded through voice-brokers, who act as intermediaries and cajole participants in the market to do deals, but do not actually trade themselves. These trades are also described as OTC. Finally, a growing part of the secondary market is traded on the Chicago Mercantile Exchange (CME), which currently lists weather derivatives for fifteen US, five European and two Japanese locations based on temperatures for each month of the year. The CME plays the dual roles of bringing transparency (the prices are freely available on the Internet) and eliminating credit risk (since you trade with the CME rather than with the other counterparty, and make margin payments on a daily basis).

Secondary trading and the Pareto optimum

Trading between speculators in the secondary market may, at first look, appear to be a zero-sum game, and have little net economic benefit. This may be the case with certain trades, but is not the case in general. A secondary market trade can quite conceivably reduce the risk of both parties to the trade, or at least reduce the total risk held by the two parties (i.e. the risk decrease on one side is greater than the risk increase on the other). And the lower the risk held by parties in the secondary market, the lower the premiums that can be charged to hedgers. In this way, it is in both hedgers' and speculators' interest for secondary trading to occur until an optimum situation has been achieved in which the total risk held by the players in

the secondary market is the least. Reaching such a situation may take many
secondary market trades, even in a market with only a few players, and this
is reflected in the fact that there are typically many more secondary market
trades than primary market trades.

Mathematical models of this idea have been studied by economists. When
considered in terms of economic utility, secondary market trading is certainly
not a zero-sum game, and one can idealise secondary trading as moving
the entire market towards the situation where the total expected utility
of the participants is the greatest possible. This is known as the Pareto
optimum.

1.1.8 Hedging and forecasts

At this point the reader may be wondering about the relationship between
the hedging of weather risk and the use of weather forecasts. Meteorological forecasts contain information about the weather a few days in advance
(in the case of weather forecasts) or a few months in advance (in the case
of seasonal forecasts). For certain business decisions, especially those on
timescales of a few days, such forecasts can be very useful. The appropriate
use of forecasts can both increase the expected profits *and* reduce the risk of
making a loss, while weather derivatives, in most cases, only reduce the risk
of making a loss. However, a company making plans for the month, quarter
or year ahead cannot make much use of forecasts. Weather derivatives, on
the other hand, are ideally suited to all periods in the future. Meteorological
forecasts and weather derivatives are thus perfect complements: what can
be predicted with accuracy should be, and action should be taken on the
basis of such predictions. Everything else can be hedged.

There are also two ways in which weather derivatives can be used to
enhance the usefulness of weather forecasts. One is that a forecast can be
used to determine the best course of action, and a weather derivative can
hedge against the possibility that the forecast is wrong. The derivative would
pay out according to the size, and possibly direction, of the forecast error.
For example, consider a supermarket that buys certain perishable fruits and
vegetables on short notice according to the weather forecast. If the forecast
is wrong and the supermarket sells less than predicted it will lose revenue
relative to the situation in which the forecast is correct. This revenue at
risk could be hedged using a weather derivative that pays according to the
forecast error.

The other way that weather derivatives can be used to enhance forecasts is
that a forecast can be used to determine the course of action, and a weather

derivative can hedge against the occurrence of forecasts that lead to a high cost being incurred. An example of this might be an oil platform in the Gulf of Mexico that evacuates staff when there is a hurricane forecast. A weather derivative could be structured to cover the cost of such an evacuation. Interestingly, in this case the actual weather does not influence the pay-out of the contract, only the forecast.

A final aspect of the relationship between meteorological forecasts and weather derivatives is that forecasts play a major role in the valuation of weather derivatives in certain circumstances. This is addressed in detail in chapter 10.

1.1.9 Hedging weather and price

The situation often arises that a company is exposed to both weather and the price of some commodity in a connected way. Consider a company that has to buy more natural gas when it is cold. If the gas is being bought at a fixed price, then this purchase involves only weather risk. The total cost of the gas bought is given by

$$\text{cost} = P_0 V \tag{1.1}$$

where P_0 is the fixed price and V is the weather-dependent amount of gas.

But if the gas is being bought at a varying price then the company is exposed not only to the weather but also to fluctuations in that price. The total cost is now given by

$$\text{cost} = PV \tag{1.2}$$

where P also varies. One can say that the level of weather risk depends on the gas price, or that the level of gas price risk depends on the weather. In some cases the variability of the weather and the gas price may be independent, which simplifies the analysis of these situations. However, often the changes in the gas price are partly affected by the weather as well (since cold weather increases demand for gas, which in turn increases the price). Hedging combined weather and price risk is more complex than hedging straightforward weather risk or price risk alone, and ideally involves contracts that depend on both the weather and the price. Only a few contracts of this type have been traded to date. The pricing of such contracts is discussed briefly in chapter 11.

1.2 Weather variables and indices

As we have seen, weather affects different entities in different ways. In order to hedge these different types of risk, weather derivatives are based on a variety of different weather variables and can also be structured to depend on more than one weather variable. The most commonly used weather variable is the temperature, as either hourly values, daily minima or maxima, or daily averages. Of these, daily average is the most frequently seen. In most countries daily average is defined by convention as the midpoint of the daily minimum and maximum. However, in some countries daily average is defined as a weighted average of more than two values of temperature per day. Definitions based on three, twelve, twenty-four or more values per day are all in use. The exact time period over which the minimum and maximum temperature are measured, and exactly how minimum and maximum are defined, also vary from country to country. To participate in the weather market one has to do thorough research into the weather measurement conventions in use in each country in which one operates.

As an example of minimum and maximum temperature values, figure 1.1 shows daily minimum, maximum and average temperatures measured at London's Heathrow Airport for the year 2000.

In addition to temperature, wind and precipitation measurements are also used as the weather variables underlying weather derivatives. Wind-based hedges are, for instance, of interest to wind farms, which want protection

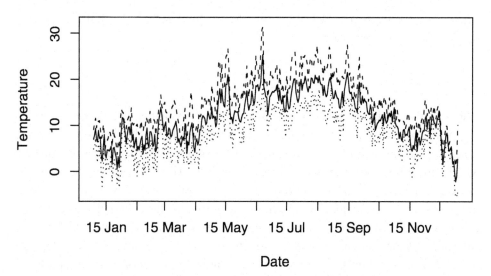

Figure 1.1. Daily minimum (dotted line), maximum (dashed line) and average (solid line) temperatures for London Heathrow, 2000.

against lack of wind, and construction companies, which may have to stop work in high winds. They can also be used to replace more traditional property insurance contracts, which cover building damage due to extreme winds. Rain-based hedges are used by the agricultural and hydropower generation industries, among others. Snow-based hedges are important for ski resorts, local councils that need to clear snow from roads, and companies that sell equipment related to snow, such as winter sports gear or snow tyres for cars.

Hedges based on other weather variables, such as the number of sunshine hours, streamflow or sea surface temperature, are also possible. All that is required is a source of reliable and accurate measurements and it is possible for a derivative structure to be created.

The exact relationship between the relevant weather variable and the impact on the business that needs a hedge will be different for different variables and different companies, and particular hedges are structured using an index that has been designed to capture the relevant dependence as well as possible. The indices most commonly in use for temperature-based contracts are degree day indices, average temperature indices, cumulative average temperature indices and event indices. These are discussed below. Indices based on other variables are discussed in chapter 13.

1.2.1 Degree day indices

Degree day (DD) indices originated in the energy industry, and are designed to correlate well with the domestic demand for heating and cooling.

Heating degree days

In winter, heating degree days (HDDs) are used to measure the demand for heating, and are thus a measure of how cold it is (the colder it is, the more HDDs there are). There are a number of different definitions of HDDs used in the energy industry, reflecting the fact that patterns of energy usage vary from location to location and that there is a trade-off between the simplicity of the definition and how well it represents the demand. The definition used in the weather market is that the number of HDDs z_i on a particular day i is defined as

$$z_i = max(T_0 - T_i, 0) \tag{1.3}$$
$$= (T_0 - T_i, 0)^+$$

where T_i is the average temperature on day i and T_0 is a baseline temperature.

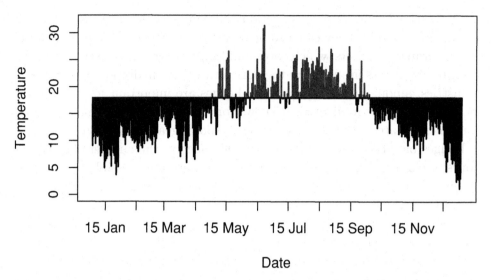

Figure 1.2. Heating and cooling degree days for London Heathrow, 2000.

In the United States, where temperature is measured in Fahrenheit,[2] the baseline is usually taken to be 65°F (18.33°C), while in all other countries, where temperature is measured in Celsius, the baseline is usually taken to be 18°C (64.4°F).

Throughout this book we will assume these definitions for daily HDDs. An HDD index x over an N_d day period is usually defined as the sum of the HDDs over all days during that period:

$$x = \sum_{i=1}^{N_d} z_i \tag{1.4}$$

The HDDs per day for London Heathrow during 2000 are shown by the lengths of the bars extending *below* the horizontal line in figure 1.2. We see large numbers of HDDs in winter, and fewer, or none, in summer.

Many of the locations commonly traded in the weather market are cold enough at certain times of year that the temperature never rises as high as the 18°C/65°F baseline, and hence the number of HDDs per day is always positive. This is the case for London Heathrow in the winter months, as can be seen in figure 1.2. Table 1.1 shows the estimated expected number

---

[2] Degrees Fahrenheit (F) and degrees Celsius (C) are related by the equations $C = 5(F - 32)/9$ and $F = 32 + 9C/5$.

Table 1.1. *Expectations of monthly numbers of days above a baseline,*
estimated using thirty years of data with linear detrending and one year of
extrapolation, at various locations in Europe and Japan (for a baseline of
18°C) and in the United States (for a baseline of 65°F).

Station/ Month	Jan	Feb	Mar	Apr	May	Jun	Jul	Aug	Sep	Oct	Nov	Dec
Amsterdam	0.0	0.0	0.0	0.2	4.4	3.8	11.5	12.1	3.1	0.1	0.0	0.0
Essen	0.0	0.0	0.1	1.0	6.0	7.8	14.9	17.5	3.5	0.8	0.0	0.0
London	0.0	0.0	0.0	0.0	3.6	6.2	17.9	19.7	4.7	0.5	0.0	0.0
Paris	0.0	0.0	0.0	0.4	8.1	13.0	23.2	24.4	6.4	1.3	0.0	0.0
Rome	0.0	0.0	0.2	0.5	16.7	28.9	31.0	31.0	27.4	13.9	2.1	0.0
Stockholm	0.0	0.0	0.0	0.1	1.4	6.9	18.9	15.0	2.6	0.0	0.0	0.0
Atlanta	0.5	0.9	3.4	12.8	25.5	29.2	31.0	31.0	27.3	15.3	2.8	0.7
Chicago	0.0	0.0	0.7	2.1	10.8	23.4	30.8	30.5	18.3	4.4	0.3	0.0
Covington	0.0	0.0	0.8	3.6	13.6	25.5	30.7	30.2	18.4	5.0	0.3	0.2
Houston	4.2	6.7	12.4	22.0	31.0	30.0	31.0	31.0	29.2	24.7	10.1	6.1
New York	0.0	0.0	0.5	1.8	10.9	26.9	30.8	30.7	24.4	7.2	0.6	0.2
Philadelphia	0.0	0.0	0.6	2.9	12.8	27.3	30.9	30.8	22.3	6.0	0.4	0.0
Tokyo	0.0	0.0	0.2	6.2	23.6	27.8	31.0	31.0	29.2	19.9	1.4	0.1

of days per month that the average temperature rises above 18°C/65°F for thirteen commonly traded locations. We see that in several of these locations the temperature never rises above 18°C/65°F during certain months. In particular, in northern Europe and the northern United States it is very unusual to see a daily average temperature above 18°C/65°F during the period from November to March. This means there is a precise relationship between HDD indices and average of average temperature indices during these periods, as we shall see below. Table 1.2 shows the estimated expected number of HDDs per month for these thirteen locations. Highest numbers of HDDs occur during the winter months, as would be expected.

HDDs are used in the United States and Europe but seldom in Japan.

Cooling degree days

Cooling degree days (CDDs) are used in summer to measure the demand for energy used for cooling, and are thus a measure of how hot it is (the hotter it is, the more CDDs there are). Although heating systems can be driven by electricity or gas, cooling is almost invariably driven by electricity, and so CDDs are most relevant to the electricity market (although more and more electricity is being generated from natural gas, and so CDDs are

Table 1.2. *Expectations of monthly sums of daily HDDs, estimated using thirty years of data with linear detrending and one year of extrapolation, at various locations in Europe and Japan (in Celsius degree days) and in the United States (in Fahrenheit degree days).*

Station/Month	Jan	Feb	Mar	Apr	May	Jun	Jul	Aug	Sep	Oct	Nov	Dec
Amsterdam	450.6	375.0	343.0	259.8	145.2	97.2	45.0	36.7	96.7	203.7	333.0	432.6
Essen	473.8	393.1	337.1	243.5	121.1	82.6	34.3	29.9	106.3	206.2	351.0	454.2
London	385.0	327.7	291.3	235.9	130.3	68.0	22.0	19.3	74.6	169.3	292.3	372.5
Paris	419.8	347.2	270.5	217.3	92.0	43.3	13.8	10.4	69.5	156.2	312.7	387.9
Rome	319.8	286.8	220.5	141.4	29.8	1.7	0.1	0.0	3.9	33.2	159.9	291.7
Stockholm	580.8	522.6	487.9	344.8	195.6	75.4	22.0	37.0	151.7	310.4	455.3	571.6
Atlanta	608.6	430.1	335.3	130.5	19.9	2.3	0.0	0.4	9.7	103.6	339.2	573.3
Chicago	1140.5	908.7	789.9	431.5	166.1	34.9	1.2	2.8	61.8	328.8	697.1	1046.7
Covington	1003.1	788.2	695.1	353.8	127.4	19.5	0.4	2.4	66.4	308.5	628.7	941.5
Houston	350.1	236.2	158.6	35.9	0.8	0.0	0.0	0.0	1.5	32.3	174.6	358.7
New York	914.0	780.7	685.9	358.2	124.2	11.4	0.4	1.0	24.9	210.6	499.6	786.3
Philadelphia	918.5	764.0	651.8	330.3	109.3	9.4	0.4	1.2	36.7	237.4	528.6	820.5
Tokyo	346.1	301.4	243.7	91.0	19.1	2.7	0.2	0.0	0.6	18.6	131.2	275.2

also becoming relevant for the gas industry). The number of CDDs z_i on a particular day i is defined as

$$z_i = max(T_i - T_0, 0) \qquad (1.5)$$
$$= (T_i - T_0, 0)^+$$

As for HDDs, a CDD index x over a period is defined as the sum of the CDDs over all days during that period:

$$x = \sum_{i=1}^{N_d} z_i \qquad (1.6)$$

The CDDs per day for London Heathrow during 2000 are shown by the length of the bars extending *above* the horizontal line in figure 1.2. We see that non-zero numbers of CDDs at this location occur only during the warmest months of the year.

Although, as we have seen, several locations never go *above* 18°C/65°F in winter, very few commonly traded locations are warm enough that the temperature never goes *below* 18°C/65°F in summer (i.e. the situation is not symmetrical). To illustrate this, table 1.3 shows the expected number of

Table 1.3. *Expectations of monthly numbers of days below a baseline,*
estimated using thirty years of data with linear detrending and one year of
extrapolation, at various locations in Europe and Japan (for a baseline of
18°C) and in the United States (for a baseline of 65°F).

Station/ Month	Jan	Feb	Mar	Apr	May	Jun	Jul	Aug	Sep	Oct	Nov	Dec
Amsterdam	31.0	28.0	31.0	29.8	26.6	26.4	19.9	19.0	27.2	31.0	30.0	31.0
Essen	31.0	28.0	30.9	29.0	25.2	22.3	16.2	13.7	26.9	30.3	30.0	31.0
London	31.0	28.0	31.0	30.0	27.7	24.1	13.1	11.4	25.4	30.5	30.0	31.0
Paris	31.0	28.0	31.0	29.7	23.0	17.2	8.3	6.8	23.8	29.7	30.0	31.0
Rome	31.0	28.0	30.9	29.6	15.0	1.7	0.2	0.1	3.2	17.3	28.0	31.0
Stockholm	31.0	28.0	31.0	29.9	29.7	23.3	12.0	16.0	27.6	31.0	30.0	31.0
Atlanta	30.7	27.3	27.9	18.6	5.7	1.0	0.0	0.1	3.1	17.1	27.5	30.4
Chicago	31.0	28.0	30.3	28.1	20.6	7.0	0.7	1.3	12.4	27.4	29.9	31.0
Covington	31.0	28.0	30.6	26.8	18.1	4.7	0.5	1.1	12.2	26.4	30.1	30.8
Houston	27.1	21.9	19.3	8.2	0.4	0.0	0.0	0.0	0.7	7.0	20.7	25.1
New York	31.0	28.0	30.5	28.5	21.2	3.8	0.2	0.5	6.4	24.4	29.7	30.9
Philadelphia	31.0	28.0	30.4	27.5	19.2	3.7	0.2	0.6	8.7	25.7	30.0	31.0
Tokyo	31.0	28.0	30.8	23.7	8.0	2.3	0.2	0.0	0.9	11.4	28.6	30.9

days per month on which the temperature falls below 18°C/65°F. Only for
Atlanta, Houston and Tokyo are there any periods when this number is zero.

Table 1.4 shows the expected numbers of CDDs for our thirteen locations.
The highest values occur in summer. By comparing with table 1.2 we can see
that the monthly totals for CDDs for summer are generally lower than the
monthly totals for HDDs for winter (except for Houston, which is the most
southerly, and warmest, of our thirteen stations). This difference between
the behaviour of HDDs and CDDs arises because the 18°C/65°F baseline is
higher than the mean temperatures for most of these locations.

CDDs are mainly used in the United States and seldom in Europe and
Japan.

Relations between HDDs and CDDs

The sum of the number of HDDs and CDDs on a particular day is simply
the unsigned magnitude of the deviation of that day's average temperature
from the baseline: one of the number of HDDs or the number of CDDs on
a particular day is always zero, and both are zero when the temperature is
exactly equal to the baseline value.

Finally, we note that neither CDDs nor HDDs can ever be negative.

Table 1.4. *Expectations of monthly sums of CDDs, estimated using thirty years of data with linear detrending and one year of extrapolation, at various locations in Europe and Japan (in Celsius degree days) and in the United States (in Fahrenheit degree days).*

Station/ Month	Jan	Feb	Mar	Apr	May	Jun	Jul	Aug	Sep	Oct	Nov	Dec
Amsterdam	0.0	0.0	0.0	0.3	7.7	7.6	25.8	31.0	2.9	0.0	0.0	0.0
Essen	0.0	0.0	0.1	1.0	10.6	18.7	49.9	54.7	7.1	0.8	0.0	0.0
London	0.0	0.0	0.0	0.0	4.3	11.9	48.1	49.3	5.7	0.4	0.0	0.0
Paris	0.0	0.0	0.0	0.4	15.6	32.5	75.5	82.8	10.3	1.4	0.0	0.0
Rome	0.0	0.0	0.2	0.3	30.4	120.4	207.2	233.0	86.4	25.1	2.1	0.0
Stockholm	0.0	0.0	0.0	0.1	1.8	12.2	54.3	44.8	4.9	0.0	0.0	0.0
Atlanta	0.6	1.2	11.8	67.2	210.6	373.3	510.3	466.1	273.1	69.2	6.7	1.3
Chicago	0.0	0.0	2.1	12.8	72.9	239.1	365.9	303.5	137.1	14.2	0.4	0.0
Covington	0.0	0.0	2.4	15.9	69.1	231.3	337.2	294.6	131.4	18.4	0.7	0.4
Houston	16.8	31.9	59.7	186.6	388.1	514.9	612.6	614.2	446.6	211.0	49.8	29.7
New York	0.0	0.0	1.6	8.5	68.5	263.7	404.0	376.7	179.2	29.0	0.8	0.2
Philadelphia	0.0	0.0	1.7	12.7	73.4	278.3	421.6	364.6	164.2	26.9	0.8	0.0
Tokyo	0.0	0.0	0.1	10.7	64.8	137.8	284.2	311.4	193.2	56.1	1.3	0.1

1.2.2 Average of average temperature indices

Average of average temperature indices are designed to be a more intuitive measure of temperature variability than the degree day measures, which are well known only in the energy industry. Average of average temperature indices are defined as the average (or mean) of the daily average temperature values over the period of the contract. Note that the first 'average' in the phrase 'average of average' refers to a mean, while the second 'average' refers to a midpoint. Writing the average of average temperature as $\overline{T}$ we have

$$\overline{T} = \frac{1}{N_d} \sum_{i=1}^{N_d} T_i \qquad (1.7)$$

Table 1.5 shows expected values for the average of average temperatures for our thirteen locations.

As discussed above, there are many locations that are cold enough that the number of HDDs per day is always positive at certain times of year because the daily average temperature is always below 18°C/65°F. If this is the case, then an average of average temperature index $\overline{T}$ and an HDD index x are simply related by

Table 1.5. *Expectations of monthly averages of daily average temperatures,
estimated using thirty years of data with linear detrending and one year of
extrapolation, at various locations in Europe and Japan (in degrees
Celsius) and in the United States (in degrees Fahrenheit).*

Station/ Month	Jan	Feb	Mar	Apr	May	Jun	Jul	Aug	Sep	Oct	Nov	Dec
Amsterdam	3.5	4.6	6.9	9.3	13.6	15.0	17.4	17.8	14.9	11.4	6.9	4.0
Essen	2.7	4.0	7.1	9.9	14.4	15.9	18.5	18.8	14.7	11.4	6.3	3.3
London	5.6	6.3	8.6	10.1	13.9	16.1	18.9	19.0	15.7	12.6	8.3	6.0
Paris	4.5	5.6	9.3	10.8	15.5	17.6	20.0	20.4	16.0	13.0	7.6	5.5
Rome	7.7	7.8	10.9	13.3	18.0	22.0	24.7	25.5	20.8	17.8	12.7	8.6
Stockholm	-0.7	-0.7	2.3	6.5	11.7	15.9	19.1	18.3	13.1	8.0	2.8	-0.4
Atlanta	45.4	49.7	54.6	62.9	71.2	77.4	81.5	80.0	73.8	63.9	53.9	46.5
Chicago	28.2	32.5	39.6	51.0	62.0	71.8	76.8	74.8	67.5	54.9	41.8	31.2
Covington	32.6	36.8	42.6	53.7	63.1	72.1	75.9	74.4	67.2	55.6	44.0	34.6
Houston	54.2	57.7	61.8	70.0	77.5	82.2	84.8	84.8	79.8	70.8	60.8	54.4
New York	35.5	37.1	42.9	53.3	63.2	73.4	78.0	77.1	70.1	59.1	48.4	39.6
Philadelphia	35.4	37.7	44.0	54.4	63.8	74.0	78.6	76.7	69.2	58.2	47.4	38.5
Tokyo	6.8	7.2	10.1	15.3	19.5	22.5	27.2	28.0	24.4	19.2	13.7	9.1

$$x = \sum_{i=1}^{N_d} max(T_0 - T_i, 0) \qquad (1.8)$$

$$= \sum_{i=1}^{N_d} (T_0 - T_i)$$

$$= N_d T_0 - N_d \overline{T}$$

The equivalent equation that relates CDDs to mean temperature indices in
the case where the temperature is always *above* 18°C/65°F is

$$x = N_d \overline{T} - N_d T_0 \qquad (1.9)$$

However, as we have seen, very few locations never go below 18°C/65°F,
even in the summer, and so this equation is less useful than equation 1.8.

Average of average temperature indices are mainly used in Japan, and
seldom in the United States and Europe.

1.2.3 Cumulative average temperature indices

Cumulative average temperature (CAT) indices are defined as the sum of
the daily average temperatures over the period of the contract

$$x = \sum_{i=1}^{N_d} T_i \qquad (1.10)$$

CAT indices are mainly used in Europe in the summer.

1.2.4 Event indices

Event indices, also known as critical day indices, are usually defined as the number of days during the contract period that a certain meteorological event occurs. A typical event would be the temperature exceeding (or going below) a threshold. Another more complex definition of 'event' counts the number of times a sequence of days of a certain length experiences temperature above or below a threshold.

Very exotic event indices are often designed in the primary market. For instance, a well-known recent weather contract (designed to provide insurance for construction workers) depended on the number of 'frost days' during the November to March period, where a 'frost day' was defined as occurring if the temperature at 7 a.m. was below -3.5^oC, or the temperature at 10 a.m. was below -1.5^oC, or the temperatures at 7 a.m. *and* 10 a.m. were both below -0.5^oC. A further complexity of this deal was that the weather on weekends and holidays was not included.

1.2.5 A general classification of indices

From the point of view of the mathematical analysis of weather contracts it is useful to classify indices in two ways. First, indices are either *additively separable* or not. 'Additively separable' means that the aggregate index is a sum of the daily indices. Second, indices are either *linear* or not. 'Linear' in this context means that the daily value of the index is a linear function of the daily weather variable.

To give some examples:

- CAT indices are both additively separable and linear;
- DD indices are additively separable but not linear – although, as we have seen above, they are often *effectively* linear if the temperature never reaches the baseline, in which case either equation 1.8 or equation 1.9 will hold;
- an event index that counts the number of days on which the temperature exceeds a certain level is additively separable, but not linear;
- an event index that counts the number of periods of three days on which the maximum temperature over the three days exceeds a certain level is neither additively separable nor linear.

These concepts are useful because, if an index is additively separable, then the expected value of the index is the sum of the expected values of the daily indices, and, if it is linear, then the expected value of the daily index is a linear function of the expected values of the daily weather variable. These concepts will be used later in our analysis when we wish to estimate the expected values of weather indices.

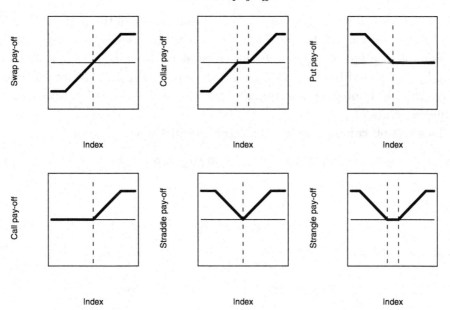

Figure 1.3. The pay-off functions for the various contracts described in the text.

1.3 Derivative pay-offs

The indices described above define how weather variability is encapsulated for the purposes of a weather derivative contract. The contract is then financially settled using the measured value of the index as the input to a pay-off function. This function defines precisely who should pay what to whom at the end of the contract. Any function could be used as a pay-off function, but in practice only a small number of simple structures, with straightforward economic purposes, are common. We will consider the pay-off for each of these structures from the point of view of the buyer of the contract, who is said to take the 'long' position. The seller of the contract, who takes the 'short' position, will have exactly the opposite pay-off. Of the contracts described, the swap, call and put options are by far the most common. All the pay-off functions described below are illustrated in figure 1.3.

1.3.1 Swaps

The pay-off, p, from a long swap contract is given by

$$p(x) = \begin{cases} -L_\$ & \text{if } x < L_1 \\ D(x - K) & \text{if } L_1 \leq x \leq L_2 \\ L_\$ & \text{if } x > L_2 \end{cases} \qquad (1.11)$$

where x is the index, D is the tick, K is the strike, $L_\$$ is the limit expressed in currency terms and L_1 and L_2 are the upper and lower limits expressed in units of the index. $L_\$$ and L_1 are related by $L_\$ = D(K - L_1)$, and $L_\$$ and L_2 are related by $L_\$ = D(L_2 - K)$. It is common practice for all types of contract to quote limits in terms of currency values (e.g. $L_\$$) rather than in index values (L_1 and L_2).

This pay-off can also be written more succinctly as

$$p(x) = max(-L_\$, min(D(x - K), L_\$))\qquad(1.12)$$

or as

$$p(x) = min(L_\$, max(D(x - K), -L_\$))\qquad(1.13)$$

or even

$$p(x) = median(-L_\$, D(x - K), L_\$)\qquad(1.14)$$

These one-line expressions are useful for calculating pay-offs in some computer languages and spreadsheets. We have set the upper and lower limits (in monetary terms) to be equal and opposite. More generally, it would be possible to structure a swap contract (and also all the other contract types considered below) with limits of different sizes on the two sides, although this is very unusual.

It is also possible to structure swaps without financial limits; the pay-off is then a linear function of the index, given by

$$p(x) = D(x - K)\qquad(1.15)$$

We call this a linear swap. Even for swaps with limits the limits are usually set at rather extreme values, and so expression 1.15 may be a good approximation. OTC contracts are usually traded with limits while the CME contracts do not have limits.

Most swaps are costless: there is no premium, and the profit or loss from a swap is equal to the pay-off. When the contract is set up the two counterparties simply exchange a contract agreeing to pay each other according to the weather at some point in the future. In this sense, a swap is like a spread bet on the future weather. A long swap contract has the economic function of insuring against high values of the index. The downside for the buyer of a swap is that he[3] has to pay the seller for low values of the index. In this way, the buyer and the seller can be said to be swapping risks, and

---

[3] Throughout this book we will use 'he' to mean 'he or she'.

they play a symmetrical role. Swap contracts traded on exchanges such as the CME involve daily settlement as the index develops during the contract period, while swap contracts traded OTC usually involve settlement only at the end of the contract. Technically speaking, the former are known as *futures* contracts while the latter are known as *forward* contracts.

If, as described above, a swap contract is to be traded without premium, then the strike would likely be set at a level where the expected pay-off is close to zero, possibly shifted slightly to compensate one or other party for the risk they are taking on. In many cases, but not all, the strike value that gives an expected pay-off of zero will be close to the expected value of the index for the swap. Swaps can also be traded with a premium paid, although this is very rare.

The 'pricing' of a costless swap prior to trading consists of determining the strike. Once the swap has been traded valuation consists of calculating the distribution of possible financial outcomes, and specific aspects of this distribution. This is covered in detail in subsequent chapters.

If a hedger is using a linear swap contract to hedge a business risk then the optimum size of the hedge (defined as the hedge that minimises the variance of the basis risk) is given by the regression coefficient obtained by regressing the profits of the business onto the weather index.

1.3.2 Call options

The pay-off, p, from a long call contract is given by

$$p(x) = \begin{cases} 0 & \text{if } x < K \\ D(x - K) & \text{if } K \leq x \leq L \\ L_\$ & \text{if } x > L \end{cases} \tag{1.16}$$

where $L_\$$ and L are related by $L_\$ = D(L - K)$.

This can also be written more succinctly as

$$p(x) = min(L_\$, max(D(x - K), 0)) \tag{1.17}$$

or as

$$p(x) = max(0, min(D(x - K), L_\$)) \tag{1.18}$$

and

$$p(x) = median(0, D(x - K), L_\$) \tag{1.19}$$

For the buyer, this has the economic function of providing insurance against high values of the index. At the start of the contract the buyer pays a

premium to the seller. At the end of the contract the seller pays the buyer
a pay-off dependent on the value of the index. For low values of the index
there is no pay-off. The buyer, if he is a hedger, presumably does not mind
this outcome: if he is using the contract to hedge these low values of the
index should be good for his business. For values of the index above the
strike the seller pays the buyer an amount that is proportional to the extent
to which the strike is exceeded. The constant of proportionality is given by
the tick. Beyond a certain financial limit, the pay-off stops increasing for
increasing index value (although, as we have already mentioned, unlimited
contracts are also possible, and the CME contracts are all unlimited). The
strike is typically set at between zero and one standard deviation above the
estimated expected index and the limit at around two standard deviations,
or at the most extreme historical value for the index. The overall profit for
the buyer of an option is equal to the pay-off minus the premium.

We have seen that both long calls and long swaps can be used to hedge
against high values of the index. The difference is that long calls involve
the payment of a single, fixed up-front premium, while for long swaps the
entire pay-off is random in both directions. Many corporations hedging their
weather risk prefer to use options rather than expose themselves to the
possibility of having to make a large and unpredictable pay-off at the end
of a swap contract.

The pricing of a call option consists of determining the premium. Once
the call option has been traded the valuation consists of calculating the
distribution of possible future financial outcomes, and specific aspects of
this distribution.

1.3.3 Put options

The pay-off, p, from a long put contract is given by

$$p(x) = \begin{cases} L_\$ & \text{if } x < L \\ D(K-x) & \text{if } L \leq x \leq K \\ 0 & \text{if } x > K \end{cases} \tag{1.20}$$

where $L_\$$ and L are related by $L_\$ = D(K-L)$.

This can also be written more succinctly as

$$p(x) = min(L_\$, max(D(K-x), 0)) \tag{1.21}$$

or as

$$p(x) = max(0, min(D(K-x), L_\$)) \tag{1.22}$$

or

$$p(x) = median(L_\$, D(K - x), 0) \qquad (1.23)$$

For the buyer, this has the economic function of providing insurance against *low* values of the index. At the start of the contract the buyer pays a premium to the seller. At the end of the contract the seller pays the buyer a pay-off dependent on the value of the index. For high values of the index, there is no pay-off. For values of the index below the strike the seller would pay the buyer an amount that is proportional to the amount by which the index is below the strike. Beyond a certain financial limit, the pay-off stops increasing for decreasing index value. The strike is typically set at between zero and one standard deviations *below* the estimated expected index.

1.3.4 Collars

A long collar position consists of a combination of a long call and a short put, usually with different strikes but the same tick and limit (although different ticks and limits are also possible). Collars have the pay-off function

$$p(x) = \begin{cases} -L_\$ & \text{if } x < L_1 \\ D(x - K_1) & \text{if } L_1 \leq x < K_1 \\ 0 & \text{if } K_1 \leq x < K_2 \\ D(x - K_2) & \text{if } K_2 \leq x \leq L_2 \\ L_\$ & \text{if } x > L_2 \end{cases} \qquad (1.24)$$

where $L_\$$ and L_2 are related by $L_\$ = D(L_2 - K_2)$, and $L_\$$ and L_1 are related by $L_\$ = D(K_1 - L_1)$.

This can also be written as

$$p(x) = max(-L_\$, min(D(x - K_1), max(0, min(D(x - K_2), L_\$)))) \qquad (1.25)$$

or by combining the expressions for calls and puts given above.

A long collar position provides a hedge against high values of the index for values beyond a certain threshold. Collars, like swaps, are usually costless.

1.3.5 Straddles

A long straddle position consists of a long call and a long put with the same strike, tick and limit. Straddles have the pay-off function

$$p(x) = \begin{cases} L_\$ & \text{if } x < L_1 \\ D(K - x) & \text{if } L_1 \le x < K \\ D(x - K) & \text{if } K \le x \le L_2 \\ L_\$ & \text{if } x > L_2 \end{cases} \qquad (1.26)$$

where $L_\$$ and L_1 are related by $L_\$ = D(K - L_1)$, and $L_\$$ and L_2 are related by $L_\$ = D(L_2 - K)$.

This can also written as

$$p(x) = min(L_\$, max(D(K - x), min(D(x - K), L_\$))) \qquad (1.27)$$

or by combining the expressions for call and puts.

A long straddle position hedges against both high and low values of the index, and is hence typically rather expensive in terms of premium since the buyer receives a pay-off for all values of the index except $x = K$.

1.3.6 Strangles

A long strangle consists of a long call and a long put but with *different* strikes (unlike a straddle, where the strikes are the same). The strike for the put is usually lower than that for the call.

Strangles have the pay-off function

$$p(x) = \begin{cases} L_\$ & \text{if } x < L_1 \\ D(K_1 - x) & \text{if } L_1 \le x < K_1 \\ 0 & \text{if } K_1 \le x < K_2 \\ D(x - K_2) & \text{if } K_2 \le x \le L_2 \\ L_\$ & \text{if } x > L_2 \end{cases} \qquad (1.28)$$

where $L_\$$ and L_1 are related by $L_\$ = D(K_1 - L_1)$, and $L_\$$ and L_2 are related by $L_\$ = D(L_2 - K_2)$.

This can also be written as

$$p(x) = min(L_\$, max(D(K_1 - x), max(0, min(D(x - L), L_\$)))) \qquad (1.29)$$

or by combining expressions for the call and the put.

A long strangle position hedges against both high and low values of the index in a similar way to a straddle, but pays out only when the index moves a certain distance. They are thus typically a little cheaper than straddles.

1.3.7 Binaries

A long binary option has a pay-off function of the form

$$p(x) = \begin{cases} 0 & \text{if } x < K \\ L_\$ & \text{if } x \geq K \end{cases} \qquad (1.30)$$

A long binary option can be considered to be a special case of a call option. In the case in which the index x is considered to be continuous, it is a call option with infinite tick. In the case in which the index x is discretised to certain values with spacing Δx the tick is equal to $\frac{L_\$}{\Delta x}$.

1.3.8 Other piecewise linear pay-off functions

Derivatives other than weather derivatives are often written on other piecewise linear pay-off functions, such as 'condors' and 'butterflies'. However, at the point of writing these are seldom seen in the weather market.

1.3.9 Non-piecewise linear swaps and options

All the pay-off functions we have seen so far have been piecewise linear. Non-piecewise linear functions are also occasionally used. Wind power production, for example, depends on the cube of the wind speed. Thus one way to structure a hedge for a wind power plant would be to define a swap or an option based on wind speed, with a cubic polynomial for the pay-off function (although a more common way to deal with this situation would be to define the index using a cubic polynomial and use a standard piecewise linear pay-off). Such structures may occur in the primary weather market, but are not seen in the secondary weather market at this point.

1.3.10 Spreads

Spreads are contracts designed with a pay-out that is a function of the *difference* of the weather between two locations. For instance, a Paris-London spread might depend on an index that is the difference in HDDs between Paris and London.

1.3.11 Baskets

Baskets are single contracts that depend on multiple locations. For instance, a US basket might depend on temperatures in New York, Chicago and San Francisco. They are appropriate for end-users who have risk at a number of locations but want to minimise the number of transactions they do to hedge that risk. Trading a single basket on ten locations may have lower transaction costs than trading ten single contracts.

1.3.12 Complex contracts

Complex contracts are contracts defined on the pay-offs from other contracts. For instance, the index for a single option contract may be taken to be the total pay-off from ten other contracts. Such structures usually occur when speculators in the weather market want to pass some of their risk on to an insurer or reinsurer. This transaction can be structured as a single complex contract that depends on the performance of a selection of contracts from the speculator's portfolio.

1.3.13 Moneyness

Once a call or a put option contract is in progress, the expected settlement index or market swap price may move towards or away from the values that would lead to a pay-off. In the jargon of derivatives trading, this is known as the 'moneyness' of the contract. 'In the money' (ITM) refers to situations where the expected index has moved into the range of values that would lead to a pay-off, while 'out of the money' (OTM) refers to situations where the expected index has moved into a range of values that lead to zero pay-off. 'At the money' (ATM) is in between. An ITM contract will typically be worth more than an OTM contract, but until final settlement of the contract a positive pay-off is still not guaranteed since the expected index can go down as well as up.

Weather contracts that depend on aggregating degree-day-type indices have the additional characteristic that the index *so far* (rather than the *expected* final index) can be in or out of the money. DD indices cannot go down, and so, once a DD index for a call option is in the money, it cannot go out of the money again and a pay-off *is* guaranteed. This does not apply to CAT indices, or average of average temperature indices, since they can also decrease with time.

1.3.14 Long and short

We have already used the phrase 'long' to describe the situation of the buyer of a contract and the phrase 'short' to describe the situation of the seller. However, these phrases are also used with respect to indices. For instance, if I buy a call option I am long the underlying index (if the index increases my expected profit increases). This occasionally creates confusion: if I buy a put contract I am long the put, but short the index underlying the put. Beware!

1.3.15 Parity relations

The prices of the options and swaps contracts described above are not completely unrelated. A combination of the pay-offs of a long call and a short put with the same strikes is equivalent to the pay-off from a long swap. This relationship is known as *put-call parity* and puts constraints on the prices of the three contracts, because the swap can be replicated using the call and the put.

Other parity relations are also possible. As we have seen above, collars, straddles and strangles are all combinations of puts and calls. Again, these relationships put constraints on the prices of these options if all the contracts are available in the market.

In financial derivatives markets such parity relations are very important. However, in the weather market the strikes of calls tend to be higher than the strikes of puts on the same index. This means that the constraint between the prices of puts, calls and swaps described above is not exact: the swap can only approximately be replicated using the put and the call, and there is some residual risk. As a result the parity relations have only a weak effect on market prices.

1.3.16 Terminology

Contract naming conventions

There are a few differences between the terminology typically used in the weather derivatives market and that used in other financial markets, and these may puzzle readers from some backgrounds. For instance, traditional financial options do not usually have limits, and options that *do* have limits are usually described either as caps, call spreads or bull spreads (for calls with limits) and floors, put spreads or bear spreads (for puts with limits). However, since weather options almost always do have limits, this is usually just assumed and not reflected in the name.

Mean and expectation

We have already used the phrases 'expected index' and 'expectation of the index' several times. We use these phrases in a purely mathematical sense, to represent the arithmetic mean of the possible values of the index. We note that the expectation of an index should not be *expected* to occur. In fact, it is easy to create cases in which the expected value can *never* occur. For example, the expected pay-off you have when buying a lottery ticket for £2 may be £1, but you cannot actually win £1.

1.3.17 Discounting

Cashflows that occur at different points in time (such as the premium and the pay-off of an option) cannot be compared directly because of the effects of interest rates. Instead they should be converted, using the process of *discounting*, to a common point in time. Given a constant interest rate r, and using continuous compounding of interest rates, a cashflow of X at time T is equivalent to a cashflow of $Y = e^{r(t-T)}X$ at time t. One common approach is to convert all future cashflows to equivalent present values, known as the net present value (NPV).

For reasons of simplicity we will ignore issues of discounting until chapter 11 of this book. The timing of the cashflows that will be discussed is very straightforward and the discounting can be applied after all other calculations are complete. For options, a premium is paid at the start of a contract, and a pay-off is paid at the end. When calculating the premium of an option from the distribution of the pay-offs, one should discount the pay-offs to the point in time at which the premium will be paid. For swaps (but not including futures) there is no initial premium, and a pay-off is made at the end. Discounting is thus not used when calculating the fair strike value for a swap. When calculating the distribution of outcomes from a swap contract, the final pay-offs should be discounted, however. For futures daily balancing payments have to be made to an exchange, and in theory these should be discounted individually. In practice this is sometimes ignored when interest rates are low and the tenor of the swap is short.

In chapter 11 we will consider trading strategies in which many trades are made at different points in time. Discounting will then have to be considered as an integral part of the pricing theory.

1.4 Principles of valuation

We will now address the main theme of this book, which is how to value a weather derivative or a portfolio of weather derivatives and how to calculate the risk associated with a portfolio of weather derivative positions.

There are three main reasons why participants in the market need to value weather derivative contracts and portfolios of contracts. The first is for pricing: to determine an appropriate strike for a costless swap, or an appropriate premium for an option prior to trading. The second is that once one or more contracts have been traded it is important to know the current value of all holdings based on the latest weather and forecasts, and how those values are likely to develop. The final reason for valuing weather derivative contracts is that both internal and external regulators often need to monitor the risk a weather trading organisation is facing due to the contracts they have traded.

To help us understand how weather derivatives might be valued we start with a quick tour of valuation principles for some other financial instruments.

Equity valuation

Equities can be valued in two ways. First, so-called *fundamental valuation* involves estimating how much money the equities will make for the investor through capital appreciation and dividends. Both the future value and the future dividends from an equity are unknown, and can take a wide range of values. A valuation depends on an assessment of that possible range, with values discounted to today.

Second, one can perform a *market-based* valuation of equities just by looking at the value of the equity quoted on an exchange. Fundamental and market-based valuation methods serve two very different purposes. Fundamental valuation is appropriate if we want to judge whether the values on the exchange are too high or too low, and whether we should be buying or selling the equity. The market-based approach is appropriate if we simply want to know the level at which we could expect to buy more equity or sell our current holding.

Insurance valuation

Insurance is valued by the purchaser in terms of how much he appreciates the reduction in his risk, and by the issuer in terms of whether, by issuing many such contracts, he can make money. Prior to selling insurance the issuer might make an attempt to estimate the probabilities of all the possible outcomes of a contract, and might then calculate the expectation and some measure of spread of these outcomes in order to derive a premium. Once a contract has been sold, the issuer might estimate the probabilities of all the possible outcomes in order to calculate how much he could lose if he has to pay out.

Equity option valuation

Equity options can be valued in three ways. First, we could apply a fundamental valuation based on a calculation of the probabilities of different pay-offs from the option. This method makes sense as an internal valuation procedure if the option is being used as a way of investing in the underlying equity. However, this is rather unusual, and fundamental valuation of equity options is not very commonly used. Second, if there is an observable market for the equity option then one could take the price from this market. Third, if there is no market price for the option but there are market prices for the equity underlying the option, and possibly for other options on the same equity, then one can use a so-called *no-arbitrage* model based on these observed prices. Such a model calculates the price that the equity option should have to avoid the possibility that someone in the market could create a risk-free profit by trading the option and then making very frequent trades of the equity (known as dynamic hedging) to hedge away the risk of the option. It is based on different principles from fundamental valuation, since it depends only on setting the price of the option correctly *relative* to other prices in the market, rather than in any absolute sense. It is far more commonly used than fundamental valuation.

Actuarial, market-based and arbitrage pricing

These three examples show two very different valuation methods. The first, used for the fundamental analysis of equities, equity options and the pricing of insurance, is based on an evaluation of the probabilities of all future outcomes of the share, option or insurance contract. We will refer to this as *actuarial* pricing. The second method, used for equities and equity options, is based on prices observed in a market, which we will call *market-based* pricing. For equities, market-based pricing consists of simply looking at the market price. For equity options, market-based pricing may consist of using the market price of the equity along with an appropriate model to derive the no-arbitrage price. This is often known as *arbitrage* or *no-arbitrage* pricing.

Which of these methods is appropriate for weather derivatives? The answer depends on the state of the market and the type of contract.

For weather swaps, there are two possible methods of valuation, analogous to the two ways of valuing equities. As with equities, they have very different purposes. First, we can calculate value on the basis of the probabilities of all possible outcomes (actuarial pricing). This is performed by using historical meteorological data and meteorological forecasts to predict the distribution of the possible outcomes of the index. Second, we can look at the prices of the swap being traded in the market. This is possible only if there is an observable market.

Now we consider weather options. In this case there are three possibilities. First, we can again, as with weather swaps, value on the basis of the probabilities of all possible outcomes, and this is usually the starting point for all weather option valuation.

Second, if an observable market for the option exists then we could consider using that market price as the value.

Third, we can also consider arbitrage pricing, as with equity options. The pay-off of a weather option depends on an index derived from meteorological variables. This index is not the price of a traded quantity and so, at first sight, weather options are *not* analogous to equity options. However, if there is also a swap contract defined on the index, then, under certain assumptions, dynamic hedging of the risk in a weather option is possible using swaps in exactly the same way that equities can be used to hedge equity options. To allow such dynamic hedging the swap market has to be fairly liquid, otherwise the costs involved are prohibitively large. At the point of writing very frequent dynamic hedging is rather difficult because of a lack of liquidity and because of the discrete sizes of swap contracts. However, this will change as the weather market develops, and even now a certain amount of dynamic hedging is possible, albeit at rather large intervals in time.

We conclude that weather option pricing is a mixture of actuarial and market-based techniques, with more emphasis on the actuarial side in most cases. For locations where the swap is not traded, and which are not highly correlated with locations on which swaps are traded, actuarial valuation of options is the only choice. For locations where the swap is traded actively arbitrage pricing has some relevance because of the possibility of dynamic hedging using the swap. Finally, for locations in which the option is actively traded one may be able to take the option valuation directly from the market.

1.4.1 Other paradigms for weather pricing

There have also been other suggestions for ways that weather derivatives could be priced, and we will mention some of them briefly here. Henderson (2002) suggests a general equation for the pricing of all weather derivatives that incorporates discounting, risk loading, the cost of hedging and the current portfolio position. To quote the author: '[This equation] is comprehensive, but too general to be applied in its current form.' The equation is a formalisation of the discussion above and in a sense the rest of this book is about methods that can be used to evaluate this equation in practice.

Cao and Wei (2000) use an equilibrium argument to conclude that the appropriate price for weather options is the expected pay-off. This idea is unlikely to be popular with speculators, since they would not make any money in the long run under such a pricing scheme but would increase their risk. We discuss the relevance of such equilibrium pricing models in more detail in section 1.4.2.

A more plausible suggestion, due to Geman (1999a), is that weather derivatives could be hedged using electricity contracts that have prices correlated with the weather and that the price of the electricity contracts could be used to fix the price of the weather derivative contracts. This cannot provide a perfect hedge since the prices of electricity contracts depend on more than just the weather, but it could potentially reduce the risk of a weather derivative position to a more acceptable level. Undoubtedly, some energy companies that trade weather and electricity contracts do attempt to create low-risk portfolios in this way. However, to our knowledge such trading does not have a strong effect on the market prices of weather derivatives, and it does not lead to an arbitrage possibility, and so it cannot be considered as a practical method for pricing.

A similar suggestion was made by Davis (2001), who proposed that weather derivatives should be priced using the utility function of a portfolio of gas and weather contracts. Again there is no doubt that certain energy companies do trade correlated gas and weather contracts in a combined portfolio (and some probably trade all gas, electricity and weather contracts in a combined portfolio), but, again, it seems that such trading does not determine weather market prices nor create an arbitrage possibility and hence the analysis of gas prices does not lead to a general method for the pricing of weather contracts.

1.4.2 CAPM and the price of weather derivatives

The capital asset pricing model (CAPM: Sharpe, 1964) is a theory of the statistical behaviour of the prices of investments. It has received a certain amount of criticism in recent years and some authors consider it not useful at all, mainly because it assumes that all investors have more or less the same portfolio of investments, and that returns are normally distributed. Nevertheless, it is interesting to consider what the theory has to say about the likely market prices of weather derivatives. The principal result of the theory is that, under certain assumptions, the excess return over the risk-free rate given by an investment is proportional to the regression coefficient between the performance of that investment and the performance of some wider market. Thus investments with high correlation with the wider market will have a return well above the risk-free rate, while investments with a low correlation with the wider market will have a return much closer to the

risk-free rate. The justification for this is that the low-correlation investments are much more desirable, and this has pushed up their price until
their return drops below that of the less desirable high-correlation investments. The market we observe is supposedly an equilibrium that results
from these effects. In this model all investments become a trade-off between
correlation and return: because of market dynamics you cannot have both
low correlation *and* high return.

As was mentioned in section 1.1.6, and is discussed further in section 1.5,
the weather is largely uncorrelated with the financial markets, and thus
the performance of weather derivatives is also largely uncorrelated with the
financial markets. Applying CAPM, this would suggest that weather derivatives should be extremely popular as an investment class, and that this
popularity would push the return on weather contracts down to the risk-
free rate.

In fact, CAPM does not apply particularly well to the real weather market. There are a number of reasons for this, including:

• weather derivatives are not considered as an investment class by the majority of
  investors, and thus there is less demand for weather derivatives as investments
  than the low correlation and CAPM might suggest;
• those organisations that do invest in weather derivatives often manage their
  weather businesses as separate entities rather than as a part of the whole business, and expect them to earn a decent return above the risk-free rate in spite of
  the low correlation with other assets;
• the prices charged for weather derivatives are strongly influenced by the targets
  for the rate of return of the various speculators in the weather market; this is
  more a managerial decision than a question of market dynamics.

To summarise, the assumptions that lie behind CAPM (and other equilibrium models, such as that of Cao and Wei, 2000) do not apply in practice.
Weather derivatives can defy the theory and give *both* a low correlation
and a high return. Equilibrium theories provide interesting frameworks for
understanding how markets may perform, and they certainly contain some
elements of truth, but they are not close enough to the real world to be
applied in practice for fixing prices.

One could also apply CAPM to the weather market alone; in this sense
the price of an individual weather contract might be considered to be proportional to the regression coefficient between the pay-off of that contract
and the wider weather market. Exotic weather contracts on exotic locations
would thus be cheaper than standard contracts on standard locations because they are uncorrelated with this wider weather market. This dynamic
may be relevant in some cases. However, it is strongly counterbalanced by

the fact that trading standard contracts is generally preferred because of the greater price transparency, the lower overhead costs and the possibility of hedging one's position in the secondary market.

1.5 The correlation between weather and the stock market

We have argued in this chapter that (a) many companies can hedge themselves using weather derivatives, and that this will reduce the volatility of their stock price, and (b) weather derivatives are a good investment because they are not correlated with the stock market. It might be said that these statements are somewhat contradictory. In fact, however, both are more or less correct. Certainly, individual stocks of companies that do not hedge themselves against weather fluctuations would be expected to be correlated with the weather that affects them. And many companies in the stock market are affected by the weather. However, each company is affected in a different way, and in a diversified portfolio of stocks of many companies the weather-driven part of the variability of the portfolio performance is likely to disappear almost completely. Thus a company investing in a diversified portfolio of stocks can indeed invest in weather derivatives under the assumption of zero correlation between the two.

1.6 Overview of contents

In this introduction we have explained the reason for the existence of the weather derivatives market, and we have introduced the various types of weather derivative contract available. The rest of the book now discusses the valuation of these contracts. In chapter 2 to chapter 12 we will focus on contracts based on average temperature, which form the bulk of the market, and in chapter 2 to chapter 10 we will concentrate on actuarial pricing methods. Chapter 2 looks in more detail at the historical meteorological data that is used for the actuarial pricing of weather contracts, and in particular describes how this data can be cleaned and detrended before use. Chapter 3 considers the pricing of a single weather derivative using the simplest possible actuarial method, known as 'burn analysis'. Chapter 4 then discusses how burn analysis can be extended to the modelling of the settlement index, a method we call 'index modelling'. Chapter 5 uses the methods described in these two chapters to address various issues that arise in the pricing of weather contracts and to introduce the greeks. Chapter 6 approaches the question of whether we can price weather derivatives using daily temperature simulation models. Chapter 7 generalises much of the material in the earlier chapters to portfolios of weather derivatives. Various issues in weather portfolio management such as risk and return, pricing against an existing portfolio and hedging the risk in a portfolio are then considered in chapter 8. Before chapter 9, no consideration is given to the use of meteorological forecasts in the pricing of weather derivatives. It is assumed that the relevant contract period is sufficiently far in advance that forecasts are not useful. After describing the relevant types of meteorological forecasts in chapter 9, this assumption is relaxed in chapter 10, where there is a detailed discussion of how to use both weather and seasonal forecasts to improve weather derivative valuation. Chapter 11 moves away from the actuarial pricing methods of chapters 2 to 10 and discusses arbitrage pricing methods based on the idea of using swap contracts to hedge, fully or partially, the risk in options. Chapter 12 then covers the subject of risk management. This is aimed at those organisations that issue weather derivatives and need to have an up-to-date picture of the performance and value of the contracts on their books. Marking a portfolio to model and to market, value at risk and expiry value at risk are discussed. Finally, in chapter 13 we briefly consider weather derivatives based on variables other than temperature.

1.7 Notes on citations

We have avoided heavy use of citations within the main text, except when we are describing a method or idea that was first suggested by a particular author or authors. At the end of each chapter we have included a short 'further reading' section in which we list references and articles that might be of use or interest to the reader. Inevitably, we have ended up citing ourselves in a large number of places; this book is, in large part, based on the research we have carried out in this area over the last four years and the technical reports we have published that describe the results of this research. However, we have tried to apply the same standards when discussing our own work as when discussing the work of others. Where possible we have given preference to citing open-access publications since these are of much greater use to the reader. Unfortunately, much of the academic literature is not open access and can be rather difficult to get hold of for non-academics. We have tried to be reasonably comprehensive in our references section: the body of work covering weather derivatives is still sufficiently small that one could reasonably try and read it all. If the reader knows of any important citations that we have missed we will be happy to include them in a future edition.

1.8 Further reading

Many articles have been written about weather derivatives, covering all aspects of the weather derivative industry. Four useful sources for such articles are the *Environmental Finance* monthly magazine, the *Energy Power and Risk Management Weather Risk Special Report* (published annually), the Social Sciences Research Network (SSRN) at http://www.ssrn.com and the Artemis Website at http://www.artemis.bm.

There are three books in English that contain collections of articles on weather derivatives. The first – chronologically – is *Insurance and Weather Derivatives* (Geman, 1999b), which has four chapters that introduce basic weather derivatives concepts. The second is *Weather Risk Management* (Element Re, 2002), which has fourteen chapters covering everything from basic meteorology to a discussion of the legal, accounting and tax issues relevant to weather derivatives. The third is *Climate Risk and the Weather Market* (Dischel, 2002), which has seventeen chapters that, again, cover a wide range of topics.

For readers of Japanese there are three books on weather derivatives published in that language: Hijikata (1999), Hijikata (2003) and Hirose (2003). The last is a collection of essays by five different authors. Finally, in French there is a book that covers the basics of the market and of valuation: Marteau et al. (2004).

The main difference between these books and this one is that we focus purely on the *valuation* aspects of weather derivatives, and consequently are able to discuss such issues in much greater depth than they receive elsewhere.

2

Data cleaning and trends

Actuarial pricing methods for weather derivatives depend on statistical modelling of stationary time series of historical meteorological data. This is described in chapters 3 to 6 for single contracts, and chapters 7 and 8 for portfolios. However, historical meteorological data is anything but stationary, and we must process it in a number of ways before the pricing methods can be applied. Firstly, we must clean the data to remove absurd values and fill gaps. Secondly, we must identify (and perhaps attempt to remove) jumps in the data that occur as a result of station changes. Finally, we may need to remove gradual trends from the data. Our discussion of the methods used for identifying and replacing absurd values, filling gaps and identifying and removing jumps will be rather cursory; a more thorough explanation is given in Boissonnade et al., 2002. We will, however, discuss the identification and removal of trends in some detail.

2.1 Data cleaning

Meteorological data measurements are usually made by national meteorological services (NMSs), and occasionally by universities, private companies or military organisations. We will restrict ourselves to a discussion of the data measured by the NMSs since this is what is generally used in the weather market. In many parts of the world measurements exist that go back at least fifty years, and in some cases much longer. However, as we shall discuss below, even very recent data already has significant problems with reliability and homogeneity, and earlier data is usually significantly worse.

The extent to which meteorological data is readily available for use by the weather derivative industry varies by country. In the United States data and information about the data, such as the logbooks kept by the observers (an example of *metadata*), are either freely available or available at a nominal

37

cost, and the infrastructure for disseminating the data is well developed. This is one of the reasons why the US weather market, and other commercial applications of meteorology in the United States, have been able to expand very rapidly. By contrast, in most countries in Europe meteorological data is expensive, and in some cases extremely so. The metadata is generally hard to obtain, and is usually available only in hard-copy format rather than digital electronic format. The infrastructure for disseminating the data is also fragmented and disorganised, with different systems operating in each country. Some of the difficulties involved in obtaining European data have been reduced, however, by the recent emergence of private sector companies acting as intermediaries between the NMSs and the rest of the private sector. Finally, in Japan data and metadata are generally expensive but are easy to obtain from a number of private meteorological companies.

We will focus our discussion on temperature data. There are two main kinds of observed temperature data that can be obtained: 'synoptic' and 'climate' data. They may or may not be derived from the same underlying measurements; this varies from country to country. Synoptic data is used primarily for feeding immediately into weather forecasts. Since it is crucial that weather forecasts are based on the latest measurements there is no time for comprehensive quality control or checking of this data, and so synoptic data does not form a particularly reliable historical record of past temperatures. Climate data, on the other hand, is created purely for the purpose of having just such a historical record, and goes through several levels of quality control and checking in most countries. Although these checking procedures often delay the release of the data by days, weeks or even months after the data has been measured, this is the data that is generally used in the weather market for the settlement of weather contracts because of its higher level of accuracy and reliability. Only in cases where quality-controlled climate data is not available, or is not available within a reasonable time-frame, is synoptic data used.

If historical climate data is obtained from an NMS or private meteorological service provider it may or may not have been cleaned to the standards necessary for use in weather pricing. This should be ascertained when the data is purchased. The various stages of the necessary cleaning are outlined below.

2.1.1 Gap filling

Almost no meteorological stations have continuous measurement series without a break during the last forty or fifty years. Any number of reasons, from power cuts to data transmission failures, can result in gaps in the historical data record. If the number of gaps is large relative to the amount of data available, and especially if there are big gaps in recent years, one may conclude that the station is not suitable for use in the weather market. This is partly because the gaps in the data will make a statistical analysis less accurate, and partly because a station that has many gaps in the past may be more likely to have gaps in the future, and this can cause problems with the final settlement of the weather contract.

If, on the other hand, the gaps are a small fraction of the available data (perhaps less than 10 per cent), then it is usually possible to proceed with using a station to structure and trade weather derivatives. Statistical methods such as detrending and distribution modelling (to be described later) can, in principle, be performed on data with gaps, and this would be the most accurate approach. However, this is usually difficult, and the preferred method is to fill the gaps using spatial interpolation procedures to create a complete data set prior to detrending and distribution fitting. When the number of gaps is a small fraction of the total amount of data this is likely to be only slightly less accurate than performing analysis on the true data including gaps, and the difference is assumed to be immaterial. Gap filling is done using spatial regression models that can estimate missing data at a particular station based on information from surrounding locations. Such models are easy to build using standard multivariate regression techniques.

2.1.2 Value checking

It is fairly common to find absurd or implausible temperature values in historical records. If left uncorrected, such values can cause severe mis-pricing of weather derivatives. Some of the types of checks that can be performed to detect incorrect values are:

- a check that the daily maximum is not less than the daily minimum (although note that in the United Kingdom this is only just about possible because minimum and maximum are measured over non-overlapping time periods);
- a check that the temperature values lie within reasonable ranges for the time of year for that location;
- a check that the temperature differences between nearby locations are not implausibly large.

Once detected, incorrect values can be replaced using the same spatial-regression-based methods as are used for gap filling.

2.1.3 Jump detection

Having filled gaps and removed obviously incorrect values, the next stage in data cleaning is the identification and possible removal of jumps. The jumps in historical temperature measurements are caused by changes at meteorological stations, and our experience suggests that all meteorological data is affected by such jumps. Such changes mainly consist of changes in the location of the station (both horizontal and vertical movements) and changes of instrumentation (updating equipment or replacing broken equipment). Other changes include changes in the housing of the equipment and changes in the immediate environment surrounding the housing (such as grass being replaced by tarmac). The jumps in the measurement series that are caused by such changes can be up to several degrees Centigrade in the worst case, and it is essential to identify these jumps before using data for weather pricing. To price weather derivatives using data containing large jumps would expose an organisation to significant disadvantages in the secondary trading market and to adverse selection in the primary market (adverse selection is the process by which, in a competitive market, the only weather deals that one succeeds in selling are those that one has unknowingly underpriced). For those stations at which large changes have occurred this single issue is more important than any other in determining reasonable weather derivative prices.

Daily data obtained directly from NMSs has, almost without exception, *not* been corrected for such jumps.[1] For some station changes, especially when measurement stations are being replaced or updated, it is common meteorological observing practice to run the new station configuration alongside the old to check that the measurements from the new station are sufficiently close to the old for the records to be concatenated. However, this does not address the problem of station changes and associated jumps fully for two reasons: (a) it is often decided that the measurements from the new station are sufficiently close to those from the original station even if there are small differences, and these small differences are not usually used to adjust the original data; and (b) such parallel measurements are performed only in certain cases, but not in cases of broken equipment or changes in the immediate environment of a station.

One of the reasons for this apparent lack of care on the part of meteorological services and the World Meteorological Organization (WMO) is that their main concern is making weather forecasts, and providing data for such

---

[1] We say *almost* without exception because the Swiss Meteorological Service has apparently carried out such an analysis.

forecasts. A change in measured temperatures of 0.5°C is more or less negligible relative to the sizes of errors in such forecasts. However, a change of 0.5°C is large relative to the size of the standard deviation of mean temperature calculated over a long time period, and is thus very important from the point of view of the weather market.

Methods for the identification of jumps usually proceed along the following lines:

- analysis of any available historical metadata (textual information about the history of the station) to identify dates when changes occurred that might have resulted in jumps;
- statistical testing of the data around these dates to determine if a jump occurred;
- analysis of all other dates in order to detect jumps due to changes not recorded in the metadata (many such jumps appear to exist in observed meteorological time series);
- estimation of the sizes of all detected jumps using data before and after the jump.

The testing and estimation procedures used for estimating the size of jumps are usually based on an analysis of the linear dependences between the target station and surrounding stations. Data from the surrounding stations can then be used to replicate the target station using regression, and a difference time series produced by subtracting the replica time series from the actual. Any jumps in the original time series show up clearly in this difference time series, and can be identified visually or using statistical tests.

Having identified a jump in a data set one has three choices:

- ignore it; this is appropriate only if the jump is too small to have a significant effect on final index values, relative to other causes of uncertainty;
- use data from after the jump only; if the jump is far back in the past this is certainly the best course of action;
- attempt to adjust the data prior to the jump to the present-day levels, using the estimated size of the jump.

Which of the second and third of these choices is more appropriate to use for the treatment of large jumps depends on a number of factors, such as the accuracy with which the size of the jump can be estimated, when the jump occurred and what contract the data is to be used to price.

Data from which jumps have been identified and removed is available from private sector companies for those stations commonly traded in the weather market, and most weather pricing is carried out using such data.

2.2 The sources of trends in meteorological data

We have described how raw meteorological data can be corrected for gaps, incorrect values and jumps. There is one more major issue to be addressed before we have a data set that can be considered representative of the likely climate during the contract period for a weather derivative: gradual trends, or shifts in the mean level of the data.

Historical meteorological data is not used in weather derivative pricing because we care about what the climate was doing twenty years ago but because we need to know what the climate might do in the near future. Studying historical data is one of the few ways we have to answer that question: the basic assumption is that the climate in the future is going to behave in ways somewhat similar to how it has behaved in the past. However, even the most cursory investigation suggests that it is not true that climate data is stationary. Almost all measurement time series appear to show trends and fluctuations on long timescales, and for temperature these trends are mostly positive (hence the phrase 'global warming'). As an example, figure 2.1 shows a CDD index at New York's LaGuardia Airport that shows a large apparent trend. There are a number of possible explanations for such trends, which we discuss in detail below.

1. *Random internal climate variability.* The simplest explanation for an apparent trend is that it is part of the random internal variability of the climate system. This is not a possibility to be taken lightly; figure 2.2 shows a short sample of white noise, representing index values for a weather derivative for the last thirty-five years. There is apparently a trend during this period, but we know that the data is actually random, and that this apparent trend has no underlying

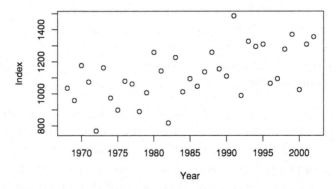

Figure 2.1. CDDs for New York LaGuardia over the last thirty-five years. There is apparently a large upward trend in the number of CDDs, indicating warming.

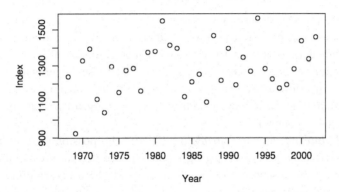

Figure 2.2. A segment of stationary white noise. The values have been chosen to look like the number of CDDs at New York LaGuardia. The apparent trend illustrates the difficulty of distinguishing between real and purely statistical trends.

cause; in this sense, the trend is not 'real'. There is no reason to suppose, if we continued this time series, that this trend would continue. Simple random models like this can be used to put error bounds on the estimates of trends, and it is quite useful to generate random numbers in a spreadsheet to become familiar with this effect.

2. *Urbanisation.* Many meteorological measuring stations are now in, or near, more urban environments than they were twenty or thirty years ago, and this may have changed their local climate. Such urbanisation generally has a warming effect and is related to (a) increased coverage of the ground surface with concrete, tarmac and buildings, which both increases the absorption of solar radiation and decreases cooling evaporation, and (b) the emission of heat from buildings, vehicles and aircraft. Urbanisation effects are not only local, and urbanisation warming can often be seen many miles downwind of major cities.

3. *Anthropogenic climate change.* This is the idea that man's activities, mainly the release of carbon dioxide (CO_2) into the atmosphere from burning fossil fuels, have had an effect on the climate system. Such effects may include warming in some regions, cooling in others, and possible changes in the atmospheric circulation. Mechanistic computer models of the climate system (known as general circulation models, or GCMs) have been used to test this idea. The models are simple relative to the real climate system, and their results cannot be entirely trusted. But to the extent that the models are realistic they prove that increasing levels of CO_2 over the last century have caused a warming, on average, over the whole globe. However, these models are not accurate enough on smaller spatial scales to tell us whether there has been a CO_2-induced warming in any particular location, or a change in any particular phenomenon (such as hurricanes or extratropical storms). As a demonstration of this inaccuracy on small scales, models

from different scientific research groups that give roughly the same warming for the planet as a whole often give very different results at individual sites. Until independent models start to agree in terms of the spatial patterns and local details of climate change, it is wise to assume that these patterns are not correct. The main objections to the theory that the observed warming is mostly due to CO_2 are that it is caused by urbanisation (see 2 above) or long-term climate variability (see 4 below).

4. *Predictable internal climate variability.* This is the possibility that predictable long-timescale changes are occurring in the climate due to internal climate processes alone. The discussion on random internal climate variability (1 above) was concerned with those trends caused by the unpredictable (random) parts of climate variability. Climate variability on long timescales of years and decades is dominated by such random effects, which arise from sampling short-timescale phenomena that occur randomly in time. However, it *may* be that there is also a component of long-term climate variability that is predictable. For instance, slow changes in the ocean, on timescales of decades, could affect the atmosphere. These oceanic changes could be oscillatory, in which case we might see periods of ten or twenty years of upward trends, followed by ten or twenty years of the reverse.

5. *Variability in solar forcing.* The radiation output from the sun varies periodically in time. This has only a small effect on climate, and can be ignored for our purposes.

For the purpose of pricing weather derivatives it is helpful, to a certain extent, to try and understand the origin of trends in order to decide whether the trends should be removed (or not) and whether they should be extrapolated appropriately into the future. To the extent that observed trends are not real but are created by sampling variability (1 above) they should not be removed or extrapolated. To the extent that they are due to urbanisation (2 above) they should possibly be removed, and also perhaps extrapolated, depending on the likely future rate of urbanisation. To the extent that they are anthropogenic (3 above) they should possibly be removed and extrapolated into the future, perhaps at an increasing rate. And finally, to the extent that they are due to predictable internal climate variability (4 above) one should attempt to predict that variability. In the absence of a prediction it probably makes most sense to remove the effects of past climate variability but not to extrapolate into the future (this is known as a persistence forecast).

How, then, are we to distinguish between the different possible causes of trends in the historical data? Unfortunately, a complete decomposition of trends into their various causes is not possible. There are, however, a few ways that we can shed some light on the issue.

2.2.1 The spatial structure of trends

Using station data for a large number of locations throughout the world
we can study the spatial variations of trends, and this can give us some
partial information about their causes. For instance, anthropogenic effects
would be expected to create fairly large-scale patterns in the trends (up to
continental scales), while urbanisation effects would be expected to be more
localised, on scales the size of urban areas. However, the distinction between
random climate variability, predictable climate variability and anthropogenic
effects will certainly not be clear simply from looking at the spatial scales
of changes, since all of these effects would be expected to impact on large
scales.

We have mapped the trends in minimum, maximum and average temperatures in winter and summer over the United States in Jewson and Brix,
2004a. As an example, figure 2.3 shows the rate of a linear trend in November
to March HDDs over the last thirty years.

The results from this study were:

- most but not all locations show warming trends;
- winter trends tend to be stronger than summer trends;
- winter trends tend to show a high degree of spatial coherence while summer trends
  do not;
- summer maxima show only very weak trends;
- summer minima show stronger trends than summer maxima;

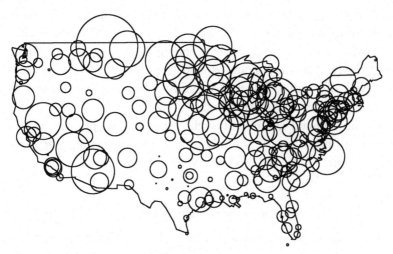

Figure 2.3. The rate of November to March HDD trends over the last thirty
years for two hundred US locations.

- in some regions winter minimum and maximum temperatures behave the same way (e.g. the northern United States);
- in other regions winter minimum and maximum temperatures behave very differently (e.g. the southern United States).

2.2.2 Climate models

We have argued above that climate models are not, at present, sufficiently accurate to give useful information about climate change trends at individual locations. However, these models are becoming more accurate as the available computer power increases, and at some point the results from different models will – hopefully – start to agree. At this point it would be possible to include information from such models into the study of local trends. The most important use of such models from the weather derivative pricing point of view is not to produce forecasts for the next fifty years but, rather, to shed light on the causes of what has already happened. The models can be run in such a way as to simulate the climate of the last fifty years, and can then be used to ask questions about the causes of different trends in different regions. Suppose, for example, that as a result of a climate modelling study using a number of different models it was concluded that the warming trend at a certain location over the past thirty years was almost entirely due to anthropogenic climate change. This would justify removing the trend and extrapolating it into the future. It would also give an idea of the shape of the trend to be removed. If, on the other hand, it was concluded that most of the trend was due to predictable climate variability as part of a twenty-year cycle then it would make sense to remove the trend using the shape of the cycle, and use any available predictions of the cycle for the upcoming year or years. Such predictions may involve increases or decreases in future temperature. Finally, if it was concluded that the apparent trend was consistent with the levels of random internal variability in the climate then it would be justifiable not to remove the trend.

It should be stressed again that such a study is, at present, not possible because of the limitations of the climate models and computer power, but may become practical in the next few years.

2.2.3 Urbanisation studies

By studying the physical environment of individual measurement sites we can decide whether or not they are likely to have been influenced strongly by

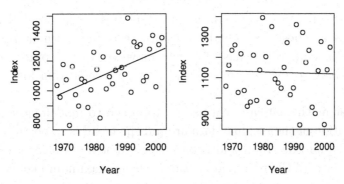

Figure 2.4. Historical values for summer CDDs at New York LaGuardia and New York Central Park. Even though these stations are physically reasonably close, one shows a very significant warming trend while the other shows no warming trend. This suggests that the trend at LaGuardia is due to urbanisation rather than large-scale climatic effects.

urbanisation. If we can find two nearby sites, one of which has experienced urbanisation while the other has not, then differences between the two can, in principle, give us an indication of the extent to which the former has been influenced by such changes. If, on this basis, it is concluded that one site has been strongly affected by urbanisation then this trend should probably be removed, unless there are reasons to believe that the urbanisation will be reversed in the near future.

As an example we will compare the CDD index for New York LaGuardia with the corresponding index for New York Central Park. These two stations are only a few miles apart, but whereas much has been built in the LaGuardia area over the last thirty to forty years not much has changed over the same period around Central Park. Figure 2.4 shows the historical CDD indices for the two locations with linear trends overlaid. Visually, the difference between the two plots is striking, and a test of the significance of the slope of the trendlines reveals that the trend for Central Park is not significant (p = 34 per cent) while the trend for LaGuardia is highly significant (p = 0.06 per cent).

2.3 Removing trends in practice

We have discussed some of the possible causes of trends, and suggested a number of ways that one can try to understand trends in more detail. It is clear that, at present, there are no easy ways to identify the origins of trends. The two most important conclusions are simply that

(a) real (not random) trends do exist in many data sets and (b) for now these trends are best accounted for using statistical methods rather than by the use of climate models. We now move on to the practical subject of how actually to identify, model and remove trends from historical time series.

The most mathematically consistent approach to modelling a trend and the distribution of the residual data around the trend is to postulate a parametric shape for the trend and a parametric distribution for the residuals and to estimate all the parameters at once using maximum likelihood methods. However, this approach is seldom used in the weather market because of its relative complexity. Rather, a simplified approach is used in which the two steps of trend and distribution estimation are performed separately, and this is the approach that we will describe below. There are some small mathematical inconsistencies in taking this separate approach, but it has some practical advantages and is easier to apply. Trend fitting is discussed below while distribution fitting is discussed in chapter 4.

In the context of weather derivatives based on daily measured values there are two possibilities for how to remove trends: (a) removing trends from the historical daily data series; or (b) removing trends from the historical index time series. Understanding daily temperature trends is more complex because of seasonality and so we will consider trends in the historical index time series first.

2.3.1 Detrending index time series

The main advantage of detrending at the index level rather than the daily level is that the effects on the index of the different types of possible trends in the underlying daily temperature are combined. In other words, if we deal with daily temperatures we should ideally consider trends in the mean, the variability, the correlation structure, the extremes, trends at different times of year, etc. If we deal with index values then, at least in terms of the estimates of the expected index, one can ignore these various sources of trends and consider simply the trend in the mean level of this single number.

There are an infinite number of different shapes of trend that can be used to detrend the index time series, and we cannot catalogue them all here. Rather, we choose a selection of the most commonly used techniques: linear, piecewise linear, quadratic, exponential, moving average and loess. To illustrate these shapes, we show these trends fitted to London Heathrow historical HDD indices in figure 2.5.

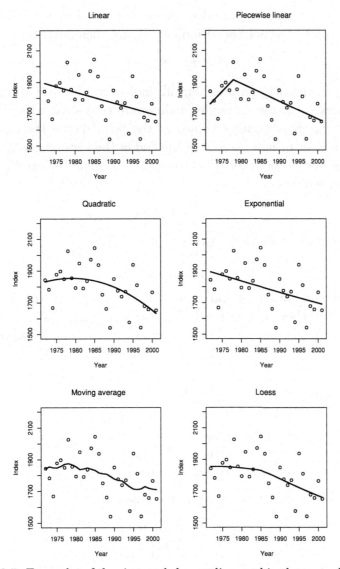

Figure 2.5. Examples of the six trend shapes discussed in the text, all fitted to London Heathrow November to March HDDs, 1972 to 2001.

For all shapes of trend our model assumption is that a historical index x_i for year i can be represented as a sum of a trend r_i and some random variation e_i.

$$x_i = r_i + e_i, \qquad i = 1, \ldots, N_y \qquad (2.1)$$

where N_y is the number of years of data.

The e_i are assumed to be independent and identically distributed with expectation zero. The detrended indices, x_i', are then defined as

$$x_i' = x_i - \hat{r}_i + \hat{r}_{N_y} \tag{2.2}$$

Adding $\hat{r}_{N_y}$ in this way ensures that all indices are brought to the level of the last index – i.e. the detrended indices are consistent with the climate in year N_y. $\hat{r}_{N_y}$ is sometimes known as the *pivot*. Often the contract will commence a year, or more, ahead of the end of the historical indices, and in such cases it may be desirable to extrapolate the trend to year $N_y + k$ using the alternative equation

$$x_i' = x_i - \hat{r}_i + \hat{r}_{N_y+k} \tag{2.3}$$

in which we have replaced $\hat{r}_{N_y}$ by $\hat{r}_{N_y+k}$.

Parametric trends

Linear, piecewise linear, quadratic and exponential trends are all parametric trends, in that they have a fixed shape that is partly adjustable with a small number of parameters. These parameters are usually estimated from historical data using either analytical or numerical minimisation of the sum of the squared errors $\sum_{i=1}^{N_y} e_i^2$.[2]

With y_i denoting the year of index i, linear, quadratic and exponential trends r_i are parameterised by

$$
\begin{aligned}
r_i &= a + by_i & \text{(linear)} \\
r_i &= a + by_i + cy_i^2 & \text{(quadratic)} \\
r_i &= a\exp(by_i) & \text{(exponential)}
\end{aligned}
$$

while piecewise linear trends are parameterised by

$$r_i = \begin{cases} a_1 + b_1 y_i & \text{if } i \leq i_0 \\ a_2 + b_2 y_i & \text{if } i \geq i_0 \end{cases} \tag{2.4}$$

The definition of piecewise linear trends also includes the constraint that the trend is continuous at the breakpoint – i.e. that $a_1 + b_1 y_{i_0} = a_2 + b_2 y_{i_0}$. The year at which the two parts of the trend join, i_0, is fitted as a parameter along with the other parameters.

---

[2] It was mentioned above that removing trends and fitting distributions to the residuals separately leads to small mathematical inconsistencies. One of these is that by fitting a trend by minimising the sum of squared errors we are essentially assuming that the residuals are normally distributed. However, later we may fit a distribution other than normal to the residuals. If the residuals are not normally distributed then fitting the trend by minimising the sum of square errors is not a maximum likelihood method. If the residuals are close to normally distributed then this does not matter. However, if they are far from normally distributed it may.

For the linear trend case, the parameters a and b are estimated by

$$\hat{a} = \frac{S_{yy}S_x - S_yS_{xy}}{\Delta}, \qquad \hat{b} = \frac{N_yS_{xy} - S_xS_y}{\Delta} \tag{2.5}$$

where

$$\Delta = N_yS_{yy} - S_y^2, \qquad S_y = \sum_{i=1}^{N_y} y_i, \qquad S_x = \sum_{i=1}^{N_y} x_i,$$

$$S_{yy} = \sum_{i=1}^{N_y} y_i^2, \qquad S_{xy} = \sum_{i=1}^{N_y} y_i x_i \tag{2.6}$$

Expressions for the parameter estimates in the other cases can be derived from the general expressions given in appendix A.

Non-parametric trends

Moving average and loess are non-parametric trends that have no fixed shape but take their shape more directly from the data. They can be used if there is reason to believe that the parametric trends do not provide a satisfactory approximation for the shape of the trend during the period considered. In practice, it often makes sense to fit a non-parametric trend when using many (i.e. forty or fifty) years of historical data. For shorter periods of data a parametric trend may be a good approximation to the real trend, but as the number of years of data is increased it becomes less likely that the approximation will remain good. The simpler of the two non-parametric trends is the moving average method, where the trend in year i is estimated as the average of the neighbouring years:

$$r_i = \frac{1}{2w + 1} \sum_{i=-w}^{w} x_{i+w} \tag{2.7}$$

The number of neighbouring years, $2w + 1$, is usually called the window length. In an extension of this method the years may be weighted such that years closer to the base year contribute more than years that are further away. The main disadvantage of moving average estimation is that it does not extrapolate the trend beyond the last historical year.

Loess trends (Cleveland and Devlin, 1988) use local parametric regression. Linear loess, for example, estimates the trend for year i by weighted linear regression, with most weight on nearby years. One advantage of the loess method over moving averages is that it does allow extrapolation beyond the last historical year. Loess has a single parameter that controls the smoothness of the fitted trend. At one extreme of this parameter the trend

Table 2.1. *The mean and standard deviation of the settlement index for London Heathrow November to March HDDs, estimated using different numbers of years of historical data and different trend assumptions.*

	10-yr mean	10-yr SD	20-yr mean	20-yr SD	30-yr mean	30-yr SD
No trend	1712.65	116.91	1764.18	140.48	1794.16	132.99
Linear	1672.92	120.72	1654.88	126.26	1694.34	120.47
Pw Linear	1672.92	120.72	1689.61	126.19	1656.36	113.46
Quadratic	1669.40	129.03	1684.19	128.86	1632.23	118.34
Exponential	1671.25	117.14	1654.68	118.72	1690.70	114.39
MA	1709.73	116.75	1709.73	131.66	1709.73	116.89
Loess	1670.84	131.01	1681.94	129.76	1660.75	117.95

comes close to passing through every data point, while at the other extreme the trend becomes linear. This allows a range of results from a single trend model just by varying this parameter.

Table 2.1 shows the estimated mean and standard deviation for HDDs at London Heathrow, calculated using ten, twenty and thirty years of data and seven different methods: no trend and the six trend methods described above. We see significant differences between the results from the different models, but it is very difficult to know which are the most accurate. We will discuss in section 2.4 some of the ways one can try and answer this question.

Combined trend models

Trend models are sometimes used that combine two of the trend types described above. One model is used to define the pivot while another defines the residuals. The justification for this approach is that some models are better at defining the correct mean index while other models are better at defining the variability about the mean.

2.3.2 The sensitivity of trends

One of the major problems with estimating parametric trends is that the parameters that result from the estimation procedure can be inexact. Using the mathematical techniques described in appendix A we can derive estimates for this uncertainty. As an example, the uncertainty in the parameter estimates $\hat{a}$ and $\hat{b}$ of a linear trend, represented by the variance of the estimates of these parameters, is given by

$$\sigma_a^2 = \frac{S_{xx}}{\Delta} \tag{2.8}$$
$$\sigma_b^2 = \frac{N_y}{\Delta}$$

These parameter estimates are correlated with correlation given by $\rho = \frac{-S_x}{\sqrt{N_y S_{xx}}}$.

It is instructive to plug in some numbers to see how large these uncertainties can be in practice. For London Heathrow and an HDD index based on November to March data for the last thirty years, we find that $\hat{a} = 3559.1$, $\hat{b} = -0.93275$, $\sigma_a = 71.04$ and $\sigma_b = 1.594$.

We see that the estimated trend parameter $\hat{b}$ is negative, indicating a downward (warming) trend, but is also extremely uncertain. This leads to significant uncertainty in our estimate of the trend values $\hat{r}_{N_y}$, the detrended indices x'_i and the mean and standard deviation of the detrended indices.

For this example the estimated expected index from this trend model has a value of 1694.34, but with uncertainty of 42.9.

These expressions for parameter uncertainty given above suggest that using more years of data is preferable because the parameters will be estimated more accurately. However, this is true only if the trend model is exactly correct, and this is *less* likely the more years of data we use. The optimum number of years for a particular trend is presumably, therefore, a trade-off between these two effects.

2.4 What kind of trend and how many years of historical data to use?

Up to now we have not addressed the question of how many years of data to use (is ten better than fifty?) or which trend to fit (linear or loess, etc.?). These two questions are closely related. If the data is good quality and we are confident that we can remove trends then we should use as many years of data as possible to make our statistical estimates more accurate. On the other hand, if we are uncertain about what the shape of the trend is then using fewer years of data may make sense: using extra data that has not had the trend removed correctly may reduce the accuracy of our results. Also, whatever the shape of the trend, then as long as it is slowly varying it will be well approximated by a linear trend over short time periods, but not over long time periods.

One way to assess the number of years to use is to plot a graph showing the mean and standard deviation of the index derived from detrending as a function of the number of years used. An example of this is given in figure 2.6. We have also shown the uncertainty around the mean and standard deviation of the index, derived using equation (2.8).

These graphs tell us, at a glance, the sensitivity of our results to the number of years of data used. They do not, however, give us any indication as to which choice is the best.

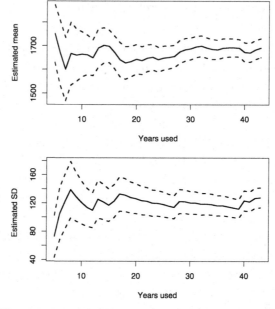

Figure 2.6. The upper panel shows the estimated mean index for London Heathrow November to March HDDs as a function of the number of years of historical data used. For each period of data a linear trend was removed. The dashed lines show the uncertainty around the estimate of the mean represented as plus and minus one standard deviation. The lower panel shows the same as the upper panel, but for estimates of the standard deviation of the HDD index.

2.4.1 Backtesting

Perhaps the only way to attempt to answer the question of how many years of data and what trend to use is to perform backtesting, or hindcasting, studies. These ask the question: what combination of trends and number of years of data would have worked well in the past?[3] The major assumption behind such a backtesting approach is that what would have worked in the past will work in the future: in other words that next year's values will be influenced by the same type of trends that affected the values over the last few years. This is not necessarily correct. Using results from backtesting does, however, free us from having to make subjective assumptions about the type of trend and length of data to be used; various types and lengths can be tried, and the optimum choices are determined by the method.

---

[3] Unfortunately, we still have to decide how far back in the past to run the backtesting comparison, and so the decision about how many years of data to use is, in some sense, only pushed to a different level.

We have attempted such a backtesting study based on temperature data for two hundred US stations, and the results are described in detail in Jewson and Brix, 2004b. For the stations and time period considered we find that using no detrending leads to a mean error, or bias, because of the warming trends in the data. This problem gets worse the longer the period of data that is used. Using detrending can remove this bias: the loess methods with extrapolation remove the bias most effectively. However, detrending introduces a different problem, which is an increase in the standard deviations of the errors. This is worst for short periods of data and non-parametric methods and is made worse still by extrapolation. Two measures that look at the size of typical errors, and hence incorporate information about both the mean and the standard deviation of the errors, are mean absolute error (MAE) and root mean square error (RMSE). When we consider these measures we find that the best of the no-trend methods are those that use between five and twenty years of data. For fewer years of data the bias is smaller, but the RMSE and MAE increase because of increases in the standard deviation of errors. For more years of data the standard deviation is smaller but the RMSE and MAE increase because of increases in the bias. The detrending methods considered (linear and loess) become better and better the more data is used, presumably because the trend is better and better estimated. Of all the methods we consider (which include methods using up to thirty years of data), the best methods overall are no trend with ten years of data and linear trend with thirty years of data. Figure 2.7, which shows the results for winter HDD values, illustrates this. The solid line shows the RMSE score for no detrending, the dashed line for linear detrending, the dot-dashed line for loess-0.9 detrending and the dotted line for loess-0.6 detrending.

In another article (Jewson, 2004i) we build a simple model to explain these backtesting results. This model makes it clear that the results of our backtesting study show the generic behaviour that is to be expected when detrending a series of data with a weak trend. The conclusion is that it is only worth trying to model the trend if we use many years of data. Modelling the trend with only a few years of data can do more harm than good even if the trend is real because of the increased standard deviation in the predictions.

2.4.2 Detrending daily time series

Up to now we have considered detrending the historical index time series. However, if we are planning to model a weather derivative pay-off by fitting

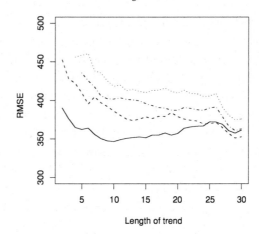

Figure 2.7. The RMSE for different detrending methods applied over the last fifty years, averaged over two hundred US locations.

a statistical model to daily values of temperature (this method will be discussed in chapter 6) then we need to use a trend model that works with these daily values rather than with the index values. Also, whatever modelling method we plan to use, for short contracts of only one month's or one week's duration modelling trends at the daily level may be better because it makes better use of the available data. Figure 2.8 shows trends calculated for the temperature at Chicago's O'Hare Airport for each week of the year using only data from that week for the past thirty years (i.e. using an index-based detrending method). The estimated trends vary widely from large positive values to large negative values. We do not believe that this is reasonable;

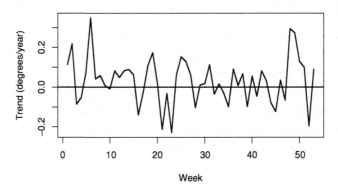

Figure 2.8. The slope of the linear trend in the average temperature at Chicago O'Hare for different weeks of the year, based on data from 1972 to 2002. We see that the trend estimates vary very widely from positive to negative, indicating the great uncertainty around such estimates.

presumably, trends are fairly constant, at least from week to week and month to month, even if they do vary from season to season. We could incorporate this idea into our index-based detrending by smoothing the weekly estimates to give a smooth curve for trends at different times of year. This would bring information about the trend from outside the week of the contract to bear on the week of the contract itself, and allow us to estimate the trends for that week more accurately. This smoothing is done automatically, however, if we use a daily-temperature-based detrending method with a trend that varies slowly with season.

As with index detrending, linear trends represent the most simple daily detrending model. We can then generalise the linear trend model to include trends that vary in slope with the time of year, and can also use more complex shapes such as loess, just as with index trends.

It would also be possible to remove trends from higher-order statistics of temperature. For instance, one might attempt to estimate trends in the standard deviation. It is certainly plausible that such trends could exist as a result of any of the underlying hypotheses for trends. Anthropogenic effects could be causing shifts in the storm track, which would certainly change variability of weather, either up or down, over large regions. Urbanisation effects could consist, in part, of daily and seasonal changes in car traffic or air traffic, which might increase variability. Predictable climate variability might also have an impact on sources of atmospheric instability and variability, and, finally, in any short time series of random noise, we would expect estimates of the standard deviation or variance based on different sections of the series to show different values, possibly giving the illusion of a forced trend with varying variance.

2.5 Conclusions

The main conclusion that we come to concerning trends is that it is difficult to analyse precisely what the best strategy is in terms of how many years of data and what trends to use. Backtesting studies have given us some indication of what would have worked well in the recent past but do not precisely determine what will work for a specific station in the future, because they involve averaging over many stations and because the future may not behave like the past anyway. Beyond that, all we can do is to make some assumptions that seem intuitively reasonable, and make sure we understand the effects of uncertainty within those assumptions, and the effects of that uncertainty on pricing.

2.6 Further reading

Unfortunately, there is no single source of information about meteorological data: the information has to be tracked down on a country-by-country basis. The only attempts to consolidate such information have been in the private sector; it is possible that the metadata for a number of countries can be purchased from private suppliers.

The differences between synoptic and climate data are discussed in Jewson and Whitehead (2001). There is a small academic literature that has looked at the question of how to identify jumps in meteorological time series in idealised situations, such as the articles by Karl and Williams (1987), Easterling and Peterson (1995) and Allen and DeGaetano (2000). A general article on the problems encountered when dealing with observational data is that by Jones (1999). Articles that discuss data issues in the context of weather derivatives are Boissonnade et al. (2002), Henderson et al. (2002) and Jewson et al. (2003c).

Much of the research into global warming is reported in the Inter-governmental Panel on Climate Change (IPCC) report (IPCC, 2001), although the economic assumptions that underlie the climate forecasts presented in this report have recently come in for heavy criticism from some economists (*The Economist*, 2003). An interesting outsider's view on the science of global climate change is given in Baker (2003). If you want to run a climate model on your PC, then you can read Allen (1999) and visit http://www.climateprediction.net. There has been a lot of research into the possible predictability of long-term climate variations, such as by Sutton and Allen (1997).

A recent review article on trends in climate, with emphasis on extremes, is by Easterling (2001). Some of the issues to do with detrending temperature indices are discussed by Brix et al. (2002) and Henderson et al. (2002).

3

The valuation of single contracts using burn analysis

We saw in the introductory chapter that, in most cases, weather derivative pricing is based on actuarial methods that estimate the probabilities of the various financial outcomes of a contract or a portfolio of contracts. In this chapter we explore the most straightforward method by which the prices and the distribution of financial outcomes of individual contracts can be estimated, which is *burn analysis*. We also investigate the level of uncertainty inherent in such estimates.

3.1 Burn analysis

Burn analysis, or just 'burn', is based, very simply, on the idea of evaluating how a contract would have performed in previous years. In its most straightforward form there is nothing more to it, and as a result it can be calculated, quite literally, with pencil and paper – or, slightly more practically, in a simple spreadsheet. We extend this basic form of burn to include those cases where we also detrend the data prior to evaluating how the contract would have performed. Burn explicitly does not include fitting distributions and using Monte Carlo simulations, however.

Although there are cases when other methods may be more accurate or give more information, burn analysis is nevertheless a good first step in pricing almost any contract. We will describe the steps involved in burn analysis for swaps and options, and then give some examples.

3.1.1 Burn analysis for swaps

Estimating the fair strike for linear swaps

The *fair strike* for a swap is defined as that strike that gives an expected pay-off of zero. Calculating the fair strike for a linear swap is trivial, since

59

the fair strike is just the expected index. This is because

$$E(p(x)) = E(D(K - x)) = DE(K - x) = D(K - E(x)) \qquad (3.1)$$

This is equal to zero if $K = E(x)$.

So, to calculate the fair strike we have to perform two operations.

1. Produce detrended historical index values x_i, as described in chapter 2. Detrending can be applied either to the daily temperatures, or to the index values.
2. Calculate the mean of the historical index values. This is an estimate for the expected index.

Estimating the fair strike for capped swaps

In most cases the caps of capped swaps are sufficiently extreme that one can ignore them, at least at the start of a contract (during the evolution of a contract the expected index can move close to or reach the caps if the weather is extreme). The fair strike can then be estimated in the same way as for uncapped swaps. However, to take the caps into account one should properly replace step 2 with another operation.

2. Calculate the strike that gives an expected pay-off of zero using an iterative procedure.

The iterative procedures that can be used for this are discussed in section 5.8.

Adding a risk loading

Given the results from the above calculations, what is the appropriate strike for a swap contract? Setting the strike to the fair strike means that neither party gains or loses in the long run if the contract is traded many times.[1]

However, the fair strike is not necessarily the appropriate level at which to trade the swap. If the swap is being sold in the primary market, and one party is a hedger and the other a pure speculator, then one would expect the strike to be shifted away from the fair value in favour of the speculator to reward the speculator for taking on the hedger's risk. The simplest method for calculating such a shift would be as a percentage of the standard deviation of the index of the swap – e.g. the strike might be set at the mean plus 20 per cent of the index standard deviation (the choice of 20 per cent is arbitrary). For a linear swap the expected pay-off for

---

[1] Although it is not commonly used, we note that an alternative definition could be that the fairest strike is that which gives a *median* pay-off of zero. Setting the strike so that the median pay-off is zero means that there is a 50 per cent chance of making or losing money for each party for this particular transaction. But, if the distribution is not symmetric, it will lead to one party having an advantage on average over many transactions.

the speculator is then 20 per cent of the standard deviation of the pay-off distribution, and the standard deviation of the pay-off distribution is the tick multiplied by the standard deviation of the index distribution. If the contract is repeated many times the speculator will now make money and the hedger will lose money on average.

Using fractions of the standard deviation as described above is just one way to add a 'risk loading'. Other ways of adding risk loading are discussed in chapter 8. In particular, we will discuss how the risk loading is more appropriately calculated by the speculator by looking at the change in the risk of his whole portfolio, rather than just the risk of the individual contract.

Based on the use of a risk loading principle, a market maker might quote two values for the strike of a swap, one at which he is prepared to sell and one at which he is prepared to buy. Typically these would be above and below the fair strike respectively. This means that buying a contract from a market maker and then selling the same contract straight back again would incur a small loss, and a small profit for the market maker.

The distribution of pay-offs

If we already know the strike of a swap and want to know the expected pay-off or the distribution of pay-offs, then we add steps 3 and 4.

3. Calculate the historical pay-offs[2] of the swap.
4. Calculate the mean of the historical pay-offs, and any other aspects of the pay-off distribution that are required. Exactly how to use historical pay-offs to estimate the pay-off distribution is discussed in section 3.1.3.

3.1.2 Burn analysis for options

What is the appropriate premium for an option? The *fair premium*, or *fair price*, is usually defined to be that for which the expected profit on the contract is zero – i.e. the premium is equal (and opposite) to the expected pay-off. We will see in chapter 11 that this is *not* what is considered the 'fair price' for an equity option, because of the possibility of arbitrage in the equity/equity option market. Arbitrage may also be possible in the weather swap/option market under certain circumstances, and we will consider that possibility later, but in most cases defining the fair price as the expected pay-off is appropriate.

---

[2] Note that we use the phrases 'historical indices' and 'historical pay-offs' even when the indices have been detrended and so are not, strictly speaking, what occurred historically.

To calculate the fair premium we can use the following steps.

2. Calculate the historical pay-offs of the option.
3. Calculate the mean of the historical pay-offs: this is an estimate for the expected pay-off.

Adding a risk loading

If the issuer charges the expected pay-off as a premium, then, in the long-run average over many trades, he will neither make nor lose money. As with swaps, this fair premium may not be the most appropriate level at which to trade. The seller of the option would probably expect a reward for taking on the risk of having to pay out, and hence the premium would probably be slightly higher than the expected pay-off by a risk loading.

The simplest method for determining this risk loading is as a fraction of the standard deviation of the pay-off of the contract, and so, for example, the price might be given by the expected pay-off plus 20 per cent of the standard deviation of the pay-offs.

As with swaps, a market maker might quote values for the premium above and below the expected pay-off by a risk loading. Unlike with swaps, it is likely that the market maker would be more willing to buy than to sell, since only selling incurs a risk of having to make a large pay-off. The prices quoted might be adjusted to reflect this, and may not be symmetric about the fair price.

3.1.3 The distribution of pay-offs

It is often useful to be able to estimate the distribution of possible pay-offs of a swap or an option contract – for example, to estimate the probabilities of various outcomes. To do this with burn analysis the historical pay-off values are sorted and used to create the cumulative distribution function (CDF) for the pay-off distribution. This is done by giving each of the sorted values a probability between 0 and 1. Because the years are considered independent, we spread the probabilities equally. To fix the probabilities precisely we need a model, and there are a number of models we can choose from. One method, which we will use throughout this book, is to put the first probability at 0 and the last at 1. The probability of the i'th sorted pay-off value is then given by $\frac{i}{N_y}$, where N_y is the number of years. This model gives unbiased estimates of the real probabilities.

Having estimated the CDF of pay-offs, we can then read off the probabilities of various events, such as hitting the strike or the limits. We can also read off the pay-off at a given percentage, such as the median pay-off (pay-off at 50 per cent).

3.1.4 Assumptions used in burn analysis

What are the assumptions we must make to use burn analysis? Prior to burn analysis the underlying historical data may be cleaned and detrended according to the methodologies described in chapter 2. We can thus assume that the historical index time series is stationary, and statistically consistent with the climate that will occur during the contract period. We then need to make just one assumption to apply burn analysis: that the data values for different years are independent and identically distributed (in fact, this assumption has already been used in the fitting of the trend: see section 2.3.1).

How valid is this assumption of the independence of years? Historical index values for one-month contracts are separated by eleven months, those for five-month contracts by seven months, etc. In Europe, the autocorrelation of climate anomalies falls to values close to zero after about one month, implying that the independence of years assumption would be valid for contracts up to eleven months in length. In the United States, climate autocorrelations last up to at least six months, principally due to the effects of the El Niño Southern Oscillation (ENSO).[3] If ENSO effects are not removed from historical data then this means that historical indices for contracts of longer than around six months cannot really be considered independent. However, in chapter 10 we will discuss ways in which the effects of ENSO can be removed from historical data (albeit imperfectly). This then justifies the use of the independence of years assumption for contracts of up to eleven months in length, as in Europe.

For twelve-month contracts it would not be completely appropriate to assume independence between years since the last days of one year are certainly correlated with the first days of the next. However, such contracts are very rare.

3.1.5 Examples

We now give an example of a burn calculation for a swap, a capped swap and an option. We consider winter contracts for London Heathrow for the period November to March, based on an HDD index. We use forty-four years

---

[3] The effects of ENSO are discussed in detail in chapter 9.

of data that has already been cleaned to remove gaps and jumps. The first stage of the analysis is to convert this data into index values: our forty-four years of data has only forty-three full November to March periods, and so we calculate forty-three historical index values based on these periods. These are shown in the first panel of figure 3.1. These index values show a clear downward (i.e. warming) trend, and we remove this trend using a linear trend model.[4] The detrended values are shown in the second panel of figure 3.1.

A linear swap example

We now define a linear swap with a tick of £5000/HDD. For pricing the linear swap, we calculate the mean and standard deviation of the detrended historical index values, giving 1698HDDs and 128HDDs. The fair strike would thus be 1698HDDs. A market maker might be willing to buy and sell the swap at 20 per cent of the standard deviation below and above the fair price, giving 1672HDDs and 1724HDDs respectively.

To estimate the distribution of outcomes for the swap with strike at 1698HDDs we convert the index values into swap pay-offs, which are shown in the third panel of figure 3.1. Since the swap pay-off is linear, the graphs of index value and pay-off are the same, except for shifting by the strike and scaling by the tick of the swap.

The fourth panel of figure 3.1 shows the estimate of the CDF of pay-outs from the swap contract.

A capped swap example

We now imagine that the swap contract described above has limiting pay-offs of £100,000. In practice, limits are set to much more extreme values than this (for this contract the limits would usually be set at £1,000,000); this value is chosen because it makes the possible effects of caps very clear. As we have mentioned, very often in practice the limits of capped swaps are sufficiently extreme that one can consider capped swaps to be linear swaps and use the methods described above.

We calculate the historical pay-offs for the capped swap and use them to estimate the CDF. Using this CDF we can calculate that setting the strike to be the expected index gives an expected pay-off of the swap of −£2572, rather than zero. This is because the historical index values are not distributed evenly around the expected index, and the pay-offs from below the expected index do not balance those from above.

---

[4] Note that our use of forty-four years of historical data and a linear trend in this example is purely for illustration. We do not necessarily think that this would be a good way to value contracts on this index in practice.

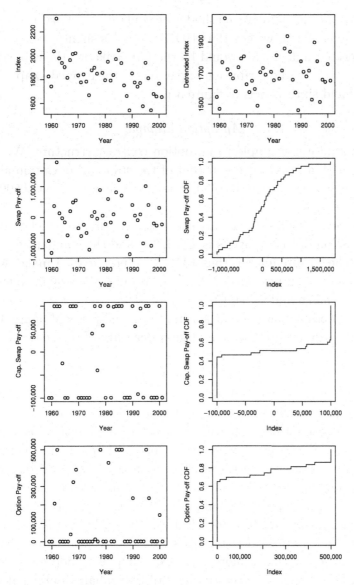

Figure 3.1. The results of burn analysis on three contracts based on London Heathrow. Panel 1 shows forty-three years of undetrended historical index values. These values show a clear trend. Panel 2 shows the same index values with a linear trend removed. Panel 3 shows the historical pay-offs of a linear swap based on this index. Panel 4 shows the CDF estimated from these historical pay-offs. Panel 5 shows the historical pay-offs of a capped swap based on this index; the cap is deliberately set at an unrealistically low level to illustrate the point. Panel 6 shows the CDF estimated from the historical pay-offs of the capped swap. Panel 7 shows historical pay-offs of a call option based on the index, and panel 8 shows the CDF of pay-offs for the call option.

When we use an iterative method to calculate the strike that gives expected pay-offs of zero we get 1694 HDDs, which is slightly below the value for the expected index. This would be the fair strike for the capped swap.

The time series and distribution of pay-offs of the capped swap are shown in the fifth and sixth panels of figure 3.1.

An option example

We now extend our example to an option contract structure. We define a call option with a strike at 25 per cent of the standard deviation above the expected index – i.e. strike at 1730. The option has a tick of £5000 and a limit of £1,000,000.

The burn pay-offs in this case are shown in the seventh panel of figure 3.1. The expectation of these payoffs is £116,731, and the standard deviation is £191,025. The fair premium is thus £116,731, and a market maker who adds a risk premium of 20 per cent of the standard deviation might offer to buy and sell at £78,526 and £154,936.

The estimated pay-off CDF is shown in the final panel of figure 3.1. Note the vertical section representing a large probability of zero pay-off.

Discussion

What are the advantages and disadvantages of burn analysis? The *advantages* are that burn analysis is very simple and, as discussed above, is based on very few assumptions. This minimal set of assumptions is important: when we make assumptions in modelling data we may add something, but no assumptions are ever exactly correct, and so we also introduce errors. Later we will show methods that are more accurate than burn analysis in some situations, because the assumptions they use add information or allow us to use the available data more effectively, or both. However, when these assumptions are wrong these methods can give worse results than burn, even though they are much more complex. Complexity does not necessarily mean accuracy. The main *disadvantages* of burn analysis are that we have no idea of the probabilities of events more extreme than those that occurred during the historical period that has been considered, and that the stepped estimate of the CDF is rather unrealistic.

3.1.6 Trading simulations, and the benefits of trading large portfolios

We now consider what kind of business can be achieved by selling only one contract at a time. Figure 3.2 shows the result of a numerical experiment in which we simulate the trading of a single option contract repeatedly. At each

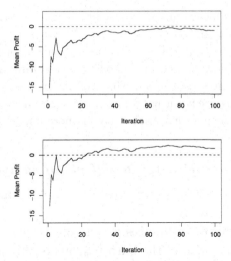

Figure 3.2. The results of a trading simulation in which we trade the same option over and over again for independent realisations of the index. In the upper panel we imagine that the option is traded at the fair price, and so the profit and loss eventually converges to zero. In the lower panel we add a risk loading of 10 per cent of the standard deviation, and so the profit eventually converges to a positive value. However, there are considerable fluctuations before we reach the final value, and there is a period where we are making a loss.

point in time the issuer issues an option contract, receives a premium equal to the fair value and pays out a claim if necessary. Consecutive settlement indices are considered independent. We plot the profit divided by the number of claims, and we see that it gradually tends towards zero.

Clearly, the issuer should charge more than the expected pay-off in order to make money in the long run. For instance, he may choose to charge a premium equal to the expected pay-off plus 10 per cent of the standard deviation. Over the long run he will now make an average profit of 10 per cent of the standard deviation. However, over the short run it is still quite possible to lose money. The second curve in the trading simulation shows this: even when we add this risk loading to the premium the speculator does not make a profit until the twenty-second year.

Most speculators are far more concerned with the results from this season's contracts than about the long run. Without good results in the short run the long run will never exist, because the business will be closed down by the owners. There are two conclusions we can draw from this.

1. Single contracts are very risky for the issuer, since there is a very significant chance of losing money. Charging a very large premium would solve this problem, but then nobody would buy the contract. In chapter 7 we consider some more

reasonable strategies for making money selling weather derivatives based on the ideas of diversification and hedging.

2. The estimated expected pay-off is not necessarily a very useful gauge for what premium to charge, nor, on its own, a good way to monitor a portfolio, since the only information it gives us is about what will happen in the long-run average. But long-run averages are not usually what we care about most. The probabilities of making or losing money this season may be more important.

3.1.7 Price uncertainty: the effects of sampling error

We now consider the effects of statistical or sampling uncertainty on burn analysis.

The mean of the historical indices is only an *estimate* of the actual expected index, and the mean of the burn pay-offs is only an *estimate* of the actual expected pay-off for a contract. In the examples above, we used forty-four years of data. These years might have been, by chance, unusually warm or cold, and our results may thus have not been very representative of the distribution of possible outcomes in the future. We now explore the extent to which such uncertainties affect our estimates of the expected index, the expected pay-off and the pay-off distribution. We assume that the index distribution follows a normal distribution with expectation $\mu = 1700$ and standard deviation $\sigma = 120$.[5]

Uncertainty on the expected index

We start by considering the expectation of the index. In the case where no detrending has been applied to the index, there is a well-known mathematical theory that tells us that our sample-based estimates of the expected index will follow a normal distribution, which has a mean equal to the actual unknown mean, μ, and a standard deviation of $\frac{\sigma_x}{\sqrt{N_y}}$, where σ_x is the actual unknown standard deviation. This standard deviation is often called the *standard error*. Applying this equation shows us that using nine years of historical data gives a standard error on the expectation of a third of the standard deviation of the index, sixteen years of historical data gives a quarter, twenty-five years gives a fifth, and so on. As an example, we tabulate the levels of uncertainty on the expectation calculated from ten, twenty, thirty and forty years of data for our example in the second column of table 3.1. We evaluate $\frac{\sigma_x}{\sqrt{N_y}}$ using our estimate of σ_x from the data.

In the case where detrending has been used this formula no longer applies exactly, because the number of degrees of freedom of the data has been

---

[5] *Roughly* the correct values for a London Heathrow November to March HDD index.

Table 3.1. *The estimated sampling uncertainty on the mean and the standard deviation of a weather index estimated using ten, twenty, thirty and forty years of data. We assume a mean of 1700 and a standard deviation of 120.*

No. of years	Uncertainty on the mean	Uncertainty on the SD
10	37.9	26.8
20	26.8	19.0
30	21.9	15.5
40	19.0	13.4

changed. Instead, for trends that are linear in the covariates (such as linear or loess) one can use either analytic expressions or Monte Carlo methods, as described in appendix A.

However, the uncertainty in the detrended case can also be estimated *approximately* using the $\frac{\sigma_x}{\sqrt{N_y}}$ rule. This will tend to underestimate the uncertainty a little, but the differences are not large in most cases, and the method is certainly much simpler.

Uncertainty on the standard deviation of the index

Now we consider the estimate of the standard deviation. This also comes from a distribution. In the case of no detrending there is, again, a simple equation for the standard deviation of this distribution: $\frac{\sigma_x}{\sqrt{2N_y}}$. This shows us, rather surprisingly, that the standard deviation is estimated more accurately than the expectation. Table 3.1 also gives us the levels of uncertainty on the standard deviation for our example.

Uncertainty on the quantiles of the index

Now we consider estimates of the quantiles of the distribution of the index. The variance of our estimate for the quantile at probability p is

$$\text{variance} \approx \frac{\sigma_x^2}{2N_y}(2 + [\Phi^{-1}(1-p)]^2) \tag{3.2}$$

where Φ^{-1} is the inverse of the CDF of the normal distribution.

Uncertainty on the option premium

What is the uncertainty on the estimate of the fair premium for an option? To illustrate how this uncertainty can be estimated we consider a call option with strike at the expected index plus 25 per cent of the standard deviation. We assume that we have estimated the mean and standard deviation of the index to be 1700 and 120, as before.

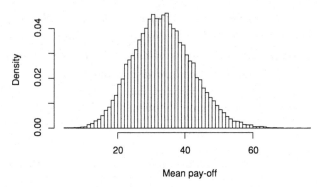

Figure 3.3. If we estimate the fair price for an option on an index with a mean of 1700, a standard deviation of 120, a strike 25 per cent of the standard deviation above the mean and a limit two standard deviations above the mean, using forty years of data, this is the distribution from which our estimate of the fair price will come. The correct value is 33.34.

In order to estimate the uncertainty on the option premium we will initially resort to the somewhat 'brute force' method of using simulations.

The simulations work as follows. We simulate a million years of indices from the fitted index CDF and then sample sections of forty years' length to simulate the burn process. We use each section of forty years to give us an estimate of the expected pay-offs of the option.

We can also estimate the mean pay-offs of the option, and the distribution of these pay-offs, using the full million years of simulated data. We consider these estimates as 'truth', and use them as a basis of comparison for the estimates based on the forty-year sub-samples.

One million years of data divided into forty-year sections gives us 25,000 series. Thus we have 25,000 estimates for the means, standard deviations and distributions of index and pay-offs.

The distribution of expected pay-offs for the option, derived from the simulations, is shown in figure 3.3. Of the 25,000 values, the lowest value is 4.0 and the highest value is 76.8. The expectation of this distribution is 33.37 and the standard deviation is 8.8. There is a 10 per cent chance that the estimate of the expected pay-off will be too high by more than 8.8, or too low by more than 8.6.

Linear theory for option pricing uncertainty

We can also *estimate* the spread of the distribution of possible option pay-offs analytically using the concept of the propagation of errors, which avoids using simulation and is much more convenient.

The standard deviation of the pay-off can be written in terms of the standard deviations of the estimates of the index mean and standard deviation. We write

$$\mu_p = f(\mu_x, \sigma_x) \tag{3.3}$$

where μ_p is the expected pay-off of the contract, and μ_x and σ_x are the mean and standard deviation of the index respectively. If we calculate an estimate $\hat{\mu}_p$ for the expected pay-off μ_p using estimates $\hat{\mu}_x$ and $\hat{\sigma}_x$ for the mean and standard deviation of the index, then the error in an estimate of the expected pay-off is

$$\mu_p - \hat{\mu}_p = f(\mu_x, \sigma_x) - f(\hat{\mu}_x, \hat{\sigma}_x) \tag{3.4}$$
$$= \frac{\partial f}{\partial \mu} d\mu + \frac{\partial f}{\partial \sigma} d\sigma + \ldots \tag{3.5}$$

where $d\mu = \mu_x - \hat{\mu}_x$ and $d\sigma = \sigma_x - \hat{\sigma}_x$.

Ignoring second-order terms, squaring both sides and taking expectations in order to calculate the variance of the error, we get

$$\sigma_{\mu_p}^2 = \left(\frac{\partial f}{\partial \mu}\right)^2 \sigma_{\mu_x}^2 + \left(\frac{\partial f}{\partial \sigma}\right)^2 \sigma_{\sigma_x}^2 \tag{3.6}$$
$$= \left(\frac{\partial f}{\partial \mu}\right)^2 \frac{\sigma_x}{N_y} + \left(\frac{\partial f}{\partial \sigma}\right)^2 \frac{\sigma_x}{2N_y}$$

We see that, under the approximation that errors in the expected pay-off are small, the variance of errors of the estimates of the expected pay-off can be written as a linear combination of the variance of the error on the estimates of the mean index σ_{μ_x} and the variance of the error on the estimates of the standard deviation of the index σ_{σ_x}. Hence errors in the estimate of the expected pay-off can be considered to be due to errors in the estimate of the mean index and errors in the estimate of the standard deviation of the index.

For our option, the partial derivatives $\frac{\partial f}{\partial \mu}$ and $\frac{\partial f}{\partial \sigma}$ have values of 0.296 and 0.204 (we will discuss ways of calculating these values in section 5.1). This gives

$$\sigma_{\mu_p}^2 = (0.296 * 120)^2/40 + (0.204 * 120.0)^2/80 \tag{3.7}$$
$$= 31.5 + 7.5$$
$$= 39$$
$$= 6.2^2$$

We see that, for this option, uncertainty in the mean index is a much greater driver of uncertainty in the expected pay-off than uncertainty in the standard deviation of the index.

We also see that this linear theory gives a reasonable approximation to the more accurate result calculated from the simulations, although it underestimates a little.

In practice, the linear theory is a useful way to calculate a quick estimate of the uncertainty around option prices, and it makes sense to calculate $\sigma_{\mu_p}^2$ using equation (3.6) whenever an option is priced to get a feel for this uncertainty.

A summary of uncertainty issues

We see that burn analysis is a reasonably inaccurate method for estimating either the expected pay-off or the distribution of pay-offs. This translates into significant uncertainty in pricing, and, in turn, into significant uncertainty about what the profit or loss from a weather contract or portfolio of contracts may be, even in the long-run average.

The pricing methods discussed in chapters 4 and 6 can reduce this uncertainty a little in some cases. However, they do not reduce it very much even in the best cases, and the analysis of uncertainty given above can reasonably be applied even if methods other than burn are being used. This uncertainty in pricing is a fundamental characteristic of the weather market, and should be borne in mind throughout the whole process of the pricing and trading of weather derivatives.

3.2 Further reading

The analysis of uncertainty on indices and on the option price comes from Jewson (2003j).

4

The valuation of single contracts using index modelling

4.1 Statistical modelling methods

We now investigate the possible use of statistical modelling in the hope that it might be more accurate than burn, and perhaps have other benefits too. We could, in principle, use a statistical model at any stage of the settlement process of a weather derivative. For example, for an HDD-based contract the settlement process consists of the following stages.

1. Collect daily Tmin and Tmax values.
2. Calculate Tavg.
3. Calculate daily HDD values.
4. Calculate the total HDD value.
5. Calculate the pay-off.

We could thus use a statistical model for any of the following.

1. Daily Tmin and Tmax.
2. Daily Tavg.
3. Daily HDD values.
4. The total HDD value.
5. The pay-off value.

We now discuss each of these in turn. The Tmin and Tmax time series could be modelled as stochastic time series. Looking at figure 1.1 we see that they show significant seasonal cycles in mean and variance, and correlations in time (autocorrelations). They are also cross-correlated at a range of lags. This is a hard statistical modelling problem, and a discussion of the methods that could be used is postponed until chapter 7. Tavg is simpler to model since there is now only one series, and hence no cross-correlations. But even modelling Tavg alone still turns out to be reasonably challenging because of the seasonality and autocorrelation of observed temperatures. Models for

73

Tavg are considered in detail in chapter 6. A daily time series of HDD values
was shown in figure 1.2 (by the lengths of the bars below the line). This is
an odd-looking time series, with many zero values. Although Tmin, Tmax
and Tavg, at least at first look, may be normally distributed, it is quite clear
that the distribution of HDDs is certainly not normal, because of the cut-off
at the baseline. For this reason it is likely to be complex to model, and hence
we will not consider any statistical models for the daily HDD time series.

Total HDD values are shown in the first two panels of figure 3.1. Consecutive years would appear to be reasonably independent (as has already been
discussed), and the distribution of values, which has the same shape as the
CDF in panel 4 of figure 3.1, would appear to be reasonably smooth and
tractable. This would imply that the total HDD values might be modelled
reasonably well using a univariate distribution, and indeed this turns out to
be the case. This is already looking like the simplest modelling solution, and
it is widely used by practitioners in the weather market. We investigate such
index modelling in detail in this chapter. As a final possibility we consider
modelling the pay-off distribution. For a swap contract the pay-off distribution is reasonably simple, and, indeed, modelling the pay-off distribution is
almost the same as modelling the index distribution. Modelling the index
distribution is, however, slightly preferable because the index distribution
has smooth tails whilst the pay-off distribution for capped swaps stops at
the limiting values. For a call option contract the pay-off distribution consists of two spikes ('point masses' to a statistician, 'delta functions' to a
physicist) at the limits of the contract, with a smooth curve in between, and
is thus difficult to model directly, so, again, modelling the index distribution
is preferable.

4.2 Modelling the index distribution

We have seen that, of all the possible statistical modelling approaches, modelling the index distribution would appear to be the simplest. Is such an
approach likely to be any better than the burn analysis of chapter 3? This
is not an easy question to answer. If we knew the distribution that should
be fitted to the historical indices, and we could estimate the parameters
of that distribution with a high degree of accuracy, then index modelling
would certainly be more accurate than burn analysis. The resulting distribution would be smoother (which is more realistic) and would extend into
the tails beyond the data in a realistic way. However, there is only a little
theory to guide us in terms of what distributions to fit to the indices, and
little data with which to estimate the parameters of those distributions (the

same data as is used for the burn analysis). As a result, there is significant danger that we fit a distribution that is not very close to the (unknown) actual distribution. In this case, modelling of the index could certainly give *worse* results than burn.

The question of whether burn or index modelling is more accurate also depends on what is being calculated. This question is addressed in some detail in chapter 5, and we will see there that the relative accuracy of burn and index modelling is different for the expected pay-off and the greeks. There is another reason to use index modelling, however, quite apart from accuracy. This is that the fitting of a distribution, especially the normal distribution, allows us to summarise data very efficiently. As we shall see, this allows us to calculate many useful results quickly and simply. We have already seen (in section 3.1.7) how summarising the index data in terms of mean and standard deviation can help us understand the uncertainty on the estimated expected pay-off, and we will see many more examples of this type of simplification below.

The index modelling methodology

We will now introduce the index modelling methodology in more detail.

The first stage of index modelling is to choose a distribution that is likely to be an accurate representation of the real unknown index distribution. The parameters of this distribution can then be estimated, the hypothesis that the observations could come from this distribution can be tested (at least for parametric models), and, if all is well, the distribution can be used to represent the unknown index distribution.

Discrete or continuous distributions?

Firstly, we ask the question: should we be using discrete or continuous distributions? Temperature variability can be considered to be a continuous random variable, but measurements of it are typically rounded to a certain degree. In the United States, temperature measurements of Tmin or Tmax are rounded to a whole number of degrees Fahrenheit. When Tavg is calculated as the midpoint, it can then be either an integer or a half-integer. In Europe, the measurements of Tmin and Tmax are usually rounded to one decimal place in Celsius, and consequently Tavg has two decimal places, with the final digit being either a zero or a five. As a result of this rounding there is only a discrete number of possible outcomes for the measured temperature during a given period, and hence only a discrete number of possible index values can be achieved. This might lead one to conclude that all index distributions should be modelled using discrete distributions. However, the actual number of different possible index values is often very large, in the thousands, and to fit a discrete distribution to such data, and run simulations, can be very slow. Instead, it is often a reasonable approximation to use a continuous distribution. We apply the following rule of thumb: in any case where there are more than one hundred possible values for the index we use a continuous distribution; in all other cases we use a discrete distribution.

Parametric or non-parametric distributions?

Secondly, we ask: should we be using a parametric or a non-parametric distribution? Parametric distributions use a particular shape, or family of shapes, for the distribution, and then use the historical data to estimate a small number of parameters that pin down the exact form within the available family. Part of the rationale for this approach is that the number of parameters estimated is much lower than the number of data points being used and so these parameters will be estimated reasonably accurately provided the model is approximately correct. The fitted distribution can also be tested for goodness of fit.

A general rule is that, if we have a good reason to believe that a certain parametric distribution is the right one before we look at the data (based on some previous experience, or theoretical rationale), then we should test that distribution against the data, and, if it cannot be rejected, we should use it. In this way we are bringing extra information to bear on the problem.

If, on the other hand, we have little a priori reason to believe that any particular parametric distribution is appropriate for the data then there is less reason to apply parametric methods, apart from the convenient way in which they summarise data. We can test a number of arbitrary parametric distributions but the data is generally insufficient for testing to be very conclusive. In such cases we can use a non-parametric method.

Non-parametric methods constrain the shape of the fitted distribution to a much lesser degree than parametric methods by doing little more than smoothing the index CDF calculated directly from the historical data. One such method is the *kernel density* approach. Kernel densities work by creating a small 'density', of specified shape, around each data point, and then combining these together. This both interpolates between points on the historical CDF and extrapolates a little at the extremes. One of the disadvantages of non-parametric methods is that the fitted distribution cannot be tested, since it always fits the data closely by design.

We will now discuss both parametric and non-parametric methods in more detail.

4.3 Parametric distributions

4.3.1 Methods for fitting parametric distributions

How should we go about fitting the parameters of a parametric distribution? There are two standard methods for fitting the parameters of distributions: the *method of moments* and the *method of maximum likelihood*. The method of moments consists of estimating the moments of the data and deriving analytical expressions for these moments in terms of the parameters of the distribution. It may be possible to solve the resulting equations to derive estimates of the parameters of the distribution in terms of the moments. Examples of such solutions are available for a number of simple distributions: see the references at the end of this chapter.

Although adequate in many cases, the disadvantage of the method of moments is that it can be difficult to derive information about the uncertainty of the parameter estimates.

This problem is overcome by the method of maximum likelihood, and hence maximum likelihood is the ideal procedure for estimating parameters, especially when the distributions get complex. It works as follows: for a given distribution, and for any set of parameters, we can calculate the probability density (for a continuous distribution) or probability (for a discrete distribution) of getting the observed data. Trying different values for the parameters may increase or decrease this probability; maximum likelihood parameter estimates for the parameters are those that give the highest probability. Studying the shape of the likelihood function around the optimum parameters can give information about the uncertainty of the parameters and the correlations between their errors. A more detailed description of the maximum likelihood method is given in appendix B.

4.3.2 Variance estimation

For many distributions the method of moments involves estimating the variance of the data. How should this be done? The detrending methods described in chapter 2 reduce the number of degrees of freedom of the historical index values, and this must be taken into account. The simplest unbiased estimator of the variance is

$$\sigma_x^2 = \frac{\sum_{i=1}^{N_y} (x_i - \mu)^2}{N_y - M} \qquad (4.1)$$

where M is the number of degrees of freedom removed in the detrending procedure. In the case where only a mean is removed the number of degrees of freedom is reduced by one, and this expression becomes the standard expression for the variance, which is

$$\sigma_x^2 = \frac{\sum_{i=1}^{N_y}(x_i - \mu)^2}{N_y - 1} \tag{4.2}$$

Getting the number of degrees of freedom right is most important either when only small amounts of historical data are being used or with non-parametric detrending methods, which remove many degrees of freedom.

4.3.3 Testing goodness of fit

Having estimated the parameters of a distribution using either the method of moments or of maximum likelihood, the next step is to evaluate whether the distribution, with these optimal parameter estimates, gives a good fit to the data. The most useful methods for doing this are graphical. First we can compare the histogram from the data with the probability density function (PDF) (for a continuous distribution) or probability mass function (PMF) (for a discrete distribution) from the model. The first panel in figure 4.1 gives an example. However, it is virtually impossible to judge whether the fit is good from this graph, and the impression depends very heavily on the number of bins used for the histogram. An improvement is to compare the cumulative distribution function from the data and from the model (see the second panel in figure 4.1). In this case both the model CDF and the empirical CDF appear as S-shaped curves. Comparison is easier than for the PDF/histogram plot, but still difficult. Better still, there are two methods that rely on a comparison of straight lines. The first of these is the QQ plot, which plots quantiles from the historical data and the model against quantiles from the model. A correct fit shows a straight line (see the third panel in figure 4.1). The second is the PP plot, which plots probabilities from the historical data and the model against probabilities from the model. Again, a correct fit shows a straight line. Both QQ and PP plots can be considered as CDF plots with one of the axes stretched by a non-linear transformation (which is based on the model, and straightens out the model CDF). For this reason it is convenient to orient the axes of QQ and PP plots so that the lines appear in the same order as in the CDF plot (as we have done in our examples). Someone used to reading a CDF can then read QQ and PP plots relatively easily, and vice versa.

We note the following rules for the interpretation of QQ and PP plots (when plotted using the convention described above).

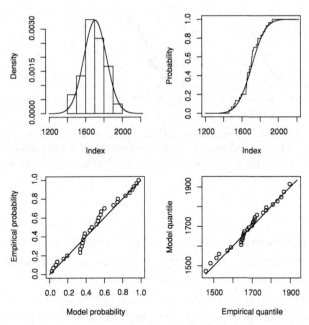

Figure 4.1. Various ways of comparing a fitted distribution with data. The first panel shows a comparison between a fitted PDF and a histogram from the data. The second panel shows a comparison between the fitted CDF and an empirical CDF from the data. The third and fourth panels show PP and QQ plots respectively. The PP and QQ plots are the easiest to use for assessing the goodness of fit of the distribution because they rely on the comparison of straight lines.

1. *Observed above model for low values, and below for high values*: this implies that the model has too low a spread.
2. *Observed below model for low values, and above for high values*: this implies that the model has too high a spread.
3. *Observed above model for low values, and above for high values*: this implies that the model is skewed to the right relative to the observations.
4. *Observed below model for low values, and below for high values*: this implies that the model is skewed to the left relative to the observations.

Confidence intervals

One of the difficulties of the graphical testing of the distributions we have described above is that it is difficult to say whether a difference between the modelled and empirical distribution is significantly large. Even if the model really is correct, the observed data will not agree with the model exactly because it comes from a finite sample. To get round this problem, confidence intervals could be attached to the observed distribution. The logic works

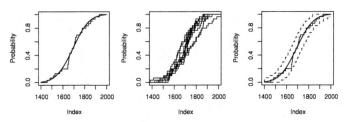

Figure 4.2. The first panel shows a CDF estimated from data and a fitted distribution. The second panel shows a number of CDFs simulated from the fitted model. The third panel shows the confidence limits around the observed CDF based on simulations.

like this: when we fit and test a distribution, we are making the assumption that the data comes from the distribution. On the basis of this assumption (that the fitted distribution is correct) we can use simulation techniques to generate an arbitrarily large number of samples from the distribution of the same length as the historical data that we started with. For each of these samples we can plot the directly estimated CDF. By comparing the CDF from historical data with these simulated CDFs, we can assess whether or not the historical CDF is consistent with the hypothesis. Rather than plotting all the simulated CDFs, we may choose to derive confidence levels at, say, 90 per cent, 95 per cent or 99 per cent. Figure 4.2 illustrates this method for the CDF, although the same can also be done for PP and QQ plots. The first panel shows a historical CDF, with the fitted distribution over the top. The second panel shows a number of CDFs generated from the fitted model, and the third panel shows 90 per cent confidence intervals based on the simulated CDFs. The confidence intervals were generated by picking the fifth lowest and the fifth highest out of one hundred simulated CDFs, for each point on the axis. In this case, we see that the historical data lies well within the range that is consistent with the model. In particular, we see that the deviation between model and observations around values of 1650 are not a cause for concern. Our conclusion is that we cannot reject this model using the historical data available. This is a much weaker statement than saying that this model is correct, which is impossible to prove. All we can ever do is to test the model with more and more tests, and if we always find that we cannot reject the model then our confidence in the model grows.

This method for generating confidence intervals does have one flaw: if we test a model with ten tests at the 90 per cent confidence interval, then we would expect it to fail at least one, on average, even if it is the correct model. To correct for this, ideally we need to change our confidence levels as the number of tests is increased. This is done occasionally but is difficult.

Standard numerical tests of goodness of fit

In addition to such graphical methods one can also perform numerical tests of goodness of fit. These tests are very specific: each test looks at one particular aspect of the distribution. They are useful if one must produce a quantitative ranking of different models, but are not necessarily better than graphical methods. The main tests in use are:

- **chi-squared** – applies to all distributions but has little power, meaning that it is very easy to pass and very hard to fail;
- **Kolmogorov–Smirnov** – also applies to all continuous distributions but, like the chi-squared, has little power;
- **Anderson–Darling** – applies to all continuous distributions, and is more powerful than the previous two tests; the drawback is that it is more difficult to apply;
- **Shapiro–Wilk** – this is a powerful test, but applies to the normal distribution only.

Each test gives a test probability. The distribution can then be accepted or rejected at different confidence levels. High values mean close agreement, and low values mean little agreement. Values below 5 per cent are typically taken to indicate failing the test. More details on these tests are given in appendix C.

4.3.4 Normality of standard degree day and CAT contracts

Is there any rationale that can help us choose distributions for standard contracts? In the next section we discuss whether it is appropriate to use the normal distribution for the standard seasonal and monthly indices.

Arguments for and against the normal distribution

The standard seasonal indices in the US weather market are HDDs for November to March and CDDs for May to September. In the European weather market they are HDDs for November to March and CAT for May to September. Each index value is a sum of daily index values for the period, which is around one hundred and fifty days in length. The number of possible different index values is in the hundreds or thousands, and hence continuous distributions are an appropriate approximation. As we shall see in the next chapter, the autocorrelation of daily temperature values reduces to 0.5 within two days, and so we might consider that these periods contain a large number of effectively independent samples. We will also see that temperature is, typically, close to normally distributed. As sums of moderately independent random variables, we might then be tempted to invoke the central-limit theorem (CLT) and argue that the aggregate index can be well modelled by a normal distribution. The fact that the individual distributions are close to normal would be expected to speed up convergence. It will be very convenient if we can conclude that we can use the normal distribution because it offers a very simple and concise method for summarising data, and a number of closed-form solutions have been derived for the normal. Before we do assume normality on the basis of the CLT, however, there are other factors that need to be taken into account: (a) because of the seasonal cycle of temperature, the daily degree day values cannot be considered a stationary process (see figure 1.2, which shows the clear seasonal cycle in daily degree day values); (b) for some stations, many of the daily degree day values may be zero; and (c) although the autocorrelations drop very quickly initially, they remain non-zero even at very long leads. As a result, the CLT is not, per se, of any use other than as a general indication that we should at least try the normal, and to find out if the normal can really be used we have to assess the data itself.

The normality of standard seasonal and monthly indices on US temperatures was analysed in Jewson (2004g), with the following conclusions:

- for winter HDD and CAT indices, and summer CDD and CAT indices, the normal distribution gives a reasonable fit at almost all locations;
- for CAT and HDD indices based on the individual winter months, November, January, February and March are well modelled by the normal distribution for most if not all locations, whereas December is definitely not normal, many locations having a heavy cold tail;
- for CAT indices based on the individual summer months the normal distribution does well everywhere;
- for CDD indices based on the individual summer months the normal distribution does not do particularly well overall, presumably because temperatures frequently cross the baseline; only in July does the normal seem to be reasonably safe.

We conclude that one may be able to use the normal distribution for seasonal contracts fairly blindly, but for monthly contracts that would not be advisable. In particular, for any contract based on December temperatures, and any contract based on summer monthly CDDs, it would be very wise to check the validity of the normal before using it.

4.3.5 Parametric alternatives to the normal distribution for standard contracts

If a distribution fails the tests for normality then theory deserts us, and it seems that if we really want to use a parametric distribution all we can do is to try a number of standard distributions in the hope that something fits. There are a range of distributions to choose from that are close to the normal distribution but include some asymmetry. These include the skew-normal distribution, the gamma distribution and the log-normal distribution.

4.3.6 Parametric distributions for event contracts

The typical index values that result from event indices are much lower than those that result from degree day indices. As a result, discrete distributions are usually appropriate. We review three parametric distributions that one might use for such contracts: Poisson, binomial and negative binomial.

The Poisson distribution

A stochastic process consisting of completely random events is known as a Poisson process. The number of events of a Poisson process during a finite period of time is distributed with the Poisson distribution, and the intervals between events of a Poisson process are distributed with an exponential distribution. At first sight, the Poisson process seems as though it may be a reasonable model for meteorological events such as temperature exceeding a certain threshold. The two problems with this are that (a) the number of times the daily temperature can exceed a threshold during a specified period clearly cannot exceed the number of days in the period, while the Poisson distribution can give an arbitrarily large number of events during any period, and (b) meteorological events are not entirely independent in time, while events in a Poisson process are independent.

The first of these problems may not kill the idea of using a Poisson distribution. As long as the average number of events is fairly small relative to the length of the period then the probability of a Poisson distribution giving silly results (more events than the number of days) is very low. The second problem with the Poisson distribution, however, turns out to be more serious. The first panel in figure 4.3 shows a QQ plot for a Poisson distribution fitted to the number of days on which temperature exceeds 20°C at London Heathrow during the summer. The mean of the distribution over the ninety-two-day period is 15.6 days. The fit is clearly very bad indeed, and the actual distribution has much fatter tails than the Poisson. This

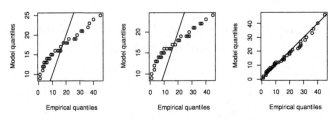

Figure 4.3. QQ plots showing the goodness of fit of Poisson, binomial and negative binomial distributions to an index of extreme weather.

means that extreme events are much more common than would be given by a Poisson process. This is exactly what we would expect if autocorrelation in the events is playing a role, and this fits with our intuition about weather: hot days come in groups. The variance of a Poisson distribution equals the mean, and one consequence of a clustering of events is that the variance of the indices will tend to be higher than would be expected for a Poisson distribution. Statisticians say that the observations are *over-dispersed* in this case.

Parametric alternatives to the Poisson distribution for event contracts

We mentioned above that one problem with the Poisson distribution is that, in theory, the model could produce more events than the number of days in the contract period. Although this may not be a practical problem if the mean number of events is much smaller than the number of days, one could still think of fixing the problem by forcing the number of events to be less than or equal to the number of days. In mathematical terms we can model this by a Poisson process conditioned on the number of events being less than or equal to the number of days. Such a process is called a binomial process, and the total number of events follows a *binomial distribution*. Use of the binomial distribution thus overcomes the first problem with the Poisson distribution (that the Poisson distribution can give an infinite number of events in a finite period) and can be used for contracts where having as many events as there are numbers of days is reasonably likely. The main disadvantage of using the binomial distribution relative to the Poisson is that it assumes so-called *under-dispersion* – i.e. the variance is less than the mean. Because of the autocorrelation that is often seen in meteorological events (and the resulting over-dispersion of the observations that we have already seen) the binomial is therefore typically less useful than the Poisson distribution. This can be seen in the second panel of figure 4.3, which shows the binomial fitted to the same exceedence data as used above, and again we see that the fit is very bad indeed.

One way to model over-dispersion for event data is by using a Poisson distribution with a random mean. This is guaranteed to produce over-dispersion, since, if we let X follow a Poisson distribution and let Y be the random mean, then

$$VX = EV(X|Y) + VE(X|Y) \geq EV(X|Y) = EE(X|Y) = EX$$

Such a model is called a mixed Poisson distribution. A common choice of distribution for the mean is a gamma distribution, which results in a *negative binomial distribution* for the number of events. We could consider our process made up of extreme autocorrelated temperature events to be a Poisson process for which the expectation is changing in time over timescales of a few days. A hot period, during which we get a larger number of extremely hot days, has a high expectation. In reality, the expectation probably does not follow a gamma distribution, but it may be a good approximation, especially since the gamma is a fairly general distribution that covers a wide range of shapes. Based on this reasoning we try fitting a negative binomial distribution to the temperature exceedences in the example considered above. The results are shown in the third panel of figure 4.3. It turns out that the negative binomial gives a very good fit to the observed data.

On the basis of this example (and other similar examples) we conclude that the negative binomial is a reasonably good candidate for modelling event indices.

4.4 Non-parametric distributions

We now consider the kernel density approach to non-parametric distribution modelling. Kernel densities estimate the unknown density using a weighted sum of densities (or kernels) that are centred around each data point. We will discuss two versions. The first, and most commonly used, simply places a density around each data point. This, however, has the flaw that the variance of the fitted distribution can be larger than the unbiased estimate of the variance. An alternative version adjusts the variance so that this is no longer the case.

The major benefits of the non-parametric approaches are as follows:

1. They involve making fewer assumptions about the overall shape of the distribution than a parametric method. Such assumptions can cause as much harm as good.
2. They can be applied to absolutely any index in any situation (although they always give a continuous distribution).

On the other hand, if the normal, or negative binomial, really is a good model for the index, they will tend to give better results. Non-parametric methods also do not provide a convenient summary of the data in the way that parametric methods do, and are more difficult to validate than parametric distributions.

4.4.1 The basic kernel density

The basic kernel density models the density as

$$f(x) = \frac{1}{\lambda N_y} \sum_{i=1}^{N_y} K\left(\frac{x - x_i}{\lambda}\right) \tag{4.3}$$

where K is a probability density. A common choice for the kernel K is the normal distribution which then gives

$$f(x) = \frac{1}{\lambda N_y} \sum_{i=1}^{N_y} \frac{1}{\sqrt{2\pi}} \exp\left(-\frac{(x - x_i)^2}{2\lambda}\right) \tag{4.4}$$

There is one free parameter in our kernel density, the *bandwidth* λ. A value of $\lambda = 0$ yields a stepped CDF equivalent to the empirical CDF, and a density consisting of delta functions (point masses) at each data point. Small values of λ smooth the CDF a bit, and typically produce finite but multimodal densities. Large values of λ create a smooth CDF and a unimodal density, and for very large values of λ the density is almost uniform.

There are a number of methods commonly used for choosing λ, all of which are more or less ad hoc. One is 'Silverman's rule of thumb', which is

$$\lambda = \frac{0.9}{1.34} \min(s, q) N_y^{-\frac{1}{5}} \tag{4.5}$$

where s is the sample standard deviation of the data x_i, and q is the interquartile range. This equation comes from Silverman (1986, equation 3.31).

Another comes from Jones (1991, equation 6):

$$\lambda = 1.034 s N_y^{-\frac{1}{5}} \tag{4.6}$$

Both Silverman and Jones give some rationale for using the expressions that they give.

An example of a kernel distribution fitted to historical HDD values for London Heathrow, for four different bandwidths, and using a Gaussian kernel, is given in figure 4.4.

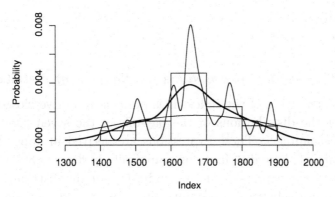

Figure 4.4. A histogram and three different kernel densities fitted to thirty years of loess detrended historical data for the November to March HDD index for London Heathrow. The bandwidths for the kernels are 10, 47.5 and 200. 47.5 is the optimal value from equation (4.5).

4.4.2 The adjusted kernel density

The variance of f is given by

$$\text{variance of fitted kernel} = \text{sample variance} + \lambda^2 \qquad (4.7)$$

We see that, as the λ increases, the variance of the fitted distribution also increases, and quickly exceeds the unbiased estimate of the variance given by $\frac{\sum x^2}{N_y - M}$, where $N_y - M$ is the number of degrees of freedom in the data after detrending. This overestimation of the variance is, perhaps, unfortunate, and certainly means that large values of λ do not make sense. To rectify this, one can force the variance to be exactly equal to the unbiased estimate of the variance. We call this method the adjusted kernel density.

In the adjusted kernel density λ becomes a pure shape parameter, and as $\lambda \to \infty$ the shape tends towards a normal distribution.

4.5 Estimating the pay-off distribution
and the expected pay-offs

We have now investigated in some detail the issues that arise when fitting distributions to historical index values. Having fitted such a distribution, we proceed by combining this with the pay-off structure to calculate the distribution of the financial outcomes of the contract and statistics such as the expected pay-off, the standard deviation of the pay-offs, the probability of hitting the strike and limit, and so on. There are a number of ways that this can be done: by deriving closed-form expressions, by numerical integration, or by simulation. Each of these is discussed below. We start by considering the closed-form expressions.

4.5.1 Closed-form expressions for the pay-off distribution

Given the distribution of the index, it is possible to derive closed-form expressions for the distributions of the pay-offs of the seven contract types described in chapter 1. These expressions are derived in appendix D. We illustrate some of these distributions graphically in figure 4.5.

We see from the expressions in appendix D that the distribution of pay-offs, over the range between the limits (for a swap) and between the strike and limit (for the call option), has exactly the same shape as the original index distribution.

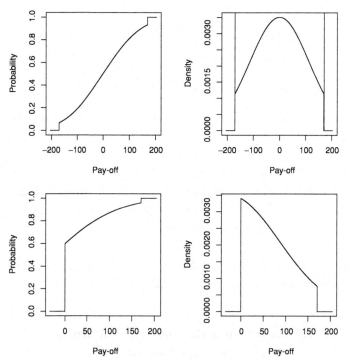

Figure 4.5. The CDFs and PDFs for the pay-off from a capped swap (upper panels) and a capped option contract (lower panels). The underlying index is London Heathrow HDDs, thirty years of historical data, detrended with loess (1,0.9). This gives a mean of 1665 HDDs and a standard deviation of 114. The swap strike is set at the mean index and the swap limit is set at 1.5 standard deviations. The option strike is set at 0.25 standard deviations above the mean, and the option limit is set at 1.5 standard deviations from the mean. Note that the limits are set unusually low for illustrative purposes.

4.5.2 Closed-form expression for the expected pay-off and pay-off variance

It is possible to derive closed-form solutions for the expectation and variance of the pay-off distribution for certain contracts and certain distributions, although not for all contracts and all distributions. The most important cases are the normal distribution and the kernel density.

Derivations for closed-form solutions for these distributions, and the expressions themselves, are given in the appendices. In appendix D we give closed-form expressions for the expected pay-off of the seven contract types for a normal distribution. In appendix E we give closed-form expressions for the pay-off variance of the seven contract types for a normal distribution. In appendix G we give expressions for the expected pay-off and the pay-off variance for the kernel density.

For other distributions it is generally more difficult, and may be impossible, to calculate exact expressions, and numerical methods are used instead.

4.5.3 Use of the limited expected value function

Our derivations of the closed-form expressions for the expected pay-off and the pay-off variance are all based on direct evaluation of the integrals that define these quantities. We now describe a slightly different but equivalent approach for deriving closed-form expressions for the expected pay-offs of weather contracts.

We define a function known as the *limited expected value* (LEV) *function* as

$$L_x(m) = Emin(x, m) \tag{4.8}$$

$$= \int_{-\infty}^{m} x dF(x) + m(1 - F(m)) \tag{4.9}$$

where m is the argument of L. The limited expected value function gives the expectation of the variable x for values of x less than m only, ignoring values of x greater than m. As m becomes large, the LEV function converges to the expectation of x.

Taking the expectations of equation (1.16) we find that the expected pay-off of a call option is given by

$$\mu_p = D(L_x(L) - L_x(K)) \tag{4.10}$$

This expression is an alternative way to write expression (D.33).

If other moments of the pay-off distribution are of interest, they can be calculated using higher-order limited expected value functions, such as $Emin(m, I)^k$.

The use of the LEV has its origins in the actuarial literature, where it is used to calculate the expected excess of loss for reinsurance programmes.

4.5.4 Numerical estimates of the expected pay-off and pay-off distribution

We now discuss how numerical integration and Monte Carlo simulation can be used to estimate expected pay-offs and pay-off distributions for any index distribution.

Numerical integration

Numerical integration works as follows. The range of possible index values is divided into intervals. These intervals may or may not be equal. One index value within each interval is converted to a pay-off using the pay-off function. A probability is also calculated for each interval using the index CDF, and a probability density using the index PDF. To estimate the distribution of pay-offs, the pay-off values are sorted and the probabilities are allocated from the CDF. To estimate the expected pay-off, the pay-offs are combined with the probability densities from the PDF.

One advantage of numerical integration is that it can be numerically efficient because the sampling of the index values can be adjusted to include only relevant values. For instance, for options the sampling of the index values need not include any index values for which the pay-off is zero. However, given that fast computers are readily available, this issue of numerical efficiency is not particularly important.

One disadvantage of numerical integration is that it does not extend very practically to large portfolios, unlike simulation.

Simulation

Simulation works slightly differently from numerical integration. First, pseudo-random numbers are generated from the index distribution using standard packages available in most computer languages or spreadsheets (details of the mathematics behind some of the commonly used simulation methods are given in appendix I). Each simulated index is converted into a pay-off. The pay-offs can be sorted to create the estimated CDF of pay-offs in the same way that historical pay-offs are used to create the CDF in burn analysis (see section 3.1.3). The mean of these pay-offs is calculated. In this

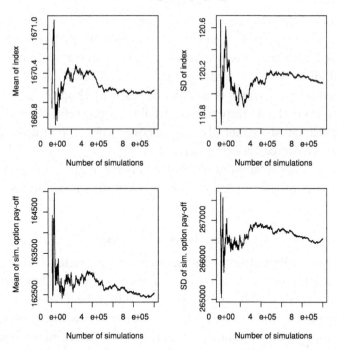

Figure 4.6. The top left panel shows the convergence of a simulation-based estimate of the mean index for an option contract versus the number of simulations. The top right panel shows the convergence of the standard deviation of the index, the lower left panel shows the convergence of the expected pay-off and the lower right panel shows the convergence of the standard deviation of the pay-offs.

case the information about the shape of the distribution is included in the random sampling, and so probabilities are not needed.

The convergence rate of the simulations is given by $\frac{\sigma_x}{\sqrt{N_s}}$ for the expected index and $\frac{\sigma_x}{\sqrt{2N_s}}$ for the standard deviation of the simulated index, where N_s is the number of simulations used (we have seen these expressions already in section 3.1.7). Convergence of the expected pay-off and the standard deviation of the pay-off are given by $\frac{\sigma_p}{\sqrt{N_s}}$ and $\frac{\sigma_p}{\sqrt{2N_s}}$, where σ_p is the standard deviation of the pay-off distribution. Figure 4.6 shows examples of the convergence of the mean and standard deviation of an index and the pay-offs of an option against the number of simulations used.

The high level of convergence that can be achieved using many simulations can be misleading if not interpreted correctly: it is the level of accuracy given by the simulations, assuming that the underlying model is exactly correct. But the underlying model is never correct. However many simulations we use we are fundamentally limited by the amount of information in the original historical data and by the sampling errors on the parameters of the distribution. These sources of error are typically much larger than the errors associated with too few simulations, and the uncertainty on the option prices is still given, more or less, by equation (3.6).

If the speed of simulations is important, then methods exist for speeding them up. However, the widespread availability of powerful computers means that such methods are generally not necessary for the simple simulation analyses that we are considering here.

One big advantage of simulation that will become apparent in chapter 7 is that it is the only practical method for the valuation of portfolios of weather derivatives.

A comparison of methods

When a normal distribution is being used for the index then for a given amount of computer time much greater accuracy can be obtained with the closed-form expressions than with numerical integration or simulation. However, the issue is moot unless extreme speed is required. For instance, most personal computers can simulate several million values from a given distribution within a few seconds, giving high accuracy to the simulation approach. Simulation has the added advantage that it can be extended to portfolios, and so it is common to use simulations for all pricing because of their general applicability to all contracts, distributions and portfolios.

The closed-form expressions still have several uses, however. First, they can be used to check that simulation or numerical integration models are working correctly. Second, they are useful in situations in which a very large number of pricing calculations are needed, which often occurs when making studies of the behaviour of weather derivative prices (we ourselves make extensive use of the closed-form solutions for this reason). Third, they are useful when 'inverting' the premium of a weather option to derive the implied standard deviation (see section 11.4.9). This is a calculation that requires many accurate calculations of the expected pay-off in succession, which could be slow with a simulation approach. Finally, closed-form solutions can be studied and allow us to develop understanding into how prices depend on the various determining factors, without having to write computer programmes and perform vast numbers of simulations to answer every question.

4.6 Further reading

Useful actuarial references for the details of some of the distributions used in this chapter are Hogg and Klugman (1984) and Klugman et al. (1998). A reference for univariate discrete distributions is Johnson et al. (1993), and for univariate continuous distributions is Johnson et al. (1994).

The closed-form expressions for the expected pay-off under a normal distribution have been in use in the weather market since the very start. Examples in certain special cases are given in McIntyre (1999), Moreno (2001b), Henderson (2002), Jewson (2003t) and Brix et al. (2002). A comprehensive set of derivations and expressions is given in Jewson (2003a), Jewson (2003c) and Jewson (2003d).

The adjusted kernel density is described in Jones (1991), and the first description of its use in weather pricing is in Jewson (2003q). The use of the LEV function for weather pricing comes from Brix et al. (2002).

5

Further topics in the valuation of single contracts

In the previous two chapters we described burn analysis and index modelling. These are the most commonly used methods for the pricing of weather derivatives. Before we consider other more complex pricing methods based on the statistical modelling of daily temperatures we now digress and look at a number of interesting issues that arise in the pricing of single weather derivatives contracts. We start by discussing the so-called 'greeks'. We then look at the relative importance of decisions concerning the choice of trend and the choice of distribution. We look at the relative accuracy of burn and index modelling, and the correlations between results from these two methods. We investigate the effects of varying the parameters of an option on the expected pay-off in order to develop some intuition about the different prices that occur for different contracts. Finally we address a number of other issues, including how to price multi-year contracts, how to use market data in pricing, how to perform static hedges and how to cope with leap-year-related issues.

5.1 Linear sensitivity analysis: the greeks

The pricing, trading and risk management of most kinds of financial options is based on the idea of maintaining a very low-risk portfolio using hedging, and, very often, frequent rehedging.[1] In order to achieve effective hedging it is useful to calculate various partial derivatives of the arbitrage price of options, known as the 'greeks'. These show us how the value of the option (or portfolio of options) can change due to small changes in the underlying price, time, interest rates or volatility. Partial derivatives are useful because

---

[1] In most cases this strategy cannot be applied to weather options because very frequent rehedging is not financially viable (this is discussed in more detail in chapter 11).

options are typically rehedged on an extremely frequent basis – frequently enough for the small changes predicted by such a linear theory to be relevant.

The derivative of the arbitrage price with respect to the underlying index is known as delta (Δ); a small value for delta implies that a contract is not greatly affected by small changes in the index. The derivative of delta with respect to the underlying is known as gamma (Γ); small values for gamma imply that delta is not greatly affected by small changes in the index. The derivative of the arbitrage price with respect to time is known as theta (Θ), with respect to interest rates is known as rho (ρ), and with respect to the volatility of the underlying index as vega (which has no symbol because it is not a real Greek letter).

We have not yet considered arbitrage pricing theories for weather. These theories involve the greeks in exactly the same way as do the arbitrage theories for other kinds of options. This will be discussed in chapter 11. For the moment, however, we will consider the relevance of the greeks to *actuarial pricing*. In actuarial pricing theory it is not possible to define exact analogues for the greeks. This is because actuarial pricing does not lead to a single price in the same way that arbitrage pricing does; as we saw in chapter 3, there may be a subjectively determined risk loading on every price. In addition, partial derivatives of prices are slightly less relevant because the actuarial management of weather contracts and portfolios is as much concerned with the final distribution of outcomes and with large changes in the underlying indices as it is with small changes.

However, there are situations in actuarial pricing and portfolio management in which it may be useful to calculate various partial derivatives of estimates of the value of contracts, and because the resulting expressions are somewhat similar to the greeks (and because many weather traders come from a financial options background) they are often given the same names. The exact definitions and actual application of the greeks are, however, often rather different from those seen in an arbitrage context.

We will now consider some of the practical questions that can be answered using partial derivatives of the actuarial value of a weather contract, and will then look at how they can be calculated.

1. *How can I best hedge an option contract using a swap contract on the same index?* One answer to this is that the tick size of the swap should be equal to the partial derivative of the value of the option with respect to the index (or the expected index), which we might call the 'delta' of the contract. Other possible answers to this question are discussed in section 5.13.2.

2. *How would my contract valuation change if the weather forecast suddenly changed?* We will describe in more detail how to use weather forecasts to value

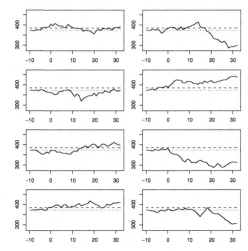

Figure 5.1. Eight realisations of the possible development of the expected index for a call option contract. See section 5.4 for details.

weather contracts in chapter 10. However, for now we imagine that we are valuing a contract in progress using a weather forecast and historical data. The partial derivative of the value with respect to the index (delta) can help us calculate the approximate sensitivity of the value of the contract to a 1° change on one day of the forecast. If we wish to know the *likely* size of the changes due to changes in the weather forecast, then we also have to consider the possible distribution of changes in the weather forecast, in combination with delta.

3. *If I change nothing in my portfolio, and the underlying indices do not change, how is the value likely to change between today and tomorrow?* To answer this we can calculate the partial derivative in time, and the result might be called 'theta' by analogy with theta from arbitrage pricing. The change of the value of the portfolio from day to day is then given approximately by theta times one day.

4. *How important is it that I estimate the standard deviation of an index accurately?* This question arises in chapter 10, where we present various methods for estimating the in-contract standard deviation. We will see that there is a trade-off between simplicity and accuracy. Differentiating the value of a contract with respect to the standard deviation can give us some indication of how errors in the standard deviation become errors in the expected pay-off.

All these questions depend on identifying some definition of the value of a weather contract. The simplest definition of value is the expected pay-off (or expected profit), and this definition has the advantages that it is independent of whether the contract is being held as a long or short position and does not have a subjective component. Also, as we will see in chapter 11, it means that there is agreement with certain arbitrage pricing theories for weather. However, it does not really represent the actual notion of value that most weather traders have in mind when they trade, which involves a trade-off between risk and return. This can be incorporated into the definition of value, by, for instance, defining value as the expected pay-off minus some fraction of the standard deviation of pay-offs. This definition has the advantage that it captures the necessary trade-off between risk and return in a reasonable way. But, using this definition, the value of a contract now depends on both the risk aversion of the trader, which is reflected in the fraction of the standard deviation used, and whether the contract is held long or short, which affects whether the risk loading is added or subtracted. Using this more complex definition of value means that calculations of the greeks would be different for different traders and different positions.

As long as value is defined as the expected pay-off, then it is additive (the value of two contracts is the sum of the values of the individual contracts). The partial derivatives of value are then also additive. If value is defined in terms of both the expected pay-off and the standard deviation of the pay-off, then it ceases to be additive and the partial derivatives are also not additive.

We now define various 'greeks' for weather. For simplicity, and based on the considerations given above, we will use definitions that are based on the expected pay-off alone and do not include a risk loading. However, practitioners may, in some cases, prefer to use a definition based on a trade-off between risk and return, and, indeed, it may be useful to look at both definitions in some situations.

Delta

We define delta as the partial derivative of the expected pay-off with respect to the current value for the index, at constant σ_x.

$$\Delta = \frac{\partial \mu_p}{\partial x} \tag{5.1}$$

This is equivalent to defining it as the partial derivative of the expected pay-off with respect to the *expected* value for the index, since changes in the current value of the index lead to changes in the expected value of the index. It is often more appropriate to consider the underlying index for an option to be our current estimate for the expected index, or even to be the market value for the swap price, rather than the current index. We will return to this point in chapters 10 and 11.

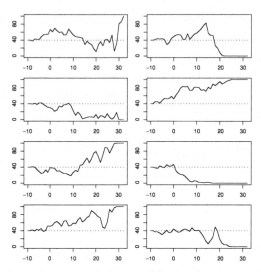

Figure 5.2. Eight realisations of the possible development of delta for a call
option contract.

Eight examples of how delta might develop during the course of an option
contract are given in figure 5.2, and are discussed in section 5.4.

Gamma

We define gamma as the partial derivative of delta with respect to the current
value for the index, at constant σ_x.

$$\Gamma = \frac{\partial \Delta}{\partial x} = \frac{\partial^2 \mu_p}{\partial x^2} \qquad (5.2)$$

Eight examples of how gamma might develop during the course of an option
contract are given in figure 5.3.

Zeta

We define zeta, which is unique to weather derivatives, to be the partial
derivative with respect to the standard deviation of the index σ_x at constant
μ_x.

$$\zeta = \frac{\partial \mu_p}{\partial \sigma_x} \qquad (5.3)$$

Zeta is sometimes called 'index vega', but we prefer to use the name 'zeta'
because it comes with a symbol.

Eight examples of how zeta might develop during the course of an option
contract are given in figure 5.4.

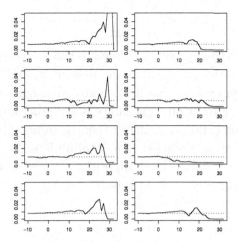

Figure 5.3. Eight realisations of the possible development of gamma for a call option contract.

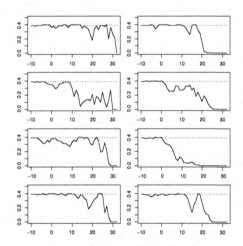

Figure 5.4. Eight realisations of the possible development of zeta for a call option contract.

Theta

We define theta to be the partial derivative of the expected pay-off with respect to time at constant μ_x.

$$
\begin{aligned}
\Theta &= \frac{\partial \mu_p}{\partial t} \\
&= \frac{\partial \mu_p}{\partial \sigma_x} \frac{\partial \sigma_x}{\partial t} \\
&= \zeta \frac{\partial \sigma_x}{\partial t}
\end{aligned}
\tag{5.4}
$$

Vega

In standard arbitrage theory vega is defined as the derivative of the arbitrage price with respect to the volatility of the underlying index. To define vega for weather derivatives we first need to create a reasonable surrogate for an underlying index. The most obvious choice is the stochastic process defined by the conditional expectation of the settlement index given our knowledge up to time t. This can be modelled as a deterministic function of Brownian motion, given by $d\mu_x = \sigma dW$ (see chapter 9 for a more detailed discussion of this), and thus it has a well-defined volatility σ. Vega is then the derivative of the expected pay-off by this volatility.

We then have

$$\text{vega} = \frac{\partial \mu}{\partial \sigma} \tag{5.5}$$

$$= \frac{\partial \mu}{\partial \sigma_x} \frac{\partial \sigma_x}{\partial \sigma}$$

$$= \zeta \frac{\partial \sigma_x}{\partial \sigma}$$

We see from this that vega is related to zeta as defined above.

Modelling the volatility

To calculate theta and vega we must relate the standard deviation of the index σ_x to the volatility σ and time t. This is discussed in detail in chapter 9, where we present a number of models for this relationship, but for now we note that the simplest relation between the standard deviation of the index and the volatility of the expected index would be that the volatility is zero outside the contract period and constant during the contract period. This is not entirely accurate, since forecasts affect our estimate of the expected index before the contract has started, but it is a useful starting point. We then have

$$\sigma_x = \begin{cases} (T - t_0)^{\frac{1}{2}}\sigma & \text{if } t \leq t_0 \\ (T - t)^{\frac{1}{2}}\sigma & \text{if } t \geq t_0 \end{cases} \tag{5.6}$$

where $T - t_0$ is the length of the contract and σ is the volatility of the expected index. We call this relation the 'volatility-variance' constraint. We give the form of this constraint for other models in chapter 9. Differentiating gives

$$\frac{\partial \sigma_x}{\partial t} = \begin{cases} 0 & \text{if } t \leq t_0 \\ -\frac{1}{2}(T - t)^{-\frac{1}{2}}\sigma & \text{if } t \geq t_0 \end{cases} \tag{5.7}$$

and

$$\frac{\partial \sigma_x}{\partial \sigma} = \begin{cases} (T - t_0)^{\frac{1}{2}} & \text{if } t \leq t_0 \\ (T - t)^{\frac{1}{2}} & \text{if } t \geq t_0 \end{cases} \qquad (5.8)$$

and hence

$$\theta = \begin{cases} 0 & \text{if } t \leq t_0 \\ -\frac{\zeta \sigma_x}{2(T-t)} & \text{if } t \geq t_0 \end{cases} \qquad (5.9)$$

and

$$\text{vega} = \begin{cases} \zeta (T - t_0)^{\frac{1}{2}} & \text{if } t \leq t_0 \\ \zeta (T - t)^{\frac{1}{2}} & \text{if } t \geq t_0 \end{cases} \qquad (5.10)$$

Temperature delta

A final point about delta is that occasionally it is useful to consider the partial derivative of the expected pay-off with respect to temperature rather than just the index. This has the advantage that deltas for different indices based on the same underlying variable (such as CAT and HDD indices for the same time period) can then be combined. To define the derivative properly it is necessary to specify exactly which temperature is being used. The most obvious case would be to consider variations in the most recently measured temperature. One could also consider varying the mean values of future temperatures, however.

Starting from

$$\mu_p = \mu_p(\mu_x, \sigma_x) \qquad (5.11)$$

and differentiating with respect to temperature T gives

$$\frac{\partial \mu_p}{\partial T} = \frac{\partial \mu_p}{\partial \mu_x}\frac{\partial \mu_x}{\partial T} + \frac{\partial \mu_p}{\partial \sigma_x}\frac{\partial \sigma_x}{\partial T} \qquad (5.12)$$

$$= \Delta \frac{\partial \mu_x}{\partial T} + \zeta \frac{\partial \sigma_x}{\partial T}$$

We see that temperature delta is, in general, related to both Δ and ζ.

Total derivatives of the expected pay-off

We now consider actual changes in the expected pay-off.

If we consider the expected pay-off to be a function of the mean and standard deviation of the index (this would apply to normal, log-normal and gamma distributions for the index, among others), then

$$\mu_p = \mu_p(\mu_x, \sigma_x) \qquad (5.13)$$

There are two kinds of derivative one can consider. The first looks at changes in μ_p due to random changes in μ_x and σ_x, such as those caused by sampling error. This gives

$$d\mu_p = \frac{\partial \mu_p}{d\mu_x} d\mu_x + \frac{\partial \mu_p}{d\sigma_x} d\sigma_x \qquad (5.14)$$
$$= \Delta d\mu_x + \zeta d\sigma_x$$

In other words, the total change depends on delta and zeta.

We have already used this expression in chapter 3 to evaluate how sampling error on μ_x and σ_x causes errors in the estimated expected pay-off.

The second kind of derivative looks at changes in μ_p due to changes in time. In this case we have to consider μ_x as a stochastic process, as described above and in more detail in chapter 9. In fact, μ_x can be considered as a kind of stochastic process known as a *diffusion* process. When differentiating a function of a diffusion process we have to use Ito's lemma, and there is an extra term relative to the expression for the total derivative of a function of deterministic processes.

Starting from a Taylor expansion of μ_p we have

$$d\mu_p = \frac{\partial \mu_p}{\partial \mu_x} d\mu_x + \frac{\partial \mu_p}{\partial \sigma_x} d\sigma_x + \frac{1}{2} \frac{\partial^2 \mu_p}{\partial \mu_x^2} d\mu_x^2 + \dots \qquad (5.15)$$
$$= \Delta d\mu_x + \zeta d\sigma_x + \frac{1}{2} \Gamma d\mu_x^2 + \dots$$
$$= \Delta \sigma dW + \Theta dt + \frac{1}{2} \Gamma \sigma^2 dW^2 + \dots$$
$$= \Delta \sigma dW + \Theta dt + \frac{1}{2} \Gamma \sigma^2 dt + \dots$$
$$= \Delta \sigma dW + dt(\Theta + \frac{1}{2} \sigma^2 \Gamma) + \dots$$

For infinitesimal changes we have Ito's lemma, which in this case gives

$$d\mu_p = \Delta \sigma dW + dt(\Theta + \frac{1}{2} \sigma^2 \Gamma) \qquad (5.16)$$

We see that changes in μ_p are driven by stochastic changes (the dW term) and by a deterministic drift (the dt term).

But μ_p is a conditional expectation, and so it cannot have a drift (this is discussed in more detail in Jewson (2003s)), and therefore the coefficient of dt in this equation must be zero.

This gives two interesting results. First,

$$\Theta + \frac{1}{2} \sigma^2 \Gamma = 0 \qquad (5.17)$$

or, re-expanding in terms of the full notation,

$$\frac{\partial \mu_p}{\partial t} + \frac{1}{2}\sigma^2 \frac{\partial^2 \mu_p}{\partial \mu_x^2} = 0 \tag{5.18}$$

We conclude that the fair price of a weather option satisfies a partial differential equation (PDE), which is a backwards diffusion type of equation. The diffusion coefficient comes from the volatility. This PDE will come up again in a slightly different context in chapter 11.

Second,

$$d\mu_p = \Delta\sigma dW \tag{5.19}$$

In other words, changes in the fair price of a weather derivative over short time horizons are normally distributed around the current fair price, and have a volatility given simply in terms of the Δ of the contract and the σ of the underlying expected index. This can be used to estimate how the value of a contract might change over a short time period, which is a question often asked in the context of risk management. We extend this idea to portfolios in chapter 12.

5.1.1 Estimating the greeks

We now discuss how the greeks defined above can be estimated.

Perhaps the simplest way to estimate delta is to price a contract twice, with a small difference in the expected index. This will lead to a small difference in the expected pay-off. Delta is then estimated as the ratio of the differences in the prices to the differences in the expected index.

$$\text{delta} \approx \frac{\mu_p(\mu_x + \Delta x) - \mu_p(\mu_x)}{\Delta x} \tag{5.20}$$

Gamma can then be estimated in a similar way from the difference between two values of delta. Zeta can be estimated by making a small change in the standard deviation.

These estimates are exact only in the case that the expected pay-off is a linear function of the index (or standard deviation), which is true only for unlimited swap contracts. For all other contracts these estimates are approximations that converge to the real value as the change in the index (or standard deviation) tends towards zero. For degree day contracts, with typical index values in the thousands, it would be reasonable to use a difference in the index of one degree day. For event contracts, where, typically, index values may be below 10, a change in the index of 1 will probably not give results close to the correct result, and a much smaller value should be used.

When calculating estimates of the greeks using these difference methods, it is wise to check that the results have converged sufficiently. The simplest way to do that is to double the spacing used and repeat the estimate. If the estimate remains the same then our original estimate was probably quite accurate. If not, then it was probably not and a smaller spacing should be used.

Closed-form expressions for the greeks

It is also possible to derive closed-form expression for the greeks for the normal distribution. We derive closed-form expressions for the seven contract types in appendix F. We also derive closed-form expressions for the greeks for the kernel density in appendix G.

5.2 The interpretation of delta and gamma

5.2.1 Delta and the probability of being in the money

We now show that for almost any index distribution, when the tick is 1, the delta of a call option is equivalent to the probability of hitting the strike but not hitting the limit.

$$\Delta = \frac{\partial \mu_p}{\partial \mu_x} \tag{5.21}$$

$$= \frac{\partial}{\partial \mu_x} \int_{-\infty}^{\infty} p(x) f(x) dx$$

$$= \int_{-\infty}^{\infty} \frac{\partial}{\partial \mu_x} (p(x) f(x)) dx$$

$$= \int_{-\infty}^{\infty} p(x) \frac{\partial f}{\partial \mu_x} dx$$

For many distributions (those for which μ_x is a location parameter – i.e. $f(x, \mu_x) = f(x - \mu_x)$) we have it that $\frac{\partial}{\partial \mu_x} f(x) = -\frac{\partial}{\partial x} f(x)$, and so

$$\Delta = -\int_{-\infty}^{\infty} p(x) \frac{\partial f}{\partial x} dx \tag{5.22}$$

Integrating by parts gives

$$\Delta = \int_{-\infty}^{\infty} f(x) \frac{\partial p}{\partial x} dx \tag{5.23}$$

For a call structure this gives

$$\Delta = \int_{-\infty}^{\infty} f(x)\frac{\partial p}{\partial x}dx \tag{5.24}$$

$$= \int_{K}^{L} f(x)Ddx$$

$$= D\int_{K}^{L} f(x)dx$$

$$= D(F(L) - F(K)) \tag{5.25}$$

And so, when $D = 1$, we have $\Delta = F(L) - F(K)$, which is the probability of hitting the strike but not the limit. In the case of uncapped calls $\Delta = F(K)$, and so delta is the probability of ending up in the money.

We note the following two points.

1. Similar relations exist for other option structures; the crucial ingredient is that the pay-off must be piecewise linear.
2. This relation is often discussed in more traditional Black–Scholes option pricing. However, in that case it is true only under risk-neutral, rather than true, probabilities. In the weather case it holds under true probabilities because delta is defined in terms of the expected pay-off under true probabilities.

5.2.2 Gamma and the curvature of the pay-off function

Because

$$\Delta = \int_{-\infty}^{\infty} f(x)\frac{\partial p(x)}{\partial x}dx \tag{5.26}$$

we see that delta can also be interpreted as the average slope of the pay-off curve, weighted by the probabilities of the different possible outcomes for the index.

Similarly, gamma is the weighted average of the curvature of the pay-off curve:

$$\Gamma = \frac{\partial}{\partial\mu}\int_{-\infty}^{\infty} f\frac{\partial p}{\partial x}dx \tag{5.27}$$

$$= \int_{-\infty}^{\infty} \frac{\partial f}{\partial\mu}\frac{\partial p}{\partial x}dx$$

$$= -\int_{-\infty}^{\infty} \frac{\partial f}{\partial x}\frac{\partial p}{\partial x}dx$$

$$= \int_{-\infty}^{\infty} f\frac{\partial^2 p}{\partial x^2}dx$$

5.3 A summary of the interpretation of the greeks

We now briefly summarise how the different greeks can be interpreted and used.

Delta:

- is the partial derivative of the expected pay-off with respect to the expected index, with the index standard deviation (or the daily volatility and time) held constant;
- is the probability of hitting the limit but not the strike for call and put options, under many index distributions, and for a tick of 1;
- is the mean of the slope of the pay-off, weighted by the probabilities of the various possible outcomes for the index;
- is (minus one times) the size of the best linear hedge of an option (where 'best' means variance minimising);
- can be used to derive a good indication of the likely size of the random changes in the expected pay-off over one day, which are given by delta multiplied by the daily volatility (see equation (5.19));
- can be used to derive an indication of the likely size of random changes in the expected pay-off over n days, by multiplying the above estimate by the square root of n;
- is an indication of the likely size of the errors in our estimate of the expected pay-off induced by an error in the estimate of the expected index of 1 (see equation (5.14) and section 3.1.7).

Gamma:

- is the partial derivative of delta with respect to the expected index, with the index standard deviation held constant;
- is the mean curvature of the pay-off, weighted by the probabilities of the various possible outcomes;
- can be used to derive a good indication of the likely size of the random changes in delta over one day, which are given by gamma multiplied by the daily volatility;
- can be used to derive an indication of the likely size of random changes in delta over n days, by multiplying the above estimate by the square root of n.

Zeta:

- is the partial derivative of the expected pay-off with respect to the standard deviation of the settlement index;
- is an indication of the likely size of the errors in our estimate of the expected pay-off induced by an error in the estimate of the standard deviation of the settlement index of 1 (see equation (5.14) and section 3.1.7);
- is used in the calculation of theta and vega (see equations (5.4) and (5.5)).

Theta:

- is the partial derivative of the expected pay-off with respect to time, holding the mean index fixed but allowing the standard deviation of the index to vary;
- for normally distributed indices, is related to gamma via equation (5.18).

Vega:

- is the partial derivative of the expected pay-off with respect to the volatility of the underlying index.

5.4 Examples of the greeks

We now show some simulations of possible realisations for the greeks through the development of a single-month call option contract, taken from Jewson (2003k).

The index has an unconditional (pre-contract) mean of 373 and a standard deviation of 48 (chosen to reflect the typical values for London Heathrow November HDDs), and the development of the expected index is simulated using a deterministic function of Brownian motion, justification for which is given in chapter 10. Figure 5.1 shows the development of the underlying expected index, and figures 5.2, 5.3 and 5.4 show the corresponding development of delta, zeta and gamma. The development of the expected pay-offs for the option, along with 10 per cent and 90 per cent quantiles of the distribution of pay-offs, are shown in figure 12.1. The development of the relative value at risk (VaR) is shown in figure 12.2. In each graph the dotted line shows the pre-contract, or unconditional, value. In figure 5.1 the dashed line shows the option strike. It is instructive to interpret these graphs in some detail: for instance, in panel 1 the expected index does not stray very far from the initial value, and finishes only slightly above the strike. Around day 0 the mean index is fairly large, and this leads to a large value for the expected pay-off at that point. Later, the expected pay-off reduces and finishes at a low settlement value, below the fair value. The quantiles of the pay-off distribution show that, until the very end, there is always the possibility that the final pay-off will be zero. Delta finishes on a high value because we finish with a non-zero pay-off, and right to the end the pay-off is still liable to change as the expected index changes. Gamma is very large just before expiry because we are fairly close to the strike at this point, and there is still a probability of a zero pay-off. The other seven panels can be interpreted in a similar way.

5.5 The relative importance of choosing data, trends and distributions

Having described the use of trends and distributions in weather pricing we can now ask the question: which of the two makes the greater difference to the final prices attained? For a linear weather swap priced at the expected index, there is no need to fit a distribution to the index values at all; the expected index is calculated directly from the detrended historical values. For capped weather swaps the choice of distribution has a small influence on the final result. For options one would expect different distributions to have a greater effect on pricing because of the non-linear shape of the option pay-off. We investigated this issue in Jewson (2004f) by studying the sensitivity of the expected pay-off of a number of option contracts to changes in the number of years of data, trend and distribution. We restricted ourselves to a small number of reasonable trends and distributions. The distributions could not be rejected using the chi-squared test. We defined a measure of the ratio of the sensitivity to trends to the sensitivity to distributions, and values for this measure are shown in figure 5.5 versus strike for four locations (London, New York, Chicago and Tokyo). The strike values in this figure are non-dimensionalised so that the mean index is zero and the standard deviation of the index is 1. We see that for values of the strike that are near the mean the expected pay-off is around twenty times more sensitive to the trend than to the distribution. As the strike moves away from the mean the distribution becomes more important until the strike is at around

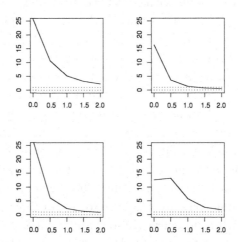

Figure 5.5. The ratio of the sensitivity of the expected pay-off of call option contracts due to changes in the trend to the sensitivity of the expected pay-off due to changes in the distribution, versus the strike in non-dimensional units, for London, New York, Chicago and Tokyo.

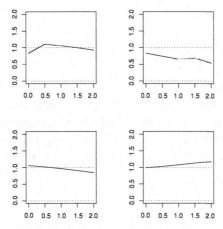

Figure 5.6. The ratio of the sensitivity of the expected pay-off of call option contracts due to changes in the trend to the sensitivity of the expected pay-off due to changes in the number of years of data used, versus the strike in non-dimensional units, for London, New York, Chicago and Tokyo.

2 standard deviations from the mean, when the trend and the distribution are equally important.

We then repeated the analysis comparing the sensitivity of the expected pay-off to changes in the trend and in the number of years of data used. The results are shown in figure 5.6. In this case we find that the two factors are equally important, independent of where the strike lies.

We conclude by suggesting that, for contracts with a strike near the mean, it is not sensible to spend a disproportionate amount of time trying to understand which the most appropriate distribution is, or what the effect of distribution is on model risk is, when the choice of trend and number of years of data used tend to dominate the final results. In these cases this conclusion justifies the use of the normal distribution whenever reasonable: if it does not make a material difference which distribution is used (as long as the distribution fits the data), then why not use the most convenient one?

For contracts with a strike far from the mean this does not apply, and the choice of distribution becomes much more important.

5.6 Comparing the accuracy of burn analysis and index modelling for option pricing

In the two previous chapters we have shown how to estimate the distribution of pay-offs and the expected pay-off using both burn and index modelling methods. Which is more accurate? We have argued so far that index modelling may be more accurate, because it smoothes the index distribution and extrapolates the tails in a reasonable way. But we have also emphasised that by enforcing a certain family of shapes onto the distribution we are making an assumption, which is bound to be at least slightly wrong and introduces an extra source of error.

Although comparing burn and index modelling in a rigorous way is practically impossible, there are certain things we can investigate. One is the question: if we fit the correct family of distributions (i.e. the data really is from a normal distribution, and we fit a normal distribution), then how much better is index modelling than burn? We call this the *potential accuracy* of index modelling: 'potential' because, in practice, we will never fit exactly the right distribution. This method shows us how much better index modelling could be in the best possible case. This question was addressed in some detail in Jewson (2003f). The conclusions from that study were:

- when estimating the expected pay-off for options with strikes that are near the expected index there is very little, if any, benefit to be had from using modelling;
- there is also very little benefit to be had when there is only a small amount of data being used (e.g. ten years or fewer);
- when more data is being used, and for options with strikes away from the mean, there may be significant benefit from using modelling;
- when estimating delta, the benefits of using modelling are greater than the benefits when estimating the expected pay-off;
- when estimating gamma, burn is almost completely useless, and modelling has to be used;
- when estimating the variance of pay-offs, modelling gives significantly better results than burn.

The results for the expected pay-off are summarised in figure 5.7, which shows the potential accuracy of modelling relative to burn for different numbers of years of data and different strikes.

5.7 The correlation between the results from burn and index modelling

Another result from the study cited above is that the correlation between the results from burn and index modelling is very high (see figure 5.8). In other words, if we estimate the fair premium for an option using burn and index modelling, and one of them is higher than the true value, then the other one is almost definitely higher than the true value too. There is no sense in which the two values will bracket the pay-offs, or in which using one method and then the other gives a useful second opinion.

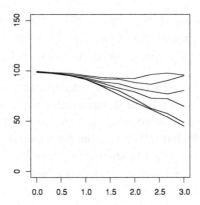

Figure 5.7. The variation of the reduction in error with number of years of historical data for index modelling versus burn against strikes for a call option in non-dimensional units. From top down the lines correspond to ten, twelve, fifteen, twenty, thirty and forty years of historical data. Values below 100 show a greater potential accuracy for index modelling than burn.

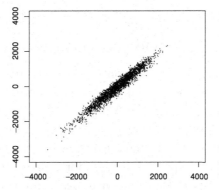

Figure 5.8. The correlation between burn and modelling estimates of the expected pay-off for a call option.

5.8 Pricing costless swaps

We have mentioned in section 3.1 that for swaps with limits it is often necessary to use iterative methods to derive the fair strike. In the case in which the index distribution is normal and the swap structure is symmetric the strike with zero expected pay-off is just the expected index. However, if either the distribution is skewed or the swap structure is not symmetric, this is not the case, and calculating the zero-cost strike can be carried out only by using iterative methods.

If we represent the expected pay-off from a swap contract as a function of the strike s as $H(s)$, then the strike at which the pay-off is zero is the solution of the equation $H(s) = 0$. Fortunately, this is a very numerically tractable problem: in almost any reasonable situation $H(s) = 0$ will have only one solution, and any gradient descent type of numerical method can be used to find it. Basically, these methods work as follows.

1. Calculate an initial estimate s (the expected index is a good start).
2. Calculate $H(s)$ (using the methods described in the previous two chapters).
3. If $H(s)$ is not sufficiently close to zero, then calculate $H(s + ds)$ and $H(s - ds)$. One of these will be less than $H(s)$. Use the corresponding argument as the new value of s – i.e. if $H(s + ds)$ is less than $H(s)$, then let s become $s + ds$.
4. Use this new value of s, and repeat from step 2, until $H(s)$ is close to zero.
5. s now gives the fair strike.

A slightly more complex method that estimated the gradient of $H(s)$ from analytical considerations would be faster. But, given the ease with which we can calculate $H(s)$, and the speed of the method given above, there is probably not much point in making the effort to derive and implement such a scheme.

5.9 Multi-year contracts

In the primary market, multi-year contracts are relatively common. These almost always consist of one partial-year deal repeated every year.

One of the reasons that such 'bulk buying' of one-year deals is common is that buying five one-year deals at once is likely to be less expensive than buying them each year for the next five years, because of diversification between the deals. The expected pay-off for a five-year deal will be five times the expected pay-off for a one-year deal, but the risk loading for a five-year deal should be closer to $\sqrt{5}$ times the risk loading for a one-year deal since the pay-offs are independent (and assuming the risk loading is proportional to the standard deviation of pay-offs).

Pricing multi-year deals gets more difficult the further out they extend into the future, mainly because the uncertainty about future temperatures increases. Different trend models, using different numbers of years of data, and the decision of whether and how to extrapolate the trend make very large differences in the prices derived. Credit risk also becomes much more important: will your counterparty still be around to pay you in five or ten years' time?

Some more exotic multi-year deals contain complex features, such as clauses that limit the total amount paid from one counterparty to the other and strikes and limits that adjust according to the weather on the way through the deal.

5.10 Derived prices

Swaps on certain indices are traded sufficiently frequently that one can observe the market swap strike for these indices. But for most swaps on most indices there is no such market price. However, it is possible that the market prices that are available on the frequently traded indices can tell us something about what the prices should be for the non-traded indices. In particular, if a non-traded index is reasonably well correlated with a traded index then the price of contracts based on the non-traded index is likely to be related to the price of contracts on the traded, index. For instance, the price of HDD swaps on Birmingham, United Kingdom, which are not traded in the market, is likely to be closely related to the price of HDD swaps on London Heathrow, which is only one hundred and twenty miles away. Similarly, the price of some event indices on London Heathrow temperatures are likely to be closely related to the price of HDD swaps on London Heathrow, since the number of events and the number of HDDs are likely to be highly correlated.

This effect arises because a speculator offering a price on the non-traded index can immediately hedge part of his risk using the traded index. The only risk this leaves him with is due to the lack of perfect correlation between the two trades, and the price on the non-traded index is likely to be higher than the price on the traded index by a factor that is proportional to this risk.

More generally, a speculator might immediately hedge himself using more than one location. In this case the price on the non-traded index is likely to depend on the market prices of all the locations used to hedge.

5.11 The pay-off integrand

The expectation of the pay-off distribution of a weather contract μ_p is defined by

$$\mu_p = \int_{-\infty}^{\infty} p(x)f(x)dx \qquad (5.28)$$

$$= \int_{-\infty}^{\infty} p(x)\frac{dF}{dx}dx$$

$$= \int_{-\infty}^{\infty} p(x)dF(x)$$

The third of these expressions is the most general because it can be used even when $F(x)$ is not smooth (i.e. cannot be differentiated). In this case $f(x)$ has the value of infinity at some points. This can be represented using

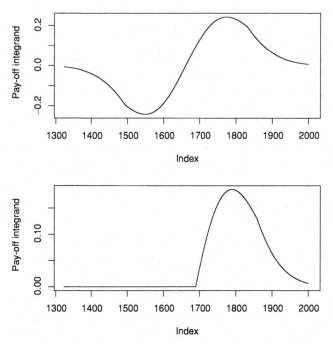

Figure 5.9. The shape of the pay-off integrand for the swap and option contracts described in the text.

the delta functions of mathematical physics. Alternatively, measure theory provides a framework for handling mixed and discrete distributions.

Note that, since the index distribution is in fact discrete, this should be a sum rather than an integral. We use integral notation on the basis that it is easier to read and manipulate.

Defining a single function of the index $fp(x) = f(x)p(x)$ the integral can be written as

$$\mu_p = \int_{-\infty}^{\infty} fp(x)dx \tag{5.29}$$

It is instructive to plot this function $fp(x)$, which we will refer to as the pay-off integrand. Figure 5.9 shows the form of this function for a swap and a call option, with a normal distribution. For the swap, the strike is at the expectation and the limits are at $+/-1.5$ standard deviations. For the option, the strike is at 0.25 standard deviations and the limit is at 1.5 standard deviations. We can use the pay-off integrand to tell us the relative importance of different parts of the index distribution in determining the expected pay-off. For instance, for the option the largest contribution to the expected pay-off comes from values of the index around 1800. This indicates that modelling the index for these values is crucial. These considerations can contribute to the decision about which distribution to use. When using graphical methods for distribution fitting one can check that the distribution gives a good fit in the most important range of values.

5.12 Pricing options using the swap price

As we have seen, one of the major challenges in pricing an option is to estimate the distribution of the underlying index. Part of this is the estimation of the expectation of the distribution. Small changes in the estimate of the expected index can cause large changes in the estimated expected pay-off. The only method we have presented so far for calculating the expectation of the index is to look at historical index data and, perhaps, remove a (fairly ad hoc) trend. In this section we describe an interesting alternative: to let the market do the work, and tell you the expectation of the index. The assumption behind this method is that there is a fairly liquid swap contract based on the index underlying the option. If we assume that (a) the distribution of the index is fairly close to normal, (b) the swap is defined symmetrically about the expected index, and (c) the swap market is trading with no risk premium, then the market strike of the swap can be taken to be the market estimate of the expected index. If we believe in efficient markets, then we might even think that this is a good estimate, and a better one than we could hope to come to ourselves by analysing historical data. At the very least, it is an estimate that a number of people apparently believe in. Note that, using the iterative swap pricing methods described in section 5.8, we can even relax the first two assumptions and derive the expected index even in the case where the index distribution is non-normal and the swap contract has asymmetric limits.

We should add that it is not uncommon for the third assumption listed above to be entirely incorrect even for the most commonly traded contracts. During January 2003, for instance, the market strike for the London January swap contract was consistently twenty degree days below the lowest reasonable estimates for the fair strike. Apparently there was a significant imbalance in supply and demand for the swap contract, which was driving the swap price well away from the expected index, and there seemed to be insufficient liquidity in the market to move it back.

However, if we do accept the market estimate for the expectation of the index we can then price the option using this expectation combined with the historical data-based estimate of the standard deviation of the index.

If we use this method then our option prices are no longer as highly sensitive to our fairly arbitrary choices of number of years of data and trend, since these now only affect the standard deviation and not the expectation.

In the next section, and in chapter 11, we will see that there may even be situations in which we should use the market swap price instead of the estimated expected index even if we do not think it is a good estimate of the expectation. This occurs either (a) when one wants to calculate liquidation values for swaps or (b) when one wants to calculate prices for options that take into account the cost of hedging.

5.13 Hedging options with a single swap

A speculator selling options on an index for which the swap contract is liquidly traded will often immediately hedge his position by trading that swap contract. The new position, consisting of a put and a swap or a call and a swap, is sometimes called a 'covered put' or a 'covered call'. This is not by any means a perfect hedge, but can nevertheless reduce the risk of holding a short option position significantly. What size should the tick of the swap be?

We offer two ways that one can think about this question. The first is to choose the tick so that small changes in the expected index will not have a big impact on the new hedged position – i.e. the size of the swap is such that, if a change in the expected index causes the value of the option to increase, the value of the swap will decrease by the same amount. This is known as delta hedging. For large changes in the expected index the hedging is not exact, because the changes in the option price cease to be linear in the changes in the expected index.

The second rationale for hedging is to think about the distribution of pay-offs at expiry and to consider reducing the risk of this distribution. This is known as static hedging.

5.13.1 Delta hedges

If we define the value of the hedged portfolio V to be the expected profit on the option plus the expected profit on the swap, we assume that the option position is short and the swap long, and that the swap is uncapped; then V is given by

$$V(\mu_x) = \mu_p(\mu_x) + D(\mu_x - K) \tag{5.30}$$

where we have written the expected pay-off of the option μ_p as a function only of μ_x, and have suppressed the dependency on σ_x.

Suppose μ_x changes by a small amount ϵ, then

$$V(\mu_x + \epsilon) = \mu_p(\mu_x + \epsilon) + D(\mu_x + \epsilon - K) \qquad (5.31)$$
$$= \mu_p(\mu_x) + \epsilon\Delta + \ldots + D(\mu_x + \epsilon - K)$$

where we have made a Taylor expansion of μ_p around μ_x and ignored terms smaller than ϵ. We can now see that if we choose $D = -\Delta$ our portfolio will be insensitive to small changes in μ_x (the ϵ terms cancel), and in this sense the risk has been reduced. We now see the reason for the name 'delta hedging': the delta of the option gives us the optimum size of hedge.

Before the speculator sells the option contract, he might want to adjust the price he charges in the knowledge that he is going to hedge with the swap. If we ignore risk loading then we can take the price to be the expected profit on the option and the swap together. This is given by

$$\text{price} = \mu_p(\mu_x) + D(\mu_x - S) \qquad (5.32)$$

If we define $e = S - \mu_x$ to be the difference between the current swap price and the fair swap price then

$$\text{price} = \mu_p(\mu_x) + \Delta e \qquad (5.33)$$
$$= \mu_p(\mu_x + e) + \ldots + O(e^2)$$
$$\approx \mu_p(S)$$

Thus we see that the price is given roughly by $\mu_p(S)$ – i.e. by calculating the expected pay-off of the option but substituting S, the current swap price, instead of the expected index, even though S does not necessarily equal the expected index.

This is now a justification for pricing an option using the swap price in place of an estimate of the expected index, even if we believe that the swap price is not equal to the expected index. It says that if the swap is overpriced then our hedge will be more expensive, and we should reflect this in the option price that we charge.

5.13.2 Static hedging

The delta hedging argument given above makes most sense when it is possible to rehedge fairly frequently during the course of the option contract. Such a situation is considered in more detail in chapter 11. If, on the other

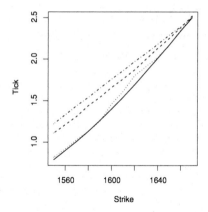

Figure 5.10. The optimum size of a static hedge for an option contract for different risk measures. The solid line applies to the standard deviation, the dotted line to the expiry VaR, the dashed line to the semi-standard deviation and the dot-dashed line to the tail VaR.

hand, rehedging is likely to be impossible then we should consider the effect of our hedge on the final pay-off distribution right from the start. This question was addressed in Jewson (2004c), where the benefits of static hedging were considered using four different possible measures of risk. The four measures of risk were standard deviation, semi-standard deviation, expiry value at risk and tail value at risk (tail VaR). Figure 5.10 shows the sizes of the optimum swap hedge in each case. We see that if the option is struck at the expected index (1660 in this case) it doesn't make any difference which risk measure we use: the size of the optimum hedge is the same. On the other hand, if the option is struck far out of the money then it can make quite a big difference. The hedges that are needed to minimise the variance are the smallest, while the hedges that are needed to minimise either the semi-standard deviation or the tail VaR are the largest. Since hedging usually costs money, it is likely to be more expensive to hedge the semi-standard deviation or the tail VaR.

In the case of static hedging in order to minimise the variance, if the index is normally distributed then the size of the hedge is exactly the same as the delta hedge of the previous section.

5.14 Sampling error and structuring

In this section we turn the discussion of sampling error from chapter 3 around and look at it from another point of view. What we considered there was the idea that we have a swap defined with the strike at exactly the true expected value of the index, or an option with the strike limit defined in terms of the exact expectation and standard deviation of the index. This is, of course, never the case in reality. Rather, whoever structures the option uses estimated values of the expectation and standard deviation to fix the position of the strike and limits. This could result in the position of the strike and limits being rather far from the intended position, due to errors in the estimates of the expectation and standard deviation of the index. We have already seen that our estimates of the expectation have a standard error given by $\frac{\sigma_x}{\sqrt{N_y}}$ and our estimates of the standard deviation have a standard error given by $\frac{\sigma_x}{\sqrt{2N_y}}$, and we can use these to derive the levels of uncertainty on the estimated strike and limits for swaps and options.

For a swap, if we are trying to set the strike at the expectation of the index then our estimate of the expectation will have a standard error of $\frac{\sigma_x}{\sqrt{N_y}}$. If we are trying to set the limit at the expectation of the index plus two standard deviations of the index then there will be uncertainty due to both the uncertainty on the expectation and the uncertainty on the standard deviation of the index. For the normal distribution these sources of uncertainty are independent, and the total uncertainty is given by

$$\text{s.e. on limit} = \sqrt{\frac{\sigma_x^2}{N_y} + 4\frac{\sigma_x^2}{2N_y}} \tag{5.34}$$

$$= \sqrt{3}\frac{\sigma_x}{\sqrt{N_y}}$$

In other words, the uncertainty on the limit is about 1.7 times larger than the uncertainty on the strike, and most of this uncertainty comes from the uncertainty on the standard deviation.

For a call option, if we are trying to set the strike at the expectation plus half of 1 standard deviation then the total uncertainty is given by

$$\text{s.e. on strike} = \sqrt{\frac{\sigma_x^2}{N_y} + \frac{1}{4}\frac{\sigma_x^2}{2N_y}} \tag{5.35}$$

$$= \sqrt{\frac{9}{8}}\frac{\sigma_x}{\sqrt{N_y}}$$

In other words, the uncertainty on the strike is about 1.06 times larger than the uncertainty on the expected index, and most of this uncertainty comes from the uncertainty on the expected index.

5.15 Leap years

The existence of leap years is slightly annoying when calculating historical indices. Consider, for instance, a January to March contract. In most years this period has ninety days ($= 31 + 28 + 31$). But in a leap year it has ninety-one days ($= 31 + 29 + 31$). When calculating historical indices, the historical HDD values for this period for leap years will therefore be higher on average, simply because they are based on more days. When performing a historical-data-based pricing analysis this is not ideal. For seasonal contracts the effect is so small it can be ignored, but for monthly contracts it is large enough to be worth addressing correctly.

One simple method works as follows:

- if the contract to be priced is not in a leap year, then one should use only ninety days of data from each historical year; these ninety days will not then have exactly the same *dates* as the dates of the contract;
- if the contract to be priced *is* in a leap year, then one should use ninety-one days of data from each historical year; again, the dates won't match exactly.

Exactly which days of data to use needs careful thought to avoid inconsistencies between burn values calculated for monthly and seasonal contracts.

5.16 Further reading

There is some discussion of the role of the greeks in weather pricing in Moreno (2003).

6

The valuation of single contracts using daily modelling

In chapter 4 we considered methods for the pricing of temperature-based weather derivatives that involve statistical modelling of the historical values of the contract settlement index. In this chapter we investigate methods that involve statistical modelling of the underlying temperature. Since the temperature measurements used for most weather contracts are daily values we will focus on the modelling of daily temperatures.

Using models of daily temperature to price weather derivatives has a number of advantages and disadvantages relative to using models of the contract settlement index.

The potential advantages include:

- more complete use of the available historical data;
- more accurate representation of the index distribution;
- more accurate extrapolation of extremes;
- more accurate mark to model estimates during the contract;
- consistent use of one model for all contracts on one location;
- easier incorporation of meteorological forecasts into the pricing algorithm.

The main disadvantage of using daily models is the added complexity; as we will see, daily models are significantly more complex than the index modelling methods of chapter 4. This, in turn, leads to greater risk of model error.

In practice, because of this disadvantage, daily models are currently used much less frequently than index models. However, as more research is done into these models their use is likely to increase.

6.1 The advantages of daily modelling

We now describe in more detail the advantages of using daily temperature modelling methods.

6.1.1 Higher potential accuracy

A desire for higher accuracy in pricing is probably the main reason why there is interest in daily temperature modelling methods for weather derivative pricing. However, the question of whether daily modelling gives higher accuracy or not is a difficult one to answer. Certainly, there are contracts for which it does, but, equally, there are contracts for which it probably never will. To help understand the issues that affect whether a model is accurate we again (as in section 5.6) distinguish between *accuracy*, which is the ability of a model to represent the real world, and *potential accuracy*, which is the ability of a model to represent the real world, if the model is correct.[1] By a model being correct, we mean that the model has the right form, even if we do not know the right values for the parameters.

Daily models very often show greater potential accuracy than burn and index models (we show this in section 6.8). To the extent that the model is correct, this then translates into actual accuracy. But all models are wrong, and so the actual accuracy is always less than the potential accuracy. The question is: how close is the actual accuracy to this potential? This is generally impossible to answer in a completely precise way. The potential accuracy of a model can be evaluated very precisely by fitting the model to its own output. The actual accuracy can be partly assessed using model validation but can only be fully assessed using out-of-sample testing on real data, which is very difficult because of the presence of trends.

More complete use of the available historical data

Consider a one-week weather contract: the index-based analyses described in chapter 4 discard the historical temperature data from all the other weeks of the year when the historical indices are calculated. Thus roughly 98 per cent of the available data, which may contain useful information, is simply being thrown away. A daily model, on the other hand, could use data from the whole year to fit the parameters of the model. If the extra data is relevant, then the model will be more accurate because the parameters will be better estimated. Of course, fitting models using more data is not necessarily better: we could price a London contract by taking extra data from Beijing, but this would be nonsensical since the statistics of temperature variability in

---

[1] Climate modellers will appreciate that this distinction is similar to the distinction between predictability and potential predictability: the former is the ability to predict the real world, the latter is the ability of a model to predict itself. If the model is correct (which, of course, they never are) then these are equal. Models always show a greater ability to predict themselves than they do the real world; there is always a danger that the skill with which a model predicts itself is mistaken for the skill of real predictions.

the two locations are very different. Similarly, if summer and winter data are not very similar then using both to fit a model intended for use on a summer contract may not increase the accuracy for that contract, and may decrease it. Assessing whether using extra data from outside the contract period improves or degrades the model is an important part of daily modelling.

To introduce another aspect of the complete use of available data possible with daily modelling, consider a CDD index based on a baseline temperature of 65°F/18°C. It may be that, for the location in question, only half the days in the contract period typically lie above the baseline. In an index-based analysis the information contained in the data below the baseline would not then be fully utilised. By using a daily model we avoid this problem of the incomplete utilisation of the data on one side of the baseline and make full use of the data from every day. However, the flip side is that the distribution we assume for the daily model may be significantly wrong for the values below the baseline, and by including those values when we fit the distribution we actually reduce the accuracy of the model. Again, evaluating whether using the data from the wrong side of the baseline improves or degrades the model is an important step.

As an extreme case of the point made in the previous paragraph, consider an event index. It may be that only one day in a hundred of the historical data gives us an event, and hence that we are not making full use of 99 per cent of the data when using an index-based pricing method. Fitting a daily model to all the data can give us accurately estimated parameters. As before, whether the model is more accurate depends on how close the distribution we fit to the daily values is to the correct distribution, and, in particular, how close the fit is for the extreme values that drive the events.

The *most* extreme case of this situation is when we are pricing a deal based on events that have never occurred historically. Neither index modelling nor burn can be used in these situations, but daily modelling could potentially give reasonable results by generating such events.

Better representation of the index distribution

The goal of both index and daily modelling is the accurate representation of the index distribution, from which accurate prices can be determined. This distribution is controlled by the distribution (both the marginal daily distribution and the dependence in time) of the daily temperature, along with the definition of the index. These two factors may combine to create index distribution shapes that cannot be represented perfectly by any of the standard parametric distributions of statistics, and in that case no parametric index model will ever do a particularly good job. A daily model that captures the distribution of the daily weather variable is less restricted, and we may, as a result, be able to get closer to the actual distribution of the index. Given the results described in section 5.5 this is most likely to be important for contracts that depend heavily on the tails of the distribution.

Better extrapolation of extremes

Index models capture extreme events by extrapolating beyond the available historical index data. For instance, if we fit a normal distribution to the historical indices then we are extrapolating using the tails of a normal distribution, etc. This extrapolation is ad hoc, and it is very hard to argue that any one distribution gives a better extrapolation than any other. Daily models overcome this to a certain extent: extremes of the index often depend on certain sequences of daily values. A daily model can create entirely new sequences of daily values that do not occur in the historical data, and that will translate to new extreme index values. If the daily model is realistic then these extremes will be realistic too. Such issues are clearly of more relevance to contracts based on indices that depend strongly on extreme values.

6.1.2 Better mark to model estimates

Marking contracts to model is the process of evaluating the current worth of a contract or portfolio of contracts given the available historical data and forecasts. This topic will be discussed in more detail in later chapters. For now we note that daily models allow better representation of the correlations between past and future temperature data than index models, and can hence potentially improve the accuracy of mark to model estimates.

6.1.3 Use of one model for all contracts on one location

If a number of different contracts are written on one location then it may be considered necessary to ensure consistent pricing between the different contracts. This is particularly important if some contracts are being used to hedge others. In chapter 7 we will discuss how index models can be extended to cover multiple contracts, but we will also see that there are some situations where the multivariate index models we describe are unable to capture the dependences between the indices exactly, while a daily model would do so.

Also, once a good daily model has been found for a particular location it can be used for all contracts on that location, whatever the index type or duration. Thus the statistical fitting process can be done once and for all, and many different types of contracts can be priced thereafter with confidence. This is not true for the index models, which have to be refitted for each new index.

6.1.4 The incorporation of meteorological forecasts

Meteorological forecasters produce forecasts of temperature in terms of daily values. It is efficient for the forecasters to produce their predictions in terms of daily temperature rather than in daily or aggregate degree days because the forecasts can then be used by everyone, from traders pricing derivatives to families planning a trip. As we shall see in chapter 10, it is easier to incorporate these forecasts into pricing models if the pricing model is also based on daily temperatures rather than on settlement indices.

6.2 The disadvantages of daily modelling

In addition to the advantages listed above, daily models have certain disadvantages relative to index models.

The complexity of the models

Daily models, are, because of the complex nature of daily temperature variability, harder to design, build, fit, validate and use. They may also be slower to run.

The risk of model error

Because of the greater complexity of daily models, there is a much greater danger of model error than with index models (index models, in turn, have a greater danger of model error than burn analysis). Model error can take two forms: first, that the mathematical model itself is a good one (i.e. close to reality) but has been implemented wrongly (i.e. coding errors); and, second, that the mathematical model itself is poor (i.e. far from reality).

6.3 Modelling daily temperatures

Having discussed the pros and cons of pricing using daily temperature models, we will now present a number of such models. The accuracy and potential accuracy of these models will be evaluated using a range of techniques. The final decision as to which model is likely to be best and whether the best daily model is likely to be better than the index models is a subjective one, based on all the available information plus a certain amount of intuition.

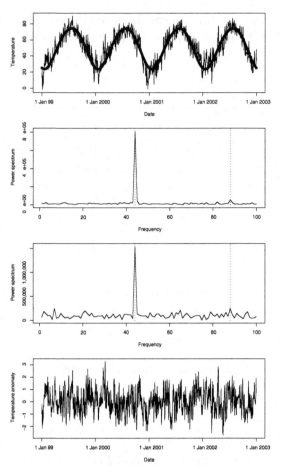

Figure 6.1. The process of the deseasonalisation of daily temperatures. The top panel shows four years of daily temperatures, with a seasonal cycle in the mean imposed. The second panel shows the fourier power spectrum of daily temperatures, with a large peak at forty-four oscillations in forty-four years of data – i.e. a period of one year. The third panel shows the fourier power spectrum of the squared intermediate anomalies, and the fourth panel shows the temperatures anomalies after the seasonal cycles in the mean and the variance have been removed.

Methods for simulation from these models are discussed briefly in appendix I.

6.3.1 Modelling the seasonal cycle

The first striking thing about time series of temperature variability in extratropical locations is that there is a strong seasonal cycle with small perturbations about it (see the first panel in figure 6.1). This motivates us to model the seasonal cycle first and the perturbations separately.[2] The hope is that, by removing the non-stationary seasonal cycle, what is left will be stationary.

The approach we take is to model the seasonal variations as deterministic and the same every year (seasonally stationary). The stochastic variability of temperature is then moved entirely into the residuals from the seasonal cycle. Such deterministic seasonal cycle modelling is the approach generally used in meteorology.

Having decided to model the seasonal cycle deterministically there are then three basic approaches one can take.

The averaging method

The simplest method for removing the seasonal cycle would consist of the following steps:

- calculate an average year by averaging together all Jan 1sts, all Jan 2nds, etc.;
- smooth this average year using a sliding window to create a plausibly smooth seasonal cycle.

The main advantage of such an approach is simplicity. The main disadvantage is that leap years are not well accounted for; the irritating occurrence of an extra day at the end of February once every four years cannot easily be dealt with in this framework.

The DFT method

When $4N$ years of temperature variability is transformed into the frequency domain using a forward discrete fourier transform (DFT) and the power spectrum is plotted, the seasonal cycle shows up as very distinct peaks at harmonics of the annual cycle of 365.25 days (see figure 6.1, panel 2). The first harmonic at one year is by far the largest, with several distinct sub-harmonics at much smaller amplitudes. A simple way to remove the seasonal cycle is to set the power of these harmonics to zero and transform the power spectrum back into real time using the inverse DFT (forward and inverse DFTs are readily available as software packages). The back-transformed temperatures no longer show the strong seasonal cycle. Our own experience suggests that removing one, two or three harmonics in this way is usually sufficient to remove all traces of seasonality in the mean. The signal that

---

[2] Although one could argue that modelling the whole lot together is more mathematically consistent.

has been removed can be constructed as the difference between the original signal and the back-transform.

Having removed the seasonal cycle in the mean as described above, we are left with residuals, which we call the 'intermediate anomalies' or the 'anomalies from the mean seasonal cycle'. These anomalies also show seasonality, now in the variance rather than in the mean, because winter temperature is more variable than summer temperature. We can remove this seasonality in almost the same way as with the seasonality in the mean:

- the variance process is calculated by squaring the time series of the intermediate anomalies;
- the power spectrum of this variance process is estimated (see figure 6.1, panel 3);
- the peaks in this power spectrum are reduced to the level of the background;
- the adjusted power spectrum is inverted back to real time.

More harmonics are needed than for removing the seasonal cycle in the mean; our experience suggests that three or four work well.

The regression method

A third method for removing seasonality is to regress the temperatures onto harmonics of 365.25 days. This has the advantage that it can be applied to any number of years of data. It can be used to remove the seasonal cycle in both the mean and the variance, as with the DFT method.

The results of deseasonalisation

The result of applying the DFT deseasonalisation process to Chicago temperatures is shown in the 4th panel of figure 6.1. We will refer to these values as 'anomalies'. These anomalies capture the random variability of weather from day to day, with most of the deterministic seasonal variability removed. We can now write the general form of the model we use for daily temperatures as

$$T_i = m_i + s_i T_i'$$ (6.1)

where T_i are the temperatures, m_i is the seasonal cycle in the mean, s_i is the seasonal cycle in the standard deviation and T_i' are the temperature anomalies.

At this stage the straightforward modelling has been done. The anomalies have complex statistical properties that cannot be modelled particularly easily, especially not in a fully general way. We will now investigate some of these statistical properties.

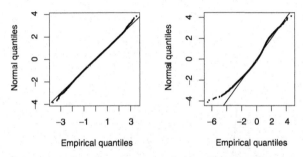

Figure 6.2. QQ plots showing the annual distribution of temperatures for Chicago and Miami. We see that Chicago is reasonably close to normally distributed (but with slightly lighter tails) while Miami is very far from normally distributed, with a very heavy left tail.

6.4 The statistical properties of the anomalies

First, we investigate the annual distribution of the the anomalies. Having removed the seasonal cycle in the mean and the standard deviation, we have, to the extent that the seasonal cycle has been modelled accurately, enforced a mean of zero and a standard deviation of one at all times of the year. The annual distributions of anomalies from Chicago and Miami are shown in figure 6.2. They are compared with normal distributions using QQ plots.

We see that in neither case is a normal distribution a perfect fit to the distribution of the anomalies: for Chicago it is fairly reasonable, while for Miami it is fairly poor.

We now break down the annual distribution into seasonal distributions. The upper panels of figure 6.3 show the winter and summer distributions for Chicago. There are slight deviations from normality in both seasons, and the deviations are different in summer and winter. Figure 6.4 shows the distributions for all four seasons for Miami. In this case, there are marked deviations from normal in all four seasons, and particularly in winter. We conclude that the annual distributions shown in figure 6.2 are composites of different distributions at different times of year.

Next, we consider the annual anomaly autocorrelation function (ACF). The ACF shows how a time series is correlated with itself at different lags. Figure 6.5 shows the annual ACFs for Chicago and Miami. We note that the ACFs do not decay to zero until beyond thirty days.

Finally, we consider the seasonality of the ACF. The lower panels of figure 6.3 show the ACFs for Chicago calculated separately using winter and summer data, along with the annual ACF. There do not seem to be big variations in the ACF from winter to summer.

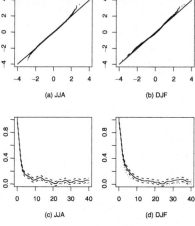

Figure 6.3. The upper panels show QQ plots of Chicago surface air temperature anomalies for summer and winter. The horizontal axes show the observed quantiles, while the vertical axes show the modelled quantiles from a normal distribution. In both cases we can see that the distribution of temperatures is close to normal, and hence that Gaussian models are reasonably well justified (although the tails of the temperature distribution in summer do show some departures from normal). The lower panels show the ACFs for Chicago surface air temperatures for summer and winter (solid line), along with the ACF fitted to data for the whole year (dotted line, the same in each graph), and with the 95 per cent confidence intervals (dashed lines) calculated using the method proposed in Moran (1947). We see that the ACF does not vary much from winter to summer, and what variations there are may be due to sampling error.

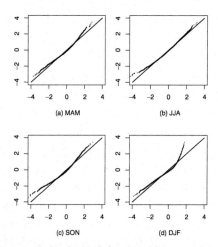

Figure 6.4. The four panels show QQ plots for temperature anomalies in Miami for the four seasons. The horizontal axis shows the observed quantiles, while the vertical axis shows the modelled quantiles. We see that in all seasons the cold tail of the distribution is heavy-tailed (cold events are more likely than predicted by the normal distribution) while the warm tail of the distribution is light-tailed (warm events are less likely than predicted by the normal distribution). The most significant departure from normal is the warm tail in winter.

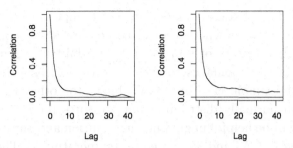

Figure 6.5. The annual ACFs for temperature anomalies in Chicago and Miami.

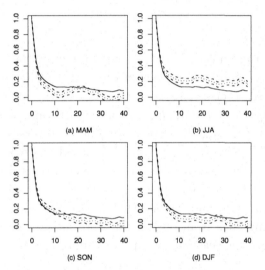

Figure 6.6. The four panels show the observed ACFs for Miami for the four seasons. In each panel the solid black line is the annual ACF, which is the same in each panel, and is included for reference. The dotted line is the observed ACF for that season. The dashed lines show the 95 per cent confidence intervals around the observed estimate. We see strong seasonality in the temperature memory, with stronger memory in summer and weaker memory in other seasons.

Figure 6.6 shows the ACFs for Miami for all four seasons, with the annual ACF. In this case there are large variations in the ACF from season to season. In particular, there is much longer memory in summer.

6.4.1 The inherited properties of the index

We now ask: how do the statistical properties of the anomalies affect the final index distribution? This is an important question, because the answer tells us which properties of the anomalies are most important to capture with our models and, in fact, whether we need to care at all about capturing the more complex aspects of temperature variability. In general, relating the properties of the anomalies to the properties of the index is difficult. However, for the simple case of a CAT index (or other linear separable index) based on normally distributed temperatures there are some simple results, which will be helpful in guiding our intuition and our choice between models. Consider a CAT index x based on temperature T. The expectation of the index $E(x)$ is given by

$$E(x) = \sum_{i=1}^{N_d} E(T_i) \tag{6.2}$$

In other words, the expectation of the index is simply the sum of the means of the temperatures. Since the means of the temperatures in equation (6.1) are fixed by the seasonal cycle, the properties of the anomalies described above are *entirely irrelevant* in fixing the expectation of the index. This means that, for calculating the expected value of a CAT index, and hence the fair price for a linear swap based on such an index, we need consider only the seasonal cycle. The same conclusion can be drawn for degree day indices when there is no chance of the temperature crossing the baseline. The benefit of using a daily model in these cases is that we are modelling the shape of the seasonal cycle using data from both inside and outside the contract period, and so may capture the seasonal mean index more accurately, especially for short contracts.

We now consider the variance of the CAT index

$$V(x) = E((x - E(x))^2 = E(x^2) - (E(x))^2 \tag{6.3}$$

where

$$E(x^2) = E\left(\left(\sum_{i=1}^{N_d} T_i\right)^2\right) \tag{6.4}$$

$$= E\left(\sum_{i=1}^{N_d}\sum_{j=1}^{N_d} T_i T_j\right)$$

$$= \sum_{i=1}^{N_d}\sum_{j=1}^{N_d} E(T_i T_j)$$

$$= \sum_{i=1}^{N_d}\sum_{j=1}^{N_d} c_{ij} + E(T_i)E(T_j)$$

where c_{ij} is the covariance between the temperature on day i and the temperature on day j. We see that the variance of the index is fixed by these temperature covariances.

Using the expansion in terms of the seasonal cycle and anomalies given by equation (6.1) gives

$$E(x^2) = \sum_{i=1}^{N_d} \sum_{j=1}^{N_d} E(T_i T_j) \tag{6.5}$$

$$= \sum_{i=1}^{N_d} \sum_{j=1}^{N_d} E((m_i + s_i T_i')(m_j + s_j T_j'))$$

$$= \sum_{i=1}^{N_d} \sum_{j=1}^{N_d} m_i m_j + s_i s_j E(T_i' T_j')$$

where $E(T_i' T_j')$ is the ACF. This now shows that the variance of the index is determined by the mean seasonal cycle, the seasonal cycle in the variance, and the ACF of temperature anomalies. Since we have assumed for this analysis that the temperatures are normally distributed, and we know that the sum of normal distributions is always a normal distribution, a CAT index will also be normally distributed. The index distribution is thus fully specified by the expectation and standard deviation. This implies that to capture the distribution for these indices we have to both model the seasonal cycle *and* the ACF of temperature correctly. This motivates us to focus on the ACF in the validation and comparison of our models below.

We note that the physical interpretation of equation (6.5) is simple: if the autocorrelation of the anomalies is high then the temperature will wander away from the seasonal cycle for long periods. This can result in both large and small values for the index, and the index standard deviation will be high.

Our discussion above is based on the assumption that temperatures are normally distributed. More generally, real temperatures are not exactly normally distributed (as we have seen), and this will lead to non-normal index distributions, even for CAT indices. The behaviour of temperatures may then not be completely specified by the mean, standard deviation and ACF. In these cases an ideal daily model would do more than just capture the seasonal cycle and the ACF, and would also capture the correct distribution of daily temperature, and temperature dependences in time more complex that those captured by linear correlations.

6.5 Modelling the anomalies

We have seen that temperature anomalies may show complex seasonal and non-normal behaviour. This means that complex models and modelling techniques are needed to represent them. First, we consider transformations that can render the daily temperature anomalies close to normally distributed in almost all cases. Then we describe linear Gaussian parametric modelling of the transformed anomalies. We will see that it works surprisingly well in many cases. For those where it does not, we will consider non-parametric modelling as an alternative. There are many other types of time series models we could have considered too, such as linear models with non-Gaussian anomalies or non-linear parametric models. Evaluation of these models in those cases where the linear parametric models do not work well is an area of active research.

6.5.1 Transforming temperature anomalies to a normal distribution

As we saw in section 6.4, temperature variability often shows a non-normal distribution. This is generally hard to model. A convenient approach is to transform the temperatures so that they are much closer to normal and then apply a normal model. The disadvantage of such an approach is that the model is not then being fitted in such a way as to maximise the likelihood of the original data, although if the temperature anomalies are close to normal, as they usually are, this probably does not matter. If the non-normality is constant throughout the year, then a fixed transformation is sufficient. However, in most cases the non-normality varies from season to season (as we have seen above) and a seasonally varying transform needs to be used. Ideally, one would use a parametric form such as the well-known Box–Cox (Box and Cox, 1964) transformations. However, the non-normality is generally sufficiently complex for such simple parametric transformations not to work. A general non-parametric transform is described by Jewson and Caballero (2003a), some results of which are shown in figure 6.7. We see that the seasonally varying non-normality apparent in figure 6.4 has largely been removed by this transformation. This means that we can now proceed to model the transformed anomalies using Gaussian models. Simulations from such models can then be transformed back to the correct distribution using the inverse of the distribution transform.

For stations such as Chicago it may not be necessary to apply a distribution transform at all, and Gaussian time series models can be used directly since the temperatures are already reasonably close to normally distributed at all times of year. For stations such as Miami, however, it

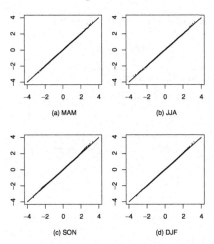

Figure 6.7. The four panels show QQ plots for temperature anomalies in Miami for the four seasons, after having been transformed using the non-parametric, seasonally varying transform described in the text. Relative to figure 6.4, we see that most of the non-normality has been removed.

would be extremely inaccurate to apply a Gaussian model without using such a transformation first.

6.5.2 Parametric modelling of temperature anomalies

Either temperature anomalies are close to Gaussian or we transform them so that they are close to Gaussian, as described above. The challenge is then to model the time dependences of the anomalies. The simplest discrete time series model for a Gaussian random time series is

$$T_i' = \epsilon_i \tag{6.6}$$

where ϵ_i is Gaussian white noise. Such a model was suggested in a weather derivative context by Davis (2001). This model gives temperature anomalies that are uncorrelated in time and normally distributed. Given the observed autocorrelations of temperature anomalies and the importance of the ACF in determining the index standard deviation, as shown by equation (6.5), this model will clearly not do.

6.5.3 ARMA models

A more complex class of models are the ARMA (autoregressive moving average) time series models of the form

$$\phi(B)T_i' = \psi(B)\epsilon_i \tag{6.7}$$

where B is the backstep operator, defined such that

$$BT_i' = T_{i-1}' \tag{6.8}$$

and ϕ and ψ are polynomials of order p and q known as the autoregressive (AR) and moving average (MA) polynomials.

They are given by

$$\phi(x) = 1 - \sum_{i=1}^{p} \phi_i x^i \tag{6.9}$$

and

$$\psi(x) = 1 + \sum_{i=1}^{q} \psi_i x^i \tag{6.10}$$

(where the two polynomials should have no roots outside the unit circle to ensure stationarity and invertibility).

Using these definitions equation (6.7) can be expanded to give

$$(1 - \phi_1 B + \phi_2 B^2 + \ldots + \phi_p B^p)T_i' = (1 + \psi_1 B + \psi_2 B^2 + \ldots + \psi_q B^q)\epsilon_i \tag{6.11}$$

and using the definition of B this gives

$$T_i' - \phi_1 T_{i-1}' - \phi_2 T_{i-2}' - \ldots - \phi_p T_{i-p}' = \epsilon_i + \psi_1 \epsilon_{i-1} + \psi_2 \epsilon_{i-2} + \ldots + \psi_q \epsilon_{i-q} \tag{6.12}$$

or

$$T_i' = \phi_1 T_{i-1}' + \phi_2 T_{i-2}' + \ldots + \phi_p T_{i-p}' + \epsilon_i + \psi_i \epsilon_{i-1} + \psi_2 \epsilon_{i-2} + \ldots + \psi_q \epsilon_{i-q} \tag{6.13}$$

In this last expression we can see that today's temperature T_i' is written as a linear combination of temperatures over the previous p days, plus a linear combination of noise terms over the previous q days.

By inverting the MA polynomial equation (6.7) can be rewritten as

$$\psi^{-1}(B)\phi(B)T_i' = \epsilon_i \tag{6.14}$$

in which today's temperature is given as a weighted sum of all previous temperatures and a single random noise term (in other words, an infinite-order AR model).

Alternatively, by inverting the AR polynomial equation (6.7) can be rewritten as

$$T_i' = \psi^{-1}(B)\phi(B)\epsilon_i \tag{6.15}$$

in which today's temperature is given as a weighted sum of all previous random forcing terms (an infinite-order MA model).

The simplest examples of ARMA models are the ARMA(1,0) or AR(1) model, which is

$$T'_i = \phi_1 T'_{i-1} + \epsilon_i \tag{6.16}$$

and the ARMA(0,1), or MA(1) model, which is

$$T'_i = \epsilon_i + \psi_1 \epsilon_{i-1} \tag{6.17}$$

Use of the AR(1) model for modelling temperatures for weather derivative pricing has been suggested by a number of authors, including Dischel (1998a), Alaton et al. (2002), Cao and Wei (2000) and Torro et al. (2001). Dornier and Querel (2000), Moreno (2000) and Moreno and Roustant (2002) suggest more general versions of the ARMA model.

ARMA models can capture autocorrelation of time series in a very flexible way. At a mathematical level one can prove that any stationary ACF can be captured to any desired level of accuracy by an ARMA model, given enough p and q terms. However, at a practical level this is not a useful result: for many ACF shapes the number of parameters required by the model is extremely large, and the parameters cannot be estimated reliably with available data.

We show the performance of some simple AR models for temperature anomaly time series. The models are fitted using the well-known Yule–Walker equations and we validate them by considering the ACF, the residuals and the index distribution. The residuals of a parametric time series model such as (6.7) are calculated as follows:

- the parameters of the model, including the noise variance, are fitted;
- the model is used to make one-step, in-sample forecasts with no innovations;
- the errors in these forecasts are calculated: these are the residuals.

The distribution of these residuals should then, for internal consistency within the model, agree with the distribution of the innovations (the ϵ terms). This can be evaluated using a QQ plot. If these distributions are not consistent, this shows that there is an inconsistency in the form of the model.

Figure 6.8 shows the observed and modelled ACF using four simple AR models. The modelled ACFs severely underestimate the observed in three out of the four cases. Figure 6.9 shows the residuals: we see that the residual distributions do not agree well with the fitted noise in any of the four cases. Finally, figure 6.10 shows the index distributions for an average temperature index for this location from historical data and the four models.

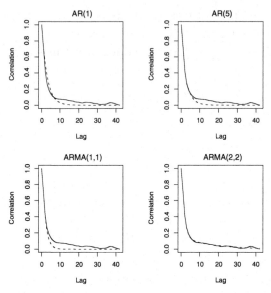

Figure 6.8. The observed (solid line) and modelled (dashed line) ACFs from ARMA models applied to Chicago daily temperatures.

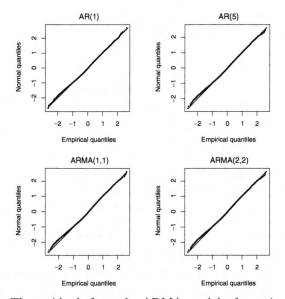

Figure 6.9. The residuals from the ARMA models shown in figure 6.8.

We can see that in three of the four cases the modelled distributions are steeper than the historical, indicating lower variance – exactly as would be expected from the underestimation of the ACF shown in figure 6.8 together with equation (6.5).

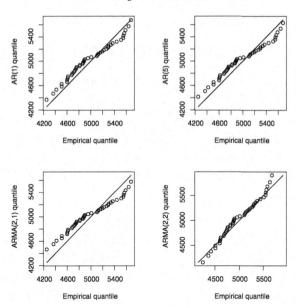

Figure 6.10. QQ plots of indices derived from the ARMA models shown in figure 6.8.

It is clear from these examples that the ARMA models do not model daily temperatures well. The best of the models considered is the ARMA(2,2) model, which gives a good fit for the ACF but at best only a reasonable fit for the residuals (our tests are based on over 16,000 days of data, so we would expect almost exactly a straight line if the model were good). In three of the ARMA models the errors show up clearly in the index distribution and would cause significant mis-pricing of weather contracts. Since any ACF can be represented if we use enough AR parameters, it would seem sensible to try more parameters. This turns out not to work in practice. Long before we get close to getting good results for both the residuals and the ACF, the number of parameters exceeds the number that can be reliably estimated.

6.5.4 ARFIMA models

Having shown that the ARMA models do not do a particularly good job in modelling daily temperatures, we now discuss another class of models, known as ARFIMA (autoregressive *fractionally integrated* moving average), which performs somewhat better. The application of these models to daily temperature was first described by Caballero et al. (2002). Independently, Brody et al. (2002) have described the use of a continuous analogue to the ARFIMA(0,d,1) model.

The ARFIMA models are specified by

$$\phi(B)(1 - B)^d T_i' = \psi(B)\epsilon_i \tag{6.18}$$

where $(1 - B)^d$ is to be interpreted as an infinite sum of powers of B

$$(1 - B)^d = \sum_{k=0}^{\infty} \binom{d}{k} (-1)^k B^k \tag{6.19}$$

where $\binom{d}{k}$ is a binomial coefficient. There are certain conditions on ϕ and ψ (see Beran, 1994).

This model is an extension of the ARMA model, and is stationary for $0 \le d < 0.5$. For $d = 0$ it is the same as the ARMA model. One interpretation of the ARFIMA model is that before we apply an ARMA model we difference the temperatures a fractional number of times d, where the meaning of fractional differencing is given by equation (6.19). Another interpretation is that ARFIMA is an ARMA model with correlated innovations ϵ_i.

The feature of ARFIMA models that makes them of use for the modelling of daily temperature anomalies is that the ACF decays very slowly at long lead times, which is exactly what we saw in the observations in figure 6.5.

As an example, we fit an ARFIMA(1,d,0) model to Chicago temperatures. The ACF of observations and the model are shown in figure 6.11; we see that the model captures the slowly decaying ACF reasonably well. The residuals are shown in figure 6.12; there is very good agreement between the residual distribution and the innovations. The results are better than those from the ARMA(2,2) model, even though there are only three parameters rather than five. Finally, we show an index distribution derived from the ARFIMA model in figure 6.13, which shows good agreement.

Our experience suggests that the ARFIMA model works well for many stations and, as such, forms a very reasonable standard model for the modelling

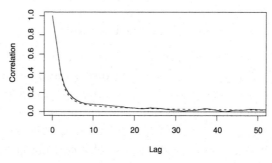

Figure 6.11. The observed and modelled ACF for Chicago temperature anomalies using an ARFIMA model.

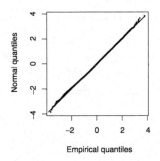

Figure 6.12. The residuals for the ARFIMA model shown in figure 6.11.

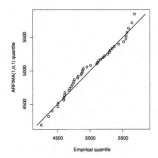

Figure 6.13. QQ plots of indices derived from the ARFIMA model shown in figure 6.8.

of temperature anomaly time series. However, for certain situations, such as Miami, we have seen that the ACF varies significantly between seasons. This cannot be captured by the ARMA or the ARFIMA models, and, indeed, using either model for Miami would give rather inaccurate results, since the models would try to fit all seasons well and end up performing badly for all of them.

6.5.5 AROMA and SAROMA models

Another class of models that appear to capture the slow decay of the ACF of temperature are the AROMA (autoregressive *on* moving average) and SAROMA (seasonal AROMA) models of Jewson and Caballero (2003a). The advantage of these models over the ARFIMA models is that they include the case where the ACF varies seasonally too. We have seen that the slow decay of the observed ACF of temperature could potentially be modelled by an ARMA model with many parameters but that many of the parameters would be unidentifiable due to over-fitting. One possible solution to this problem would be to put restrictions on the parameter space. One can think of many such restrictions, such as setting some parameters to zero or

Table 6.1. *Eight US weather stations, with the optimum lengths of the four moving averages, as selected automatically as part of the fitting procedure for the AROMA model.*

Location	m_1	m_2	m_3	m_4
Chicago Midway	1	2	3	17
Miami	1	2	4	28
Los Angeles	1	2	9	33
Boston	1	2	5	32
New York Central Park	1	2	4	18
Charleston	1	2	4	22
Detroit	1	2	3	24
Atlanta	1	2	7	27

requiring some subsets of the parameters to be equal. Since it usually not possible to base such restrictions on physical mechanisms they inevitably become somewhat arbitrary. The class of AROMA models is one such attempt to impose restrictions on the parameters of AR models with many lags; the choice of restrictions is still arbitrary, but the model is easy to interpret.

The AROMA$(m_1, m_2, \ldots, m_M)$ model is specified by

$$T_i' = \sum_{n=1}^{M} \alpha_n \sum_{j=i-1}^{i-m_n} T_j' \tag{6.20}$$

In other words, the temperature on day i is written as a weighted sum of M running means of previous temperatures. The first running mean covers days $i-1, i-2, \ldots i - m_1$, the second covers days $i-1, i-2, \ldots, i - m_2$, and so on. Optimum values for the m_i when M is set to 4 are given for a number of US locations in table 6.1.

Figure 6.14 shows the observed ACF for Chicago, along with the simulated ACF from the AROMA model and the ARFIMA model. We see that the AROMA model simulates the observed ACF as well as the ARFIMA model.

Extension to SAROMA

The advantage of the AROMA model over the ARFIMA model is that it can be readily extended to include seasonality in the ACF. This is achieved by making the coefficients α_i vary slowly from season to season.

Figure 6.15 shows the seasonally varying coefficients of a SAROMA model applied to Miami. We see that these coefficients vary significantly from season to season.

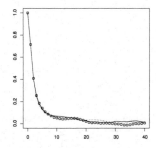

Figure 6.14. The observed (solid line) and modelled ACFs for Chicago. The modelled ACFs were produced using the ARFIMA model (dotted lines) and the AROMA model (circles). We see that both models give a good fit to the observed ACF.

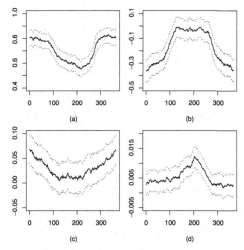

Figure 6.15. The seasonal variation of the four regression parameters for the SAROMA model for Miami. The solid lines show the estimated parameter values, while the dotted lines show the 95 per cent error bounds. We see that each of the parameters shows a strong seasonal cycle, corresponding to the strong seasonal cycle seen in the observed and modelled ACFs.

Figure 6.16 shows the seasonal ACFs for Miami from observations and from the SAROMA model. We can see that the SAROMA model does reasonably well in capturing the seasonal variation in the ACF.

6.6 Non-parametric daily modelling

We have described daily models that do a good job of modelling temperature in many cases, but in some cases these models fail, particularly for stations that show strong non-normality and seasonality. We now present a non-parametric model that can be used in these difficult cases.

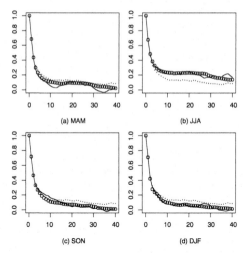

Figure 6.16. The four panels show observed and modelled ACFs for Miami for the four seasons. The observed data is the same as in figure 6.6. In each panel the dotted line is the annual ACF, which is included for reference. The solid line is the observed ACF for that season, and the circles are the modelled ACF for that season. We see that the observed and modelled ACFs show good agreement, and that the model captures the seasonality well. Confidence limits are omitted for clarity, but it seems likely that the differences between the observed and modelled ACFs can probably be explained by sampling errors.

6.6.1 Sliding window resampling

Consider again a one-week contract. We have argued that standard index modelling throws away 98 per cent of the historical data. ARFIMA modelling, on the other hand, uses all the data. In some cases this may be beneficial but in others it may be inappropriate, especially when there is strong seasonality and the summer data has a very different distribution from the winter data. SAROMA modelling is an improvement: because the parameters vary seasonally, only data that is reasonably local in terms of the time of year is used. However, if the distribution or ACF is changing *very* rapidly with season then neither the distribution transform of section 6.5.1 nor the SAROMA model can capture that. As an alternative, the sliding window resampling method (described in Jewson and Caballero, 2003a) allows a flexible way to use exactly the data desired. It works as follows:

- the methods described above are used to separate the seasonal cycle and the anomalies;
- plots of the seasonal variation in the skewness, kurtosis and ACF are used to determine the 'relevant data period' – the period during which the distribution

and ACF of the data are reasonably close to the distribution and ACF during the contract period;

- a window of the same length as the contract is moved through all the possible positions within the relevant data period;
- for each position of the window, an index value is calculated by adding anomalies from within the window to the seasonal cycle for the contract period;
- these index values are used to define the estimate of the index distribution.

It must be emphasised that the very many historical index values calculated using this method are not independent. Nevertheless, they can be used to create an estimate of the index distribution, since they come in groups from different years, and the different years are independent.

The advantages of this method are that it allows the user to control exactly how much data is used and from what part of the year, it can allow the use of much more data than index modelling, it automatically accounts for seasonality and non-normality in the temperature distribution and seasonality in the ACF, and it is extremely simple to implement. It will tend to extrapolate and smooth the index distribution more than the basic index method, but in very realistic ways (any extrapolation is based on a real period of days). The main disadvantage comes if we try and combine this method with forecasts in a sophisticated way.

6.7 The use of daily models

When should daily models be used to price contracts in preference to the burn or index models of chapters 3 and 4? This is a very difficult question to answer. The only clear answer we can give is that, in cases where the daily models clearly do *not* work for some reason (i.e. the seasonal ACFs or seasonal distributions from the model do not agree well with reality), they should *not* be used. In cases where they work very well (all the relevant statistics have been thoroughly checked) they can be used confidently, and the results given more weight than the results of the index-based approaches. For cases in between these two extremes the most sensible approach is probably to use a combination of index and daily models.

6.8 The potential accuracy of daily models versus index models

Finally, we investigate the question of the potential accuracy of daily models. As discussed above, high potential accuracy, combined with a realistic model, gives accurate results. The realism of the model can be judged using the methods described above: the comparison of distributions and ACFs

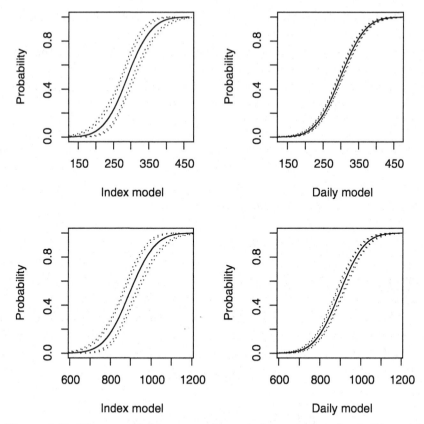

Figure 6.17. The potential accuracy for an index model and a daily model applied to a thirty-day (top two panels) and a ninety-day contract (bottom two panels).

with reality. Potential accuracy is calculated by fitting a model to its own simulated output in an imitation of the way that the model is fitted to historical data. If this is done many times one can build up a picture of the statistics of the accuracy of the model, under the assumption that the model is perfect.

The potential accuracy of daily modelling in this way has been investigated in Jewson (2004h). Figure 6.17 shows the potential accuracy of a daily model and an index model for a thirty-day and a ninety-day contract. We see that the potential accuracy of the daily model is higher in both cases, but the difference is greater for the thirty-day contract. The reason for this is that the potential accuracy of the daily model depends on the amount of data available *relative to the length of the contract*. For a thirty-day contract we have twelve times as much data as the length of the contract, while for the ninety-day contract we only have four times as much. For a one-year contract, the potential accuracy of a daily model is therefore the same as that of an index model.

6.9 Further reading

A standard reference on the statistical modelling of time series, covering the ARMA model but not the ARFIMA model, is Box and Jenkins (1970). A standard reference on long-memory modelling of time series, including the ARFIMA model of Granger and Joyeux (1980), is Beran (1994). Other useful references are Brockwell and Davis (1999) and Davison and Hinkley (1997); the latter has a section on non-parametric time series modelling.

There has been interest in the statistical modelling of daily temperatures for many years for use in crop growth simulation models. Models developed for this purpose are reviewed by Wilks and Wilby (1999). A discussion of the importance of using the correct frequency when deseasonalising daily temperatures is given in Villani et al. (2003).

Finally, we note that a shorter discussion of some of the issues presented in this chapter is given in Brix et al. (2002).

6.10 Acknowledgements

Figures 6.3, 6.4, 6.6, 6.7, 6.14, 6.15 and 6.16 and table 6.1 are reproduced from Jewson and Caballero (2003a) with the permission of the editor of *Meteorological Applications*.

7

Modelling portfolios

Up until now we have looked exclusively at individual weather contracts, and how to model and price them on a stand-alone basis. However, we saw in chapter 3 that, from a speculator's point of view, individual weather contracts are very risky investments. For swaps there is around a 50 per cent chance of losing money while for short options there is typically a 20 per cent to 40 per cent chance, depending on the location of the strike. The addition of risk loading can make these risks a little less severe, but these are still worse risks than even the lowest-rated junk bonds.

There are two ways that speculators can overcome this problem and use weather derivatives to have a favourable impact on their overall levels of risk and return. The first is to view the weather derivative business as part of a larger enterprise. Although the weather business on its own might have a large risk relative to return, it could be that the marginal contribution to the total risk and return of the whole business makes it a good investment. This is possible because of the lack of correlation between weather events and other forms of investment. For instance, an insurance company that writes weather derivatives may value them because they are uncorrelated with the other forms of insurance being written; a bank that writes weather derivatives may value them because they are uncorrelated with most of the other trading the bank is doing; and a hedge fund that invests in weather derivatives may value them because they are uncorrelated with the other investments the fund holds.

The second way that organisations can build a reasonable business from writing weather contracts is by viewing weather as a stand-alone business, and building a portfolio of weather contracts that is sufficiently well diversified or hedged that the risk/return profile of that part of the business alone justifies it as a reasonable investment.

There are, then, a number of different strategies a speculator can follow, including the following.

1. Originating primary market end-user deals, passing off the risk immediately to other speculators in the secondary market, and keeping some of the premium as profit (known as a back-to-back strategy).
2. Trading swaps and options in such a way that the total portfolio risk is very low because of hedging effects.
3. Building a large, diversified book of contracts on many different locations, variables and time periods.
4. Attempting to price using forecasts and historical data more accurately than the other traders in the secondary market, and trading on that basis.
5. Trading weather with correlated gas, electricity or emissions contracts in such a way that the total risk is very low.

In this chapter and the next we consider the weather derivatives trading activities of a business as a stand-alone venture, and consider the behaviour, in terms of risk and return, of a portfolio of weather contracts.

Portfolio-based analysis changes many things about the way we view weather contracts: in particular, it changes the way that risk loading is calculated, and it changes which contracts we decide to trade. It also tells us what the sources of risk are within our portfolio, and gives us ways of reducing that risk.

In this chapter we focus mainly on the modelling issues related to portfolios, while in the next we focus on portfolio management.

7.1 Portfolios, diversification and hedging

Before we delve into the details of how to model a weather portfolio we will first review the basic mathematical principles behind portfolios, diversification and hedging. Much of this can be introduced using the equations for the mean and variance of the sum of two random variables.

$$mean(a + b) = mean(a) + mean(b) \tag{7.1}$$

and

$$var(a + b) = var(a) + var(b) + 2cov(a, b)$$

or

$$\mu_{a+b} = \mu_a + \mu_b \tag{7.2}$$
$$\sigma_{a+b}^2 = \sigma_a^2 + \sigma_b^2 + 2\rho\sigma_a\sigma_b$$

where a and b are random variables with means and standard deviations of μ_a, μ_b, σ_a and σ_b, and ρ is the linear correlation between them.

We will come back to these equations several times during this chapter. We start by considering a to be the pay-offs from a portfolio, and b to be the pay-offs of a contract to be added to the portfolio. We consider the variance to be a measure of risk, and the mean to be a measure of the (expected) return. We can rearrange the above equations to emphasise the changes in the portfolio when contract b is added.

$$\text{change in mean} = \mu_{a+b} - \mu_a = \mu_b \tag{7.3}$$

and

$$\text{change in variance} = \sigma_{a+b}^2 - \sigma_a^2 = \sigma_b^2 + 2\rho\sigma_a\sigma_b$$

The equations show that when we add the contract b to the portfolio the return increases by the return of the new contract, while the risk changes through the effects of two terms. The first term (term A, σ_b^2) shows that the variance increases with the variance of the added contract. This term is always positive. In the diversified case, where the contract and the port-folio are uncorrelated, this is the only term, since the second term is zero. The second term (term B, $2\rho\sigma_a\sigma_b$) encapsulates the interaction between the risk in the contract and the risk in the portfolio. This term can be either positive or negative, depending on whether the contract and the portfolio are positively or negatively correlated. This is the term that can be used to create hedged portfolios, with even less risk than diversified portfolios.

We can compare the sizes of these two terms. If term A is greater than term B, then the overall effect of adding contract A to the portfolio is to in-crease the risk. If, however, term A is *less* than term B, then the overall effect is to *reduce* the risk in the portfolio. This is unusual, and can happen only when the correlation between the contract and the portfolio is sufficiently negative. In particular, for the total variance to reduce, the correlation has to obey

$$\rho < -\frac{\sigma_b}{2\sigma_a} \tag{7.4}$$

In other words, the larger the size of the new contract relative to the size of the portfolio (where size is measured in terms of the standard devia-tion of pay-offs), the more negatively correlated it has to be to reduce the overall risk. Very small contracts need to be only very slightly nega-tively correlated to reduce the risk, but will reduce the risk only by a small amount.

If we apply equation (7.2) contract by contract to all the contracts in the portfolio we find that

$$\mu_{total} = \sum_{i=1}^{N_c} \mu_i \qquad (7.5)$$

where N_c is the number of contracts, and

$$\sigma_{total}^2 = \sum_{i=1}^{N_c} \sum_{j=1}^{N_c} c_{ij} \qquad (7.6)$$

$$= \sum_{i=1}^{N_c} \sum_{j=1}^{N_c} \rho_{ij} \sigma_i \sigma_j$$

$$= \sum_{i=1}^{N_c} \sum_{j \neq i}^{N_c} \rho_{ij} \sigma_i \sigma_j + \sum_{i=1}^{N_c} \sigma_i^2$$

The double sums run over all pairs of contracts in the portfolio. The terms c_{ij} form the covariance matrix, and the terms ρ_{ij} form the correlation matrix. What we see is that the total return of the portfolio is the sum of the returns on the individual contracts while the total variance of the portfolio pay-off is given by the sum of all the terms in the covariance matrix: the diagonal terms are the variances of each individual contract, while the off-diagonal terms are the covariances between contracts. If all the correlations between contracts are zero, then the correlation matrix is diagonal ($\rho_{ij} = \rho_{ii}\delta_{ij}$) and the portfolio is diversified. We can see clearly in these equations how the interactions between contracts in a portfolio contribute to creating the total risk, while the total return does not depend on interactions between contracts at all.

Let us interpret these ideas in greater detail. We will now switch to measuring risk using the standard deviation of the profit rather than the variance. Variance and standard deviation are not necessarily the best risk measures in practice but are useful for simple examples because the mathematics is very easy. The mathematics of standard deviations is slightly more complicated than that for variances, but we prefer to use the standard deviation because it has the same units as the pay-off. We have already seen other ways of measuring risk in section 5.13.2, and will discuss the issue further in chapter 8.

First, let us consider building a portfolio with a large number of identical contracts. As the portfolio gets larger, how do the expectation and standard deviation of the profits change? We have N_c contracts in our portfolio, each with expected profit μ and with standard deviation of profit σ. Because the contracts are identical the correlation matrix is full of 1s. Equations (7.5) and (7.6) show us that the expected profit of the portfolio increases as $N_c\mu$ and the standard deviation of the profit increases as $N_c\sigma$. The ratio of these two, which is the simplest way to trade off risk against return, is a constant value of $\frac{\mu}{\sigma}$. There is no diversification effect whatsoever: increasing the size of the portfolio has no impact on this ratio and the whole portfolio behaves like one large contract.

Secondly, let us consider building a portfolio with a large number of independent contracts. How do the risk and return increase in this portfolio? The return is the same as in the previous example and increases as $N_c\mu$. However, all the off-diagonal elements in the correlation matrix are now zero and the risk increases much more slowly than before, as $\sqrt{N_c}\sigma$. The ratio of return over risk is now given by $\sqrt{N_c}\frac{\mu}{\sigma}$, which increases as N_c increases. This shows that, the bigger the portfolio, the more diversified it becomes, and the better it becomes as an investment. This is the principle behind most of investment theory, and explains why there is a natural economy of scale for insurance and reinsurance companies that sell many uncorrelated insurance contracts.

Finally, let us consider building a portfolio with a large number of contracts that have been chosen so that the risk in the various contracts cancels out completely. One way to do this would be to trade contracts in pairs. Within each pair, identical contracts are bought and sold. Assuming the returns are equal, the return of this portfolio is given by the same equation as the other two cases ($N_c\mu$), while the risk is now zero for all sizes of the portfolio. The contracts in the portfolio are perfect mutual hedges. The risk/return ratio goes to infinity.

These are three limiting cases that illustrate how diversification and hedging work in portfolios. Shares in different companies typically have correlations of between zero and one, and hence portfolios of shares lie somewhere between the first two cases: completely undiversified and diversified. The portfolios of insurance contracts held by insurance companies are typically much closer to the second, diversified, case. Finally, the portfolios of derivatives and underlying instruments held in banks are much closer to the third example, with almost no risk (at least in principle).

How weather derivative portfolios behave depends entirely on how they are managed. A (foolish) company that decides to issue only one type of contract, in one direction, will be completely undiversified. More realistically, a company that issues only long options on various locations, variables and time periods, as an insurance company might, would be more diversified. A company that trades both sides of contracts, and concentrates on reducing its own risk, could be quite well hedged; and, finally, a company that trades only back to back will end up holding no risk at all (bar some credit risk).

7.2 Index dependences

The correlations between the pay-offs of different weather contracts arise because of statistical dependences between the indices that underly the contracts, and these dependences arise because of dependences between the fundamental weather variables – such as temperature and precipitation – at different times and different locations. Temperature is correlated for a few days in time (if it is warm today, it will probably be warm tomorrow) and for many hundreds of kilometres in space (if it is a warm summer in London, it is probably also a warm summer in Paris).

In figure 7.1 we show correlations and lag correlations between Chicago and other locations in the United States for daily temperatures. We see patterns over large areas in space, and decaying in time. These correlations in temperature lead to similar patterns of correlation for HDDs and CDDs.

As well as correlations between the same index across different locations, there are significant correlations between different indices at the same location, and there may be correlations between different indices at different locations. Indices that only partially overlap in time will also be correlated, and indices that are adjacent in time but do not overlap are also often correlated.

As some simple examples, we show the correlations for winter HDD indices between US cities in table 7.1, between London Heathrow and various US locations in table 7.2 and between various European locations in table 7.3. These correlations were estimated using thirty years of data.

7.2.1 Relating index and temperature correlations

Relating the correlations between fundamental weather variables to correlations between indices is, in general, very difficult. This is partly because there are a number of different aspects to the correlations between the weather variables: all weather variables are correlated because of the seasonal cycle, but this is not the correlation that creates correlations between annual indices; rather, it is the differences from the seasonal cycle (i.e. the anomalies) at different locations that create index-to-index relationships. The non-linear nature of many index definitions also affects the correlation between indices.

Table 7.1. *Winter HDD correlations between a number of US locations.*

Location	Atlanta	Chicago	Cincinatti	Houston	Miami	New York CP	New York LGA	Philadelphia
Atlanta	1.00	0.60	0.78	0.82	0.73	0.71	0.72	0.75
Chicago	0.60	1.00	0.88	0.49	0.50	0.79	0.82	0.85
Cincinatti	0.78	0.88	1.00	0.62	0.61	0.88	0.89	0.92
Houston	0.82	0.49	0.62	1.00	0.56	0.52	0.57	0.56
Miami	0.73	0.50	0.61	0.56	1.00	0.52	0.57	0.64
New York CP	0.71	0.79	0.88	0.52	0.52	1.00	0.95	0.93
New York LGA	0.72	0.82	0.89	0.57	0.57	0.95	1.00	0.95
Philadelphia	0.75	0.85	0.92	0.56	0.64	0.93	0.95	1.00

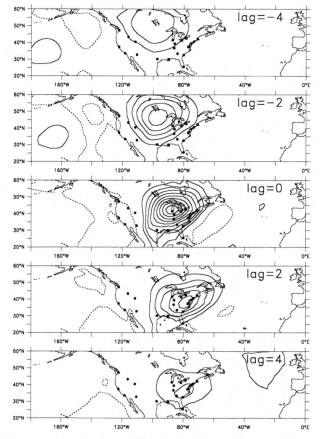

Figure 7.1. Correlations between Chicago temperature and temperature at other locations in the United States at different daily lags. Positive correlations are shown with solid lines and negative correlations with dashed lines. The zero correlation line has been omitted and the contours show correlations on intervals of 0.1.

Table 7.2. *Winter HDD correlations between London and a number of US locations.*

Heathrow	1.00
Atlanta	0.38
Chicago	0.60
Cincinatti	0.47
Houston	0.28
Miami	0.50
New York CP	0.44
New York LGA	0.48
Philadelphia	0.54

Table 7.3. *Winter HDD correlations between a number of European locations.*

Location	Amsterdam	Essen	Heathrow	Paris	Rome	Stockholm
Amsterdam	1.00	0.97	0.93	0.87	0.22	0.83
Essen	0.97	1.00	0.91	0.91	0.28	0.83
Heathrow	0.93	0.91	1.00	0.87	0.21	0.77
Paris	0.87	0.91	0.87	1.00	0.46	0.72
Rome	0.22	0.28	0.21	0.46	1.00	0.25
Stockholm	0.83	0.83	0.77	0.72	0.25	1.00

However, in the simple case of two CAT indices we can break the index correlation down very simply as follows. The covariance between indices x and y is defined as $E(xy) - E(x)E(y)$. Plugging the definitions of the two indices into $E(xy)$ we get

$$E(xy) = E\left(\sum_{i=1}^{N_d} T_i \sum_{j=1}^{M_d} U_j\right) \quad (7.7)$$

where T_i is the temperature on day i of the first contract and U_j is the temperature on day j of the second contract. Rearranging the sums gives

$$E(xy) = E\left(\sum_{i=1}^{N_d}\sum_{j=1}^{M_d} T_i U_j\right) \quad (7.8)$$

$$= \sum_{i=1}^{N_d}\sum_{j=1}^{M_d} E(T_i U_j)$$

$$= \sum_{i=1}^{N_d}\sum_{j=1}^{M_d} (c_{ij} + E(T_i)E(U_j))$$

where c_{ij} is the cross-covariance matrix between temperature at the two locations. What we see is that the covariance (and hence the correlation) between these two indices depends on the cross-covariances between the daily variables. This equation is a general case of equation (6.5), which showed the relationship between the autocorrelation function of the variable and the variance of a single index. Setting $U = T$ in the above expression recovers that equation. To interpret equation (7.8) in words: when the indices are aggregates over time, a relationship whereby temperature in Chicago is correlated with temperature in New York a day later (such as we see in figure 7.1) contributes to the correlation between the indices.

7.2.2 Relating index and pay-off correlations

Relating correlations between indices to correlations between pay-offs is easy in some cases. Two unlimited swaps will have pay-offs that are correlated in exactly the same way as the underlying indices. The pay-offs from pairs of call and put options will have different *linear* correlations from their underlyings, but the *rank* correlation will stay the same because applying the pay-off function does not change the ordering of outcomes. However, no simple relation exists for the pay-off correlations between straddles and strangles and other contracts.

We have made some progress in deriving closed-form expressions for the correlations between the pay-offs of weather contracts; this is described in Jewson (2004b).

7.3 Burn analysis for portfolios

We now address the question of how to calculate the distribution of the pay-offs of a weather portfolio, and how to calculate the risk and return.

When we were looking at methods for estimating the pay-off distribution for a single weather derivative contract the simplest method presented was burn analysis. This is also the simplest method for analysing portfolios. The historical data for all the indices underlying the contracts in a portfolio is converted to index values (possibly with detrending of either the daily temperature or the index values), and these indices are converted into historical pay-offs. Using thirty years of data will give thirty historical pay-offs for the whole portfolio. The time lags between the contract settlement periods must be translated into appropriate time lags in the historical data when the pay-offs of the individual contracts are aggregated to make the pay-offs of the portfolio. For instance, if a two-contract portfolio consists of a winter contract and a summer contract for the *following* summer, then the historical indices for the two contracts must be aligned in such a way that the summers follow winters. The thirty historical pay-off values for the portfolio can then be used to estimate the distribution of the pay-offs for the portfolio and various parameters that summarise that distribution, such as the expectation and the standard deviation of the pay-offs.

As with burn analysis for single contracts, portfolio burn has certain advantages and disadvantages relative to more complex modelling methods. The advantages are that it is simple to implement and involves assumptions only at the detrending stage. The biggest disadvantage of burn analysis for portfolios is with respect to the estimation of extreme outcomes. Thirty years of data will give us enough data only to estimate the probability of a one-in-thirty-year extreme event. This is also a problem for single contract analysis, but much less so: most weather derivatives are capped, and so we know what the largest extreme outcome will be and can typically make a reasonable estimate of the probability of it from the available data. For a portfolio, the most extreme outcome would occur when all the contracts hit their limits at once (i.e. all give maximum profit or all give maximum loss); this is very unlikely to have happened in the historical record.

Since financial institutions usually like to estimate their extreme risks at much smaller probability levels (higher risks) than one in thirty (often up to levels of one in five hundred) it becomes *essential* to go beyond burn analysis.

Extended burn analysis

In the portfolio case there is an extension to burn analysis, which we will call *extended burn analysis*, that, in some cases, goes some way towards providing information about the extremes. Extended burn analysis involves running a standard burn analysis and then fitting a normal distribution to the portfolio pay-offs. The fitted distribution then gives probabilities of profit and loss at any required probability level. This method works, however, only if the pay-off distribution really is normally distributed, or close to normally distributed. This is extremely unlikely to be the case for the following reasons:

- even in a situation where a portfolio consists of independent and identically sized option contracts, the convergence to a normal distribution is fairly slow because of the non-normality of the option pay-offs (see Jewson, 2003g, for some numerical tests we have performed on this case);

- most real weather portfolios are very unbalanced in terms of the sizes of the contracts, and the portfolio distribution is often driven by a small number of such contracts;
- there are certain situations in which the dynamics of trading encourage the distribution of portfolio pay-offs to become non-normal (in particular, risk management using only the expectation and VaR).

We conclude that extended burn analysis is not a useful practical tool for the modelling of extreme loss quantiles of real weather portfolios, except in very unusual circumstances.

7.4 Modelling the multivariate index distribution

We now consider how the index modelling methodology, described for single contracts in chapter 4, can be extended to a portfolio. The added complexity is that, as we saw in section 7.2, the indices for the contracts in a portfolio may well be correlated. We have to take this into account: not doing so would be acceptable if we were interested only in the expected pay-off for the portfolio, but not if we are interested in the distribution, or the standard deviation, of pay-offs. How, then, to model the correlations between indices? We start by considering the special case in which all the indices within a portfolio can be assumed to be normally distributed.

7.4.1 Normally distributed indices

In this case, modelling the portfolio consists of the following steps.

1. Estimate the expectation and standard deviation for each index in the portfolio.
2. Estimate the linear correlation matrix between these indices.
3. Simulate, for example, 100,000 years of surrogate data that captures these correlations using standard simulation methods.

By using 100,000 years of simulations (or more) we can, hopefully, create extreme scenarios in which many of the contracts hit their downside limits at once. If it is crucial to capture the absolute worst-case scenario, then the number of simulations should be increased until there are a few instances where *all* contracts hit their limits. This might entail a vast number of simulations for large portfolios.

The simulation methodology used in step 3 can work as follows. We write the historical index values for the contracts in the portfolio in a single matrix X with dimensions n (number of contracts) by t (number of years). Removing the mean gives us X'. We imagine we can factorise this matrix into the form

$$X' = AB^t \qquad (7.9)$$

where A is an n by k matrix (of k patterns across the various indices), B is a t by k matrix (of k time series that correspond to each of the patterns) and k is the rank of X' (the number of independent rows or columns). We also add the constraint that $B^t B = I$ (i.e. that the time series in B are orthogonal), which means that $X'X'^t = AA^t$. Is this factorisation actually possible? In fact, there are an infinite number of ways of doing this factorisation, as can be seen by counting the number of equations and the number of unknowns. Having found any one of these ways, we can simulate surrogate X''s, which will have the correct covariance matrix, by replacing the matrix B with normally distributed random numbers.

To see that the covariance matrix of the simulated indices is correct, let the simulated values be $\hat{X}'$, where

$$\hat{X}' = A\hat{B}^t \qquad (7.10)$$

where the time dimension of $\hat{X}'$ and $\hat{B}$ is as long as desired (e.g. 100,000).

The covariance matrix of the simulated data $\hat{X}'\hat{X}'^t$ is given by

$$\hat{X}'\hat{X}'^t = A\hat{B}^t\hat{B}A^t \qquad (7.11)$$
$$= AA^t$$
$$= X'X'^t$$

and we see that the simulated data has the same covariance matrix as the original data. The reason this works is that the factorisation in equation (7.9) splits X' into the index-to-index correlation information in A (which we want to keep) and the temporal correlation information in B (which we can ignore because we are treating years as independent).

Of the infinite number of ways of factorising a given matrix X', only two seem to be in common use: Choleski factorisation, in which the equations are made uniquely solvable by setting as much of A to zero as possible, and singular value decomposition, in which the equations are made uniquely solvable by adding the extra constraint that $A^t A = I$.

In cases where one or more of the index distributions are not normally distributed the method described above does not work, and so it is not really useful in practice except in special cases. There are, however, two generalisations that extend the method to the cases we are interested in. These methods are rank correlations and copulas.

7.4.2 Rank correlations

Rank correlation (also known as *Spearman's rank order coefficient* or *Spearman correlation*) is an alternative to linear correlation for measuring dependence. It is more appropriate than linear correlation when the variables being considered have non-normal distributions. In the normal distribution case, rank and linear correlations are equivalent (up to a simple transformation) and have a range from -1 to 1. In the non-normal case the range of possible values of linear correlations may be reduced, and this then makes it unhelpful to use linear correlation to measure dependence. Rank correlations, on the other hand, have a range from -1 to 1 whatever the distributions being considered. As an example consider $y = e^x$, where x is normally distributed. This fixes y to be log-normally distributed. Clearly, y is totally dependent on x, but the linear correlation is only 0.76. The rank correlation, however, is 1. One way of defining rank correlation is as the linear correlation of the ranks of the data. It is obvious from this definition why rank correlation works for all distributions: the actual values of the data are ignored, and only the ordering matters. The actual values can be adjusted to change the distribution, but as long as the rank ordering remains the same the rank correlation is unchanged.

There is a simple simulation method for use with rank correlations that allows us to simulate indices with whatever distributions we require.

1. Transform the historical values of each index to a normal distribution using a combination of the modelled CDF for that index and the inverse of the CDF for the standard normal distribution.
2. Simulate from the resulting multivariate normal distribution (e.g. using the method given above in section 7.4.1).
3. Transform the simulated values back to the correct marginal distributions using the CDF for the standard normal distribution and the inverse CDF for the index.

Why does this work? Step 1 will not affect the rank correlations, since it does not affect the rank ordering of the data. In step 2 we simulate linear correlations; but for a multivariate normal distribution there is a one-to-one relationship between linear and rank correlations, and so we are also simulating the right rank correlations. In step 3 we ensure that the marginal distributions are correct without changing the simulated rank correlations.

This method can be simplified further, since there is a known algebraic relationship between rank and linear correlation values for multivariate normal distributions, given by

$$\rho_{rank} = \frac{6}{\pi}\arcsin\left(\frac{\rho_{linear}}{2}\right) \tag{7.12}$$

Using this, the first step can be simplified, and the method becomes:

1. Calculate the rank correlations and convert them to linear correlations using equation (7.12).
2. Simulate a multivariate normal distribution with these linear correlations.
3. Transform the simulated values back to the correct marginal distributions.

7.4.3 Copulas

Rank correlation provides a useful way of modelling dependences between indices but does not completely specify the possible structure of that dependence. For instance, two pairs of indices could have the same rank correlations but a different dependence structure in detail.

One way to give a complete specification is by using a copula, which is the multivariate distribution of the indices once they have been transformed to uniform distributions using their CDFs. By using the rank correlation simulation method we are actually making an ad hoc choice of one particular copula (the Gaussian copula), whereas, in fact, another copula could – in theory – be a better representation of the observed relationships. This is, however, rather a technical point: there is typically not enough data to distinguish satisfactorily between different copulas, and so it makes sense to use the one that can be handled most easily. The main practical use for alternative copulas in this context seems to be as a sensitivity test. By replacing the Gaussian copula with another copula we can get a rough idea of the impact of the assumption that the Gaussian copula is the correct one. A simple copula to use as an alternative is the multivariate t copula.

7.4.4 Conversion to pay-offs

Having created a large number (e.g. 100,000 years) of simulated indices (x_{ij}) using the methods described above we convert these to simulated pay-offs for each contract in the portfolio:

$$p_{ij} = p_j(x_{ij}) \tag{7.13}$$

where p_{ij} is the $i'th$ simulated pay-off for the $j'th$ contract. These p_{ij}'s can then be used to calculate the pay-offs for the entire portfolio, as

$$P_i = \sum_{j=1}^{N_c} p_{ij} \tag{7.14}$$

where P_i is the $i'th$ simulated pay-off for the whole portfolio. Sorting the P_i's gives the distribution of outcomes for the portfolio. The P_i''s can also be used to calculate the expectation, standard deviation and quantiles of the portfolio pay-off distribution. Furthermore, we can use the individual contract pay-offs, the p_{ij}'s, to derive a wide variety of diagnostics for our portfolio, which can help us understand, for example, what the main factors are driving the risk and return. Many of these diagnostics are explored in the next chapter.

7.4.5 The consistency of simulations and constraints

We now discuss one of the limitations of the rank correlation and copula methods described above. Consider a portfolio of three contracts on the same location. The indices for the three contracts are November HDDs, December HDDs and November to December HDDs. Clearly, the number of HDDs for the two-month contract is the sum of the numbers of HDDs for the other two contracts. Thus, one can exactly hedge a linear swap position on the two-month contract with two individual monthly linear swap contracts.

Now consider simulations for this example portfolio. If we fit normal distributions and use linear correlations then the simulations will preserve the sum of HDDs constraint exactly; they have to, since to run the simulations we specify the means, variances and covariances, and the multivariate normal distribution is exactly specified.

However, now consider fitting non-normal distributions to each index and using the rank correlation or copula simulation methods. In this case the simulation will probably not satisfy the sum of HDDs constraint exactly. There is no reason why they should, because the information provided to the simulation algorithm is not enough to define the multivariate distribution uniquely. Thus the simulation algorithm produces simulations that have the right marginal distributions and rank correlations or copula but may not satisfy other constraints, such as the sum of HDDs constraint. In fact, this is not usually a problem, and the constraint will *almost* be satisfied anyway; the information provided does pin down the possible multivariate distributions to a fairly narrow range (in some sense). But, in a situation where one is attempting to model complete cancellation of risk between these contracts, it could matter. There are a number of solutions to this problem:

- to use normal distributions and linear correlations;
- to simulate indices for individual months only and construct the two-month indices as a sum of the simulated monthly indices;
- to simulate daily values for the whole two-month period, and build all the indices from the same set of daily values (i.e. use a daily model).

7.5 The daily modelling of portfolios

In the same way that daily modelling offered an alternative to index modelling for single contracts, so it can be used for portfolios. In addition to the advantages of daily modelling described in chapter 6, the daily modelling of portfolios offers the additional benefit that dependences between indices may be estimated more accurately, especially for short contracts. There are two reasons for this, which are analogues of two of the reasons given as benefits of the use of daily modelling for single contracts. The first is that we can bring more data to bear on the estimation of the dependence. To illustrate this, consider two one-week contracts. Using the index-based methods, the correlation is estimated using only historical data from that week of the year; 98 per cent of the data is discarded. One would imagine that correlations between adjacent weeks are likely to be very similar, and that using these weeks as extra data could improve our estimates. A daily modelling method can allow the use of all the available data for calculating these correlations. The second reason is to do with the shape of this dependence. If the dependence between two indices is not simple, then rank correlations, however much data is used to estimate them, will never be able to capture the detailed structure of the dependence; this relates to the discussion in section 7.4.3 on copulas. Dependences estimated and simulated at the daily level, however, will be more able to capture such details.

7.6 Parametric models for multivariate temperature variability

In the single station case we presented the ARMA models as a simple and straightforward time series model. We also showed that these models do not work well for temperature, but showed two other classes of models, the ARFIMA and SAROMA models, that work well in many cases.

The multivariate equivalents of the ARMA models are the so-called VARMA (vector ARMA) models, in which the single temperatures T_i are replaced by a vector of temperatures at multiple locations $\mathbf{T}_i$, and the autoregressive and moving average polynomials become polynomials of matrices. The simplest of these models is the VARMA(1,0) model (or VAR(1) model), which has the form

$$\mathbf{T}_{n+1} = \mathbf{A}\mathbf{T}_n + \mathbf{E} \qquad (7.15)$$

This model can capture exponentially decaying autocorrelations at each location, as well as lag zero and lag one cross-correlations. The cross-correlation functions (CCFs) are also exponentially decaying beyond lag one. The problems with VARMA models for use in modelling daily temperatures

Modelling portfolios

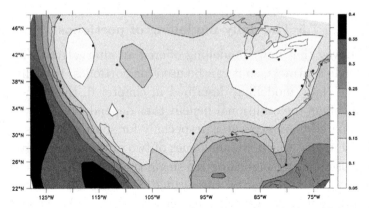

Figure 7.2. The d parameter from the VARFIMA model.

are very similar to the problems seen with the ARMA models for single
stations: the observed autocorrelation and cross-correlation functions decay
much more slowly than those of the VARMA model.

In the same way that the slow decay of the observed autocorrelations
can be modelled using the ARFIMA model, so the slow decay of the
cross-correlation functions can be modelled using the VARFIMA (vector
ARFIMA) model (Jewson and Caballero, 2002), which is a multivariate extension of the ARFIMA model. This model allows each location to have a
different value for the fractional differencing parameter d. Values of d for the
whole of the United State are shown in figure 7.2. It can be seen that d has
the largest values near the coasts and in lower latitudes. This is presumably
because much of the long memory is due to the influence of the ocean on
the atmosphere, which depends on ocean temperature and is hence greater
near the equator, where the ocean is warmer.

Figure 7.3 shows the observed and modelled ACFs and CCFs for a group
of three US locations modelled using a VARFIMA(1,d,1) model. Both the
ACFs and the CCFs are captured reasonably well.

The VARFIMA model can be fitted as follows:

- an ARFIMA model is fitted at each location separately
- the d's from each location are used to fractionally differentiate the temperatures
  at that location;
- the differentiated temperatures are fitted using a VARMA model.

7.7 Dimension reduction

A potential problem with VARMA and VARFIMA models is that the number of parameters in the model increases very rapidly as we use the model

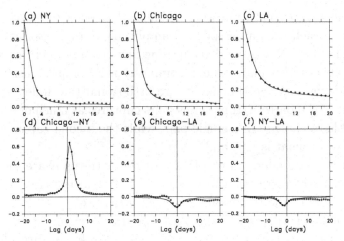

Figure 7.3. ACFs and CCFs from observations and from the VARFIMA model fitted to these three US locations.

for more locations. A VARMA(1,1) model applied to N stations has $2N^2$ parameters. As we add more stations the amount of data being used increases with N, but the number of parameters increases as N^2. The ratio of data to parameters gets worse and worse, and the model fitting time increases dramatically. Our experience suggests that it is not possible to fit VARMA models to more than five stations at once because of these problems.

One way around this is to pre-filter the data so as to reduce the number of dimensions in the data set. The reasoning behind this in the current application is that temperature variability is highly correlated in space. The temperature variability across a hundred locations can be accurately approximated by many fewer than a hundred independent patterns and variables.

Mathematically this works as follows. We write the historical temperature anomalies at one hundred locations using a single matrix X with dimensions space n by time t.

Applying singular value decomposition (SVD) to this matrix we can decompose it into three matrices:

$$X = E\Lambda P^t \tag{7.16}$$

where $E^t E = I$, Λ is diagonal and $P^t P = I$. The dimensions of E are n by k, the dimensions of Λ are k by k and the dimensions of P are t by k. This decomposition can be understood more clearly if we write the matrix multiplication out in terms of sums:

$$x_{ij} = \sum_{n=1}^{k} e_{in} \lambda_n p_{jn} \tag{7.17}$$

From this sum representation we see that X has been written as the sum of k patterns, each with an associated amplitude and time series. There are an infinite number of ways of decomposing any given matrix into a product of three matrices. Singular value decomposition is uniquely useful because (a) the patterns and the time series are orthogonal (i.e. independent) and (b) the first of the pattern/time series pairs captures as much of the variance as is possible to capture in a single pair, while the second captures as much as is possible of what is left, and so on.

Another way to understand SVD is that the patterns E are the eigenvectors of the spatial correlation matrix $C_s = XX^t$ and the time series P are the eigenvectors of the temporal correlation matrix $C_t = X^tX$.

The number k is the rank of the matrix X. In our example it is extremely unlikely that the matrix is not full rank, and hence $k = min(t, n)$.

Because of the variance-maximising property of SVD we can use it as an efficient filter. By constructing an approximation for X,

$$\hat{x}_{ij} = \sum_{n=1}^{k'} e_{in} \lambda_n p_{jn} \tag{7.18}$$

using only the first k' pattern/time series pairs (ordered by the largest singular values), we can capture a large amount of the variability in X using only a small number of patterns. Since it is usually patterns with large spatial scales that contribute the most to the overall variance, this truncation effectively truncates small-scale features.

Our multivariate time series modelling methodology can then be applied to the time series corresponding to the leading patterns, while univariate modelling is applied to the rest. The multivariate problem now has a much reduced dimensionality compared to modelling the original data, and it is more likely that VARMA or VARFIMA can be successfully applied.

We have obtained good results using the following sequence of steps:

- pre-filter the temperature data to remove the long memory;
- apply the dimension reduction algorithm above;
- model the first few time series using VARMA, and the rest using ARMA;
- simulate VARMA and ARMA time series;
- convert back to patterns by reversing the dimension reduction step;
- add back the long memory.

As an example, we show results from the modelling of twenty locations of temperature variability in the United States using VARFIMA(1,d,1). Without dimension reduction we would have to estimate 800 parameters. In fact, just five patterns capture 72 per cent of the total variance. We thus choose to truncate at five patterns and model the time series using five

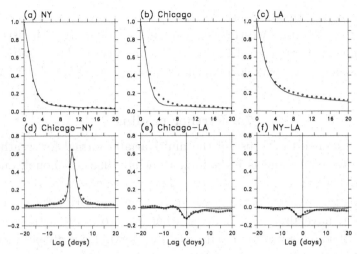

Figure 7.4. ACFs and CCFs from model and observations for three US locations; the model is the SVD-VARFIMA model fitted to twenty US locations.

dimensional VARMA(1,1). Figure 7.4 shows the ACFs and CCFs as captured by this model for three of the stations; all are simulated reasonably well.

7.8 A general portfolio aggregation method

We present one final method for modelling portfolios of weather derivatives that is a hybrid between the index and daily modelling methods described above and is the most practical approach for modelling large and varied portfolios.

In a large portfolio of weather derivatives there are likely to be contracts based on a number of underlying variables, with a number of different index definitions. For some of these contracts the best modelling method may well be to use daily simulations. For others index modelling may be better, or may even be the only available option. We would like to be able to mix these different approaches for different contracts. In fact, this is very easy to do.

The general aggregation method consists of the following steps:

- use whatever is the most appropriate method to estimate the marginal distribution of the index for each contract in the portfolio (this could be index or daily modelling);
- estimate the rank correlations between these index distributions using historical index data;
- simulate from these marginal index distributions using the estimated rank correlations.

The advantage of this method is that it allows us to combine distributions that have been accurately estimated using daily modelling with distributions for other contracts that are based on index modelling. The disadvantage is that the estimates of rank correlation are made entirely at the index level.

7.9 Further reading

The first reference to the use of the multivariate normal for weather portfolios that we could find is in Goldman-Sachs (1999), although one would imagine that it was in use before then. The first reference to the use of rank correlations for weather portfolios is in Jewson and Brix (2001), although, again, it may have already been in use when we wrote that article. A general discussion of some issues to do with weather portfolios is given by Zeng and Perry (2002). Simulating using rank correlations was apparently originally suggested by Iman and Conover (1982), and it has been described more recently by Wang (1998) and Embrechts et al. (2002). The general method for combining daily and index modelling was first described in Jewson et al. (2002a).

A useful reference for discrete multivariate distributions is Johnson et al. (1997), and for continuous multivariate distributions see Kotz et al. (1994).

8

Managing portfolios

In the previous chapter we discussed the methods that can be used to model the pay-offs of a portfolio of weather derivatives, taking into account the distributions of each weather index and the correlations between the indices. We now turn to the question of how portfolios can be managed. We start with a discussion of some of the different ways for measuring the performance of a portfolio. These methods are then applied to the question of how to expand a portfolio (which contracts to add) and how to price contracts against a portfolio. We then discuss various methods for understanding portfolios, and look at the hedging of portfolios using swap contracts.

8.1 Risk and return

Having modelled a portfolio using either an index-based method, a daily-simulation-based method or the general method of section 7.8 that mixes the two, there are a lot of questions we can ask to understand better what is creating the total risk and return profile in the portfolio. However, before describing these questions, and how to answer them, we need to look in more detail at how actually to measure risk and return.

Defining return

The word 'return' itself is used in a number of different ways in finance. First, we can look back at the performance of an investment that has now run its course. We might calculate the *absolute return*, which is simply the profit, in monetary units, that the investment yielded. More commonly this is expressed as a percentage relative to the amount of money invested and is called the *relative return*. This percentage can also be given in terms of the excess relative to the risk-free rate of return (the interest rate paid by safe government bond issues), known as the *excess relative return*. Making

169

£110 in one year on a £100 investment would be a £10 absolute return, a 10 percent relative return, and would be 6 per cent in excess of a risk-free rate of 4 percent. This is also referred to as a spread of 600 basis points over the risk-free rate.

Second, we can look forward at the *likely* levels of return an investment may yield in the future. The actual returns, in the senses of the word used above, are now random variables, and all we can do is to attempt to estimate the distributions, or aspects of the distributions, of these random variables. For instance, we could estimate the expected profit. If we know the initial investment, we can convert that into the expected relative return, and if we are confident about estimating the risk-free rate over the future period we could express it as the expected excess relative return above the risk-free rate.

As we have seen already, the 'expected profit' is the value that you would receive on average if you could repeat an investment in identical circumstances many times over. Since you cannot do this, it can be said that the expectation is not a very good measure of the future performance of an investment. We have already argued that it may be more important to know the probabilities of various levels of return *this time round*. In that case, a reasonable alternative to the expected profit is the median profit: this has a precise meaning in terms of this particular investment cycle, and is the level of profit that you will get with a probability of 50 per cent.

In practice, we will often refer to measures of the likely future performance of an investment simply as the 'return'. The context will make clear whether the word 'return' is being used in a backward- or forward-looking sense.

Defining risk

Just as the return can be defined in a number of different ways, so can the risk. Looking forward or backward, the risk is usually defined as some measure of the spread, or dispersion, of the distribution of possible outcomes.

The most common measures of risk, both of which we have seen already, are the variance and the standard deviation. They have the benefit of being extremely tractable mathematically (using equation (7.1)) and are a good starting point for understanding many of the mathematical issues pertaining to risk. Furthermore, the standard deviation has the nice property that the total standard deviation cannot be more than the sum of its parts (this property is sometimes known as 'coherency'). To illustrate this, consider a portfolio with two weather derivatives in it. If the standard deviations of the pay-offs are £100 and £50 respectively, then by equation (7.1) there is no way that the total standard deviation can be more than £150, however highly correlated these two derivatives are. Even without knowing anything about the details of the risks and their interdependences, we can quickly get an upper limit for the total risk. We will see that not all risk measures possess this nice property. One disadvantage of the standard deviation is that it does not tell us very succinctly how much money we could lose. Consider an investment with an expected profit of £100 and a standard deviation of £80. What could we lose? If we can assume that the distribution of profit is a normal distribution then we can say that there is a 2.5 per cent chance of losing £60 or more. But in the general case of non-normal distributions we cannot say anything without further information. Another shortcoming of the standard deviation (and the variance) is that it can lead to ridiculous decisions in certain circumstances. Examples of this are given in section 8.1.2.

To overcome the limitation of the standard deviation that it does not tell us clearly how much we could lose, it is common to use profit/loss quantiles at certain levels of probability. So, for example, we might consider the 2.5 per cent level of loss. In the example above, this would be a loss of £60 in the case of a normal distribution, or maybe £30, or £90, for other distributions. The advantage of quantiles is that they communicate very clearly how much could be lost, especially if we use several levels (maybe 5 per cent, 1 per cent and 0.1 per cent). The major disadvantage of quantiles is that the total *can* be more than the sum of the parts: a portfolio of two weather derivatives with 5 per cent quantiles of −£100 and −£50 could have a portfolio 5 per cent quantile of *less* than −£150.

Loss quantiles can be presented in several different ways.

1. As the quantile itself, with positive values for profit and negative for loss (i.e. 'the 5 per cent quantile is a profit of −£200').
2. As a loss value, with positive values for loss (i.e. 'the 5 per cent quantile is a loss of £200').
3. Relative to either the expectation or the median of the distribution. If the median is £500, and the 5 per cent loss level is −£200, we could represent this relative to the median as −£700.

How quantile loss levels relate to the well-known VaR is described in more detail in chapter 12.

In addition to evaluating the pay-off at a certain quantile one can also monitor the quantile of a certain pay-off – e.g. monitor the probability of losing more than £10 million.

Two other risk measures that are less commonly used than the standard deviation, variance, or quantiles, but that have certain advantages, are the downside semi-standard deviation and the downside semi-variance.

Whereas variance of a random variable x with density $f(x)$ is defined as

$$\sigma^2 = \text{variance}(x) = \int_{-\infty}^{\infty} f(x)(x - E(x))^2 dx \qquad (8.1)$$

downside semi-variance is defined as

$$\sigma_d^2 = \text{downside semi-variance}(x) = 2\int_{-\infty}^{E(x)} f(x)(x - E(x))^2 dx \qquad (8.2)$$

And while standard deviation is defined as

$$\sigma = \text{standard deviation}(x) = \left(\int_{-\infty}^{\infty} f(x)(x - E(x))^2 dx\right)^{\frac{1}{2}} \qquad (8.3)$$

downside semi-standard deviation is defined as

$$\sigma_d = \text{downside semi-standard deviation}(x) = \left(2\int_{-\infty}^{E(x)} f(x)(x - E(x))^2 dx\right)^{\frac{1}{2}} \qquad (8.4)$$

For a normal distribution (and other symmetric distributions) these are equal to the standard deviation and the variance respectively, while for other distributions they may be different, and emphasise departures from the expected value on the side of losses rather than profits.

Risk and return

We have discussed how to measure risk and return separately. We will now review three frameworks that can be used for managing risk and return at the same time. These frameworks are *risk-adjusted return*, *utility theory* and *stochastic dominance*. We will also consider some of the connections between these three frameworks. Then, in sections 8.2 and 8.3, we will describe how to apply each of the frameworks to the practical decisions that portfolio managers have to make, such as whether to trade a particular contract, given the premium, or at what level to set the premium of a new contract. Finally, in section 8.6, we will discuss some of the ways that complex portfolios can be understood, and look at how total portfolio risk can be reduced.

8.1.1 Risk-adjusted return

Managing a weather portfolio – or, indeed, any portfolio of investments – is about creating the greatest return (however measured) for the least risk (however measured). Portfolio managers must decide how much risk is justified for a given increase in return, or how much return should be expected for a given increase in risk. This can be done on a purely intuitive basis, but there are also a number of ways to attempt to answer this question analytically.

One simple method is to define a single number that increases with return and decreases with risk. The goal is then to maximise this number, which we will call the risk-adjusted return (RAR).

The simplest formulae that encapsulate this basic idea are

$$RAR = \mu - \lambda\sigma^2 \tag{8.5}$$

which uses the expectation to measure return and the variance to measure risk, and

$$RAR = \mu - \lambda\sigma \tag{8.6}$$

which uses the expectation to measure return and the standard deviation to measure risk.

For dimensional consistency, λ in equation (8.5) has the units of $\$^{-1}$, while λ in equation (8.6) is unitless.

Using downside semi-variance instead of variance and downside semi-standard deviation instead of standard deviation these definitions become:

$$RAR = \mu - \lambda\sigma_d^2 \tag{8.7}$$

and

$$RAR = \mu - \lambda\sigma_d \tag{8.8}$$

In all these formulae λ must be specified by the portfolio manager. A large value indicates low tolerance for risk and a small value indicates high tolerance for risk. These formulae use absolute values of return, and hence can be used when we do not know the exact level of initial investment (this is not uncommon: if weather derivatives trading is part of a larger business it is not necessarily possible to say how much capital has been set aside for it). One shortcoming of these formulae is that, precisely because we do not know the initial level of investment, we cannot compare with the risk-free rate of return. If we *do* have the initial investment then the *Sharpe ratio* (SR) is a more appropriate definition of RAR, because we can relate risk to returns in excess of the risk-free rate (and only returns above the risk-free rate should entail taking on risk). The Sharpe ratio can be written in terms of the expected pay-off, the standard deviation of the pay-off, and the expected pay-off μ_r that would be achieved from a risk-free investment:

$$SR = \frac{\mu - \mu_r}{\sigma} \tag{8.9}$$

Dividing the numerator and denominator of the right-hand side by the initial investment, we can rewrite using relative values of return (this is more standard).

With any of the above definitions, the goal is to increase the RAR, or to keep it above a certain level. When we evaluate whether the contracts in our portfolio are good or bad, we look at their contribution to the RAR. When we are considering whether or not to trade a new contract, we look at the impact it would have on the RAR. And, finally, when we are setting the premium to be charged we must set it high enough that the RAR either increases or stays above a certain specified level.

We look at all these situations in more detail later in this chapter.

8.1.2 Problems with mean-variance and mean-standard deviation approaches

We now investigate one of the shortcomings of the mean-variance and mean-standard deviation approaches to risk-adjusted return, which is that in certain circumstances they lead to obviously ridiculous decisions.

Imagine that someone offers you a free lottery ticket with pay-off L and probability of winning p. Of course you should take it, under any framework for measuring risk and return, since it will increase your return with no adverse effects. When we apply the mean-variance framework we find that

$$\mu = Lp, \sigma^2 = L^2 p(1-p) \tag{8.10}$$

and so

$$\text{RAR} = \mu - \lambda\sigma^2 \tag{8.11}$$
$$= Lp - \lambda L^2 p(1-p) \tag{8.12}$$
$$= Lp(1 - \lambda L(1-p)) \tag{8.13}$$

If $L > \frac{1}{\lambda(1-p)}$ the RAR becomes negative: very large free lottery tickets reduce our RAR! This is clearly a failure of the mean-variance framework to indicate the right decision. A similar problem occurs if we try and use the mean-standard deviation framework.

These problems arise because the distribution of pay-offs being considered in this example is highly skewed, and both standard deviation and variance do not distinguish between the upside and the downside.

The downside semi-variance and downside semi-standard deviation can also lead to problems of this type.

Are these problems with RAR likely to occur in practice? In most cases, probably not. But it is clear that certain contracts, with low probabilities of large pay-outs, are not well represented using a RAR based on either mean-variance or mean-standard deviation, and this is a reasonable argument for investigating the possibility of using other methods.

8.1.3 Utility theory

In the previous section we discussed how to manage risky investments under a framework in which we separate risk and return. One can argue, however, that this is not entirely adequate, and that it would make more sense to consider the whole distribution of possible outcomes, their relative probabilities, and our reaction to each possible outcome. This is the approach taken in utility theory. Utility theory is a mathematical framework used by economists to understand risk preferences in theoretical models of economic behaviour. It is more general than the measures described above, but is usually considered too abstract to use in practice. However, we will see that it can help us understand some of the limitations of the RAR methods, and will lead to a useful new way of analysing risk. It is also necessary to understand utility theory to some extent in order to understand many of the academic papers on option pricing in incomplete markets, including some academic papers on weather pricing.

The basic idea of utility theory is that every level of wealth has a level of utility (usefulness, or value) to the holder of that wealth. Writing the wealth as w and the utility as u we have $u = u(w)$. The function $u(w)$ describes one person's (or one organisation's) risk preferences. By definition, decisions are then made on the basis of the expected utility, where expectations are calculated over all possible values of w. If the probabilities of different levels of wealth lead to one decision having a higher expected utility than another, then it is to be preferred. If the expected utilities are the same, then we are indifferent.

There are a number of properties that utility functions are usually required to have in order to give a reasonable representation of real attitudes to risk.

1. Wealth preference: more wealth is always better. As w increases, so u increases – i.e. $u' > 0$.
2. Risk aversion: the marginal benefits of increasing wealth decrease with increasing wealth. As w increases, u' decreases – i.e. $u'' < 0$. To put it another way, losing a fixed amount of wealth becomes worse the poorer you are.
3. Ruin aversion: the poorer you are, the more risk averse you become. Putting it another way, as w increases, u'' increases, or $u''' > 0$.

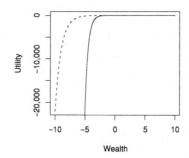

Figure 8.1. Graph of exponential utility for values of a of 1 and 2.

The most commonly used function with these properties is the so-called exponential utility

$$u(w) = 1 - e^{-aw} \tag{8.14}$$

where a is a positive parameter that measures risk aversion and has units of inverse money. The shape of this utility function is given in figure 8.1 for two different values of a (1 and 2).

Utility can be used to compare risk-free and risky choices using the certainty equivalent c, defined by

$$u(c) = E(u(w)) \tag{8.15}$$

The certainty equivalent for a certain distribution of wealth is the single fixed value of wealth that would give the same expected utility; c is the maximum price we would pay to attain a certain distribution of wealth.

The relation between utility and risk-adjusted return

We can attempt to interpret the simple risk measures described in section 8.1 in terms of utility.

For small changes w' in wealth around the current wealth w_0 we can expand the utility function using a Taylor expansion:

$$u(w) = u(w_0) + w'u'(w_0) + \frac{1}{2}w'^2u''(w_0) + \ldots \tag{8.16}$$

Taking the expectations of this equation gives

$$Eu(w) = u(w_0) + u'(w_0)Ew' + \frac{1}{2}u''(w_0)Ew'^2 + \ldots \tag{8.17}$$

The units in which utility are measured are arbitrary, and so we can assume that $u(w_0) = 0$ and $u'(w_0) = 1$, which gives

$$Eu(w) = Ew' + \frac{1}{2}u''(w_0)Ew'^2 + \ldots \tag{8.18}$$

If we neglect the higher-order terms, this equation is now of the same form as equation (8.5), in that it measures value using the mean and variance, with a negative weight on the variance (since u'' is negative). This shows that for small changes in the level of wealth (for which approximating the utility function locally with a quadratic is a good approximation) the mean-variance approach is consistent with a utility approach. There are various other insights that come from this comparison, such as the observation that the λ in equation (8.5) should perhaps reduce as wealth increases in the same way that u'' does.

8.1.4 Stochastic dominance theory

The main difficulties of applying utility theory directly in practical situations are that (a) nobody knows what shape utility function they have (e.g. what value a they should take in equation (8.14), or even if exponential utility is the right class of shapes at all) and (b) the whole method is reasonably 'black box'; it may give an answer, but it is difficult to see how that answer arises.

The authors are not aware of any organisation that uses utility theory in practice to make pricing decisions in the weather market. However, we now describe an extension of utility theory, known as stochastic dominance theory (SDT), that overcomes these problems, and that *is* occasionally used in practice. The idea behind SDT is to accept that, while it is difficult to identify one's utility function, it does seem reasonable to assume that we possess the three properties often required of utility that were described above: wealth preference, risk aversion and ruin aversion. It turns out that assuming that our unknown utility function satisfies these properties can still help us make decisions without having to specify exactly which utility function we have.

Stochastic dominance, then, is applied by testing for dominance, and first-, second- and third-degree stochastic dominance. We consider how to use stochastic dominance to compare two scenarios, which might be (1) keep our current portfolio unchanged and (2) add a new contract to our portfolio.

Dominance

The dominance test is applied by comparing the worst outcome of scenario 2 with the best outcome of scenario 1. If the worst outcome of scenario 2 is better than the best outcome of scenario 1, then we say that scenario 2 dominates scenario 1. If this is the case, then we should choose scenario 2. Otherwise, we should test first-degree stochastic dominance, which is more subtle.

First-degree dominance

The first-degree stochastic dominance test is applied by comparing the CDF of the pay-off under scenario 1 with the CDF of the pay-off under scenario 2. If the CDF under scenario 2 is less than the CDF under scenario 1 for all values of wealth then scenario 2 stochastically dominates scenario 1 at the first degree, and we should choose scenario 2. Otherwise we should test second-degree stochastic dominance.

Second-degree dominance

The second-degree stochastic dominance test is applied by comparing the indefinite integral of the CDF of the pay-off under scenario 1 with the indefinite integral of the CDF of the pay-off under scenario 2. If the integral of the CDF under scenario 2 is less than the integral of the CDF under scenario 1 for all values of wealth then scenario 2 stochastically dominates scenario 1 at the second degree, and we should choose scenario 2. Otherwise we should test third-degree stochastic dominance.

Third-degree dominance

The third-degree stochastic dominance test is applied by comparing the second indefinite integral of the CDF of the pay-off under scenario 1 with the second indefinite integral of the CDF of the pay-off under scenario 2. If the second integral of the CDF under scenario 2 is less than the second integral of the CDF under scenario 1 for all values of wealth, then scenario 2 stochastically dominates scenario 1 at the third degree, and we should choose scenario 2. Otherwise we conclude that the two scenarios are equivalent.

Possible outcomes of stochastic dominance testing

We denote the result of each test as:

- 'F' (fail) if scenario 1 dominates scenario 2;
- 'N' (neutral) if neither scenario dominates;
- 'P' (pass) if scenario 2 dominates scenario 1.

We can then write the results of the four tests as a string of four characters, such as 'NNNF', which means that the first three tests are neutral and the last is failed. Outcomes such as 'FF' are equivalent to 'F', since once we fail the dominance test there is no point in applying the first-degree stochastic dominance test, and so the number of possible outcomes reduces to nine.

1. F
2. NF

3. NNF
4. NNNF
5. NNNN
6. NNNP
7. NNP
8. NP
9. P

If we are considering switching from scenario 1 to scenario 2 then we would do so under outcomes 6 to 9. A useful stochastic dominance score can be created by subtracting five from all the numbers above. Negative scores mean 'do not switch', and positive scores mean 'switch'. A zero score means that we are ambivalent about switching.

Relations between SDT and mean-variance approaches

There are various relations between SDT and the mean-variance approaches to managing risk. These are discussed in Ogryczak and Ruszczynski (1997).

Pricing using SDT

In order to price a (short) option contract using SDT the minimum premium charged should be the amount that ensures that we are (just) better off with the new contract than without, where 'better off' means we achieve at least dominance at the third level. This can be found by starting with a low premium and increasing it until third-degree dominance is achieved.

Comparing RAR, utility theory and SDT

The main practical differences between making decisions using risk-adjusted return or utility theory on the one hand and SDT on the other are that (a) RAR and utility theory both need us to specify an arbitrary parameter that measures our risk aversion while SDT does not, and (b) utility theory and RAR always give a clear-cut decision, while SDT is often undecided.

For many classes of investment stochastic dominance is often not considered particularly useful, because it can be applied only if we have an estimate of the whole CDF of outcomes. However, in weather we always do have an estimate of this CDF as an output of the modelling methods described earlier, and so stochastic dominance can be used particularly easily. SDT is so easy to apply, and so objective, that it is hard to argue that one shouldn't use it to help with all portfolio decisions (perhaps in addition to other methods).

8.1.5 The significance of stochastic dominance results

One final extension of the stochastic dominance framework described above is to attempt to add statistical significance tests to the differences between the various curves that we are comparing.

Without significance tests the results of a first-degree SDT analysis are:

- scenario 1 is better than scenario 2;
- we are uncertain which decision is better;
- scenario 2 is better than scenario 1.

If we use statistical testing on the differences this then expands to five possibilities:

- scenario 1 is significantly better than scenario 2;
- scenario 1 is better than scenario 2, but not significantly;
- we are uncertain which decision is better;
- scenario 2 is better than scenario 1, but not significantly;
- scenario 2 is significantly better than scenario 1.

These significance tests can be generated using simulation methods.

One disadvantage of using such tests is that one has to set a subjective level at which the test is passed or failed.

8.1.6 Examples of stochastic dominance

To illustrate SDT, consider the following example. We have two fair six-sided dice, A and B.

Dominance

If A is labelled with 1 to 6 and B with 7 to 12, then B dominates A. Whatever happens, B will be higher than A.

First-order stochastic dominance

If A is labelled with 1 to 6 and B with 2 to 7, then B does not dominate A, but it does *stochastically* dominate it. It is very possible that A will end up higher than B, but at any fixed level of probability B is higher than A. B should be preferred to A by anyone who thinks more wealth is better.

Second-order stochastic dominance

If A is labelled with 1 to 6 and B is labelled with all 4s, then B does not dominate A, nor does it stochastically dominate A. However, by looking at the integrated values, which are 1, 3, 6, 10, 15, 21 and 4, 8, 12, 16, 20, 24, we see that B does dominate A stochastically at the second order.

Third-order stochastic dominance

If A is labelled with 1 to 6 and B is labelled with all 3s, then B does not dominate A, nor does it stochastically dominate at the first or second order. However, by looking at the *twice* integrated values, which are 1, 4, 10, 20, 35, 56 and 3, 9, 18, 30, 45, 63, we see that B does dominate A stochastically at the third order. Even though the mean outcome of B (3) is lower than that of A (3.5), B is preferred by anyone who is ruin-averse.

8.2 Expanding a portfolio

We now have all the information we need to apply the various frameworks described above to practical portfolio management decisions. First we look at expanding a portfolio.

Let us imagine that we have a large portfolio of weather contracts, and are considering adding one more. The premiums for this contract have been fixed and are non-negotiable. Should we add the contract or not? We can use either RAR, utility theory or SDT for addressing this question.

Applying risk-adjusted return

There are two ways we can apply the RAR approach to answer this question. In the first, we stipulate that we will trade this contract only if the RAR of the portfolio increases. In the second, we stipulate that we will trade this contract only if the RAR remains above a fixed level. Either approach is very easy to implement in practice: we model the portfolio with and without the contract, and evaluate the risk-adjusted return in both cases.

Applying utility theory

In this case we would model the portfolio and evaluate the portfolio utility with and without the contract. If the expected utility increases, then we should add the contract.

Applying SDT

With SDT we would model the portfolio and compare the distributions of pay-offs before and after adding the contract. If the new distribution dominates, or stochastically dominates at the first, second or third level, then we should add the contract. If the old distribution dominates, or dominates at the first, second or third level, then we should not add the contract. If neither dominates, then it does not matter what we do, and we can make the decision based on factors other than the financial returns.

Efficient modelling

When modelling a portfolio first without and then with a contract, as we have to in all these cases, there are efficient ways of performing the necessary calculations that avoid having to simulate the whole portfolio twice. This can save time for large portfolios. These methods are described in section 8.5.

8.3 Pricing against a portfolio

Let us imagine that we have a large portfolio of weather contracts and that, again, we are considering trading one more contract, but this time we are in the position to set the premium. What level should we set it at? As we have seen, it is very important to consider this question in the context of the whole portfolio: if the contract is very highly correlated with what we already have then trading it will be a good idea only if we can charge a high premium. Similarly, if this contract is very anticorrelated with what we already have, and might even reduce our risk, then we should be happy to charge a lower premium. We can calculate appropriate premiums in any of the decision frameworks described above. Again, we model the portfolio with and without the contract.

Applying risk-adjusted return

When selling an option contract, we choose the premium (which we will receive) so that the RAR must either increase, or must stay above a certain level.

In the mean-standard deviation framework, applying the first of these rules gives

$$RAR_2 > RAR_1 \tag{8.19}$$

or

$$\mu_2 + p_s - \lambda\sigma_2 > \mu_1 - \lambda\sigma_1 \tag{8.20}$$

where p_s is the premium, μ_1 and σ_1 are the expectation and standard deviation of the pay-offs of the portfolio before adding the contract, and μ_2 and σ_2 are the standard deviations of the pay-offs after adding the contract, but without the premium. Rearranging this gives

$$p_s > \mu + \lambda(\sigma_2 - \sigma_1) \tag{8.21}$$

where $\mu = \mu_1 - \mu_2$ is the expected pay-off of the contract (with the sign convention defined so that μ is positive). We see that the minimum premium to be charged is given by the marginal changes in the expected pay-off and the standard deviation of pay-offs of the portfolio. Both of these terms would usually be positive, in which case the selling price would be above the expected pay-off of the contract by a factor dependent on the marginal change in the risk. For this value of the premium our RAR would stay the same. For premiums above this value the RAR would increase.

For a contract that is very beneficial to our portfolio $\sigma_2 - \sigma_1$ might be negative; trading the contract would reduce our risk. In this case, we can charge a premium *below* the expected pay-off and still increase our RAR.

When *buying* an option contract for a premium p_b we get

$$p_b < \mu - \lambda(\sigma_1 - \sigma_3) \qquad (8.22)$$

where σ_3 is the standard deviation of the pay-offs of the portfolio after adding the contract, and $\mu = \mu_3 - \mu_1$ is the expected pay-off of the contract (again, defined with the sign convention so that μ is positive). The $\sigma_1 - \sigma_3$ term is usually positive, in which case the buying price would be *below* the expected pay-off of the contract by a factor dependent on the marginal change in the risk.

Again, for a contract very beneficial to our portfolio $\sigma_1 - \sigma_3$ might be negative, and we could pay a premium *above* the expected pay-off and still increase our RAR.

Applying utility theory

In the utility context, the minimum price at which we would sell a contract, or the maximum price at which we would buy, would be the price at which our expected utility does not increase. This argument is sometimes known as a utility-indifference argument.

Applying stochastic dominance theory

With stochastic dominance, the minimum price at which we would sell a contract would usually be set by the point at which the new portfolio starts to dominate at the third level (although the second or first level could also be used).

Sources of uncertainty

It is useful to appreciate that there is additional sampling uncertainty when pricing contracts against a portfolio relative to pricing a contract on a 'stand alone' basis. When pricing a single contract stand alone, the source of sampling uncertainty is the uncertainty in the estimation of the distribution of the contract index. When pricing against a portfolio, there is an additional source of uncertainty due to the estimate of the correlation between the contract and the portfolio.

8.4 Market making

Making markets is very similar to pricing against a portfolio, except that we price both long and short positions. As we saw in section 8.3, the selling price for an option would typically be above the expected pay-off, and the buying price would typically be below the expected pay-off.

In the unlikely case that the new contract is exactly uncorrelated with the old portfolio then the buying and selling prices are symmetrical about the expected pay-off (at least in the mean-standard deviation framework). However, in the general case of non-zero correlations they will not be symmetrical: the market maker will have a preference for buying or selling depending on the sign of the correlation between the new contract and the portfolio. In the extreme case where trading the contract in one direction actually reduces the risk in the portfolio then the expected pay-off will lie outside the buying and selling prices.

A market maker who rigorously follows such a quantitative approach should adjust his prices every time he does a new trade, because each trade changes the base portfolio.

When making markets for swaps, rather than calculate the premiums that give a change in the RAR of zero, a market maker calculates the swap strikes for long and short positions that give a change in the RAR of zero. These strikes can be calculated using iterative methods similar to those described in section 5.8, but now considering the RAR of the whole portfolio.

8.5 Efficient implementation methods for adding single contracts to a portfolio

In sections 8.2 and 8.3 we considered the question of whether or not to add contracts to our portfolio. The answer to this question involved evaluating either the risk-adjusted return, the utility or the CDF with and without the extra contract. If we use burn analysis then the necessary calculations can be performed very quickly. However, if we are using index modelling then, for a large portfolio, modelling the whole portfolio twice in this way could be extremely time-consuming, and we might need to ask this question many times every day. Fortunately, there are ways that we can make the modelling more efficient. We present two methods by which this can be done. The first, and preferred, method we call 'index regression'. This involves saving all the simulations of the original portfolio and using these to price subsequent contracts without resimulation. It relies on the ability to store a large number of simulations. If this is not possible, one can use the second method, which we call 'pay-off regression', which saves only the portfolio pay-offs.

Index regression

The basic idea behind the index regression method for efficient pricing against the portfolio is to extend the rank correlation simulation method described in section 7.4.2. The normally distributed simulations used in that method are stored. When a new contract needs to be priced, linear combinations of these simulations are combined with random numbers to create a simulation for the new contract with the correct correlations with the original portfolio. These new simulations are then transformed to the correct marginal distribution and converted to pay-offs for the contract. This method gives the same results (up to differences in the random number feeds used) as repricing the whole portfolio with and without the extra contract, but is much faster because it avoids resimulating all the contracts in the portfolio. More details of this method are given in appendix J.

A limitation of this method is that the matrix of stored simulations could be very large: for a portfolio of one hundred contracts, using ten thousand simulations and storing as eight-byte floating-point numbers, this would need eight million bytes of storage. Although such storage is readily available, reading such large arrays into computer memory can be very slow, and may even be slower than a resimulation of the whole portfolio. To circumvent these problems, one can use a slightly different method.

Pay-off regression

The basic idea behind this method is to extend the rank-correlation-based simulation method by modelling the new index as a linear combination of the portfolio *pay-offs* and random numbers. Details are given in appendix J.

This method is extremely light on storage and processing, and is hence extremely fast. The disadvantage is that the assumptions in the method are slightly different from the assumptions in the original rank correlation simulations. Whereas we originally assumed that the dependences between *indices* are best captured by using rank correlations, in this method we use rank correlations for the dependence between the new index and the *pay-offs* of the other contracts. This may give different results from repricing the whole portfolio with and without the extra contract. Although these different assumptions may not be any less justifiable, it is generally better to stick with one approach to avoid contradictory and confusing results.

8.6 Understanding portfolios

We now consider techniques that can be used to understand what is going on in a portfolio of weather derivatives. When portfolios are small, with only a handful of contracts, it may not be necessary to apply mathematical methods in order to understand what drives the risk and return, since it may be obvious. But for large portfolios, of tens or hundreds of contracts, it rapidly becomes extremely difficult to understand these issues without further analysis. There are many different aspects of portfolios that we can look at, and a few of these are discussed below.

8.6.1 Breaking down risk and return (risk budgeting)

The first question we ask is: which of the contracts in our current portfolio contribute the most to the risk and return? Identifying contributions to the return is easy if we are measuring return using the expectation, since the total return is then the sum of the returns on the individual contracts. A contract with return that is a high percentage of the portfolio return can be said to be driving that percentage of the total return.

Identifying contributions to risk is more complicated, since a contract may have a high risk when considered alone, but this risk may be wholly or partly cancelled by other contracts and the contribution to the total risk of the portfolio can then be zero or negative. We can avoid this difficulty by noting that we are usually considering adding or removing contracts one by one; it is then the *marginal change* in the risk that matters. Although the marginal changes in risk due to all the contracts in the portfolio do not sum to give the total risk, they can still tell us which individual contracts we should hedge to reduce the total portfolio risk by the largest amount.

In practice, we might tabulate the marginal contribution to the expected pay-off and the marginal contribution to the standard deviation of the pay-off for all contracts in our portfolio. We might also look at the marginal contribution to the RAR or the utility. Contracts with a large positive marginal contribution to the RAR or the utility are good, those with a large negative marginal contribution are bad. If we see that a small number of contracts are distinctly worse than others we may consider taking proactive steps to hedge the risk in those contracts. This is addressed in section 8.7.

The second, and very similar, question we ask is: which of the *groups* of contracts in our current portfolio contribute the most to the risk and return? The analysis described above can be repeated but for the marginal effects of whole groups of contracts. There are a number of situations in which this may interest us: we may want to know whether we have a particularly high level of exposure to one counterparty or region, or whether one trader is taking on more risk than the others.

8.6.2 Portfolio beta

In section 5.1 we introduced delta, and explained that it can be used either to give a quick estimate of how a new forecast might affect the value of a portfolio, or to indicate the size of swap contract that should be used as a hedge. It would be useful to extend the concept of delta to portfolios. For a portfolio of contracts on one index this is easy: the delta of the portfolio is equal to the sum of the deltas on the individual contracts. However, deltas for different indices should not be added together. The appropriate extension to portfolios based on a number of different indices is to *beta*, or *regression*, analysis.

The vector of pay-offs for a whole portfolio, P_i, can be regressed onto a single index, x_i, as

$$P_i = \alpha + \beta x_i + \epsilon_i \qquad (8.23)$$

The regression coefficient β is the equivalent of delta with respect to the index x for the whole portfolio. In the case in which all the contracts in the portfolio are based on the same index, and the index is normally distributed, this is exactly the delta. In the general case, the value of beta depends in a complex way on the non-linear pay-off functions in the portfolio and the correlations between locations. As with delta, beta can be used either to assess the impacts of weather forecasts on the portfolio or to design hedging strategies.

Multiple beta values can be calculated for different indices. This can be done using multiple regression rather than several steps of univariate regression:

$$P_i = \alpha + \sum_{j=1}^{N_c} \beta_j x_{ij} + \epsilon_{ij} \qquad (8.24)$$

The beta values for each location are now different from the values calculated at single locations. These values can be used to understand how to hedge a portfolio using more than one contract at once.

There is a difference in interpretation between the univariate and the multivariate values for the beta. The univariate values apply if we are considering changes in one index, while still allowing other indices to vary. If, however, we want to understand how the portfolio responds to changes of one index, with other indices held fixed, we should use the multivariate beta values. Holding the other indices fixed reduces the extent to which the main index can vary, because of the correlated variability of indices, and so the multivariate values are generally smaller.

8.6.3 Portfolio greeks

In chapter 5 we discussed the greeks for individual contracts. We now discuss how greeks can be used for portfolios.

For a portfolio of contracts on a single index only all the greeks can be calculated, and are simply the sums of the greeks for the individual contracts. The whole portfolio behaves like a single contract. More generally, however, for a portfolio of contracts on different indices one has to be slightly more careful. Delta, gamma and zeta should not be added together for contracts on different indices, and the only greeks that can be added across the contracts in a portfolio are theta and rho. The appropriate generalisation of delta is, instead, the portfolio beta that we discussed in section 8.6.2, and one could consider generalising gamma in the same way. It is less obvious how to generalise zeta.

8.6.4 The dominant patterns of risk

We have described in section 8.6.1 how we can analyse the impact of individual contracts on our portfolio. However, it could be that no individual contract has much of an impact, while a group of contracts together might be creating a very large risk. Although we described how to assess the impacts of groups of contracts too, the groups were prescribed by us in advance. It could be that a group of contracts that we have not considered are conspiring together, through the covariance matrix, to have a major effect on the risk. How could we detect this? There are a number of possible methods, but one particularly simple one is based on a mathematical technique known variously as principal components analysis (PCA), empirical orthogonal analysis (EOF analysis) or singular value decomposition analysis.[1] The application of PCA to weather portfolios has been described in Jewson (2004a). It works as follows.

---

[1] We have already come across the mathematical process of SVD in section 7.4; however, in that case we applied it to indices, not pay-offs.

We calculate the matrix of pay-offs of the whole portfolio, P, with elements P_{ij}. We then remove the expected pay-off of each contract, so that the expected pay-offs are all zero, and we are left only with the risk:

$$p'_{ij} = p_{ij} - \frac{\sum_{i=1}^{N_c} p_{ij}}{N_c} \tag{8.25}$$

Singular value decomposition is then applied to the matrix P' with elements p'_{ij}:

$$P' = E\Lambda Q^t \tag{8.26}$$

The first of the patterns (the first column in matrix E, which is the first singular vector) is the dominant pattern of risk. The contribution it makes to the total risk is given by the first singular value in matrix Λ.

When PCA analysis is used for portfolios of liquidly traded contracts such as equities one can proceed to hedge the first principal component by trading an appropriately weighted basket of contracts. This is usually not possible for weather, however, because the necessary basket of contracts may not be tradable at any reasonable price.

8.7 Reducing portfolio risk

Having explored a number of ways in which we might better understand the sources of risk and return in our portfolio we finally turn to the question of what we might do with that knowledge: how we might trade further contracts in an attempt to make things better.

The simplest solution to that question is to consider all the contracts available in the market, and to apply the pricing against the portfolio methodology developed in section 8.3. This will tell us which of these contracts would benefit our portfolio, and to what extent. If there are contracts that give a large benefit, we can trade them, and then repeat the exercise iteratively. One can also consider adding groups of contracts at once, although the number of permutations to be tested rapidly becomes very large.

However, it may well be that none of the contracts in the market is very effective in reducing the risk of our portfolio. In that case it might be worth creating new contracts based on what risk we really need to hedge, and then trying to find a willing counterparty. There are a number of ways one might attempt this.

The most general approach would be to consider all possible contracts, on all possible indices, and see which would benefit us most. This is likely to be very impractical in terms of calculation time. The challenge is to develop a streamlined version of this approach.

One simpler possibility is to compare the pay-offs of our portfolio (either historical or simulated) with a number of indices based on different locations using the univariate beta analysis described above. This reduces the number of comparisons that have to be made. If one further restricts the number of comparisons to only commonly traded indices (e.g. in the United States one might consider degree day indices for monthly contracts), the resulting algorithm becomes quite feasible to apply quickly. Having found an index that correlates or anticorrelates highly with one's portfolio, it is then easy to design a contract – either a swap or an option, and either long or short – on that index such that the pay-offs will be anticorrelated with the portfolio. Trading such a contract may lead to a significant reduction in risk, and if it can be traded at a reasonable price it may result in an increase in the RAR.

Beta neutrality

A special case arises when liquidly traded swap contracts are available on a certain number of locations. If we assume that these are trading at fair value then trading such contracts affects only our risk, not our return. A portfolio manager can endeavour to stay 'beta-neutral' to each of these contracts as follows. On a frequent basis, the portfolio beta is evaluated relative to these contracts. If any of the beta values are significantly non-zero, then the appropriate contracts are traded to reduce those betas to close to zero. The main limitation to achieving exact beta neutrality in the current weather market is that even the most liquidly traded contracts are traded only in discrete sizes. Until one's beta is large enough to justify trading one lot of a contract, it cannot be reduced. This is often known as 'gapping'.

The portfolio start-up problem

One of the difficulties with all the portfolio management techniques described above is that they work well only when one has already built a large portfolio of contracts. If one starts from a position of an empty portfolio then applying pricing against the portfolio methods will tend to lead to rather extreme prices, and there would be a danger of never doing any trades as a result. There is no easy answer to this problem. A work-around is to price the first few contracts using assumptions about what the composition of the final portfolio will probably be. In this way one can take advantage of likely future diversification of the portfolio and offer much lower prices.

8.8 Further reading

The theory behind mean-variance modelling of portfolios comes from Markowitz (1952) and Markowitz (1959). There are many books in economics and finance that discuss utility theory and stochastic dominance; two examples are Wolfstetter (2000) and Elton and Gruber (1995). A recent overview paper is by Tsanakas and Desli (2003). The use of stochastic dominance theory in the weather market seems to have come from the (no longer extant) weather derivatives group at Aquila, Inc. We learnt about it from Heyer (2001).

9

An introduction to meteorological forecasts

In this chapter and the next we will consider how *weather* forecasting and *seasonal* forecasting can potentially improve our valuation of weather derivative contracts. This chapter starts with a discussion of which weather forecasts are relevant to weather derivatives, and how these forecasts are made. We discuss forecasts of the expected temperature first, and forecasts of the whole distribution of future temperatures (*probabilistic forecasts*) after that. In each case we describe how to compare two forecasts to find out which is better, and briefly mention statistical methods with which one can try to improve forecasts. In the second part of this chapter we give a brief description of seasonal forecasts.

It is interesting to note that weather is somewhat different from financial market prices in the extent to which it is predictable. Forecasts of changes in financial market prices are possible, and may be successful, but there is a feedback between the forecast and the price, which means that, over time, all forecasting systems are likely to fail. Weather, on the other hand, is not affected by weather forecasts, and the dynamics of weather is constant.[1] This allows forecast systems to be constructed that will continue to make useful predictions now and into the future. There is, however, a parallel between the unpredictability of changes in market prices and weather in that changes in *expected* weather are unpredictable. We have touched on this idea in chapter 5 and will elaborate on it further in chapter 10, as it has some useful applications.

9.1 Weather forecasts

We will now look in some detail at weather forecasts – that is, forecasts that cover the immediate future up to around fifteen days.

---

[1] At least on the timescales that we are interested in.

9.1.1 Physical background

Meteorological forecasts are possible because of the predictability of the physical processes that drive the weather and climate. In the case of weather forecasts the dominant process that creates predictability is the dynamics of air masses in the atmosphere. Fifteen-day weather forecasts that are on average better than either random guessing or predictions of 'normal' conditions are possible mainly because it is possible to predict the motions of large air masses around the planet that far in advance. Other relevant physical processes are solar radiation, the behaviour of clouds, the capacity of the ground to retain heat and moisture, and the effect of the ocean on the atmosphere.

9.1.2 Forecasting methods

Most weather forecasts are produced by dynamical models of the atmosphere known as atmospheric general circulation models (AGCMs). These models are based on discrete numerical methods for attempting to solve the continuous equations that are believed to govern large-scale atmospheric flows. The calculations are made on a grid that divides the whole global atmosphere into boxes with perhaps a hundred values in the east–west direction, a hundred values in the north–south direction and twenty levels in the vertical. The models step forward in time with steps of around ten minutes. In addition to those parts of the model explicitly representing atmospheric dynamics, there are statistical representations of clouds and other processes that are too small or too fast to be resolved by these discrete spatial and temporal grids.

To make a prediction the models are started off from a best guess of the current state of the atmosphere. This best guess, known as an 'analysis', is based on a combination of previous forecasts and recent measurements. Much of the time and effort spent in making a forecast is involved in creating this initial state. The forecast is then produced by integrating the equations of the model forward in time, generating simulations of subsequent atmospheric states. At this stage the forecast consists of predictions of atmospheric variables such as temperature, pressure and wind on the grid of the numerical model. The final stage of making the kinds of prediction that are useful for the weather derivatives industry is that these grid forecasts are downscaled, using statistical methods, to produce predictions at individual locations, such as at the meteorological station at London's Heathrow Airport.

Ensemble forecasts involve running an AGCM a number of times in different configurations. This then gives an ensemble of alternative forecasts, and the mean of this ensemble is almost always a better forecast than any of the individual members. The different configurations in the ensemble are usually created by varying the initial conditions slightly to represent the uncertainty in the estimates of the current state of the atmosphere. It is also possible to create different configurations by perturbing the physical representations in the model using random numbers.

9.1.3 The leading models

At the time of writing, the leading ensemble weather forecasting systems are (in alphabetical order):

- CMC (Canadian Meteorological Centre), based in Canada (http://www.msc-smc.ec.gc.ca/cmc/op_systems/global_forecast_e.html);
- ECMWF (European Centre for Medium-range Weather Forecasting), based in the United Kingdom (http://www.ecmwf.int);
- NCEP (National Centers for Environmental Prediction), based in the United States (http://www.emc.ncep.noaa.gov/gmb/ens/).

The leading single forecast systems (again in alphabetical order) are:

- Canadian (http://www.ec.gc.ca);
- DWD (Deutsche Wetterdienst) (http://www.dwd.de);
- ECMWF (http://www.ecmwf.int);
- JMA (Japan Meteorological Agency) (http://www.jma.go.jp);
- Meteo-France (http://www.meteo.fr);
- NCEP (http://www.emc.ncep.noaa.gov/gmb/ens/);
- UKMO (United Kingdom Meteorological Office) (http://www.metoffice.com).

Both ECMWF and NCEP create a single forecast with their best (highest-resolution) model, and an ensemble forecast with a slightly inferior (lower-resolution) model.

We have deliberately not given information about the sizes of the ensembles, the lengths of the forecasts or the frequency at which forecasts are produced, since these details are liable to frequent change.

Organisations involved in pricing weather derivatives do not usually obtain forecasts directly from the above organisations but buy them through intermediary commercial forecast providers, who perform value-added services such as converting the forecasts on the model grids to site-specific forecasts. Users of forecasts do *occasionally* buy forecasts directly from the modelling agencies listed above and produce their own site-specific forecasts, but this is a costly and difficult activity.

Commercial forecast providers typically use a selection (but seldom all) of the models listed above to produce the forecasts that they sell. The NCEP forecasts are the most commonly used, mainly because they are available free of charge, and, at this point, are the longest. The ECMWF forecasts are often believed to be the best because the ECMWF has the largest ensemble and the highest resolution models. However, the ECMWF forecasts are expensive.

9.1.4 Downscaling

The process by which forecasts on a dynamical model grid are converted to forecasts at specific physical locations is known as 'downscaling'. The simplest methods for downscaling involve linear regression models between AGCM grid values and observed values (Leith, 1974). It is also possible to convert model values to site-specific forecasts using subjective methods, and this is what a number of forecasting agencies employ meteorological forecasters to do. The argument for subjective methods is that a skilled forecaster can learn which models do well in certain weather situations, and what types of errors the various models typically make, and adjust for those more efficiently than objective algorithms can.

9.1.5 An example forecast

For all our illustrations of weather forecasts we will use ECMWF zero- to ten-day ensemble forecasts for London Heathrow for 2002.[2] These forecasts have been downscaled to the London Heathrow location using linear interpolation from the model grid, but with no regression or bias correction. We calculate the mean of this ensemble forecast as an example of a single forecast.

9.1.6 Forecast terminology: lead time, target day and forecast day

Imagine that today is a Monday, and we obtain a forecast early in the morning that predicts the weather over the next few days. The first day of the forecast will be a forecast for today, which we will refer to as a lead 0 forecast. The forecast for Tuesday will be lead 1, etc. The day on which

---

[2] Kindly provided to the authors by Ken Mylne and Caroline Woolcock.

the forecast is made (Monday in this case) is the 'forecast day'. The day being predicted we will call the 'target day'. The number of days in between the target day and the forecast day is the 'lead time'.

9.2 Forecasts of the expected temperature

The simplest kind of meteorological forecast is a single number (for example, that the day after tomorrow will be 15°C in London), and we will start by considering this type of forecast. Forecasts for general use do not usually specify a very precise location or precisely defined weather variable. Weather derivatives, however, are based on precisely defined measurements made at individual stations, and consequently the forecasts used in weather derivative pricing need to reflect that. For example, the forecast might be one for London Heathrow, weather station WMO 03772, maximum temperature between 9 a.m. and 9 a.m. the following day.

Forecasts are sometimes presented as anomalies, and such anomaly forecasts are often much easier to understand than full-field forecasts. An anomaly forecast would say that tomorrow is going to be 3°C *warmer than normal*, rather than just 15°C. However, there is a lot of subjectivity about how 'normal' is defined. If you receive an anomaly forecast it is *crucial* to understand what normal, or *climatology*, has been used. The common meteorological practice of using climatologies based on thirty-year periods can be misleading, since almost all measured temperature series show upward trends and will appear warm relative to such a long-term average. Use of the detrending and deseasonalisation methods described in chapters 2 and 6 may be a more reasonable way to define anomalies.

Figures 9.1, 9.2 and 9.3 show forecasts from our example data. In each figure the left panel shows full values and the right panel shows anomalies, the climatological mean is shown as a solid straight line and the climatological range (plus and minus two standard deviations) is shown using straight dotted lines. Figure 9.1 shows a ten-day forecast for a fixed forecast day. The solid line shows the forecast and the dotted line the actual. We can see that the forecast starts off well, does poorly in the mid-range and, perhaps by chance, does well at the end. Figure 9.2 shows fifteen days of forecast for a fixed lead time of two days – i.e. the forecasts shown were made on different days, but were all two-day forecasts. We can see reasonably good agreement between the forecast and the actuals, as would be expected for such a short-lead forecast. Figure 9.3 shows ten days of forecast for a fixed target time – i.e. all the forecasts shown are attempting to predict the temperature on one

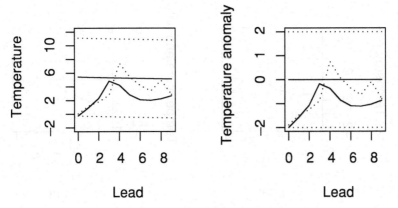

Figure 9.1. An example forecast (solid line), with climatological mean and range, and observed temperatures (dotted line), for a fixed forecast day.

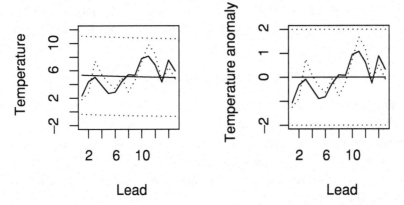

Figure 9.2. An example forecast (solid line), with climatological mean and range, and observed temperatures (dotted line), for a fixed lead time of two days.

particular day, and as we move across the graph from right to left we get closer and closer to the day itself.

9.2.1 The interpretation of single forecasts

What does a single temperature forecast mean? Is it the most likely temperature? Is it the mean of the possible distribution of temperatures? Or is it something else? Very often meteorological forecasts are provided without a clear mathematical definition of what they represent. This may be adequate for many purposes, but is certainly not adequate for weather derivative pricing. For our purposes it is most useful if single forecasts represent the mean or expectation of the distribution of possible future outcomes. Fortunately,

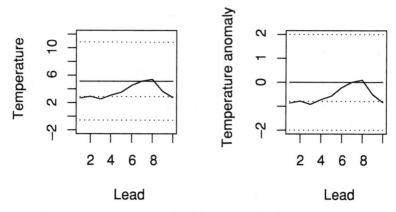

Figure 9.3. An example forecast (solid line), with climatological mean and range, and observed temperatures (dotted line), for a fixed target day.

it is possible to check whether a forecast represents the mean, and, if it does not, to correct it so that it does; this will be described in section 9.4.

9.2.2 Ensemble means

If we take an ensemble forecast and calculate the mean of the ensemble at each lead time this usually turns out to be a better single forecast than the individual ensemble members. This is because the forecast errors in the different members of the ensemble are, typically, reasonably independent, and so the error of the mean is smaller than the error of an individual member of the ensemble.

Very often the single forecasts provided by forecasting agencies are actually derived from a combination of ensemble means and single forecasts from higher-resolution models. At shorter leads the higher-resolution models tend to be more useful, while at longer leads the ensemble mean may be more useful.

Figure 9.4 shows an ECMWF ensemble forecast made on 1 January 2002 with target days from 1 January to 10 January, along with the actual outcome. It is tempting to try and interpret the spread of the ensemble members as indicating the range of possible outcomes, but this is not advisable until corrections have been applied. This is discussed further in section 9.5.

9.3 Forecast skill

As we have seen above, forecasts can be obtained from a number of different sources. Users of forecasts thus need to be able to compare forecasts to work

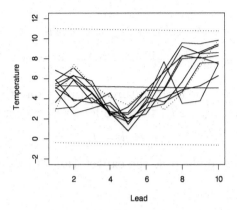

Figure 9.4. An example of an ensemble forecast. The spread of the members of the ensemble should *not* be taken to indicate the range of possible future values until further processing has been applied.

out which is best. They also need to be able to determine how many days of each forecast they should be using, based on how many days of the forecast are better than use of the climatological mean or random guessing.

We will now imagine that we have a long record of past forecasts with which to estimate the 'skill' of a forecast. We will assume that past skill implies future skill, and so by comparing past forecasts we can decide which forecast is likely to perform well in the future. This assumption is reasonable most of the time, but forecasting systems are continually updated, and one sometimes finds that a forecast that does well for one period does not do well for the next. Because of this the decision of which forecast to use needs to be continually revisited.

9.3.1 Skill measures based on full temperature values

The simplest methods for measuring the skill of forecasts are those that involve comparisons between the full (not anomaly) temperatures from the forecast and from the observations. The first such measure that we will consider is the bias, and the others are the root mean square error and the mean absolute error. Because of the seasonal cycle of temperature it does not make sense to calculate the correlation between the forecast and the observed temperatures. This correlation will be dominated by the seasonal cycle and will usually be very high, since even very poor forecasts can succeed in predicting warm temperatures in summer and cold in winter. This problem can be overcome by looking at the correlation between anomalies rather than full values, which we discuss in section 9.3.5.

9.3.2 Bias in the mean

The simplest measure of the skill of a temperature forecast is bias in the mean.

Writing the forecast for temperature on target day i as f_i, and the real temperature for that day as T_i, then the forecast error is given by

$$e_i = f_i - T_i \tag{9.1}$$

Bias in the mean is defined as the expectation of this error, i.e.

$$E(e_i) = E(f_i - T_i) = E(f_i) - E(T_i) \tag{9.2}$$

A practical system for estimating the bias in the mean of a forecast is to take the previous N days of forecast, along with the corresponding N days of observations, and calculate the mean error during this period, defined as

$$\bar{e} = \frac{1}{N} \sum_{i=1}^{N} e_i = \frac{1}{N} \sum_{i=1}^{N} (f_i - T_i) = \overline{f_i} - \overline{T_i} \tag{9.3}$$

Bias often varies seasonally and so N should not be taken larger than, say, ninety days to avoid the possible cancellation of opposing biases from different seasons.

Bias has the same units as the forecast, and can take positive and negative values.

We show the bias for our example forecast in figure 9.5. We see that there is a large negative bias at all lead times. This is not surprising, since our forecast was generated directly from an AGCM and had not been previously corrected for bias. Most commercially available forecasts would (hopefully) have already been corrected for bias, and so would be close to bias-free.

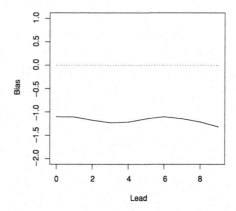

Figure 9.5. The bias versus lead time for our example forecast.

Just because a forecast is bias-free does not mean it is a good forecast: the climatological mean itself is bias-free, as is the climatological mean plus very large random numbers with mean zero. Thus we also need to know about the ability of the forecast to represent fluctuations around the climatological mean value. The RMSE and MAE tell us something about this.

9.3.3 Mean square error and mean absolute error

The mean squared error (MSE) of a forecast is defined as

$$MSE = E((f_i - T_i)^2) \tag{9.4}$$

and can be estimated from N days of past forecast as

$$MSE = \frac{1}{N} \sum_{i=1}^{N} (f_i - T_i)^2 \tag{9.5}$$

The RMSE is the square root of the MSE.

The RMSE is an attempt to measure the size of typical forecast errors, and, as such, has the same units as the forecast itself. The RMSE of using the climatological mean temperature is σ_T, which is the benchmark for other forecasts. A single forecast has no skill if it does not have a lower RMSE than this.

A (seldom used) alternative to the RMSE is the MAE, defined by

$$MAE = E(|f_i - T_i|) \tag{9.6}$$

and estimated by

$$MAE = \frac{1}{N} \sum_{i=1}^{N} |f_i - T_i| \tag{9.7}$$

The MAE is less affected by large errors than the RMSE. Whether this is good or bad is partly a matter of taste and may vary from one application to another.

The RMSE is strongly affected by the level of temperature variability at a particular location. Forecasts at different locations cannot be compared in terms of their RMSE because they may have different background levels of weather variability.

Figure 9.6 shows the RMSE for our example forecast (the sloping line) along with the RMSE for the climatological mean (the horizontal line). We see that the forecast RMSE is much lower than that for the climatological mean at short lead times, but gradually approaches the climatological RMSE and is scarcely any better than climatology at longer lead times.

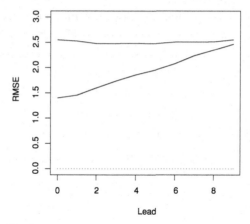

Figure 9.6. The RMSE for our example forecast and for the climatological mean.

9.3.4 Skill measures based on anomaly temperatures

Very often one does not need to go beyond the forecast skill measures described above in order to decide which the best forecast is, and the simplest approach is to use the RMSE alone. However, if one wishes to gain further insight into the performance of a forecast then one can do so by considering anomalies rather than full temperatures. This then allows us to calculate the correlation between forecast and observed temperatures.

9.3.5 Anomaly correlation

Anomaly correlation (AC) is based on the linear correlation between observed and forecast temperature anomalies.

The correlation between a forecast f and temperature T is defined by

$$\rho = \frac{E(f'T')}{\sqrt{(E(f'f'))(E(T'T'))}} \qquad (9.8)$$

where

$$f' = f - E(f), T' = T - E(T) \qquad (9.9)$$

Given N days of past forecasts this can be estimated in terms of forecast and temperature anomalies f^a and T^a as

$$\rho = \frac{\sum_{i=1}^{N} f'_i T'_i}{\sqrt{(\sum_{i=1}^{N} f'^2_i)(\sum_{i=1}^{N} T'^2_i)}} \qquad (9.10)$$

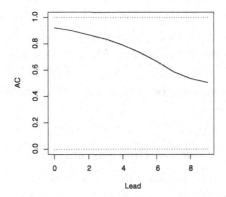

Figure 9.7. The anomaly correlation versus lead time for our example forecast.

where

$$f_i' = f_i^a - \bar{f_i^a}, T_i' = T_i^a - \bar{T_i^a} \tag{9.11}$$

One can also use $f_i' = f_i^a - T_i^a$, which is more convenient since more data is available to define T_i^a than f_i^a.

Anomaly correlation is unitless and varies between -1 and $+1$.

An example is given in figure 9.7, showing the AC as a function of lead time for our example forecast. We see that our example forecast has very high initial values for the AC, which decrease gradually throughout the forecast but are still significantly better than no forecast (which would have an AC of 0) at the end of the forecast.

Anomaly correlation captures whether the forecast is a good indication of the direction and relative size of the fluctuations around normal. However, it does not contain any information about the overall size of anomalies; note that if we double the amplitude of the forecast anomaly the AC stays the same. Anomaly correlation is also not affected by a bias: a forecast could have very good AC but be a very bad forecast because of large bias. Only if we can assume that bias has been corrected, and that the variance of the forecast has been set correctly (see the next section for an explanation of how that can be done), will a forecast with high AC be a good forecast. For these reasons, anomaly correlation is not terribly useful for our purpose of comparing forecasts. It is used mainly because it provides a way to present forecast skill on a universal scale.

9.4 Improving forecasts of the expected temperature

It may be the case that simple statistical processing can improve the forecasts that one is receiving. This depends on the extent to which the forecast provider has already applied such corrections. The simplest such calibration scheme is to correct any biases. This can be applied to full temperatures without the need to define anomalies. More complex schemes based on regression can improve both the bias and the RMSE but usually depend on using anomalies. We consider both bias correction and regression-based correction schemes below.

9.4.1 Bias correction

Once we have estimated the bias, it would seem sensible to correct future forecasts using the estimated value. However, this can actually be somewhat dangerous because of the risk of *overcorrection*: correcting a forecast that has already been corrected. Overcorrection can do more harm than good by increasing the standard deviation of forecast errors. We distinguish four typical cases.

- Case 1. If you are reasonably sure that (a) the forecast has *not* already been corrected for bias, and (b) the system used to create the forecast does *not* automatically compensate for bias (for example, if the forecast is interpolated from AGCM values), then you can assume that the forecast will have a bias. The bias should be estimated using, say, ninety days of previous data, and then corrected in future forecasts. Since estimating bias is so simple this can be repeated for every forecast, so that the estimated bias is always based on the forecasts and observations over the immediately preceding period.
- Case 2. If you know that the forecast *has* been corrected for bias, but for the wrong measurement, then you can assume that the forecast has a bias, and this should be corrected as in case 1. This situation is a common occurrence: many forecasts are corrected for bias using data that is measured over a different time period from that which is used for settling weather derivatives. In particular, many forecasts are corrected for bias using observed synoptic data, while most weather derivatives are settled on climate data. This can create bias if the measurement periods of the two types of data are out of step by a few hours, as they are for a number of countries.
- Case 3. If you are unsure as to whether the forecast has been corrected for bias or not, and are not able to get that information from your forecast provider, then you can test the forecast for significant bias. If a significant bias is detected, then the forecast should be corrected. The significance level should, perhaps, be set at around 50 per cent, to reflect the prior uncertainty about whether the forecast has been corrected or not.
- Case 4. If you are reasonably sure that the forecast has been corrected for bias, you can either not test for bias (which is rather dangerous, given the many things that can go wrong in forecast production) or you can test for bias, but this time using a rather higher significance level, perhaps at 95 per cent. If a significant bias

is detected, one should not necessarily take this as proof of the existence of bias, since one in twenty of such tests of even bias-free forecasts would be expected to give positive results. Rather, one should contact the forecast agency to check whether the bias really has been removed.

9.4.2 Correcting forecasts using regression

If one is prepared to take the step of converting all values to anomalies then one can use more sophisticated correction schemes than the bias correction described above. These schemes are based on regression, and improve not only the bias but also the RMSE. The simplest such scheme would involve building a linear regression model between recent observed anomalies and recent forecast anomalies, where 'recent' is usually taken to be around ninety days.

We write this model as

$$T_i^a \sim \Phi(\alpha + \beta f_i^a, \sigma) \qquad (9.12)$$

In other words, we model temperature anomalies on day i as being from a normal distribution with mean given by $\alpha + \beta f_i^a$, where f_i^a is the original forecast and the standard deviation is given by σ. If α is significantly different from zero, or β is significantly different from one, then this implies that correcting future forecasts using this regression will improve them. The case-by-case considerations for whether to correct the forecast or not are the same as for correcting the bias alone, as discussed above.

A more complex scheme (Jewson, 2004d) allows us to use more of the past forecast data by allowing the regression parameters to vary seasonally:

$$T_i^a \sim \Phi(\alpha_i + \beta_i f_i^a, \sigma_i) \qquad (9.13)$$

where

$$\alpha_i = \alpha_0 + \alpha_s \sin\theta_i + \alpha_c \cos\theta_i \qquad (9.14)$$
$$\beta_i = \beta_0 + \beta_s \sin\theta_i + \beta_c \cos\theta_i$$
$$\gamma_i = \gamma_0 + \gamma_s \sin\theta_i + \gamma_c \cos\theta_i$$

and θ_i indicates the time of year.

9.4.3 Combinations of single forecasts

Single site-specific forecasts are available from a number of different forecast vendors. These forecasts are often somewhat different, due to the different underlying models and methodologies used to create the forecasts. One (cost-effective) approach is to assess the skill of all the available forecasts over a period of three months and then purchase only the best. An alternative, and potentially more accurate, method is to attempt to combine the various forecasts into a single, better forecast. There are various ways this can be done.

Subjective combinations

A skilful forecaster can learn to recognise those weather situations in which one forecast outperforms others. He can then make a subjective combination of the available forecasts, using this knowledge to produce his own best forecast.

Linear combinations

A more objective (but not necessarily better) way to combine forecasts is to make a multivariate linear regression model with the various forecast anomalies as input and a single 'best' forecast as output. Such a model cannot, however, capture situations where one model outperforms the others in certain weather conditions.

Non-linear combinations

In theory, a better objective approach would be a non-linear model that could capture the fact that forecast performance is weather-dependent. One might use a neural network, or other non-linear system, that could 'learn' which model does best under certain atmospheric states. However, fitting such models needs more past forecast data than is usually available.

9.4.4 A summary of the strategy for evaluating single forecasts

The simplest strategy for evaluating the performance of a single forecast is to calculate the RMSE alone. If the RMSE is less than the standard deviation of historical temperatures σ_T then the forecast has skill and can be used. The danger of monitoring only the RMSE is that one might miss a good forecast that has a poor RMSE simply because of bias in the mean, which can be easily corrected. For this reason it is useful to monitor both the RMSE and the bias. Finally, the anomaly correlation is a useful general measure of forecast skill on a universal scale. We emphasise again, however, that AC should not be used alone, since a high AC does not necessarily mean that a forecast has a low RMSE, only that it has the *potential* to have a low RMSE if the mean and variance are set correctly (which can be done using equations (9.12) and (9.13)).

9.5 Probabilistic forecasts

The previous section described single forecasts, representing the mean or expectation of the distribution of possible future outcomes. A shortcoming of such forecasts for some applications is that they include no indication of the uncertainty or the *width* of the distribution of future outcomes. There is a big difference between 15°C +/− 1°C and 15°C +/− 15°C.

A forecast consisting of a mean and a standard deviation about the mean is an example of a *probabilistic* forecast – one that provides a distribution rather than a single value. Given the probabilistic methods used in the valuation of weather derivatives it is clear that such methods are likely to be useful for us. Probabilistic forecasts have recently become available commercially, but the methods for producing them are still developing rapidly and our own experience suggests that some of these commercial products are not correctly calibrated and can be used only after further corrections have been applied. The alternative to buying a probabilistic forecast is to make one oneself, and, fortunately, this is easy to do.

9.5.1 Making probabilistic forecasts

The most straightforward method for making probabilistic forecasts for temperature is to use the regression models described in section 9.4.2. Previously we had interpreted the output from equation (9.12) as an optimal forecast for the expected temperature $(\alpha + \beta f_i^a)$. However, if we take $\alpha + \beta f_i^a$ as the mean and σ as the standard deviation, then we have a probabilistic forecast. Such forecasts assume that the conditional distribution of temperature is normal, which is unlikely to be exactly true. However, we have looked into this and have found no evidence that it is a shortcoming (Jewson, 2003i), although the results presented in Denholm-Price (2003) suggest that it may be.

An example of a probabilistic forecast created using regression is given in figure 9.8. The forecast is the same one as shown in the left panel of figure 9.1, but now the dashed lines show plus and minus two standard deviations.

9.5.2 Measuring the skill of probabilistic forecasts

How should we compare the skill of two different probabilistic forecasts? One of the most natural measures to use is the probability of the observations

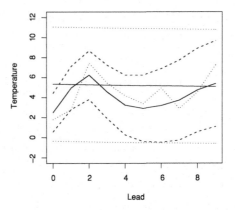

Figure 9.8. A probabilistic version of the forecast in figure 9.1.

given the forecast. The forecast that gives the higher probability can be taken as the better one. Interpreted as a function of the unknown parameters, this is what in classical statistics is called the 'likelihood function' for the observations given the forecast (from Fisher, 1912, and Fisher, 1922), and we have adopted this terminology and refer to this quantity as the *likelihood*.[3] Likelihood evaluates the performance of a probabilistic forecast over the whole range of predicted and observed values, which is typically what we are interested in. However, it is also possible to define versions of the likelihood that work for special situations, such as predicting the distribution of temperatures only over certain thresholds.

It is usually more convenient to use log-likelihood rather than likelihood, since log-likelihood gives a more manageable range of values but still preserves the ranking of forecasts. There are also versions of the likelihood that normalise by the amount of data used and others that correct for over-fitting, such as the Akaike Information Criterion, the Bayes Information Criterion and the Schwartz Criterion (Akaike, 1974).

If one is considering buying a commercial probabilistic forecast product, one should compare the likelihood from the commercial forecast with that from the simple regression models described above. Our own experience, based on work we have done for forecasts for London Heathrow, has been that the regression models are very hard to beat.

Other skill measures

A host of very specific methods are used in the meteorological research community for comparing probabilistic forecasts. Most of them are concerned

---

[3] Note, however, that Murphy and Winkler (1987) call this object the *calibration*.

with the evaluation of the skill or usefulness of probabilistic forecasts that predict whether a certain event will occur or not (often called *binary forecasts*), and the rest are concerned with forecasts of the probability of various categories. Since we are interested in the whole continuous distribution of temperatures, rather than particular categories, such binary and categorical forecasts are not particularly useful for the weather derivatives community (except perhaps in the context of event indices), and so we only mention these methods briefly here. They include:

- *the Brier score* (Brier, 1950) – a method for comparing two binary forecasts; we believe this method can give counter-intuitive decisions as to which of two forecasts is the better one, and should not be used unless there is a very specific reason to do so (see Jewson, 2003n);
- *ROC curves* (Swets, 1988) – a method for calculating the amount of information in a continuous forecast that involves first converting it into binary forecasts; the ROC cannot be used for forecast comparison because it is blind to biases;
- *Reliability diagrams* (Hamill, 1997) – a method for understanding biases in binary forecasts;
- *Cost-loss scores* (Richardson, 2000) – a method for evaluating the value of binary forecasts in a simple decision model;
- *Rank probability scores* – a method for measuring the skill of multi-category probabilistic forecasts;
- *Spread/skill relationships* (Talagrand et al., 1997) – a method for identifying the presence of information in the spread of an ensemble forecast; spread/skill relationships cannot be used for forecast comparison because they do not consider actual forecast skill (in the same way that correlation can't be used for the comparison of single forecasts);
- *Rank histograms* – a method for identifying biases in categorical forecasts.

Details of these measures are given in Jolliffe and Stephenson (2003) and at http://www.bom.gov.au/bmrc/wefor/staff/eee/verif/verif_web_page. html.

9.6 The use of ensemble forecasts for making probabilistic forecasts

The regression-based probabilistic forecasts described above predict a distribution that has dispersion that varies in time with the seasonal cycle. But on any one particular day of the year the dispersion is fixed. It has often been suggested that, in fact, forecast skill varies with the state of the atmosphere – i.e. that some atmospheric situations are more predictable than others. If this could be predicted one could then make a probabilistic forecast in which the dispersion varied with the state of the atmosphere, and these variations might improve the forecast by increasing the likelihood achieved.

Ensemble forecasts were initially designed to improve the forecast of the expected temperature, and they definitely achieve that goal. However, it has also been shown that the spread of ensemble forecasts contains information about how the range of possible outcomes varies with weather state. This raises the possibility that one could use this spread to make an improved probabilistic forecast that beats the regression models. At this point it seems that such a forecast has never been achieved, although this is an active area of research (for us at least). It is, however, difficult to extract the information from the ensemble spread, and the amount of information is apparently rather small (see Jewson et al., 2003a, and Jewson, 2003e). Certainly, without extensive adjustment the raw ensemble spread (as shown in figure 9.4) should definitely not be used. We have managed to do slightly better than the regression models by using the ensemble spread as an extra predictor in *in-sample* tests, but did not beat regression in a significant way in *out-of-sample* tests (see Jewson, 2003m).

9.6.1 Predicting correlations

A complete ten-day probabilistic forecast consists not only of distributions of temperature for each day but also of dependences between days. For normally distributed temperatures this means the forecast consists of ten means, ten variances and a ten by ten correlation matrix. We shall see in chapter 10 that, ideally, all this information is available when calculating option prices.

We have looked at predictions of the mean and variance, but where can we get forecasts of these correlations? The starting point is to save past forecasts of the expected temperature and use them to derive the correlations between the forecast errors for different days. There is also the possibility that ensemble forecasts can contribute: one can calculate correlations between the forecasts on different days using the ensemble members. Some of our own recent research suggests that ensembles can indeed add something to the predictions of correlations (Jewson, 2003h). In the one example we looked at (forecasts for temperature at London Heathrow) we found that the correlation forecasts based on past forecast error statistics could be improved slightly by weighting them with correlation forecasts based on the ensemble, with relative weightings of 80 per cent on the past forecast error statistics and 20 per cent on the ensemble. However, in most cases predicting these correlations with high accuracy is probably not required, and one can simply use the past forecast error statistics.

In a similar way, a complete probabilistic forecast for several locations at once should consist not only of a distribution at each location but also of dependences between locations. Again, all of this information should, ideally, be used when estimating the value of weather portfolios, and again the starting point should be past forecast error statistics.

9.6.2 A summary of the strategy for evaluating probabilistic forecasts

If one is interested in using probabilistic forecasts then we believe that, at this point, the best alternative is to produce one's own using the regression models described above. Having developed a regression-based forecast one can use that as a basis for comparison for the forecasts available commercially. Comparison can be performed using the likelihood.

9.6.3 Predicting changes in weather forecasts

A forecast for changes in the expectation cannot be predicted in advance; if it could then this information should have been included in the forecast (this is a mathematical tautology). The assumption that available forecasts are expectations is known as the 'efficient forecast hypothesis' (EFH) because of the similarity to the efficient market hypothesis (EMH) of economics.

Although, if we assume the EFH is true, forecast changes cannot be predicted in advance, it has been shown that the width of the distribution from which forecast changes are drawn *can* be predicted (Jewson and Ziehmann, 2003). Such predictions are based on the ensemble spread; a larger than usual ensemble spread implies that the size of changes in the ensemble mean will be larger than usual, and a small ensemble spread that they will be smaller than usual. As an example, figure 9.9 shows the relationship between ensemble spread and the standard deviation of the distribution of forecast changes for the NCEP ensemble forecast for London Heathrow at lead 4. The relevance of these change predictions is that they can potentially help us to predict the likely sizes of changes in values of weather derivatives over short time periods.

Furthermore, it is also possible to predict the ensemble *spread* in advance. Such predictions are based on the autocorrelation of the spread in time. As with forecasts of changes in the mean, such forecasts can, in principle, also help us predict the sizes of changes in the value of weather derivatives.

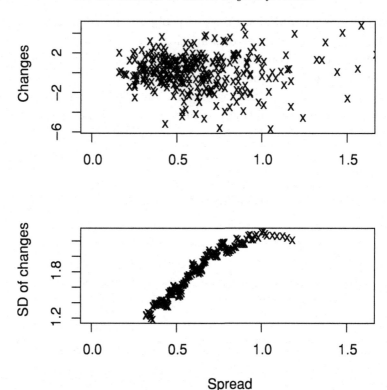

Figure 9.9. The empirical relationship between spread and volatility for the NCEP forecast. The upper panel shows actual forecast changes as a function of ensemble spread, and the lower panel shows the standard deviation of these changes calculated using a running window with a width of seventy days. We see that there is a clear relationship between ensemble spread and the standard deviation of subsequent changes in the ensemble mean, and this can be used to predict this standard deviation in advance.

9.7 Seasonal forecasts

Whereas weather forecasts attempt to predict the atmosphere over zero to ten days, seasonal forecasts attempt to predict it over zero to ten *months*. In the same way that the weather forecasts described above do not attempt to predict the variability of temperature *during* the day, but only the average temperature *over* the day, seasonal forecasts do not attempt to predict the temperature on individual days *during* the month or season, but the average of temperature *over* months and seasons.

These are the most important differences between weather and seasonal forecasts, but there are also others. One is that weather forecasts show *roughly* the same level of skill everywhere in the world. Seasonal forecasts, on the other hand, work very well in some regions and very poorly in others.

Another difference is that weather forecasts show *roughly* the same levels of skill at all times, while for seasonal forecasts the skill varies hugely both from season to season and from year to year. A final difference between weather and seasonal forecasts, linked to the different time scales over which the predictions apply, is that whereas weather forecasts can be thoroughly checked and evaluated this is impossible with seasonal forecasts, simply because there are too few past examples available for analysis. This means that the kinds of statistical methods that work very well for the calibration of weather forecasts (such as the regression models described in section 9.4.2) cannot be used so easily because the parameters cannot be estimated as reliably. A pure statistical approach to seasonal forecasting might thus reject the forecasts as being useless. However, there is a lot of circumstantial scientific evidence that seasonal forecasts do contain useful information, such as studies from computer models. The challenge of how to interpret seasonal forecasts is thus more of a scientific and intuitive problem than a purely statistical one.

We start our discussion of seasonal forecasts with a description of the physical processes that underly the ENSO phenomenon (ENSO is defined below) and a discussion of ENSO indices and the impacts of ENSO. We then move on to a discussion of seasonal forecasts. We will focus on seasonal predictions of changes in the mean temperature, although it is also possible in principle for seasonal forecasts to contain information about changes in the variability, and this would also be useful for weather derivative valuation. However, as we shall see, even predicting changes in the mean is rather difficult.

9.7.1 The physical background

The main source of seasonal predictability is a phenomenon known as El Niño Southern Oscillation. The 'El Niño' part of ENSO is a fluctuation in the surface temperatures of the eastern half of the equatorial Pacific Ocean, while the 'Southern Oscillation' part is a shift in the wind and pressure patterns over the whole of the Pacific. In fact, the two phenomena are intimately linked through a cycle of cause and effect, and hence they are usually discussed as part of the same phenomenon: hence the name ENSO.

The fluctuations that make up ENSO can be described and understood as follows.

The mechanics of ENSO

The eastern equatorial Pacific Ocean surface temperature varies significantly from year to year on very large spatial scales. Fluctuations away from the

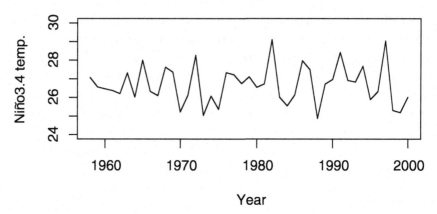

Figure 9.10. The November to March average temperature for the Niño3.4 region of the equatorial Pacific.

mean temperature often last many months and may cover areas of the ocean as large as North America. The average temperature in two well-defined geographical regions of the Pacific known as Niño3 (defined as the region between 5°S and 5°N and 150°W and 190°W) and Niño3.4 (defined as the region between 5°S and 5°N and 170°W and 120°W) are often used as indicators of these fluctuations. The fluctuations in these two regions are highly correlated (see the scatter plots of one against the other in Jewson, 2004e). Figure 9.10 shows historical fluctuations of winter temperatures in Niño3.4.

During 'normal' conditions the equatorial winds blow from east to west, towards a region of warm ocean, atmospheric convection and heavy rainfall situated near Indonesia. The easterly winds tend to reinforce the warm waters in the west, and the warm waters in the west tend to drive the convection, the rain and the winds, creating a fairly stable and self-reinforcing pattern. However, this pattern is not *completely* stable, and occasionally it breaks down. The eastern equatorial ocean then warms up, and can become as warm as the western ocean. The rainfall patterns move further to the east and the winds weaken or reverse. In this new configuration the weaker winds encourage warmer waters in the east, which in turn supports the changed convection, rain and wind patterns. It is this changed state that is known as El Niño, and the opposite state is known as La Niña.

One way to understand El Niño is that the atmosphere and ocean spend most of their time in the 'normal' state described above but occasionally flip to the El Niño state for a few months before reverting to normal. The changes into and out of the El Niño state are affected by large, slow-moving waves in the ocean, and it is the long time scale of these waves that

Table 9.1. *El Niño (left column) and La Niña (right column) winters since 1950.*

El Niño	La Niña
1957–58	1954–55
1965–66	1955–56
1968–69	1964–65
1972–73	1970–71
1982–83	1973–74
1986–87	1975–76
1991–92	1988–89
1997–98	1998–99

lead to a partial ability to predict these changes, at least a few months in advance.

In figure 9.10 we can see that particularly large El Niño events occurred in the winters of 1982/1983 and 1997/1998.

Almost all El Niño events start in the boreal (northern hemisphere) autumn, peak during the boreal winter, and decay during the boreal spring. A list of recent El Niño and La Niña winters is given in table 9.1.

9.7.2 The effects of El Niño

The changes in the atmosphere associated with El Niño cause changes in the weather around large parts of the globe. In particular, El Niño has very strong effects in other parts of the tropics: this is because atmospheric signals travel most easily along the equator. Certain parts of South America and Australia experience very strong El Niño effects, while parts of Africa and the Indian Ocean also feel some effect.

The impact of El Niño on the extratropics (which is the area currently of most interest to the weather market) is weaker. Among these weaker signals, the strongest are those in North America. Many studies have been carried out to quantify such effects, although precise quantification is very difficult for a number of reasons, such as (a) every El Niño is slightly different, (b) there have only been a small number of El Niño events during the last forty years and (c) the effects are not necessarily simple in structure. However, the two basic features of the response to El Niño over the United States during the winter seems to be fairly uncontroversial:

- a warming over most of the northern United States;
- increased rainfall in the southern United States and coastal California.

There are a number of scientific groups that post maps of these effects on the Internet, such as http://www.cpc.ncep.noaa.gov/products/analysis_monitoring/lanina.

9.8 Predicting El Niño and its effects

The science of seasonal forecasting can be broken down into two stages. The first stage is predicting El Niño itself, and the second is predicting the effects of El Niño. We will see that the first stage is much easier than the second.

9.8.1 Predicting El Niño

Predictions of El Niño, or of the Niño3 and Niño3.4 indices, are made using many different kinds of models. The simplest models are purely statistical, such as those of Penland and Magorian (1993). At the other end of the spectrum there are complex, coupled ocean-atmosphere simulation models, such as those of Stockdale et al. (1998), Mason et al. (1999) or Barnston et al. (2003). In between there are a multitude of hybrid models that combine dynamical and statistical aspects. A good source of forecasts, and information about how the forecasts are produced, is the Experimental Long-Lead Forecast Bulletin, available at http://www.iges.org/ellfb. Some of the prediction models are better than others, but there is little to choose between the statistical and the dynamical models, and the best models in each class do very well. The main characteristics of the predictions these models make are that predictions that start in summer and autumn perform very well, with very high levels of skill at three months and significant skill out to six months or more, while predictions that start in winter and spring perform much less well. It is fortuitous that it is this way round, since it is the autumn predictions that are the most useful because it is in autumn that El Niño typically starts to grow.

9.8.2 Predicting the impact of El Niño

Given a forecast for El Niño, what can we say about the likely impacts on weather in the United States? This is the hard part of the puzzle. One approach is to attempt to use statistical models that relate Niño3 or Niño3.4 temperatures to the US temperature indices of interest. We have attempted this ourselves, the results being published in Jewson (2004e). We found that it is slightly easier to see a relationship with US temperature using Niño3.4 than Niño3, but that it doesn't make any material difference if

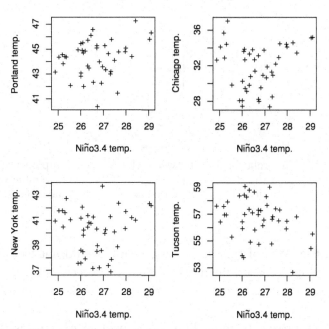

Figure 9.11. The relationship between the winter temperature in the Niño3.4 region and the winter temperature in four US cities (November to March averages).

we use December to February (which is what meteorologists tend to prefer) or November to March (which is more suitable for the weather derivative industry). Figure 9.11 shows a scatter plot of Niño3.4 temperatures against November to March temperatures at four US locations. The conclusions we draw from these results are that it is not possible to discern a clear relationship between Niño3.4 and US winter temperatures at these locations, and that it is not possible to fit a simple statistical model to this data. In particular, it would not seem reasonable to assume a linear response of the winter temperature to Niño3.4 temperatures (which would be very convenient if it were justifiable).

Figure 9.12 looks in more detail at the relationship between Niño3.4 temperatures and temperature in Chicago. We have drawn two vertical lines on this graph to suggest a possible model for the relationship. It seems that both El Niño and La Niña lead to warmer temperatures, that there is no relationship at all for moderate Niño3.4 temperatures, and that the variability during La Niña is greater than that during El Niño but less than the climatological variability.

The exact changes in the distribution of winter temperatures, which is what we would really like to understand, cannot be established very reliably,

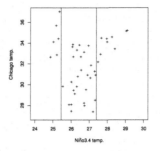

Figure 9.12. The relationship between the winter temperature in the Niño3.4 region and the winter temperature in Chicago (November to March averages). The vertical lines are added to suggest a possible statistical model.

however, on the basis of this data. As a result, we do not feel able to offer any robust recipes for producing probabilistic forecasts in the same way that one can for weather forecasts. One has to make a mainly subjective assessment.

The other approach to modelling the impact of El Niño is to take predictions from the simulations of the atmosphere in the coupled ocean-atmosphere simulation models. In addition to forecasting El Niño these models also include simulations of the atmospheric circulation and temperatures over the United States. This approach is very promising in the long run, but is at an early stage of development. We ourselves have not been able to produce satisfactory predictions in this way. There is much work to be done in terms of understanding how best to extract the information from the simulations. For instance, the best predictors for the real winter temperature in Chicago may not be the winter temperature in Chicago in the model, but could be the winter temperature at a slightly different location.

9.9 Other sources of seasonal predictability

Our discussion of seasonal predictability has focused on the effects of ENSO. ENSO is the strongest of the seasonal signals, and the most predictable, but it is not the only one. Significant amounts of research have gone into trying to understand and predict the North Atlantic Oscillation (NAO), for instance. The NAO is a pattern of atmospheric variability that affects many aspects of the weather in the North Atlantic region. Unlike ENSO, however, the NAO is almost completely unpredictable. Nevertheless, it may be that a small percentage of the variability of the NAO *is* predictable. We consider such research as preliminary at this stage, but the interested reader may wish to investigate further. There are many articles on this subject, such as those by Qian and Saunders (2003) and Lloyd-Hughes and Saunders (2002).

We note that the methods for portfolio simulation described in chapter 7 naturally incorporate the correlation structure of the NAO, and any other relevant modes of variability, in the correlation matrices used.

9.10 Further reading

There is a vast meteorological literature on weather forecasting, the models used for weather forecasting, and methods for the assessment of weather forecasts. Unfortunately, much of it is printed in academic journals that cannot easily be obtained by non-academics. Accessible review articles, with emphasis on the weather market, and many further references, are those by Roulston and Smith (2002), Dutton (2002) and Banks (2002). Other relevant articles are those by Dutton and Dischel (2001), Dischel (1998c), Dischel (1998b) and Dischel (2000).

A good non-mathematical book on meteorology is that by Thompson (1998) and short overviews of many interesting aspects of meteorology are given in Banks (2002), Smith (2002), Gibbas (2002) and Dutton (2002). A discussion of general forecasting issues is given in Roulston and Smith (2002) and some seasonal forecasting issues are discussed in Shorter et al. (2002).

A recent collection of articles on the assessment of forecast skill is contained in Jolliffe and Stephenson (2003) and general discussion on the evaluation of forecasts is given in Livezey (1999). The use of the likelihood and other information criteria to measure the skill of probabilistic forecasts comes from Jewson (2003r) and subsequent articles.

We advocate using regression to make probabilistic forecasts, but other methods have also been suggested, such as the 'dressing' method of Roulston and Smith (2003) and the methods described in Mylne et al. (2002).

Papers on the methods used to generate ensemble forecasts are those by Toth and Kalnay (1993) and Molteni et al. (1996).

A recent discussion of the causes of variability in the US climate is given in Rajagopalan and Kushnir (2000). Many articles have been written about the Pacific Decadal Oscillation (PDO) and the NAO, such as those by Mantua (2000) and Ambaum et al. (2001) respectively.

10

The use of meteorological forecasts in pricing

Chapters 2 to 8 have described methods for the actuarial pricing of weather derivatives when no meteorological forecasts are available. In practice, these methods are used when pricing well before the start of a contract. We will occasionally refer to values calculated in this way as *par* values. Relevant meteorological forecasts then start to become available around six months before the start of contracts in the United States and around three weeks before the start of contracts in Europe.

The availability of skilful forecasts changes the methods that one must use for the pricing of weather contracts. A skilful forecast means that the range of meteorological outcomes that are considered possible is reduced, and their probabilities changed. When the forecasts are weak this reduction is small, and when the forecasts are highly skilful this reduction is large.

The simplest case of forecast-based pricing is when a forecast is available that covers the whole remaining period of a contract. The contract can then be priced using the forecast alone. In many cases, however, the available forecasts will not cover the whole remaining period of the contract, and a mix of historical data and forecast must be made. As we will see below, making this mix in an accurate way is not always a trivial exercise.

Unfortunately for those involved in the development of algorithms to price weather derivatives, meteorologists tend to provide weather and seasonal forecasts separately, and in very different formats. Often they come from entirely different sources. As an example, weather forecasts usually come as daily values, while seasonal forecasts are more often presented as monthly values. Trying to combine these forecasts into a single consistent forecast over all timescales is one of the challenges that must be addressed.

We will approach the topic of how to use forecasts in pricing models by considering weather forecasts first. We will then very briefly consider the use of seasonal forecasts, which is of primary relevance only to contracts based in the United States and, to some extent, Japan. One of the methods we present for the merging of forecasts and historical data is a general method that can, in principle, be used to combine all weather forecasts, seasonal forecasts and historical data.

One final issue is the question of how much of a forecast to use. If a fifteen-day weather forecast is available, should we use all of it or should we use only the first five, or maybe ten, days? If we calculate the forecast skill diagnostics described in chapter 9, then we know for how long the forecast is better than using distributions derived from historical data. This is how much of the forecast we should use. The methods described below have all been designed to incorporate forecasts in this way and, thus, to get the greatest possible information from the forecasts. Using any less of the forecast than this will simply give less accurate results. For weather forecasts this typically means using around fifteen days. For seasonal forecasts the number of months to use is more variable, and will depend strongly on location.

10.1 The use of weather forecasts

We will start by considering the simplest case of using weather forecasts in weather derivative pricing, which is the calculation of the fair price of a linear swap contract on a separable and linear index (e.g. a CAT index). We will see that, in this case, only forecasts of the expected temperature need to be used and probabilistic forecasts are not necessary.

The next special case we consider is the calculation of the fair price of a linear swap contract on a separable non-linear index (e.g. HDDs). Probabilistic weather forecasts must now be used, but there is no particular difficulty in merging historical data and the probabilistic forecast.

Finally we consider the general case, which includes the calculation of the fair price for all other contracts (non-linear swaps and options) and the calculation of the distribution of outcomes for all contracts. This is the most difficult case, and we will present three techniques for solving this problem.

The first technique is based on the index modelling methods. These are the most commonly used methods for pricing weather derivatives, and so it makes sense to attempt to extend them to include forecasts. We will present a straightforward way in which forecasts can be used in conjunction with such models. The second technique we present is based on the daily modelling of temperature. In some cases, merging forecasts with daily models may be more accurate than merging them with index models. However, the methods that result are reasonably complex. Finally we present an entirely different approach, which makes a number of rather strong assumptions but, as a result, is able to incorporate forecasts into pricing in a very simple and intuitive way. This final approach is of particular interest as it leads on directly to much of the discussion on arbitrage pricing in chapter 11 and risk management in chapter 12, and uses methods that are very similar to methods used in the wider financial community for modelling share prices. This method allows the use of single rather than probabilistic forecasts for all types of contracts and for the calculations of both the prices and distributions of outcomes.

10.2 Linear swaps on separable linear indices

We now consider the estimation of the fair strike of a linear swap on a separable linear index based on daily temperatures. This includes linear swaps on CAT indices, and also linear swaps on HDDs and CDDs in those cases where there is no chance of the temperature crossing the baseline. By definition, the fair strike of a linear swap is given by the expectation of the index distribution

$$\text{fair strike} = E(x) \tag{10.1}$$

Since we are considering a separable index, we can write the aggregate contract index x in terms of daily indices z:

$$x = \sum_{i=1}^{N_d} z_i \tag{10.2}$$

and hence the expected index is the sum of the mean daily indices:

$$E(x) = \sum_{i=1}^{N_d} E(z_i) \tag{10.3}$$

For a CAT index

$$z_i = T_i \tag{10.4}$$

If we are part way through the contract then evaluating $E(x)$ involves using measured temperature, forecasts, and expectations from historical data. If we are using a forecast with N_f values in it, then on day N_0 of the contract

$$E(x) = \sum_{i=1}^{N_d} T_i \tag{10.5}$$

$$= \sum_{i=1}^{N_0-1} T_i^{hist} + \sum_{i=N_0}^{N_0+N_f-1} m_i^{fc} + \sum_{i=N_0+N_f}^{N_d} m_i^{clim}$$

where T_i^{hist} are the known historical temperatures, m_i^{fc} are single forecasts giving the expected temperature over the forecast period, and m_i^{clim} are climatological mean temperatures from historical data.

We see that in this case there is no need for probabilistic forecasts since only the expected temperature is needed. The third term in the above sum can be estimated using either burn or daily modelling methods. For daily modelling methods, m_i^{clim} is just the seasonal cycle of temperature; statistics of the anomalies are not important in this case.

As the contract progresses the number of days in the first sum increases while the number of days in the third sum decreases. From some point on the third sum disappears altogether and the expected index is estimated from forecasts alone. As the contract progresses still further the number of days of forecast used reduces until the outcome of the entire contract is known.

10.3 Linear swaps on separable indices

We now consider a slightly more complex case in which the index is not necessarily linear. This now includes HDD and CDD indices for which there is some chance that the temperature will cross the baseline. We can no longer express the mean of the daily index in terms of the mean temperature, but rather it becomes a function of the whole distribution of daily temperature, $f(T)$:

$$E(z_i) = \int_{-\infty}^{\infty} f_i(T) z_i(T) dT \tag{10.6}$$

For normally distributed temperatures this integral can usually be evaluated in terms of the mean and the standard deviation of temperature. For HDDs

$$E(z_i) = \int_{-\infty}^{\infty} \phi_i(T) z_i(T) dT$$

$$= \int_{-\infty}^{T_0} \phi_i(T) T dT$$

$$= (T_0 - m_i)\Phi_i(T_0) + s_i\phi_i(T_0) \tag{10.7}$$

where Φ_i is the cumulative normal distribution of temperatures on day i, $\frac{1}{s_i}\phi_i$ is the density of temperatures on day i, and m_i and s_i are the mean and standard deviation of temperatures on day i.

Fair value for the swap contract for an arbitrary distribution of temperature is now given by

$$E(x) = \sum_{i=1}^{N_0-1} z_i(T_i^{hist}) + \sum_{i=N_0}^{N_0+N_f-1} \int f_i(T)z_i(T)dT$$

$$+ \sum_{i=N_0+N_f}^{N_d} \int f_i(T)z_i(T)dT \tag{10.8}$$

The first term is the accumulated index due to historical temperatures. The second term is the expected contribution due to forecasts, and the third term is the expected contribution due to temperature beyond the end of the forecast. The distribution of temperature in the second term can be taken from a probabilistic forecast, and in the third term from historical data. The days in the third term could be treated together as one block, and the mean of the aggregate index estimated from historical values of the aggregate index (i.e. index modelling, but for part of the contract only). Alternatively, the distribution of temperature on each day could be estimated (i.e. using the seasonal cycle and marginal distribution fitting steps of the daily modelling approaches of chapter 6).

For normally distributed temperatures and for HDDs this equation becomes

$$E(x) = \sum_{i=1}^{N_0-1} max(T_0 - T_i^{hist}, 0) + \sum_{i=N_0}^{N_0+N_f-1} (T_0 - m_i^{fc})\Phi_i(T_0') + s_i^{fc}\phi_i(T_0')$$

$$+ \sum_{i=N_0+N_f}^{N_d} (T_0 - m_i^{clim})\Phi_i(T_0'') + s_i^{clim}\phi_i(T_0'') \tag{10.9}$$

where $T_0' = \frac{T_0-m_i^{fc}}{s_i^{fc}}$ and $T_0'' = \frac{T_0-m_i^{clim}}{s_i^{clim}}$.

The probabilistic forecast comes in via the mean and the standard deviations of temperature on each day during the forecast (m_i^{fc} and s_i^{fc}), and the historical data used in the third term comes in via the mean and standard deviation of historical temperatures (m_i^{clim} and s_i^{clim}).

10.4 The general case: any contract, any index

Thus far, the incorporation of forecasts into pricing has been fairly simple. However, the two cases we have considered are special cases because they involve only the calculation of the expectation of the index distribution and only for separable indices. As soon as we need to estimate the standard deviation or shape of the index distribution, or the expectation for a non-separable index, things become more difficult. This is the case when we need to calculate the distribution of outcomes of a linear swap contract, or when we need to calculate anything about a non-linear contract, including the expected pay-off of all option types. To illustrate the issues, we will initially focus on calculating the expected pay-off of an option on a separable linear index (e.g. a CAT index) with normally distributed temperatures. The expected pay-off depends on both the expectation and the standard deviation of the index. Estimating the expected index is easy, as we have seen in the previous two examples. It is estimating the standard deviation of the index that creates the difficulty.

10.4.1 Estimating the index standard deviation

The standard deviation of the index is the square root of the variance of the index. For a separable index the variance is the sum of the terms in the covariance matrix of daily index values during the contract period. For a CAT index (the example we will use for illustration) it is the sum of the terms in the covariance matrix of the daily temperatures. For a contract covered partly by forecast and partly by historical data we can split the terms in the covariance matrix into those that involve the forecast only, those that involve historical data only, and those that involve a mix of historical data and forecast.

$$\sigma_x^2 = \sum_{i=1}^{N_d} \sum_{j=1}^{N_d} E(T_i' T_j')$$

$$= \sum_{i=N_0}^{N_0+N_f-1} \sum_{j=N_0}^{N_0+N_f-1} E(T_i' T_j') + \sum_{i=N_0+N_f}^{N_d} \sum_{j=N_0+N_f}^{N_d} E(T_i' T_j')$$

$$+ 2 \sum_{i=N_0}^{N_0+N_f-1} \sum_{j=N_0+N_f}^{N_d} E(T_i' T_j')$$

$$= \sum_{i=N_0}^{N_0+N_f-1} \sum_{j=N_0}^{N_0+N_f-1} c_{ij} + \sum_{i=N_0+N_f}^{N_d} \sum_{j=N_0+N_f}^{N_d} c_{ij} + 2 \sum_{i=N_0}^{N_0+N_f-1} \sum_{j=N_0+N_f-1}^{N_d} c_{ij}$$

$$= \sum_{i=N_0}^{N_0+N_f-1} \sum_{j=N_0}^{N_0+N_f-1} s_i^{fc} s_j^{fc} \rho_{ij} + \sum_{i=N_0+N_f-1}^{N_d} \sum_{j=N_0+N_f-1}^{N_d} s_i^{clim} s_j^{clim} \rho_{ij}$$

$$+ 2 \sum_{i=N_0}^{N_0+N_f-1} \sum_{j=N_0+N_f-1}^{N_d} s_i^{fc} s_j^{clim} \rho_{ij}$$

$$= \sigma_{fc}^2 + \sigma_{pfc}^2 + \sigma_{cov}^2 \qquad (10.10)$$

The first of these three terms (σ^2_{fc}) depends on forecast variances and correlations between temperatures during the forecast period. As we saw in section 9.5, forecast variances are produced as part of a probabilistic forecast, and in section 9.6.1 we also discussed how correlations can be predicted.

The second of these terms (σ^2_{pfc}) represents climatological temperature variances and correlations. This term can be estimated most easily from historical values of the index for this period (i.e. index analysis). It can also be estimated from daily historical temperature data or from a daily temperature model fitted to historical data, such as the ARFIMA model. As usual, the daily modelling approach would be recommended when the number of days in this term is small.

The third of these terms (σ^2_{cov}) represents forecast variances, climatological temperature variances, and correlations between temperature during the forecast and the post-forecast period. This third term complicates matters significantly: if it were not for this term we could model the index variance as the sum of the index variance due to the forecast period (which can be calculated from a probabilistic forecast) and the index variance during the post-forecast period (which can be calculated from historical data). However, the dependences between these two periods, combined with the inherent positive autocorrelations of temperature, mean that this would always underestimate the total index variance.

An expression similar to equation (10.10), but slightly more complex, can also be derived for degree day indices. The essence is the same: the total variance of the index depends not only on the variances of the index during the forecast and post-forecast periods but also on the covariances between these periods.

10.4.2 Estimating the size of the covariance term

How large is this awkward forecast/post-forecast covariance term? If it is small then perhaps it could be neglected without harm and the modelling could be significantly simplified. Results of an estimation of the size of this term using simulations are shown in figure 10.1, upper panel. We see that, the longer the post-forecast period, the lower the correlation between the two periods – as would be expected. Most of this correlation comes from the long-memory property of temperature variability, which has been described in chapter 6. Figure 10.1 also shows the values for the correlation for $d = 0.0, 0.1$ and 0.2.

Figure 10.1, lower panel, shows the size of this correlation effect in terms of the percentage underestimation of the total index variance that would result

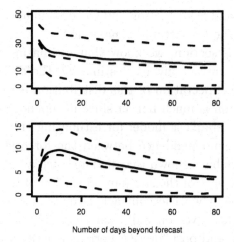

Figure 10.1. The upper panel shows the correlation between cumulative temperature over a period of eleven days and a subsequent period of N days, where N is given on the horizontal axis. The correlations are based on (a) simulations from the ARFIMA temperature simulation model fitted to Chicago temperatures and (b) correlations from simulations based on the same model but with d readjusted to have the values $0.0, 0.1$ and 0.2. The lower panel shows the error in the estimate of the standard deviation of cumulative temperature over a period of $N + 11$ days that is made if the first eleven days, and the subsequent N days, are assumed to be independent. The error is expressed as a percentage of the total actual standard of the whole period. All the calculations were based on temperatures simulated from the ARFIMA temperature simulation model fitted to Chicago temperatures, but with the value of the long-memory parameter d reset to $d = 0.0, 0.1, 0.2$.

from assuming that the forecast and post-forecast periods are independent. For each value of d we can see that the maximum error in the standard deviation would occur for a post-forecast period of length around ten days. The maximum at ten days can be understood from the expression for the total variance of the index. The error in the estimation of the total variance is given by

$$\text{error} = \sigma^2 - \sigma_{fc}^2 - \sigma_{pfc}^2 = \sigma_{cov}^2 = 2\rho\sigma_{fc}\sigma_{pfc} \qquad (10.11)$$

where ρ is the correlation between the forecast and post-forecast periods, as shown in figure 10.1, upper panel. We see that the error depends both on the correlation between the forecast and post-forecast period and also on the size of the standard deviation of the post-forecast period. For post-forecast periods of much less than ten days the standard deviation of the post-forecast period is small and so the error is small. For periods of much greater than ten days the correlation is small, and so the error is small. For ten days both the standard deviation and correlation have reasonable values, and the product of the two attains a maximum.

To summarise this section, we know that estimating the fair price of a non-linear weather contract involves estimating the distribution of the index. Estimating the expectation of this distribution is easy, but estimating the standard deviation is much harder since it depends on autocorrelations of temperature. The simplest model for estimating the standard deviation would be to assume independence between the forecast and post-forecast periods. However, we have shown that making such an assumption does not give an accurate estimate of the standard deviation of the index in all cases, and is least accurate when the contract extends around ten days beyond the end of the forecast. We conclude that the assumption of independence between the forecast and post-forecast periods may lead to underestimation of the index standard deviation and should be avoided if a high level of accuracy is required.

Non-normal temperatures

The above discussion has focused on normally distributed temperatures to illustrate the issues that arise in trying to estimate the index standard deviation for the whole of the contract period. The same issues also apply to non-normal temperature distributions: the distribution for the whole period depends not only on the distributions of the forecast and post-forecast period but also on the dependences between temperatures in those two periods. Equation (10.10) applies to non-normal temperatures too. The only difference is that we may need more than the standard deviation to describe the whole distribution shape.

We now present a number of methods that allow us to combine probabilistic forecasts and climatological models in such a way as to calculate estimates of the distribution of the index. Estimates of the index distribution then allow us to calculate prices for weather derivatives.

10.4.3 Short contracts

The simplest case occurs when the remaining part of the contract is short enough to be covered entirely by a probabilistic forecast. The contract can then be priced as follows.

- a probabilistic forecast is created for the period in question, using the methods discussed in chapter 9; in particular, this forecast should include forecasts of the correlations between days;

- the probabilistic forecast represents a single multivariate distribution of temperatures over the period of the contract; a large number of samples are taken from this distribution;
- each of these samples is then converted to an index value.

It has been suggested that ensemble forecasts could be used *directly*, without going through the stages of creating a probabilistic forecast (see Smith et al., 2001, and Palmer, 2002). This has been called 'end to end' use of ensembles. However, we would note that

- the members of the ensemble would have to be calibrated in terms of both mean and spread;
- it does not seem to be possible to calibrate the correlation, and the correlation inferred directly from the ensembles does not seem to be as accurate as that inferred from past forecast error statistics (as discussed in chapter 9); as a result, the correlations used in this method are likely to be less accurate than those from the probabilistic forecast route;
- the ensemble sizes are small relative to the typical sizes of Monte Carlo simulations used in weather pricing, and do not do a good job of sampling the tails.

10.4.4 Long contracts: methods based on index modelling

We now proceed to discuss the general question of how to price contracts for which the remaining period is longer than available probabilistic forecasts. We will start by describing methods that are based on index modelling.

The part of the contract covered by a probabilistic forecast can be analysed as in section 10.4.3 – i.e. we sample the probabilistic forecast and convert into index values. This gives an index distribution for that part of the contract and an estimate of σ_{fc}^2 from equation (10.10). The part of the contract not covered by a forecast can be analysed using index modelling based on historical data. This gives an index distribution for that part of the contract, and an estimate of σ_{pfc}^2 from equation (10.10). These two index distributions can then be combined to give an estimate for the index distribution for the whole contract period. For normal distributions the distributions can be combined by adding the means and the variances. For non-normal distributions the best method for combining distributions is simply to simulate from both distributions (e.g. a thousand values from each) and sum the simulated values in pairs (creating, e.g., a million simulated values for the combined distribution).

The shortcoming of this method is that it has neglected the third term in equation (10.10): σ_{cov}^2. Since weather is almost always positively correlated in time, this will lead to an underestimate of the total spread of the index, as we have explained in section 10.4.1. There are two ways that this problem can be addressed.

Ignore the cross-correlation term

Notwithstanding the discussion in section 10.4.2, ignoring the covariance may not be a terribly bad thing to do in certain circumstances, especially when (a) the location in question shows only weak long memory and (b) the remaining contract period is either very long or very short relative to the length of the forecast. The covariance term σ_{cov}^2 is, in most cases, the smallest of the three terms in equation (10.10).

Estimate the covariance term using historical indices

Alternatively, we can estimate the covariance term. Historical indices can give us an estimate of the correlation between the forecast and post-forecast periods that, along with the standard deviations of the distributions for the two periods, can be used to estimate the cross-correlation term using equation (10.11). The variance of the total index distribution can then be increased by this amount. Note that this can be applied even in cases in which the index distribution, or the distributions for the two parts, are not normal.

10.4.5 Long contracts: methods based on daily modelling

We now describe how weather forecasts can be combined with methods based on daily modelling. Combining forecasts with daily models is perhaps the most elegant way to incorporate forecasts into weather pricing because of the natural way that daily models cope with the issue of time dependence and the evaluation of the σ_{cov}^2 term in equation (10.10). However, as we will see the methods – although elegant – are reasonably complex. Implementing these methods is probably only justifiable economically if an organisation is trading options very frequently on the basis of forecasts.

Pruning

The so-called 'pruning method' (due to Jewson, 2000, and Jewson and Caballero, 2003b) works as follows. First, we use a daily temperature model of the sort discussed in chapter 6 to generate a large number of temperature tracks, which cover the whole remaining period of the contract. These tracks should be initialised from the most recent historical data. We also calculate the probability density associated with each track from the daily temperature model. Second, we calculate another probability density for each track using a probabilistic forecast. These probabilities contain the forecast information. Third, we convert each track into an index value. The index values are weighted using a weight that is proportional to the second (forecast) density divided by the first (historical) density. The weighted index values then define the index distribution. In statistics the weighting of simulations in this way is called 'importance sampling' (Ripley, 1987).

This method is not limited to normally distributed temperatures; if the daily model is being used on temperature that has previously been transformed using a distribution transform, then the same transform should also be applied to the forecast before calculating the weights and all simulated temperatures should be transformed back to the correct distribution before calculating index values.

The advantage of the pruning method is that the covariance term between forecast and post-forecast periods is incorporated automatically because we are using temperature tracks that run throughout the remaining period of the contract. This method can, in principle, be adjusted to include both weather forecasts and seasonal forecasts simultaneously, and can thus be considered both the most accurate and the most flexible of all the methods we will present for pricing with forecasts.

The mathematical basis for the pruning method is the following.

Let $p(\mathbf{T})$ be the pay-off due to temperature track $\mathbf{T}$, $f(\mathbf{T})$ be the climatological probability of $\mathbf{T}$, and $g(\mathbf{T})$ be the forecast probability of $\mathbf{T}$. Then the climatological expected pay-off μ_p^{clim} is given by

$$\mu_p^{clim} = \int p(\mathbf{T})f(\mathbf{T})d\mathbf{T} \tag{10.12}$$

where the integral is over all possible tracks for $\mathbf{T}$. The forecast expected pay-off μ_p^{fc} is given by

$$\mu_p^{fc} = \int p(\mathbf{T})g(\mathbf{T})d\mathbf{T} \tag{10.13}$$

To evaluate μ_p^{clim} we choose a set of tracks that are equally spaced along the climatological CDF, $F(\mathbf{T})$. In other words, all the values of $dF(\mathbf{T}) = f(\mathbf{T})d\mathbf{T}$ are equal, so $dF(\mathbf{T}) = dF = \frac{1}{N}$ where N is the number of tracks. The integral becomes

$$\mu_p^{clim} = \int p(\mathbf{T})dF \tag{10.14}$$

$$\approx \frac{1}{N}\sum p(\mathbf{T}) \tag{10.15}$$

where the sum is over all the tracks in a discrete set of possible tracks.

If we evaluate μ_p^{fc} using the same set of tracks,

$$\mu_p^{fc} = \int p(\mathbf{T})g(\mathbf{T})d\mathbf{T} \qquad (10.16)$$

$$= \int p(\mathbf{T})g(\mathbf{T})\frac{dF}{f(\mathbf{T})} \qquad (10.17)$$

$$= \int p(\mathbf{T})\frac{g(\mathbf{T})}{f(\mathbf{T})}dF \qquad (10.18)$$

$$= \int p(\mathbf{T})w(\mathbf{T})dF \qquad (10.19)$$

$$\approx \frac{1}{N}\sum p(\mathbf{T})w(\mathbf{T}) \qquad (10.20)$$

where the weights $w(\mathbf{T})$ are given by

$$w(\mathbf{T}) = \frac{g(\mathbf{T})}{f(\mathbf{T})} \qquad (10.21)$$

In other words, we sum the pay-offs for all possible tracks, but with weights. The weighting to be used is the forecast probability density of a certain track divided by the climatological probability density of that track.

Grafting

An alternative to the pruning method is 'grafting' (Jewson and Caballero, 2003b). In the grafting method a probabilistic forecast is sampled a large number of times to create realistic temperature tracks during the forecast period. These temperature tracks are then used as initial conditions for a daily model, which is integrated to the end of the forecast period. As with pruning, the troublesome cross-correlation term is incorporated automatically by the algorithm.

Grafting has the advantage over pruning that it is slightly simpler, since it does not involve calculating probability densities. It has the disadvantage, however, that it is not easy to include seasonal forecasts as well.

10.4.6 Methods based on Brownian motion

The final method that we will describe for incorporation of forecasts into pricing is markedly different from the previous methods and is much simpler. It relies on the following strong assumptions:

- that the index is separable and linear;
- that temperature, and forecasts of temperature, are normally distributed;
- that the statistics of forecast uncertainty are not flow dependent;
- that the forecasts are efficient (according to the definition of section 9.6.3).

Although these assumptions are quite restrictive, and eliminate many kinds of contracts, they are a good approximation for almost all contracts traded in the secondary market.

Since we assume that the temperature is normally distributed and the index is separable and linear, the index distribution must be normal, and we need only consider the expectation and the standard deviation of the index rather than the whole shape of the distribution. The expectation of the index can be calculated using a single forecast, as described in section 10.2. Calculation of the standard deviation is more complex. Up until now we have thought of the standard deviation of the index as arising due to the combination of the uncertainty around the temperatures on the remaining days of the contract. Understood in this way, the standard deviation depends on all the terms of the covariance matrix of daily temperatures (see equation (10.10)), and, as we have seen, the analysis becomes rather complex. However, there is another way to understand the standard deviation that is much more tractable, and is based on consideration of the stochastic process for the expected index.

10.4.7 The stochastic process for the expected index

Since an estimate of the expected index is just a sum of forecasts (as we saw in section 10.2), a *change* in the expected index is simply a sum of *changes* in the forecasts.

Writing the expected index on day j as $\mu_x(j)$ and a change in the expected index from day j to day $j + 1$ as

$$\Delta\mu_x(j) = \mu_x(j + 1) - \mu_x(j) \tag{10.22}$$

then substituting in equation (10.5), we get

$$\Delta\mu_x(j) = (T_j^{obs} - T_{j,j}^{fc}) + \sum_{i=j+1}^{j+N_f} (T_{i,j+1}^{fc} - T_{i,j}^{fc}) + (T_{j+N_f+1,j}^{fc} - E_j(T_{j+N_f+1}))$$

$$\tag{10.23}$$

The first pair of terms is the difference between the actual value for T_j, which becomes known on day $j + 1$, and the forecast for T_j made on day j. The second term is the sum of the differences between the forecasts for days $j + 1, \ldots, j + N_f$ made on days $j + 1$ and day j. The third term is the difference between the forecast for day $j + N_f + 1$ made on day $j + 1$ and the mean value for T_{j+N_f+1} estimated from historical data. In short, the change in the expected index is driven by new historical data, changing forecasts and a forecast that extends one day further into the future.

Since temperature and forecasts are normally distributed, these changes will also be normally distributed. Combining this with the assumption of efficiency we see that changes in the expected index are independent and normally distributed. We can thus represent them as a Brownian motion, which we write as

$$\Delta\mu_x(j) = \sigma(j)\Delta W(j) \tag{10.24}$$

or as

$$d\mu = \sigma dW \tag{10.25}$$

The volatility of this Brownian motion depends on the sizes and correlations between the changes of the forecasts on each day, and the extent to which the forecasts overlap the contract period. We will assume that σ is deterministic and ignore the fact that forecast uncertainty actually varies stochastically to a very small extent from day to day.

Figure 10.2 shows the sizes of the terms in equation (10.23) as estimated from one particular forecast (taken from Jewson, 2002b). Perhaps surprisingly, we see that for this forecast these terms are roughly equal in size. Figure 10.3 shows the correlations between one of these terms (the sixth) and the others. We see that the terms at the different leads are positively correlated with the sixth term within two or three days of lead time.

The stochastic process for the expected index (equations (10.24) and (10.25)) is the process that defines how the expected index changes on a daily basis up to the end of the contract. At the end of the contract the expected index becomes the same as the final settlement index for the contract. This means that the distribution of the final values of the stochastic process for the expected index is just the distribution of the settlement index.

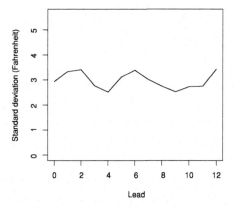

Figure 10.2. The standard deviation of forecast changes versus lead time.

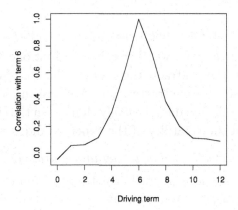

Figure 10.3. The correlation of forecast changes between different lead times.

Summing equation (10.24) from day j to one day after the end of the contract gives

$$\mu_x(N_d + 1) - \mu_x(j) = \sum_{i=j}^{N_d} \sigma(i)\Delta W \qquad (10.26)$$

But $\mu_x(N_d + 1) = x$, since on the day after the end of the contract we have all the information we need to calculate the settlement index, and so

$$x - \mu_x(j) = \sum_{i=j}^{N_d} \sigma(i)\Delta W \qquad (10.27)$$

The standard deviation of the settlement index $\sigma_x(j)$ is defined by

$$(\sigma_x(j))^2 = E[(x - \mu_x(j))^2]$$

$$= E[\left(\sum_{i=j}^{N_d} \sigma(i)\Delta W\right)^2]$$

$$= \sum_{i=j}^{N_d} \sigma^2(i) \qquad (10.28)$$

We call this the volatility-variance constraint since it relates the daily volatility of the expected index to the variance of the settlement index. We have used this already in section 5.1 and it will prove very useful below.

Given $\sigma^2(i)$ for all i we can now calculate $\sigma_x(j)$ for any day during the contract. In particular, we see that, under our assumption that $\sigma(j)$ is deterministic, σ_x is also deterministic and can be determined for the whole contract period in advance of the start of the contract.

This leads to three phases in the evolution of the expected index.

Volatility of the expected index just before the start of the contract

As we approach the start of a weather contract, first one day of the weather forecast will overlap the contract, then two, and so on, increasing until the whole forecast overlaps the contract period. As more and more of the forecast overlaps the contract day on day, the likely changes in the size of the expected index get larger and the volatility of the expected index will be increasing.

Volatility of the expected index during the central part of the contract

From some point on the forecast will lie entirely within the contract, and all the forecast will be used in our estimate of the expected index. From day to day the amount of forecast being used does not change, just the days on which it is being used. Thus for short contracts the volatility of the expected index will stay roughly constant. For long contracts seasonal changes in the sizes of forecast change terms may lead to gradual changes in the volatility during this period.

Volatility of the expected index at the end of the contract

As we approach the end of the contract the last days of the forecast will start to extend beyond the end of the contract, and only the start of the forecast will be relevant. Less and less of the forecast will be used day on day, the changes in the expected index will get smaller and the volatility of the expected index will gradually reduce.

10.4.8 The trapezium model

The actual shape of the increasing and decreasing parts of the volatility curve is complex and depends on the relative sizes of the various changes in the forecast and the correlations between them. A simple parameterisation of this shape is to use a trapezium for the shape of the squared volatility, following Jewson (2002b). A comparison of this trapezium model with the standard deviations of actual forecast changes for a particular example taken from that paper is shown in figure 10.4.

The three parts of the trapezium correspond to the three phases of the evolution of the index volatility described above. If the forecast changes at different leads were independent and equal in size the trapezium would be exactly correct. If they were perfectly correlated and equal in size then the volatility itself, rather than the volatility squared, would show a trapezium shape. In reality, as we have seen in figures 10.2 and 10.3, the forecast change terms are roughly equal in size, and somewhat correlated. The correlation probably explains why the trapezium model overestimates the volatility slightly during the first and third phases in figure 10.4.

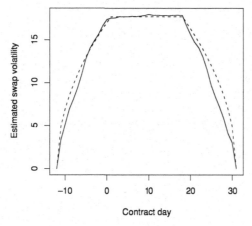

Figure 10.4. The swap volatility from the trapezium model (dashed line), and calculated from forecasts (solid line).

The area under the trapezium is given by the historical variance of the index, which can be calculated before the start of the contract. This fixes the entire trapezium. We thus know the squared volatility of the expected index at any point in time during the contract, before the contract has even begun, because we can read a value off the trapezium. And, since the variance of the index at any point during the contract is just the area remaining under the trapezium, the standard deviation of the index at any point in time is also fixed before the contract has begun. In other words, we have a deterministic model for the rate of decrease of the standard deviation throughout the contract period. The rate of decrease is initially slow but accelerating, then levels off, then reduces near the end of the contract.

So far we have ignored seasonality, but seasonal effects can also be incorporated fairly simply using the method described in Jewson (2003p); as an example, figure 10.5 shows the seasonal trapezium model applied to a November contract, while figure 10.6 shows it applied to a November to March contract. In the November contract case the volatility is increasing during the contract due to the increasing variability in the underlying temperatures. In the November to March contract the volatility first increases and then decreases again towards spring.

The trapezium models allow for the very simple pricing of contracts during the contract period, in the following steps:

- the expected index is calculated using a single forecast, as in section 10.2;
- the *par* value for the historical index variance is calculated using historical data, as in chapter 4;
- this par value fixes the height and shape of the trapezium;

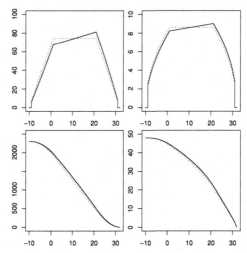

Figure 10.5. The volatility from a seasonal trapezium model (solid line), with a non-seasonal trapezium model (dotted line), for a one-month contract in November. Both models are fitted to a pre-season par value of the index standard deviation of 48, representing roughly the value for London Heathrow November HDDs. The four panels show the volatility squared, the volatility, the conditional index variance (conditional on all the available information at that point in time) and the conditional index standard deviation.

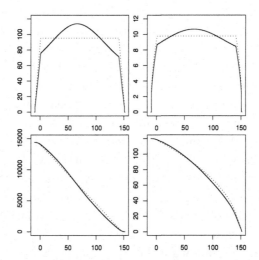

Figure 10.6. The volatility from a seasonal trapezium model (solid line), with a non-seasonal trapezium model (dotted line), for a November to March contract on London Heathrow, and fitted to a par value of the index standard deviation of 120 HDDs.

- from the trapezium we can obtain the *current* value for the index variance as the area remaining under the trapezium;
- contracts can now be priced using the expected index and the current standard deviation of the index.

The main advantage of this method for pricing during the contract period relative to the previous methods described is that we do not have to use a probabilistic forecast but only a single forecast. The probabilistic information is automatically incorporated in our model for the volatility. We also do not have to calculate the covariance term between the forecast and the post-forecast period; again, this is automatically included in the model. This makes the method extremely simple. The disadvantage is the rather strong assumptions that we have to make, which are not accurate for all contracts.

In the next chapter we will discuss the relevance of these ideas for arbitrage pricing, and in chapter 12 we will discuss how these ideas can be extended to provide a very simple algorithm for calculating value at risk.

Limitations of the trapezium model

The trapezium models are most appropriate for locations where seasonal forecasts are not important. For locations where seasonal forecasts *are* important the release of such forecasts creates an additional source of volatility, characterised by large jumps in the price around once a month (when the forecasts appear). This could easily be modelled in the framework given above by including a deterministic 'spike' in the volatility at the time of the release of the forecast.

10.4.9 Which method to use?

We have presented three rather different methods for the incorporation of forecasts into pricing models. Which method should be used? In the end, this is a matter for individual institutions or traders to decide for themselves. However, certain guidelines can be given.

1. If a material fraction of the indices being traded cannot be modelled well using a normal distribution, then one cannot use the method based on Brownian motion.[1] But, otherwise, it is the easiest method to use.
2. For general use, the index modelling approach is reasonably good.
3. In the case where frequent trading of options is taking place during the contract period, and very precise valuation is needed, then the daily modelling methods potentially give the most accurate results, if used with care.

---

[1] In principle one could extend such methods to event indices, but characterising the stochastic process for the expected index is more difficult, since it is no longer just a deterministic function of Brownian motion. We are working on it.

10.5 Seasonal forecasts

We now briefly discuss how one might use seasonal forecasts in pricing. This is much more difficult than using weather forecasts because it is so hard to create a probabilistic forecast of site-specific temperatures from a seasonal forecast. As a result, it is hard to specify any kind of general quantitative methods.

In practice, one might choose to use the following approach. We consider pre-winter season valuation in September or October.

1. Check a number of available seasonal forecasts, and estimate the chance that there will be an El Niño or La Niña event during the upcoming winter.
2. If there is apparently no chance of an El Niño or La Niña then one might want to eliminate El Niño and La Niña years from any historical analysis.
3. If there is a strong chance of El Niño or La Niña then one might want to shift the expected index distribution according to scatter plots, such as those shown in section 9.8.2.
4. This is sufficient for swap contracts, for which we need only an estimate of the mean index. For options contracts one also needs an estimate of the standard deviation of the index. This is very hard to achieve in a rigorous scientific way; the starting point might be to reduce the climatological standard deviation by a certain amount.

A slightly more sophisticated approach might use probabilistic forecasts of Niño 3.4 temperatures. How to produce such forecasts has been investigated in Jewson et al. (2003b).

Clearly, this approach is somewhat basic. These are all areas of current research.

10.6 Further reading

Much of this chapter comes from our own work. The discussion from section 10.1 to 10.4.5 comes mostly from Jewson and Caballero (2003b), while the discussion from 10.4.6 to 10.4.8 comes mostly from Jewson (2002b). Other articles we have written on this subject include those in Jewson (2000), Jewson and Ziehmann (2003) and Jewson et al. (2002b).

The only other article we have been able to find that addresses similar issues is that by Shorter et al., 2002.

10.7 Acknowledgements

Figure 10.1 is reproduced from Jewson and Caballero (2003b) with the permission of the editor of *Meteorological Applications*.

11

Arbitrage pricing models

Thus far this book has described the use of actuarial principles for pricing weather derivatives. This chapter will now discuss the application of arbitrage pricing ideas. The main difference between actuarial and arbitrage pricing theories is that actuarial pricing is based on diversification while arbitrage pricing is based on hedging. The anticipation of following a hedging strategy can affect the prices we charge for weather contracts.

A useful context in which to explain arbitrage pricing is that of equity options. The issuer of an equity option can trade the underlying equity in order to hedge his/her risk. If the underlying equity market is liquidly traded, then many such hedging transactions can be performed between the issuance and expiry of the option, and the risk will be hedged almost perfectly. Many hedging trades are necessary because the risk from the equity option depends on the share price and hence varies as the share price fluctuates in time. The cost of the hedging combined with the distribution of payoffs on the option determines the price initially charged for the option, and this price, which we call the 'arbitrage price', is generally different from the price that would be charged if no such dynamic hedging were to be undertaken and the option were priced actuarially. In particular, the arbitrage price is *not* the expectation (although we will see below that it is possible to recover the fact that the price is the expectation, but only by redefining 'expectation').

A market maker has to charge the arbitrage price for an option because if he/she does not then other players in the market can make a risk-free profit by trading the options the market maker is offering and then replicating them using equity. In this way the market can be said to *enforce* arbitrage pricing under certain conditions.

Temperature itself cannot be traded, and so one cannot form a parallel between temperature and equities. However, weather derivatives can, in principle at least, be hedged with other weather derivatives on the same or similar indices, and this is the main concept behind arbitrage pricing for weather derivatives. Since dynamic hedging requires frequent trading, and at the time of writing the only weather contracts that can be frequently traded without incurring extremely large transaction costs are weather swaps, we will restrict ourselves to the situation where weather swaps are used to dynamically hedge weather options. However, in principle, given appropriate market liquidity, one could also conceive of using options to hedge swaps, or options to hedge other options.

We will first give a brief review of standard arbitrage pricing theory, and comment on some of the attempts to extend it to include transaction costs, market slippage and hedging at discrete intervals. We will then develop a price process for weather swap contracts, and, by modifying the standard theory, develop expressions for the price of dynamically hedged weather options. We will then discuss how the extensions of standard theory can also be applied to weather.

At the end of the chapter we will discuss a few extensions and related topics, such as the pricing of dual-trigger contracts and the pricing of contracts on highly correlated locations.

11.1 Standard arbitrage theory

We imagine that we trade an equity option, and are hedging the risk in that option by using the underlying equity.

The first assumption is that the equity price S follows a stochastic differential equation given by

$$dS = \mu S dt + \sigma S dW \tag{11.1}$$

where μ is the drift, t is time, σ is the volatility and W is Brownian motion. The first term on the right-hand side denotes a drift (usually upward), while the second term denotes random fluctuations driven by the arrival of new information in the market and fluctuations in supply and demand. The effect of new information is random, because if it were not random it would be predictable and already included in the price. If share prices usually drift upwards then why does not everybody invest in shares? The answer is that the random fluctuations are large, and over any finite time period there is significant risk that the share price may fall.

We can also consider how the discounted value of the share price changes in time. The discounted value of the share at time t_0 is

$$S_d = e^{r(t_0 - t)} S \tag{11.2}$$

and the stochastic process for the discounted value is then

$$dS_d = (\mu - r)S_d dt + \sigma S_d dW \qquad (11.3)$$

We can 'solve' equation (11.1) to give the share price in terms of the Brownian motion. The solution is

$$S = S_0 e^{(\mu - \frac{\sigma^2}{2})t + \sigma W} \qquad (11.4)$$

Note that when differentiating equation (11.4) to give equation (11.1) we have to use Ito's formula for evaluating the derivatives of functions $f = f(W, t)$ of stochastic processes, which gives

$$df = \frac{\partial f}{\partial t} dt + \frac{\partial f}{\partial W} dW + \frac{1}{2} \frac{\partial^2 f}{\partial W^2} dt \qquad (11.5)$$

The extra term on the right-hand side arises because although W is continuous it is not differentiable, and makes jumps of size $dt^{\frac{1}{2}}$ in time dt.

Standard arbitrage pricing theory can be presented mathematically in a number of different ways. We will start with a partial differential equation (PDE) approach similar to the original derivation of Black and Scholes (1973). We will then present a more succinct approach based on measure theory.

11.1.1 Delta hedging and the PDE approach

Imagine that at time t we own, in addition to the option position, a short position Δ in shares, and an amount of cash cB invested in a risk-free bond B with interest rate r. The total value of our holding, Π, is then given by

$$\Pi = V - \Delta S + cB \qquad (11.6)$$

where $V(S, t)$ is the unknown value of the option, S is the value of one share, Δ is the number of shares being held and B is the value of the bond.

Moving forward an infinitesimal time step, the value of our holding changes by

$$d\Pi = dV - \Delta dS - S d\Delta + c dB + B dc \qquad (11.7)$$

Thus the value of our portfolio changes because the value of the option changes, the share price changes, the number of shares we are holding changes, the value of the bond changes, and the number of bonds we are holding changes.

If we assume that the number of shares changes only because we bought or sold them with or for cash, and the amount of cash changes only because we used it to buy or sell shares, then we see that the changes in value due to changes in the number of shares are cancelled by the change in value due to a change in the number of bonds held. This is known as self-financing of the portfolio, and is written as

$$Bdc = Sd\Delta \tag{11.8}$$

Thus the change in our portfolio reduces to

$$d\Pi = dV - \Delta dS + cdB \tag{11.9}$$

The bond increases at interest rate r, so

$$dB = rBdt \tag{11.10}$$

and hence

$$d\Pi = dV - \Delta dS + crBdt \tag{11.11}$$

We can expand dV in terms of dS and dt (taking care to use Ito's lemma), so that

$$dV = \frac{\partial V}{\partial t}dt + \frac{\partial V}{\partial S}dS + \frac{1}{2}\sigma^2 S^2 \frac{\partial^2 V}{\partial S^2}dt \tag{11.12}$$

If we now expand S using the model for the share price given in equation (11.1), we get

$$dV = \left(\frac{\partial V}{\partial t} + \frac{1}{2}\sigma^2 S^2 \frac{\partial^2 V}{\partial S^2} + \mu S \frac{\partial V}{\partial S} \right) dt + \left(\sigma S \frac{\partial V}{\partial S} \right) dW \tag{11.13}$$

The change in the portfolio value then becomes

$$d\Pi = \left(\frac{\partial V}{\partial t} + \frac{1}{2}\sigma^2 S^2 \frac{\partial^2 V}{\partial S^2} + \mu S \frac{\partial V}{\partial S} - \mu S \Delta + crB \right) dt + \left(\sigma S \frac{\partial V}{\partial S} - \sigma S \Delta \right) dW \tag{11.14}$$

This change has a deterministic component (the dt term) and a random component (the dW term). If we now choose Δ as

$$\Delta = \frac{\partial V}{\partial S} \tag{11.15}$$

then the random term in dW and the drift term in dt both cancel out and the total portfolio change becomes

$$d\Pi = \left(\frac{\partial V}{\partial t} + \frac{1}{2}\sigma^2 S^2 \frac{\partial^2 V}{\partial S^2} + crB \right) dt \tag{11.16}$$

The cancellation of the random and drift terms is the essence of continuously hedging with shares.

Since changes in the value of the portfolio are now deterministic, the change must be the same as what would be earned by putting the same money into safe bonds with interest rate r. If this were not the case someone would be able to make a risk-free profit by either buying the option and hedging or selling the option and hedging. This equality between the return on our portfolio and the return on safe bonds can be written as

$$d\Pi = \Pi r dt \qquad (11.17)$$

Equations (11.17), (11.16) and (11.6) give

$$\left(\frac{\partial V}{\partial t} + \frac{1}{2}\frac{\partial^2 V}{\partial S^2} + crB\right) dt = (V - \Delta S + cB)r dt \qquad (11.18)$$

Rearranging terms, we get the famous Black–Scholes (BS) partial differential equation for the option price, as a function of the share price and time:

$$\frac{\partial V}{\partial t} + \frac{1}{2}\sigma^2 S^2 \frac{\partial^2 V}{\partial S^2} + rS\frac{\partial V}{\partial S} - rV = 0 \qquad (11.19)$$

Given appropriate boundary conditions, which specify the final pay-off structure, this equation has an analytical solution. For an unlimited call option contract with strike at K this solution is

$$V(S,t) = S\Phi(d_1) - Ke^{-r(T-t)}\Phi(d_2) \qquad (11.20)$$

where

$$d_1 = \frac{log(S/K) + (r + \frac{1}{2}\sigma^2)(T-t)}{\sigma\sqrt{(T-t)}} \qquad (11.21)$$

$$d_2 = \frac{log(S/K) + (r - \frac{1}{2}\sigma^2)(T-t)}{\sigma\sqrt{(T-t)}}$$

11.1.2 Replication and the measure theory approach

There are several ways of deriving equation (11.20), in addition to the PDE-based method described above. One popular approach comes from probability theory. It is based on the following steps (taken from Baxter and Rennie, 1996). These steps will be readily understood only if the reader has a basic understanding of the branch of mathematics known as measure theory. Our treatment of this approach will be brief, since it is covered very well elsewhere. We will include just enough detail to see how the theorem can be extended to the weather case later in the chapter.

Using a theorem known as Girsanov's theorem we can find a change of measure (a change of the probabilities of events) such that the drift in the discounted share price process given in equation (11.3) becomes zero. The discounted share price process in this new measure is then given by

$$dS_d = \sigma S_d dW \tag{11.22}$$

A stochastic process with no drift such as this is known as a *martingale*.

Using the new measure we can define another stochastic process E_t (where the subscript t denotes a function of time) based on the discounted final pay-off of the option by using expectation to work backwards in time. The expectation is calculated using all the information available at time t:

$$E_t = E_Q(B_T^{-1}X) \tag{11.23}$$

where E_Q denotes expectation under the new measure Q and B denotes discounting of the final pay-offs X. As we move forward in time the share price evolves, and hence our prediction of X, and E_t, will change.

We can show that this new process is also a martingale (since all expectations are martingales). By definition, the initial value of this pay-off process is just the expectation of the discounted final pay-off of the option under the new measure, and the final value of this pay-off process is just the discounted pay-off of the option.

Now we have two martingales (the discounted share price process and the pay-off process) based on the same underlying source of randomness (the randomness in the share price). According to another theorem, known as the martingale representation theorem, any two such martingales can be written in terms of each other. This means that we can write the option price process in terms of the discounted share price process. In financial terms this means that the option pay-off can be replicated using the shares and bonds. The initial amount of cash needed to start this replication is the initial value of the option price process, which, as we have seen, is just the expectation of the option pay-offs under the new measure. This means that the value of the option is just the discounted expected pay-off of the option, under the new measure.

$$V(S,t) = B_t E_Q(B_T^{-1}X) \tag{11.24}$$

Again, the expectation is calculated using all information available at time t. All the complexity has been moved into the question of finding the new measure. In fact, finding this new measure is easy (in this case, although not always). We have seen that the new measure is the measure in which the discounted share process is a martingale. This means that the drift in the *undiscounted* share in this measure must be r. The option price can thus be calculated as the discounted expectation of pay-offs of the option using a share price that has an adjusted drift r instead of μ.

We can simulate final share values in the adjusted measure using

$$dS = rSdt + \sigma SdW \qquad (11.25)$$

and calculate the discounted expected pay-off of the option across these final share values.

11.2 Comments on the standard theory

Uniqueness

The striking thing about arbitrage pricing compared to actuarial pricing is that arbitrage prices are unique, and do not depend on the trader. This is because all risk is hedged away and so risk preferences do not play a role; there is no role for risk loading, as there is in actuarial pricing theory.

Risk neutrality

We saw in section 11.1.2 that the option can be priced simply by setting the drift in the share price process to r and then calculating the discounted expected pay-off.

Making this temporary artificial change in the drift of the share in order to price options is known as 'risk-neutral pricing', because it means we can price an option in the following way:

- assume that we live in a world in which everyone is risk-neutral (there is no risk aversion, or no marginally increasing utility);
- since share traders are risk-neutral, share prices grow at the risk-free rate, and we can use equation (11.25) for the share price;
- since option traders are risk-neutral, they do not hedge their positions;
- option prices can then be calculated as the discounted expected pay-off of the option with no risk loading.

This method of pricing can also be derived from the observation that equation (11.20) does not contain the drift of the share price.

In this artificial risk-neutral world we can price the option stand-alone, without having to consider the cost of the hedge, and we get the same result as if we considered the cost of the hedge in the real world.

We note that risk-neutral pricing does not involve *becoming* risk-neutral. A real risk-neutral trader would not hedge his positions at all, and would probably invest all his money in unhedged option positions. Risk neutrality is just a useful mathematical short cut to getting to an expression for the option price.

The phrase 'risk-neutral pricing' is also often extended to refer to arbitrage pricing in general, although we note that the arguments used in section 11.1.1 to derive the arbitrage price do not follow a line of argument that uses the assumption of risk neutrality, and from a historical perspective the concepts of risk-neutral pricing came later.

Intuitive arguments and the relation to actuarial pricing

Neither of the derivations of the arbitrage price for options given above is particularly intuitive: one says that the price of the option is the solution of a partial differential equation, and the other says that it is the expectation under a set of probabilities that are different from real probabilities.

A less rigorous but more intuitive expression for the price can be derived as follows. The total discounted profit made from selling an option and continuously hedging with shares is given by the sum of the premium, the discounted profit made on the option and the discounted profit made on the shares, or

$$p = p_r - p_o + p_s \tag{11.26}$$

where p is the total discounted profit, p_r is the premium, p_o is the discounted pay-off of the option and p_s is the discounted net result of the share trading.

Because of arbitrage the total profit must be exactly zero, and so

$$p_r = p_o - p_s \tag{11.27}$$

We see that the premium of the option is balanced by the discounted pay-off of the option and the discounted loss on the shares. The terms on the right-hand side are random variables, while the premium is a constant.

Taking expectations of this expression under *any* measure we get

$$p_r = E(p_o) - E(p_s) \tag{11.28}$$

Thus we see that the price of the option is the discounted expected pay-off on the option plus the discounted expected cost of trading the shares. This result is reasonably intuitive (we think).

We can also now see that the arbitrage price is simply a special case of the actuarial pricing rules based on the expectation and the risk loading. Since the risk has been hedged away, the risk loading term is zero and the price is just the expectation of the profit on the combined portfolio of option and swap trades.

Finally, we note that if we choose the measure used in equation (11.28) to be one under which the discounted expected loss on the shares is zero then we recover the result of section 11.1.2, that the option price is the expected pay-off under a measure in which the share price is a martingale. The effect of the change of measure is to set $E(p_s) = 0$.

The relation to the expected pay-off of the option

How does the arbitrage price on an equity option relate to the expected pay-off of that option? We have seen in section 11.1.2 that the option price is the discounted expected pay-off when the share drift is set to r. Consider a call option and assume that the share drift is greater than r, as is usual. If we reduce the share drift to r then we are making high values of the final share price less likely and so the option is less likely to pay out. We conclude that the arbitrage price must be less than the expected pay-off. If call options are trading at below the expected pay-off, why then don't people buy them and hold them, without hedging, to expiry, since this would presumably make a profit on average? Now consider a put option. Reducing the share drift to r makes low values of the final share price more likely and so the option is *more* likely to pay out. We conclude that the arbitrage price must be *greater* than the expected pay-off. Why then don't people *sell* put options and hold them to expiry? On average, buying call options and selling put options in this way *would* make money, and such a trading strategy can indeed be used: it is just a way of betting on the share price. Relative to just buying or selling the shares themselves, it is more leveraged: a small amount of money can give a bigger profit or loss.

Conserved quantities

Much of physics and meteorology is concerned with identifying conserved quantities. Purely for interest's sake we note that, in the BS system, the discounted value of the portfolio (option, shares and bonds together) is conserved. This follows directly from the assumption that the portfolio must appreciate at the risk-free rate.

$$d(e^{-rt}\Pi) = 0 \qquad (11.29)$$

Delta hedging versus replication

The PDE derivation of the BS price emphasised hedging the risk at each infinitesimal time step. Because each small step of risk is hedged, the total risk is zero. The derivation of the same result using measure theory emphasised using shares and bonds to replicate the final pay-off of the option. Because the final pay-off is replicated exactly, there is no total risk. Thus continuous hedging and replication are microscopic and macroscopic views of the same idea of removing all the risk.

Assumptions

It is useful to highlight some of the assumptions underlying the derivations of the arbitrage price above. Later we will discuss how to relax some of these assumptions in order to make the model more realistic.

1. The hedging is continuous in time.
2. Trading shares and bonds has no transaction costs.
3. Hedging does not affect the share price.
4. Shares can be traded in any amount.

Although in practice many of the assumptions underlying the above derivations are clearly wrong, the BS price plays a vital role in many derivatives markets as a reference price.

The role of volatility

One of the crucial aspects of the BS model is the role of volatility. There is a one-to-one relationship between the volatility and the price for call options: higher volatilities give higher prices because options are more likely to pay out. As a result, volatilities can be quoted instead of prices.

Options traders in the weather market, especially those with a background trading other options in more liquid markets, often also think more in terms of volatility than price, even though this may not be justifiable on a rigorous basis because of the lack of liquidity in weather. We investigate this further in section 11.4.9.

Volatility and standard deviation

Much of the discussion in previous chapters about pricing weather options involved estimation of the standard deviation of the settlement index. This quantity has not appeared in the BS derivations given above. In fact, however, equation (11.21) can be written using something similar to the standard deviation of the settlement index.

From equation (11.4), the standard deviation of the log of the share price is $\sigma_x = \sigma\sqrt{T-t}$. Equation (11.21) can be rewritten in terms of this standard deviation, rather than in terms of the daily volatility of the share price σ, as

$$d_1 = \frac{log(S/K) + r(T-t) + \frac{1}{2}\sigma_x^2}{\sigma_x} \tag{11.30}$$

$$d_2 = \frac{log(S/K) + r(T-t) - \frac{1}{2}\sigma_x^2}{\sigma_x}$$

We see that using the standard deviation of the settlement index σ_x and using the volatility of the log of the daily share process σ are interchangeable. Since for equities σ is what is usually estimated from data, it makes more sense to use σ. In weather, however, it is the standard deviation σ_x that can be estimated more easily.

Relations between the greeks

The greeks are defined as partial derivatives of the price of an option. Equation (11.19) is a relation between partial derivatives of an option, and is hence a relation between the greeks. In particular, equation (11.19) can be rewritten:

$$\Theta + \frac{1}{2}\sigma^2 S^2\Gamma + rS\Delta - rV = 0 \tag{11.31}$$

The market price of risk

In liquidly traded markets, relationships between the prices of contracts can often be understood using the so-called 'market price of risk', which links the sizes of risks (volatility) and returns (drifts). If there are two contracts that are both liquidly traded and that have stochastic fluctuations driven by the same source of randomness then they can be used to hedge each other and eliminate the randomness. One can then show (Hull, 2002) that the two contracts have the same value for the market price of risk:

$$\text{mpr} = \frac{\mu - r}{\sigma} \tag{11.32}$$

where μ and σ are the drift and the volatility of the contract price.

In the above derivation of the arbitrage price we have, in fact, considered that we know the drift and the volatility of one of the contracts (the underlying shares). We thus know the market price of risk for the shares, and hence we know the market price of risk for the option.

11.2.1 The Black (76) model

Rather than hedge an option with shares, one could imagine hedging an option with forward contracts on the shares. A simple static hedging argument gives the forward price in terms of the share price as

$$F = e^{r(T-t)}S \tag{11.33}$$

Following Black (1976) we can then rewrite equation (11.19) in terms of F rather than S using the following relations:

$$\left.\frac{\partial V}{\partial t}\right|_S = \left.\frac{\partial V}{\partial t}\right|_F - \left.\frac{\partial V}{\partial F}\right|_t \left.\frac{\partial F}{\partial t}\right|_S \tag{11.34}$$

$$\left.\frac{\partial V}{\partial S}\right|_t = \left.\frac{\partial V}{\partial F}\right|_t \left.\frac{\partial F}{\partial S}\right|_t \tag{11.35}$$

and

$$\left.\frac{\partial^2 V}{\partial S^2}\right|_t = \left.\frac{\partial^2 V}{\partial F^2}\right|_t \left.\left(\frac{\partial F}{\partial S}\right)^2\right|_t \tag{11.36}$$

The BS equation then becomes

$$\frac{\partial V}{\partial t} + \frac{1}{2}\sigma^2 F^2 \frac{\partial^2 V}{\partial F^2} - rV = 0 \tag{11.37}$$

We note that the $rS\frac{\partial V}{\partial S}$ term has disappeared. One way to understand this is that this term relates to the interest lost because of having to invest in shares. When one is hedging with forwards this term disappears because no money changes hands until the end of the contract, and one does not have to worry about lost interest on forward contracts.

If we now write the option price in terms of the accrued value at time T (which involves discounting forward in time),

$$V_T = e^{r(T-t)}V \tag{11.38}$$

then equation (11.37) simplifies even more to

$$\frac{\partial V_T}{\partial t} + \frac{1}{2}\sigma^2 F^2 \frac{\partial^2 V_T}{\partial F^2} = 0 \tag{11.39}$$

In terms of the greeks (now redefined using V_T, not V) this equation can be written as

$$\Theta + \frac{1}{2}\sigma^2 S^2 \Gamma = 0 \tag{11.40}$$

This relation can be understood rather simply. The stochastic nature of the underlying forwards price creates gamma, which would tend to change the option price. However, the option price must stay fixed to ensure a lack of arbitrage opportunities.

11.3 Extensions to the standard theory

There is a vast academic literature dedicated to extending the basic BS model described above to more realistic markets. Some of these extensions are discussed below.

Discrete time hedging

One of the assumptions in the BS model is that options are hedged continuously. In practice, this is not realistic. If hedges are made very frequently relative to the rate of change of the underlying then this may be a good approximation. If they are made less frequently then it may not be.

Once discrete time hedging is being used the risk in the option cannot be hedged perfectly and there will be a residual risk; the final outcome of the hedged position is then partly stochastic. There is then no exact arbitrage price, and the price will depend on the risk preferences of the traders involved. This is reflected in the mathematical models by the need to make fairly arbitrary assumptions about risk preferences. In discrete time hedging models, the size of the optimum hedge may also change, and is no longer given exactly by the delta.

Studies that have looked at these issues include those by Boyle and Emanuel (1980), Wilmott (1994) and Mercurio and Vorst (1996).

Adding transaction costs

In the BS model it is assumed that transaction costs are zero. In reality, most share trades go through brokers or exchanges, who charge a small fee, often proportional to the size of the trade.

Adding transaction costs means that very frequent delta hedging is no longer possible. A trade-off arises between reducing risk by hedging as frequently as possible, on the one hand, and reducing transaction costs by hedging as infrequently as possible, on the other.

As with discrete hedging there is a residual risk, and risk preferences come into play. Given a model for risk preferences and a model for transaction costs, one may be able to find a trading strategy that is optimum. This strategy then gives the price of the option and the sizes of the hedges.

There have been many articles on this subject, including those by Leland (1985) and Hoggard et al. (1994).

Adding market feedback

In the BS model the price process for the underlying is specified and fixed. However, in thinly traded markets the trades that are made to hedge options can affect the underlying itself. The fundamental assumptions about the (fixed) dynamics of the underlying are no longer valid. This has been explored in the work of Schönbucher (1993) and Frey and Stremme (1995), among others.

Shares can trade in any amount

In the BS model it is assumed that shares can be traded in any amount, including fractional amounts. This is not exactly correct in practice, but for equity options it is not a bad assumption, since the size of the options relative to the size of individual shares is such that the error is minimal.

Complete models

Ideally, one would price options taking into account all the above effects. This can be achieved only by using numerical methods; one would want a numerical method that can take all of these factors into account, and (quickly) give the optimal hedging strategy and the price, or price range, to be charged for the option. One attempt in this direction are the methods described in Potters et al. (2001) and Bouchaud et al. (1996), and other papers by the same authors.

11.4 Weather swap price processes

Having given a brief overview of standard option pricing theory, we now move on to see how such theories can be developed in the case of hedging a weather option with a weather swap. The key stage is to develop a price process for the swap. Once we have that, it will be easy to apply slightly modified versions of the standard theory to derive an option price. We will present three price processes for the swap, from simple (and a little unrealistic) to complex (and more realistic).

We will assume that all swaps are linear, without caps, and are based on CAT or linear degree days. This greatly simplifies the analysis, and is a reasonably good model for most commonly traded contracts.

We will also use a mathematical trick of dealing with swap *prices* rather than strikes, in order to make the similarity with the standard BS theory (where shares have prices) more clear. In other words, rather than entering into a costless swap with tick 1 and strike K that pays $x - K$ if the index settles at x, we will imagine paying a premium to buy a swap that will pay us x at settlement. The premiums that would be paid for such premium-based swaps are given by arbitrage arguments in terms of the strikes of the costless swaps as

$$\text{premium} = S = Ke^{r(t-T)} \qquad (11.41)$$

These imaginary premium-based swaps are to equities as costless swaps are to equity forwards. In other words, we can think of these fictional premium-based swaps as analogous to equities, and real costless swaps as analogous to forwards on these equities.

11.4.1 The balanced market model

In order to develop our first price process for the swap we will make the assumption that the swap market is balanced in terms of supply and demand.

This leads to our imaginary premium-based swaps trading at the discounted expected pay-off, and the costless swap trading at the expected index. If our estimate of the discounted expected pay-off does not change then the swap price will grow only at the risk-free rate. This argument would not make sense for equities, since the fundamental reason for buying equities is as an investment: no one would invest unless there was a good chance of the equity price growing at a faster rate than the risk-free rate. However, the fundamental reason for trading swaps is as a hedging instrument, and one does not expect capital growth from a hedge. In a balanced market hedgers exchange swaps between themselves through an exchange or through a market maker. The market maker would require a small premium to justify trading, but we will ignore that for now.

How is the expected pay-off of the swap calculated? Initially we assume that all market participants use the same historical data and forecasts to estimate the expected index of the swap.

As we saw in section 10.4.7, the expected index μ then changes as a deterministic function of Brownian motion given by

$$d\mu = \sigma dW \tag{11.42}$$

where σ is the index volatility.

By equation (11.41), the *price* (of the premium-based swap) is given by

$$S = e^{r(t-T)}\mu \tag{11.43}$$

and so

$$dS = rSdt + e^{r(t-T)}\sigma dW \tag{11.44}$$
$$= rSdt + \sigma_s dW$$

where $\sigma_s = e^{r(t-T)}\sigma$ has been defined so as to remove the discounting term.

Discounting the price at time t back to time t_0,

$$S_d = e^{r(t_0-t)}S \tag{11.45}$$

and so

$$dS_d = e^{r(t_0-T)}\sigma dW$$
$$= \sigma_d dW \tag{11.46}$$

where $\sigma_d = e^{r(t_0-T)}\sigma$ has also been defined to swallow the discounting term. We see that the discounted swap price is a Brownian motion and hence a martingale.

Equations (11.44) and (11.46) are the stochastic processes for the swap price and the discounted swap price that follow from our assumptions, including the efficient forecast assumption that says our forecasts are expectations. Unlike the share price process in equation (11.1), the random part of the change in the swap price is not related to the swap price. This is because the random part is entirely driven by changes in forecasts and temperatures. Note also that, although we have seen in chapter 6 that temperature shows significant autocorrelations and long memory, these have entirely cancelled out in the swap price process. This is because the autocorrelation of temperature is known about by the forecast and hence has been included in our estimate of the index. This effect is illustrated by an example below.

Finally, we note that the swap price can go negative. This would be unacceptable for shares: if a share price goes negative, then one can buy the share (for a negative amount – i.e. by receiving money), throw it away and make a risk-free profit. However, buying a swap at a negative price still involves committing to the possibility of having to pay out at the end of the swap term, and so no such risk-free profit is available.

One of the assumptions made in the derivation of the swap price was that all market players use the same forecasts and data to estimate the expected index. This is, of course, not true, since one of the main ways that secondary market participants seek to gain advantage is by using more accurately cleaned historical data or more accurate forecasts. However, we argue that the swap price given by equation (11.44) still holds. We assume that market participants will rationalise the price in terms of the data they have available. Price *changes* will still be driven by the changes in the forecasts and data as described above.

11.4.2 A toy model for swap prices

In order to elucidate the disappearance of the temperature autocorrelations in the swap price, we consider the following toy model for temperatures and prices.

We imagine that real temperature develops according to a stationary AR(1) process

$$T_{n+1} = \alpha T_n + \epsilon_n \tag{11.47}$$

where $0 < \alpha < 1$. This is autocorrelated to represent the autocorrelations of real temperatures.

We imagine that we are trading a contract that will settle on temperature on day $n + m$. On day $n + 1$ we know temperatures only for up to and including day n. Our best forecast for the settlement index (the temperature on day $n + m$) is thus

$$f_1 = \alpha^m T_n \tag{11.48}$$

Ignoring discounting, and assuming a balanced market, this gives the price on day $n + 1$. On day $n + 2$ we have a better forecast, which is

$$f_2 = \alpha^{m-1} T_{n+1} \tag{11.49}$$

This gives the price on day $n + 2$. The change in price is given by

$$
\begin{aligned}
f_2 - f_1 &= \alpha^{m-1} T_{n+1} - \alpha^m T_n \\
&= \alpha^n (T_n + \epsilon_n) - \alpha^m T_n \\
&= \alpha^m \epsilon_n
\end{aligned}
\tag{11.50}
$$

We see that the change in prices is random even though our model temperatures are autocorrelated. The autocorrelations cancel because they are included in the forecast.

11.4.3 Option pricing in the balanced market model

Given the swap price process in equation (11.44) we can now price options on the same index based on the assumptions that the swap is tradable without transaction costs and is used to continuously hedge the option. Replacing equation (11.1) with our new price process (11.44) we can rederive equation (11.19). This gives

$$\frac{\partial V}{\partial t} + \frac{1}{2}\sigma_s^2 \frac{\partial^2 V}{\partial S^2} + rS\frac{\partial V}{\partial S} - rV = 0 \tag{11.51}$$

which is the equation analogous to the BS equation for weather swaps trading with premium S. Note that the only difference from the actual BS equation is the coefficient in front of the second derivative term.

In section 11.2 we showed that the BS equation can be rewritten as a relation between the greeks. The same is true of equation (11.31), which can be rewritten as

$$\Theta + \frac{1}{2}\sigma_s^2 \Gamma + rS\Delta - rV = 0 \tag{11.52}$$

We must now transform this equation so that V is a function of the swap strike K and t rather than S and t, since K is what we actually observe in the swap market. This is analogous to the set of transformations that gave the Black (76) model in section 11.2.1.

Equation (11.37) becomes

$$\frac{\partial V}{\partial t} + \frac{1}{2}\sigma^2 \frac{\partial^2 V}{\partial K^2} - rV = 0 \tag{11.53}$$

We have lost the $rS\frac{\partial V}{\partial S}$ term and the σ_s has become a σ again.

This equation is the same as equation (11.37) but with the coefficient in front of the second derivative changing from $\sigma^2 S^2$ to σ^2.

This is the PDE satisfied by the price of the weather option. If we write this price in terms of the accrued value of the option at time T

$$V_T = e^{r(T-t)}V \tag{11.54}$$

then the equation simplifies to

$$\frac{\partial V_T}{\partial t} + \frac{1}{2}\sigma^2 \frac{\partial^2 V_T}{\partial K^2} = 0 \tag{11.55}$$

Like the BS equation, this equation can also be solved analytically. We derive the solution by noting that the Green's function solution of this equation is

$$V_T = \frac{1}{\sqrt{2\pi}}\frac{1}{\sigma}(T-t)^{-\frac{1}{2}}\exp\left(-\frac{(x-\mu)^2}{2\sigma^2(T-t)}\right) \tag{11.56}$$

We can verify that this is a solution by calculating the derivatives:

$$\frac{\partial V}{\partial t} = V\left[-\frac{(x-\mu)^2}{2\sigma^2(T-t)^2} + \frac{1}{2(T-t)}\right] \tag{11.57}$$

$$\frac{\partial V}{\partial x} = V\left[-\frac{(x-\mu)}{\sigma^2(T-t)}\right] \tag{11.58}$$

$$\frac{\partial^2 V}{\partial x^2} = V\left[\frac{(x-\mu)^2}{\sigma^4(T-t)^2} - \frac{1}{\sigma^2(T-t)}\right] \tag{11.59}$$

and substituting into equation (11.55).

Letting $t \to T$ in (11.56) we get the boundary condition

$$V(x, t = T) = \delta(x - \mu) \tag{11.60}$$

(note that equation (11.56) is one of many functions that converge onto the Dirac delta function: see Arfken, 1985, p. 481).

Since equation (11.55) is a linear PDE, to satisfy a more general boundary condition $V_T(x, T) = p(x)$ we just have to superimpose solutions, and so the more general solution is

$$V_T = \frac{1}{\sqrt{2\pi}}\frac{1}{\sigma}(T-t)^{-\frac{1}{2}}\int_{-\infty}^{\infty} p(s)\exp\left(-\frac{(s-\mu)^2}{2\sigma^2(T-t)}\right)ds \tag{11.61}$$

Letting $\sigma_x^2 = \sigma^2(T-t)$ gives

$$V_T = \frac{1}{\sqrt{2\pi}}\frac{1}{\sigma_x}\int_{-\infty}^{\infty} p(s)\exp\left(-\frac{(s-\mu)^2}{2\sigma_x^2}\right)ds \tag{11.62}$$

which is just the expected value of $p(s)$ under the normal distribution with expected value μ and standard deviation σ_x. The price of the option V is then just the discounted expected value.

As an alternative to the above PDE-based derivation we can also apply the replication and measure theory argument of section 11.1.2 to the weather case. Our discounted swap price given in equation (11.46) is *already* a martingale. In the standard theory we have to change measure to make the discounted share price a martingale; with our swap price we do not have to. The option price is therefore simply the discounted expected pay-off under the *natural* measure.

Curiously, the arbitrage price we have derived using the PDE and measure theory approaches is exactly the same as the actuarial fair price, without a risk loading. This was not true for the equity option case. Comparing with equation (11.28), we may ask what happened to the expected loss on the swap trading. When hedging equity options this expected loss (in the natural measure) is not zero because share prices drift and, as a result, option prices are not the same as the actuarial fair price. With weather swaps, however, there is no drift in the discounted swap price and the expected loss on the swaps is zero. Equation (11.28) then tells us that the actuarial fair price and the arbitrage price agree.

The equivalence between the actuarial fair price and the arbitrage price means that we can reuse the same closed-form expressions for both. Expressions for the arbitrage price and the greeks are thus given in appendices E and F.

The market price of risk

It is interesting to apply the market price of risk ideas described in section 11.2 to the weather case. Because the drift in equation (11.44) is just r, the market price of risk for the swap contract is zero. Hence the market price of risk on the option must also be zero, and the drift on the option price must also be r. Thus the drift on the discounted option price must be zero. Since the final option price is the expected pay-off, the initial option price must also be the expected pay-off.

11.4.4 Pricing weather options

This model justifies the following algorithm for calculating the arbitrage price for options.

1. Take the market swap strike as the expected index.
2. Calculate the option expected pay-off using this expected index.
3. Discount this option expected pay-off to give the arbitrage price.

In order to evaluate the expected pay-off of the weather option, we must know the standard deviation of the settlement index. In a liquid market there are a number of ways this could be determined:

- from historical data, as described in chapters 4 and 6;
- from an implied standard deviation calculated from other options in the market;
- from the trapezium model given in section 10.4.8, but used in reverse; the observed daily volatility of the swap is used to fit the model and then the model is used to calculate the standard deviation.

11.4.5 The linear imbalance model

Given all our assumptions, the arbitrage prices derived above are the prices that market dynamics would enforce for weather options. However, our assumptions are not close to being correct for the real weather market: in particular, the swap is both illiquid (trading swaps incurs transaction costs, and moves the swap price) and lumpy (not any size of swap contract can be traded, only discrete sizes). Both of these will prevent exact hedging, which is likely to create a bid-ask spread around the arbitrage price. Furthermore, the swap price process may not be entirely realistic. We now investigate the possibility that the market is imbalanced in one direction.

The simplest way to add an imbalance in the swap market is to imagine a constant level of imbalance in supply and demand, and assume that this leads to a linear drift in the swap price. This gives a swap price for which equation (11.43) is replaced by

$$S = e^{r(t-T)}(\mu - \lambda(T - t)) \qquad (11.63)$$

with a stochastic differential equation (SDE) for the price process

$$dS = rSdt + \sigma_s dW + \lambda_s dt \qquad (11.64)$$

where $\lambda_s = e^{r(t-T)}\lambda$.

The discounted swap price is then

$$S_d = e^{r(t_0 - t)}S \qquad (11.65)$$

with a price process

$$dS_d = \lambda e^{r(t_0 - T)}dt + e^{r(t_0 - T)}\sigma dW \qquad (11.66)$$
$$= \lambda_d dt + \sigma_d dW$$

where $\lambda_d = \lambda e^{r(t_0 - T)}$.

We can calculate the value of λ by comparing the current swap price with the expected index μ:

$$\lambda = \frac{\mu - e^{r(T-t)}S}{T - t} \tag{11.67}$$

11.4.6 Option pricing in the linear imbalance model

Under this more general model we do have to consider changes of measure to price options, since the discounted swap price is no longer a martingale but has a drift of λ_d. This justifies the following algorithm for calculating the arbitrage price:

- integrate $dS_d = \sigma_d dW$ to get the risk-neutral distribution of outcomes for the swap price; this is *not* the actual distribution of outcomes for the swap price, since we have set the drift to zero;
- calculate the discounted expected pay-off of the option under this risk-neutral distribution; this is the arbitrage price but not the real expected pay-off of the option.

In practice this method becomes:

- take the current swap strike (which we are *not* assuming is the expected index);
- calculate the discounted expected pay-off of the option using this swap strike; this is the arbitrage price, but now is *not* the expected pay-off of the option.

To illustrate this, imagine a case where the market imbalance has driven the swap price below the discounted expected pay-off. The swap price must drift up (on average) to reach the final pay-off distribution. Thus buying swaps will now make money on average. If we are hedging a short call option we have to buy swaps. Since these swaps make money on average, the arbitrage price of the option is lower than the expected pay-off of the option. This is effectively the same argument as was given in section 5.13.1, except that now we are hedging continuously rather than just once, and the mathematics is exact and doesn't involve an approximation.

11.4.7 The stochastic imbalance model

In the linear imbalance model for swap prices we allowed for a constant level of imbalance in supply and demand, leading to a price with a linear drift relative to the discounted expected pay-off of the swap. A more realistic model for the swap price process would allow for stochastic fluctuations of this imbalance. A simple version of this would be

$$S = e^{r(t-T)}\mu - \phi(t)W_2 \tag{11.68}$$

where W_2 is a new Brownian motion and ϕ is a deterministic function that tends to zero as $t \to T$, an example of which would be $\phi(t) = \lambda(T - t)$ for some constant λ.

Another plausible model for ϕ is that it should be proportional to the uncertainty in the estimate of the expected index, which decreases as $\sqrt{t}$. This would give $\phi(t) = \lambda(T - t)^{\frac{1}{2}}$.

The justification for this model for the supply/demand fluctuations is that the swap price can never move too far from the discounted expected pay-off. If it did, then this would offer an investment opportunity with low risk and high return. This creates bands around the discounted expected pay-off within which the price must lie. These bands get narrower as expiry approaches. In particular, at time T market supply and demand effects disappear and the distribution of swap prices is affected only by the weather.

This argument is an insurance version of the ideas about arbitrage. Rather than fixing an exact price, this arbitrage argument fixes a range of prices. The reason we can apply such an argument (which could not be applied so readily to equities, for instance) is that weather swaps are fundamentally tied to a distribution of pay-offs that is unaffected by market sentiment.

Equation (11.68) now contains two sources of randomness: the randomness in the expected pay-off due to weather and weather forecasts (W) and the randomness in the price due to random fluctuations in supply and demand (W_2).

Because of these two sources of randomness it is no longer possible to hedge the risk completely using just one hedging instrument (the swap contract), and the prices are no longer unique.

11.4.8 Stochastic volatility issues

Up until now we have assumed that the volatility in equation (11.42) is deterministic and can be determined from past forecasts by assessing the statistics of forecast errors. This is not entirely true. As discussed in chapter 9, the predictability of the atmosphere does depend, to a small extent, on the state of the atmosphere itself. On some days it may be possible to make better forecasts than others. Thus the volatility is partly dependent on the state of the atmosphere. This dependence is partly predictable, using forecasts of prediction error from ensemble forecasts based on numerical models that were discussed in chapter 9. However, these forecasts are not entirely accurate, and there remains an error in the prediction of forecast error. This term could be represented as a stochastic volatility term.

The presence of stochastic volatility disrupts the neat derivations of arbitrage price given above in the balanced and linear imbalance cases and creates a source of risk that cannot be hedged away with only one asset. Again, prices are no longer unique. In some financial markets this is a large effect: in foreign exchange, for instance, volatility varies a huge amount. However, it would seem to be such a small effect in weather that it is probably reasonable to ignore it.

11.4.9 Volatility and risk loading

Options traders in the weather market who have a background in more liquid options markets may choose to derive implied standard deviations of indices from observed options prices. However, these prices may have been initially created by a trader adding a risk loading onto the fair price. This raises the question as to whether there is any simple relation between implied volatility and risk loading. This question has been investigated in detail in Jewson (2003o) for a simple standard-deviation-based risk loading model. The conclusions from that study are as follows:

1. If one is considering uncapped options of a single type and position then varying the standard deviation of the underlying is *roughly* equivalent to adding a risk loading to the option price. Thus if one derives an implied volatility from an uncapped long call option and uses it to price another uncapped long call option one will be applying roughly the same risk loading to the second contract as was applied to the first. The exact relationship between the standard deviation and risk loading for this case is shown in figure 11.1, with different lines for different

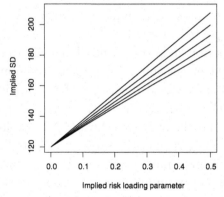

Figure 11.1. The relationship between the standard deviation of the settlement index and the risk loading.

option strikes. This relationship could be considered as a justification for using implied volatilities even in an illiquid market such as the weather market.

2. This rough equivalence breaks down, however, when capped options are considered, and also does not work if one uses the implied volatility from one type of contract to price another type of contract.

Extensions to the standard theory for the weather case

The discussion up until now has focused on the rather unrealistic world in which the weather swap is traded continuously, with infinite liquidity, no transactions costs and in any amount. We have also assumed that swaps are linear, while in practice they may be capped.

The question that really needs to be answered is: given the nature of the real weather market, with only finite sizes for swaps contracts and significant transaction costs and feedback effects, is it worth hedging at all with swaps? If so, how many hedges should be made, of what size, and when? And, finally, what price should we charge for options in the knowledge that we are going to do some hedging?

Many of the studies mentioned in section 11.3 could be converted to the weather case for the balanced market model and the linear imbalance model, and this would go some way towards answering these questions.

One particular example of addressing the question of incomplete market effects in the context of the balanced market model is given by Jewson, 2003t. The study in this paper considered the possibility of hedging a weather option with a linear weather swap on the same location in the presence of transaction costs, and asked how many hedges needed to be done to maximise the value of the trading strategy in a mean-standard deviation risk/return framework. Transaction costs were modelled as being proportional to the size of the trades. Some of the results are shown in figure 11.2. As the number of hedging transactions is increased the cost of the hedging increases and the expected profit decreases, as shown in the first panel of the figure. The reduction in profit is not linear in the number of hedges made because the hedges get smaller and smaller the more that are made. At the same time, the standard deviation of the profits from the hedged portfolio decreases; this is the point of the hedging (panel 2). Combining the expected return and the standard deviation of profit into a measure of risk-adjusted return, there is an optimum (risk-adjusted-return-maximising) hedging strategy for a finite number of hedges, as shown in panel 3. Panels 4 and 6 show how the optimum number of hedges varies with the size of the transaction costs and the level of risk aversion. The higher the transaction costs the fewer the hedges that should be made, and the greater the level

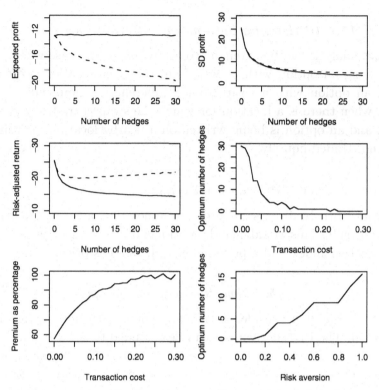

Figure 11.2. All panels relate to the modelling of the effects of transaction costs as discussed in the text. The first panel shows the variation of the expected profit versus the number of hedging transactions with no transaction costs (solid line) and transaction costs (dashed line). The second panel shows the variation of the standard deviation of the profit, again versus the number of hedging transactions with no transaction costs (solid line) and transaction costs (dashed line). The third panel shows the variation of the risk-adjusted return of the profit versus the number of hedging transactions with no transaction costs (solid line) and transaction costs (dashed line). The fourth panel shows the optimum number of hedging transactions against the cost of hedging. The fifth shows the minimum premium to be charged when selling an option such that the RAR does not decrease, and the sixth panel shows the optimum number of hedging transactions against the risk aversion parameter.

of risk aversion the more should be made – as one would expect. Panel 5 shows the premium that should be charged so that the risk-adjusted return does not decrease, as a function of transaction costs. When transaction costs are small, the hedging reduces the premium that can be charged by over 40 per cent relative to the case with no hedging. This is an example of the possible beneficial effects of secondary market trading, as were discussed in chapter 1.

11.4.10 Hedging options on different locations

The above analysis can be extended to the more general case where, rather than hedging an option with a swap from the same location, we consider hedging an option with a swap from a different location. This arises in practice when there is a location for which the swap is traded particularly liquidly, and an option is being written on a nearby location for which the swap is not traded liquidly.

11.5 Pricing dual-trigger contracts

We will now briefly discuss some of the issues that arise in pricing dual-trigger contracts. This would include contracts based on two weather indices, or on a weather index and a price index such as a gas price.

11.5.1 Two liquid underlyings

The first case we will consider is the case where both underlyings are liquidly traded. The PDE derivations can be extended to cover two underlying contracts, and the measure theory arguments can also be extended by using a two-dimensional version of the martingale representation theorem. The price of options can then be calculated either as the solution of the differential equation, or as the discounted expectation in a measure in which both underlying processes are martingales.

11.5.2 One liquid, one illiquid underlying

In the case of one liquid and one illiquid underlying the approach to hedging is to hedge using the liquid contract as well as possible. This will, however, leave significant residual risk because of the dependence of the pay-out on the illiquid underlying. This risk cannot be hedged away; the price to be charged for the option should include a risk loading to cover this.

11.5.3 Two illiquid underlyings

Finally, in the case of two illiquid underlyings no hedging is possible and pure actuarial pricing should be used; the price should be the expected pay-off plus risk loading for the entire risk, none of which is hedged.

11.6 Further reading

For those who like differential equations, any of Wilmott's books, such as Wilmott et al. (1995) or Wilmott (1999), give a good introduction to the mathematics of arbitrage theory. For those who prefer a martingale-based approach, the book by Baxter and Rennie (1996) is better. Other textbooks on the subject include those by Hull (2002) and Björk (1998). A standard book on the mathematics of stochastic processes is the one by Gardiner (1985).

The details of the adaptation of the standard theory to the weather case are taken from a number of our own articles, including Jewson and Zervos (2003b), Jewson (2003t) and Jewson (2002a).

The only article we have been able to find on the question of how to price dual-trigger weather/commodity contracts is that by Carmona and Villani (2003).

12

Risk management

This chapter discusses various aspects of risk management for companies that deal with weather derivatives. The simplest aspect of risk management is estimating the value of currently held positions. This is known as either marking to model or marking to market, depending on how 'value' is defined. Mark to model involves calculating expected pay-offs while mark to market looks at the current market value of the contracts held. Having evaluated current positions it is often desirable to understand the risk that these positions could pay out less than the expected pay-offs, or that the expected pay-off could deteriorate with time. We will call these two risks 'expiry risk' and 'actuarial value at risk' respectively. It can also be useful to understand how much we could lose if we are forced to liquidate our positions as soon as possible. We will call this the 'liquidation value at risk', which will often be different from the actuarial value at risk. Finally, one may wish to evaluate risk by counterparty (counterparty credit risk) or the risk of a temporary cashflow shortage (liquidity risk).

Before we describe how these values can be estimated for weather portfolios we will look briefly at how similar quantities are estimated for portfolios of more traditional financial products such as equities. Many of the ideas used in the analysis of equities have been adapted for use in the weather market. We will also see, however, that because of certain peculiarities of the weather market various other considerations also have to be taken into account.

12.1 Risk management in liquid markets

In a liquid equity market the value of current equity holdings can be estimated simply by using current market quotes. Bids and offers are often so close that there is little point in distinguishing between them, but if there is a spread then one can use bids to value long positions and offers to value short positions. Market value at risk is then defined as one of the lower quantiles of the distribution of possible changes of the current value over a specified time period, where the time period is often fixed by the length of time it would take to liquidate the portfolio. This VaR can be calculated using a model for the fluctuations in the equity price, where the model is fitted using past data for such price fluctuations. This data is generally available in abundance, and except for very large positions one can reasonably assume that equity price is not affected by the liquidation trades that one would be making.

Calculating VaR for a portfolio of equities is thus reasonably straightforward. The main issue that arises is that the system being modelled is non-stationary and the future doesn't always behave like the past.

The methods used to calculate equity VaR cannot be converted immediately to weather for a number of reasons.

1. Many weather contracts are not traded at all and so there are no market quotes.
2. Even the most liquidly traded weather contracts are traded only rather thinly and market prices can be moved by trading very easily. Thus market quotes are not necessarily very useful even when they do exist, and building models of likely price movements based purely on past data is not necessarily very helpful.
3. The value in weather contracts is often related to the level at which they are likely to expire, rather than the level of a market.
4. Liquidation of positions may be practically impossible, or may require the payment of a very high risk premium, and may take a long time (days or weeks).

The problem with non-stationarity that arises for equities is less important in weather because weather data can more reasonably be assumed to be stationary, except for the problems to do with station changes and trends that we have described in chapter 2.

We now look at the weather case in more detail.

12.2 Marking positions

The value of a portfolio of weather derivatives gradually changes as new weather data, new weather and seasonal forecasts and new market data become available. An organisation that is holding a large portfolio of weather derivatives of different types is likely to want to calculate the value of that portfolio on a regular basis. This could be as often as several times as day, or as infrequently as once a season. There are various methods by which such calculations can be made, and the differences between them mostly hinge on different definitions of 'value'. We will distinguish between two such definitions, which we call 'expected expiry value' and 'expected liquidation value'.

We believe that it is extremely important to distinguish between these two and, if necessary, to produce both values on a daily basis. The differences between the two may or may not be large, depending on the types of contracts being held and the state of the market. It is often the case that the first value is of most interest to traders, who are primarily interested in how much money they will make or lose at the end of the season, while the second is of most interest to risk managers, who are primarily interested in worst-case scenarios and how much the company could lose.

12.2.1 Expected expiry value

Our first concept of value is the answer to the question 'given all the information we currently possess, what is the expectation of the value of our portfolio of contracts at expiry?'

This question can be answered using the valuation methods described in the earlier chapters of this book. For each contract we choose a valuation method that we believe is appropriate, including using the latest weather and seasonal forecasts. We calculate the distribution of possible outcomes, and the mean of this distribution is the expected expiry value. For instance, for a single contract, long before the start date, we could use any of burn analysis, index modelling or daily modelling, the relative merits of which we have discussed in some detail in chapters 3 to 6. For a portfolio of contracts we could use burn, index modelling or daily modelling, or a combination of these methods using the general aggregation method, all as described in chapter 7.[1] As we approach the start of the first contract in the portfolio then we would need to start using weather forecasts, and, for certain parts of the world, seasonal forecasts, as described in chapters 9 and 10. As a forecast of future out-turns the expected pay-off can be said to be the best forecast because it minimises the root mean square error.

One wrinkle in the definition of value as expected expiry value is that some of the contracts in a portfolio may have been traded on the assumption

---

[1] Although to calculate *only* the expected expiry value the portfolio methods of chapter 7 are not strictly necessary, since the expected expiry value of a portfolio is just the sum of the expected expiry values for the different contracts in the portfolio. However, we usually want to calculate risk measures for the portfolio as well (see section 12.3), for which modelling the correlation is essential.

that they will be hedged on the way through the contract, as described in chapter 11, and expected expiry value ignores this. As an extension one can thus consider expected expiry value with the likely cost of anticipated hedging and the likely outcomes of the hedges included.

As with all estimates, it would be useful to accompany the expected expiry value with an estimate of the likely error. There are two ways that this can be done. The first is to estimate the likely size of differences between our estimate of expected expiry value and the actual expected expiry value that we would calculate if we had an infinite amount of historical data and perfect models. The sampling error component of this can be estimated using the methods given in chapter 3, and the model error component can be estimated by trying a number of different plausible modelling assumptions. This latter would typically involve varying the numbers of years of historical data used, the trends, the distributions, the sources of forecasts, the methods for incorporating forecasts and the method for aggregating the portfolio.

The second method for estimating the error on the expected expiry value is to estimate the likely range of actual outcomes for the portfolio. This is the subject of expiry risk, discussed in section 12.3. One might also want to know how rapidly the expected expiry value is likely to change: this is the subject of actuarial value at risk, discussed in section 12.4.

The use of market data

Calculating expected expiry value is fundamentally an actuarial question, and the expiry value of weather contracts is affected only by the weather and not by market dynamics. However, there are occasionally situations in which market data can also be used in the calculation. For instance, if we believe that the current market price for a swap contract is a better estimate of the expected index than our models, we can use that market price in the valuation of swaps and options in place of our model estimate. If we believe that both market and model values contain useful information, then we can combine them in a weighted average, with the weights adjusted to reflect our confidence in each. Also, if we believe that market premiums for options are a better indicator of the expected pay-off of an option than our model then we can use these instead of, or in combination with, our model values. Finally, if we believe that market premiums for options are close to the expected pay-off then we can use them to derive implied values for the index standard deviation, which we might then use instead of our modelled standard deviation, and use to price other options on the same index.

We do, however, urge caution in the use of market values in this way. There have been clear examples in the history of the weather market where the market swap price has moved significantly away from the expected settlement index because of imbalances in supply and demand (we described such a case in chapter 5). In these cases, using market values to estimate the expected index would have been very misleading. Similarly, the market prices for options can often be very far from reasonable estimates of the expected pay-off, presumably because of risk loading.

12.2.2 Expected liquidation value

Our second definition of value is the answer to the question 'given all the information we currently possess, what is the expectation of the range of values at which we would be able to liquidate our current holdings?' The expected expiry value described in the previous section can be taken as a first estimate of the expected liquidation value. However, there are also a number of other issues that must be taken into account, and these are discussed below, first for traded contracts and then for non-traded contracts.

The liquidation value of traded contracts

If some of the contracts in our portfolio are being traded then it may be possible to liquidate these contracts in the trading market. A small contract can probably by liquidated at the market prices; a long position should be valued at the bid and a short position at the offer, just as with equities.

For larger positions it is likely that trading would move the market itself. In this case one should add a loading to the current market price to represent such slippage. Exactly how much trading of a position is likely to move the market, and hence how much loading to add, is, however, very difficult to estimate; the estimate can be made only on the basis of experience of the market.

The liquidation value of non-traded contracts

For non-traded contracts no one in the market is likely to want to buy contracts at fair value. In doing so they would be taking on risk, but with no return. In very unusual circumstances it may be that we can sell some of our contracts to other hedgers or speculators as hedges for their current positions, but this would certainly not be the normal situation. More usually one would have to pay a premium on top of fair value to persuade other counterparties to take on the risk of our positions. It is very hard to estimate what this premium is likely to be. Furthermore, if a large portfolio is broken up into small pieces and sold to a number of counterparties, at once the total premium is likely to be larger because much of the diversification of the portfolio will be lost. For the largest market players total liquidation may be effectively impossible, and there may be no choice but to hold at least some contracts to expiry. Another issue that affects the possibility of liquidation is the extent to which contracts are based on standard locations and reliable data sets. For instance, a precipitation contract based on synoptic data from a small town in South Korea would be harder to liquidate than a temperature contract based on London or New York.

It always takes time to liquidate contracts, and during this time both the expected pay-off and the market value of contracts can change. This means that possible future liquidation values are best understood as a distribution rather than as a single number. This is investigated in section 12.5, where we discuss liquidation VaR.

12.3 Expiry risk

In section 12.2.1 we discussed calculating our best estimate of the expiry value of a portfolio of contracts. This number is of limited use on its own without some indication of the possible error in the estimate, and one way to quantify this is to give some indication of the likely range of possible values at expiry. We term this the 'expiry risk' or 'expiry distribution'. Methods for calculating the expiry distribution, using the latest data and forecasts, have been described throughout this book.

Rather than presenting the whole of the expiry distribution, it may be preferable to present a few summary numbers. These could include:

- the expected pay-off;
- the median pay-off, which will be close to the expected pay-off unless the pay-off distribution is skewed;
- the probability of making a loss;
- the x per cent quantile of the distribution (sometimes called the x per cent expiry VaR); this is most likely to be a loss quantile near the tail – the 5 per cent or 1 per cent quantile, for instance;
- the probability of exceeding a pre-specified loss (e.g. the probability of losing $10 million or more);
- the x per cent tail VaR, defined as the expected loss conditional on exceeding the x per cent quantile (i.e. given that the losses are in the worst x per cent, what is the expected loss?); this quantity is also called the 'mean excess VaR';

- the \$x expected shortfall, defined as the expected loss conditional on a loss exceeding \$x (i.e. given that the losses are worse than \$x, what is the expected loss?).

All of these quantities can be accompanied by error bars. These can be calculated in a number of ways, such as:

- using the linear error propagation theory of section 3.1.7;
- using simulations;
- using an ad hoc selection of different models.

The first two of these methods estimate the uncertainty associated with having only a finite number of years of historical data to work with, but do not estimate the uncertainty associated with the choice of one model rather than another. The third of these methods estimates the uncertainty associated with the choice of model, but does not estimate the uncertainty associated with having only a finite number of years of historical data to work with. Ideally, we would combine both these sources of uncertainty.

As an example of expiry VaR, figure 12.1 (reproduced from Jewson, 2003k) shows eight realisations of the development of the expected pay-off for a monthly call option contract, with the 10 per cent and 90 per cent quantiles from the conditional distribution of pay-offs shown at each point in time (these results are from the same simulations described in section 5.4). We see that in some cases (2, 3, 6 and 8) the option is out of the money before

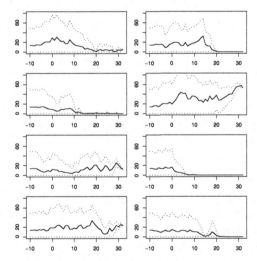

Figure 12.1. Eight simulations of possible outcomes for the expected pay-off and the 10 per cent and 90 per cent quantiles of the pay-off distribution for a single call option contract (see section 5.4).

the end of the contract and the distribution width collapses to zero. In the other cases there is still some uncertainty about the distribution of possible pay-offs right to the end of the contract.

12.4 Actuarial value at risk

As well as calculating expected expiry value and the expiry distribution it can also be useful to understand how the expected expiry value might change over short time periods. In particular, it can be useful to understand whether the expected expiry value might drop rapidly and by how much. We call these changes in the expected expiry value (and in particular the lower quantiles of the distribution of these changes) the 'actuarial VaR'. Another name would be the 'actuarial horizon VaR', which emphasises the necessity for a specific time horizon, in contrast to the expiry VaR, which has a time horizon given by the end of the last contract.

We will discuss four different models for calculating actuarial VaR, ranging from extremely complex to extremely simple.

The temperature-based approach

In this model for actuarial VaR we consider the value of a portfolio today to depend on the most recent historical data, the most recent weather forecasts, and estimates of the distribution of outcomes for the remainder of contracts beyond the end of the post-forecast period. Changes in the value between today and tomorrow, or today and next week, then depend on new recent historical data, new forecasts, and changes in our estimates of the post-forecast distribution. To calculate the distribution of changes in value, we could thus attempt to model these three change terms. This, it turns out, is extremely difficult to do directly. Such a model would have to take into account:

- the autocorrelations in changes in forecasts for each location;
- the cross-correlations in changes in forecasts between locations;
- the autocorrelations and cross-correlations between changes in forecasts and recent historical data.

Even modelling such effects for a single station is already much more difficult than the type of statistical modelling that we considered for daily temperatures in chapter 6, because it involves modelling both temperature and forecasts, not just temperature. Modelling changes in forecasts, in particular, is difficult because records of past forecasts are typically short and non-stationary, due to changes in the forecast models. Because of these complexities it is necessary to consider various ways that we can make approximations and simplify this problem.

The index-based approach

Rather than considering daily temperatures we can consider that the value of our portfolio today depends on updated estimates of the expectation and standard deviation of the indices for our weather contracts. We have described and tested this approach to calculating actuarial VaR in a series of articles (Jewson, 2003k, and Jewson, 2003l). It is much simpler than trying to model daily temperatures and forecasts, because:

- our current estimate of the expected index already includes both historical temperatures and forecasts;
- the dynamics of the expected index are *much* simpler than the dynamics of temperature; changes in temperature are highly autocorrelated, while changes in the expected index can be considered to be totally uncorrelated, as discussed in chapter 10.

An approach to calculating actuarial VaR based on the dynamics of the expected index thus consists of:

- choosing models for the dynamics of the mean and standard deviation of the index, such as the trapezium models described in chapter 10;
- integrating a multivariate Brownian motion for the expectations of all the indices underlying the portfolio; the variances of the individual processes, and the covariances between them, are fixed by the model;
- integrating a deterministic model for the standard deviation of each index;
- converting the resulting distributions of the future values of the expected index, and the deterministic future values of the standard deviations, into a distribution of expected pay-offs.

The limitations to and assumptions behind this approach are:

- since we are dealing with indices in terms of expectation and standard deviation this approach works well only for index distributions that can be characterised by their expectation and standard deviation;
- this model assumes that index volatility is deterministic, which, as we have previously discussed, is not entirely correct;
- the guts of this model lies in the models used for the volatility of the expected index; if these models are realistic, then the model will give good results – otherwise not.

We now give two examples of this approach. The first is taken from Jewson, 2003k, and shows eight realisations of the relative 5 per cent actuarial VaR

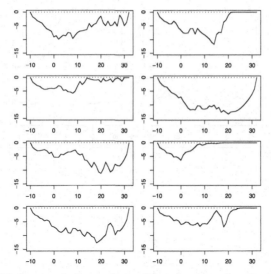

Figure 12.2. Eight simulations of possible outcomes for the 5 per cent relative actuarial VaR for a single call option.

versus time for a single call option. The simulations are the same as those described in section 5.4. In those cases where the call option ends up out of the money before the end of the contract the actuarial VaR is very small. In case 4, where the option ends up extremely in the money, the actuarial VaR is very large right to the end. For the last ten days of this realisation the option is far enough in the money that it is is behaving more or less like a swap contract.

The second example (taken from Jewson, 2003l) considers a portfolio of two contracts: a long call option on London Heathrow and a short call option on Paris. Figure 12.3 shows the expected pay-off and actuarial VaR results from eight simulations of this portfolio. We see that both the expected pay-off and the VaR fluctuate considerably during the contract in several of the examples.

In example 1 both indices settle out of the money. From around the twentieth day they are so far out of the money that the deltas are both zero. From this point on there is no range of possible future pay-offs, and the relative VaR is zero.

In example 3 both contracts end in the money. For the last ten days or so they are so far in the money that the deltas are near to one and they have effectively become linear contracts. As a result, changes in the pay-offs are highly anticorrelated and the relative VaR is very small, because if one contract goes up the other contract will probably go down. A similar situation is seen at the end of example 8.

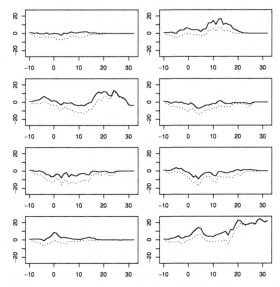

Figure 12.3. Eight simulations of possible outcomes for the expected pay-off and the actuarial VaR of a portfolio of two contracts.

The greeks-based approach

We can simplify the index-based approach still further by considering only *small* changes in the expectation and standard deviation of the index. We can then linearise the changes in the portfolio pay-offs in terms of changes in the expectation and the standard deviation. This has been discussed for single contracts in section 5.1, where we saw that if we write

$$\mu_p = \mu_p(\mu_x, \sigma_x) \tag{12.1}$$

then the total derivative is given by

$$d\mu_p = \frac{\partial \mu_p}{\partial \mu_x} d\mu_x \tag{12.2}$$
$$= \Delta d\mu_x$$

We can now reinterpret this equation so that μ_p is the pay-off of the whole portfolio. Δ is then a vector of derivatives of μ_p with respect to each index. If the distributions of the random changes $d\mu_x$ are normal then the distribution of random changes $d\mu_p$ is also normal, and we can derive the VaR as a quantile of this normal distribution.

The main limitation of this method is that it is valid only for small changes in the expected index, which limits it to calculating actuarial VaR over short time horizons. Over longer time horizons equation (12.2) is not a good approximation of the change in the portfolio pay-off.

The whole-portfolio-based approach

Finally, we present an extremely simple approach for estimating portfolio actuarial VaR that relies on a number of rather strong assumptions. If we have a large portfolio of contracts of many different types, spread out in time roughly equally, and with the portfolio pay-off distribution close to normal, then we would expect the value of the portfolio to change from day to day roughly as a Brownian motion with constant volatility. But we know the distribution of final values of the portfolio from our calculations of the expiry distribution. Thus we can calculate the daily portfolio volatility required to achieve that distribution of final values simply by scaling the final portfolio variance appropriately.

12.5 Liquidation value at risk

We saw in section 12.2.2 that liquidation value cannot really be considered without taking into account the time over which liquidation can be achieved and how much modelled and market values might change over that time period. We will call the distribution of possible liquidation values, and in particular the lower quantiles of this distribution, the 'liquidation VaR'.

Modelling the liquidation VaR involves extending the calculations of expected liquidation value to allow for fluctuations in the values of all quantities during the time it takes to liquidate positions. These fluctuations lead to a distribution of the estimates of the liquidation value. Estimating the change in the actuarial parts of the valuation can be carried out using the methods described above for actuarial VaR. The biggest difficulty comes when we try and estimate the liquidation VaR for liquidly traded contracts, because the market may move more than the change in the pure actuarial value.

In a very simple model the pure market term can be modelled as a multivariate Brownian motion multiplied by a scaling factor, as we have already described for one contract in the stochastic imbalance model in section 11.4.7. The scaling factor ensures that the market-driven variability disappears as we approach settlement. The difficulty of modelling the pure market process then boils down to how we specify the volatility and covariance matrix of the Brownian motion.

What is the volatility of the market prices likely to be many months before the start of a contract? There seem to be two (competing) arguments. The first argument is that many months before the start of a contract there is typically very little trading of that contract, and so there is very little trading-induced volatility; the volatility of market prices is thus very low. It then increases as we approach the contract, and decreases again towards the end of the contract. The second argument is that many months before the start of the contract there is a great amount of uncertainty about how to calculate prices for that contract. As a result, different market participants will calculate very different prices, and market prices are likely to move in a very volatile fashion as different traders influence the market. Volatility thus starts at a very high level and decreases as we approach the contract.

Without extensive market data it is very difficult to distinguish between these two scenarios. For this reason, the only model that we feel confident in suggesting for pre-contract market volatility is one in which the volatility level is constant. This market-driven volatility can then be combined with our actuarial estimates of volatility, and the whole model used to derive a very approximate estimate of the liquidation VaR.

12.6 Credit risk

So far we have discussed modelling the effects of weather risk and market risk on weather portfolios. We will now briefly consider the question of modelling credit risk. Credit risk is that risk that one of your counterparties will go bankrupt while they still owe you some money, and that you will not be able to claim very much of what they owe. Credit risk is often divided into the probability of counterparty default and the distribution of possible sizes of loss given default. The probability of default can be estimated in a number of ways, but often the simplest is to convert a credit rating into the probability of default using standard tables. The distribution of possible sizes of loss given default is much more complicated. First, one must estimate the total exposure to each counterparty. This is relatively straightforward: the simulations of the contract pay-offs from the portfolio simulation methods described in chapter 7 simply need to be aggregated on a counterparty-by-counterparty basis. Second, one should estimate the likely percentage of the exposure that would be recovered. This is much more difficult and depends on the particular situation of each counterparty. A conservative approach is to assume 100 per cent loss.

There are also some extensions to the above credit risk analysis that one can consider, such as an analysis of likely future credit risks versus time.

12.7 Liquidity risk

Liquidity risk is the risk that at some point in the future you may suffer a temporary cashflow shortage. This can happen because of an unlikely conjunction of payments that have to be made even if your current mark to model or mark to market position is good. As with credit risk, one can model liquidity risk by appropriate aggregation of the simulations from the portfolio simulation methods we have discussed in chapter 7, in conjunction with the timings of the payments related to each contract.

12.8 Summary

We have attempted to describe a mathematical framework within which one can understand risk management for weather derivatives, and we have been very careful with our terminology to try and avoid much of the confusion that surrounds this subject. In addition to the issues discussed above, there are also a number of practical and regulatory issues that affect what is actually calculated by each institution. Trading strategy also influences the importance of the various numbers: for a passive (buy and hold) trading strategy only expiry values are important, whereas for an active trading strategy only market values are relevant. We also note that for a truly conservative view of all risk management numbers one should try a number of models, and select the worst results. This can, however, be a rather sobering experience.

12.9 Further reading

There are many books on general financial risk management, such as Dowd (1998).

Articles that focus on risk management for the weather market include Vandermarck (2003), Banks and Henderson (2002) and McIntyre (2000). The VaR models discussed in this chapter come from a number of our own articles. Jewson (2002b), Jewson (2003p), Jewson (2003k) and Jewson (2003l).

13

Modelling non-temperature data

In chapters 2 to 12 we have considered how to model and price weather derivatives that depend on temperature as the underlying variable. Such contracts are by far the most common, accounting for about 85 per cent of all contracts traded in 2002 according to the WRMA.[1] However, a number of other weather variables are used too. These include precipitation, snow depth, snow fall, river flow and wind. Of these, the most commonly seen are precipitation and wind, and we focus on these two variables in this chapter. Contracts based on these variables can be priced using the same basic methods as used for temperature-based contracts (burn analysis, index modelling and daily modelling), and as with temperature one may wish to detrend the data before applying any of these methods. Burn analysis works in exactly the same way as for temperature; index modelling may involve using new index distributions to cope with the different distribution shapes that arise; daily modelling may involve new kinds of time series models.

The purpose of this chapter is not to discuss precipitation and wind modelling in the same kind of detail as we have for temperature. Rather, we provide a brief overview of some of the modelling techniques available. In each case we first discuss the most common index types and show some examples of their index distributions. We then look at models for higher-frequency variables.

13.1 Precipitation

Figure 13.1 shows the daily precipitation at Chicago O'Hare from 1958 to 2002. The first thing to notice about the plot is that although the average is only 0.1 inches per day (0.3 inches if only rainy days are considered) there

---

[1] In Japan, though, temperature contracts account for only around 50 per cent of all deals.

Table 13.1. *The daily precipitation statistics for Chicago O'Hare, 1958 to 2002, in inches.*

Mean	SD	% zeros	Q50	Q75	Q90	Q95	Q99	Max
0.1	0.3	66	0.0	0.04	0.29	0.58	1.37	6.49

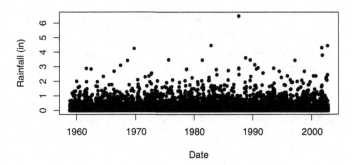

Figure 13.1. Daily precipitation at Chicago O'Hare, 1958 to 2002.

are a significant number of days with precipitation vastly exceeding the daily average. This is also seen in table 13.1, which shows some statistics for the historical distribution of daily precipitation.

The distribution of daily precipitation amounts is very different from that of daily temperatures in that 66 per cent of the observations have the same value (zero). Furthermore, the vast majority of the daily precipitation amounts are less than 1 inch, but the remaining days can have much higher values. The main characteristics of the distribution of daily precipitation are thus skewness and a point mass at zero. We illustrate this in figure 13.2, where we have overlaid the empirical CDF for daily precipitation with the CDFs of normal and gamma distributions, both with mean 0.1 and standard deviation 0.3. Note how the normal CDF has a significant part below zero and increases slowly compared with the observed CDF, while the gamma CDF follows the data remarkably well. The close fit of the gamma distribution is despite the fact that it is a continuous distribution that does not have a point mass at zero.

13.1.1 Precipitation index modelling

Figure 13.3 shows November to March and May to September average indices for the Chicago O'Hare data with a loess trend overlaid. There seems to be a tendency for the smallest November to March indices to increase

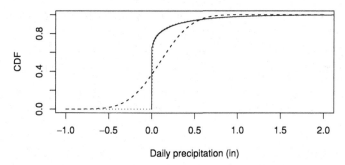

Figure 13.2. The empirical CDF for daily precipitation at Chicago O'Hare, 1958 to 2002. The CDFs of normal (dashed) and gamma (dotted) distributions with the same mean and standard deviation have been overlaid.

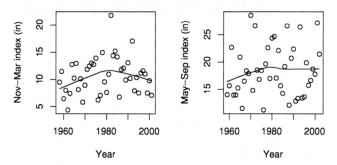

Figure 13.3. Precipitation at Chicago O'Hare, 1958 to 2002, with a loess trend superimposed. Left panel: cumulative precipitation for November to March. Right panel: cumulative precipitation for May to September.

over time but there is no obvious increasing or decreasing trend over the whole time period. For the May to September indices there is also no clear trend. This is in contrast with the temperature data, which shows strong positive trends at almost all locations over the same time period.

We now consider the index distributions of the loess detrended indices. We have seen that daily precipitation values are well modelled by a gamma distribution, but this does not help us guess what might work for the seasonal indices since sums (or averages) of gamma distributed variables do not in general follow any common parametric distribution. We might, however, hope that the central-limit theorem applies sufficiently well for a normal distribution to be a good approximation. Figure 13.4 shows the index CDFs for the winter and summer periods with normal and gamma distributions overlaid. Both distributions seem to fit the data reasonably well but the fit of the gamma distribution is slightly better than that of the normal in this case. Figure 13.5 shows the corresponding QQ plots for the gamma

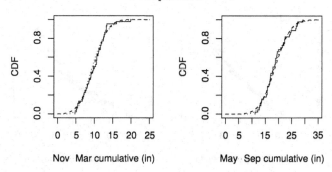

Figure 13.4. The index CDFs for cumulative precipitation at Chicago O'Hare, 1958 to 2002. Left panel: November to March. Right panel: May to September. Moment matched CDFs for normal (dashed) and gamma (dotted) distributions have been overlaid.

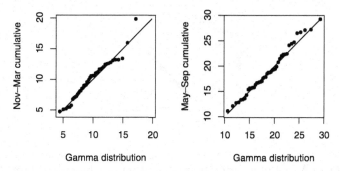

Figure 13.5. The index QQ plots for gamma distributions for cumulative precipitation at Chicago O'Hare, 1958 to 2002. Left panel: November to March. Right panel: May to September.

distribution, which confirms the good fit. If we look at average indices over shorter periods the CLT works even less well. Figure 13.6 shows that the normal distribution gives a significantly worse fit than the gamma for a January contract.

13.1.2 Daily precipitation modelling

Figure 13.2 indicated that the distribution of daily precipitation may be approximated by a gamma distribution (see, e.g., Wilks and Wilby, 1999, for more evidence of this). However, extreme rainfall cannot be modelled accurately with gamma distributions, since the tail of the gamma is too thin (see, e.g., Coles and Pericchi, 2003, Koutsoyiannis, 2003, Wilks, 1993, and Katz, 2001). One example of this is the 6.49 inches that fell at Chicago O'Hare on 14 August 1987, which shows up clearly in both figure 13.1 and in

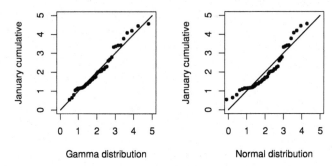

Figure 13.6. The index QQ plots for a gamma (left) and a normal (right) distribution for total January precipitation at Chicago O'Hare, 1958 to 2002.

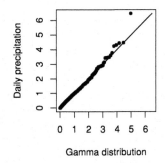

Figure 13.7. A QQ plot for daily precipitation at Chicago O'Hare, 1958 to 2002. The theoretical distribution is a gamma distribution.

the QQ plot for daily precipitation in figure 13.7. Using the estimated gamma distribution the return period for such extreme rainfall is more than 100,000 years. Indices that depend on extreme precipitation distributions other than the gamma may thus need to be considered. Extreme value modelling (see Coles, 2001, Embrechts et al., 1997, Leadbetter et al., 1983) may be a good alternative in such cases.

Traditionally, daily precipitation modelling has followed one of two approaches: single gauge modelling, where the temporal development of rainfall is modelled for a particular location and spatial modelling, where the rainfall footprint at a fixed time is modelled. The two approaches can be extended so that the final results are similar: the spatial approach can be adapted to emulate the results of fronts of rain cells crossing an area, in which case it is possible to simulate rainfall development in time. Likewise, the single gauge approach can be extended to multiple gauges, in which case the result is not unlike that of the spatial approach. We will now review some of the models that have been suggested in the literature for these two approaches.

Time series modelling

Traditional time series models usually assume the distribution of the observed variables to be well approximated by a normal distribution, which we have seen is not the case for precipitation. There are several ways in which such models can be adapted to take care of this problem. One possibility is to transform the observed precipitation in such a way that the usual time series models will work (Allcroft and Glasbey, 2003). The disadvantage of this is that the model fitting is no longer by maximum likelihood. Another option that has been suggested is to model the occurrence of dry and wet periods as a Markov process, and use generalised linear models to model the rainfall intensity of wet periods (Chandler and Wheater, 2002). A similar model has been described by Moreno, 2001a, in the weather derivative context.

Rain cell modelling

One model for rainfall clouds is to represent them as the aggregate effect of many small rain cells, which are themselves taken to represent the smallest structures that can be seen on weather radar images. Rain cells are created, merge, separate and disappear all the time during a rainstorm, and it has been suggested that they could be modelled in a space-time point process framework (LeCam, 1961, Rodriguez-Iturbe et al., 1987, and Rodriguez-Iturbe et al., 1988). In such models the spatial-temporal point process consists of the centres of the rain cells, and each cell is a random shape reflecting the rain intensity from the cell. The footprint of a rainstorm over a period of time is the sum of the intensities of all the rain cells in that period.

13.2 Wind

From a weather market perspective wind is somewhat different from temperature and precipitation since there is less interest in cumulative and average daily values. This is because very few businesses are affected by the average daily wind speed. For example, external construction work and offshore work are typically halted when the peak gusts are large, but not because of the level of the average wind speed. Similarly, wind power generation, which is the main application of wind derivatives, is not very highly correlated with the average wind speed. This is because wind power generated during a day

Table 13.2. *The daily average wind speed statistics*
for Philadelphia International, 1961 to 2003.

Mean	SD	% zeros	Q50	Q75	Q90	Q95	Q99	Max
9.5	3.4	0	8.9	11.3	14.1	19.8	0.0	30.0

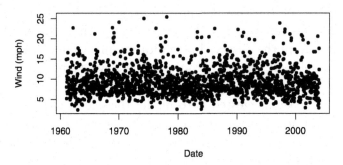

Figure 13.8. The daily average wind speed at Philadelphia International, 1961 to 2003.

is roughly proportional to the daily average of the *cube* of the wind speed.[2] As a result, hourly rather than daily wind measurements are often used. Wind speed modelling is complicated by the fact that wind has a direction and is much more affected by the surrounding terrain, such as buildings and trees, than are precipitation and temperature. This results in wind speed distributions that are much more spatially inhomogeneous than is the case for the other variables. In the following we will show examples of how wind speed modelling can be approached, but because of the spatial inhomogeneity it is very important that distribution assumptions are validated carefully for each location; the 'one size fits all' approach to modelling is even less true for wind than it is for temperature and precipitation.

Although we argue above that daily average wind speeds are not much used in practice for weather derivatives, we will use them as a starting point for our analysis for illustrative purposes. Figure 13.8 shows the daily average wind speed at Philadelphia International Airport from 1961 to 2003. Compared to the precipitation data in figure 13.1 it is noticeable how regular daily average wind speed is in this case, and how few extreme observations are present. This is also seen in table 13.2, which shows some statistics for the historical distribution of daily average wind speed at the same location. We note that this lack of extremes is certainly not a generic feature of wind;

[2] The kinetic energy of a moving particle of mass m and velocity v is $\frac{1}{2}mv^2$, and the mass of the air passing an area A during a time interval t is $A\rho tv$, where ρ is the density of the air. Combining these two facts we see that the energy of air passing an area A during a time interval t is $\frac{1}{2}A\rho tv^3$. Power is energy per time unit, so wind energy power is given by $\frac{1}{2}A\rho v^3$.

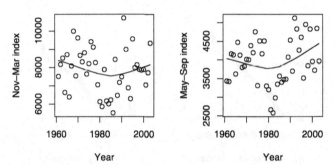

Figure 13.9. The November to March and May to September indices of cumulative cubed hourly wind speeds at Philadelphia International, 1961 to 2003. A loess trend estimate has been imposed.

locations affected by tropical cyclones, for instance, can experience very extreme wind speeds.

13.2.1 Wind index modelling

We will now consider cumulative indices of hourly wind speeds cubed, since these are approximately proportional to potential wind power production. Figure 13.9 shows such indices for the period 1961 to 2003 for Philadelphia International for the summer and winter periods.

The indices are higher in the winter than in the summer by a factor of two. Curiously, the estimated trends both show a clear dip in the early 1980s. It is possible that this dip is the result of a change in the measurement instruments or their surroundings. Such changes are important to detect if a weather derivative is to be traded on these indices, and in principle methods similar to those described in chapter 2 could be used. However, due to the more erratic nature of wind (changing direction and speed) it can be much more difficult to detect such changes than it is for temperature.

Since the indices are sums of many daily variables the normal distribution might seem to be an appropriate choice of distribution for this kind of data. It turns out, however, that normal distributions do not fit the data for this station very well. On the other hand, as we show in figure 13.10, gamma distributions do provide quite a good fit to both the summer and the winter index distributions.

13.2.2 High-frequency wind modelling

We now consider modelling wind at higher frequency than seasonal. We could try and build models for daily average wind, but, as argued above, average daily wind speed is not often used for weather derivatives. Instead,

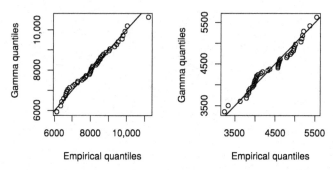

Figure 13.10. QQ plots for daily indices of cumulative cubed hourly wind speeds at Philadelphia International, 1961 to 2003. Left panel: November to March. Right panel: May to September.

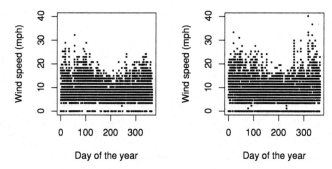

Figure 13.11. Hourly wind speeds for two years of data at Philadelphia International. Left panel: 1961. Right panel: 2003.

we could consider modelling hourly wind speed or peak gusts. One could also use finer-resolution data than hourly, but then storage capacity and data availability could become problematic. Since hourly data is generally the finest resolution that is easily available, we will consider hourly data here.

Figure 13.11 shows hourly wind speeds for two years of data for Philadelphia International – 1961 and 2003. The figures highlight a common problem for wind data, namely that data is often discrete and on a fairly coarse scale. All measurements of all variables are discrete in the sense that there is a limit to the accuracy with which we can measure. However, it is more common for wind than for temperature and precipitation that the measurement scale is very coarse. In this case the wind speed measurements are made in jumps of size 1 mph, and there are almost no measurements between 0 and 3.4 mph.

In the wind modelling literature there is a long tradition for modelling hourly wind speeds using Weibull distributions. There does not seem to be

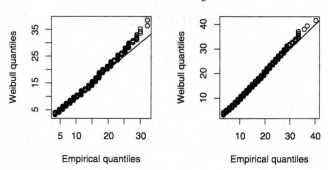

Figure 13.12. QQ plots for hourly wind speeds for two years of data at Philadelphia International. Left panel: 1961. Right panel: 2003.

any theoretical rationale for this, but often this distribution may provide reasonable approximations to the observed data. However, the distribution of wind speeds varies significantly by location and time of year, and may even vary from year to year. For this reason it is most prudent to verify carefully any distributional assumptions. Figure 13.12 shows Weibull QQ plots for data from Philadelphia International Airport for the years 1961 and 2003. The Weibull distribution fits the 2003 data reasonably well but the fit for the 1961 data is less good. There are many possible reasons for this, such as equipment changes, measurement height changes, other station changes and long-term trends.

13.3 Further reading

The business side of hedging precipitation is discussed in Ruck (2002), and some agricultural examples are given in Turvey (2001).

Appendix A
Trend models

A.1 A general theory for trend modelling and the uncertainty of trend estimates

For a large class of trend types (those that are *linear in their covariates*, which is a much more general class than the linear trend considered in chapter 2) there is a useful general theory, which gives trend parameters, the uncertainty in the estimated parameters and the uncertainty in the de-trended index values. The linear theory given in section 2.3 is a special case of this general theory.

The theory applies to all trends for which the estimated trend lines are linear functions of the observed indices. This applies to all the parametric trends described in chapter 2 because the parameter estimates are (approximately) normally distributed, and it applies to loess and moving average trends by construction.

Before exploring this further we first review some results from the statistical theory of linear models, which shows that our parameter estimates are normally distributed.

We will consider linear models of the form

$$X = A\theta + e \tag{A.1}$$

where $X = (X_1, \ldots, X_N)^T$ is the vector of index values and e is a vector of independent and normally distributed random variables with expectation 0 and variance σ^2. The mean vector (trend) of the indices is given by the known $N \times p$-matrix A, called the *design matrix*, and the vector θ of p unknown parameters. The values in the row i of the design matrix A are related to observation X_i and are often called the covariates for X_i.

For instance, the linear trend is of the form (A.1), with $\theta = (a, b)^T$ consisting of the intercept and slope, and the design matrix of the form

$$A = \begin{pmatrix} 1 & t_1 \\ 1 & t_2 \\ \vdots & \vdots \\ 1 & t_N \end{pmatrix} \tag{A.2}$$

The quadratic trend has the same design matrix with an additional column consisting of $(t_1^2, \ldots, t_N^2)^T$, whereas the exponential trend can be approximated by a trend of the form (A.2) if we model the logarithm of X instead of X. We would then have to transform the estimated trend back by the exponential function.

One of the fundamental results of the theory of linear models (Casella and Berger, 2002) is that the least square estimator of θ is given by

$$\hat{\theta} = (A^T A)^{-1} A^T X \sim \Phi\left(\theta, \sigma^2 (A^T A)^{-1}\right) \tag{A.3}$$

The expected index is the trend at time T corresponding to the covariate vector $a_T = (a_{T1}, \ldots, a_{Tp})$ and can be estimated by equation (A.3). The detrended expected index is then given by

$$\hat{X}_T = a_T \hat{\theta} \sim \Phi\left(a_T \theta, \sigma^2 a_T^T (A^T A)^{-1} a_T\right) \tag{A.4}$$

which is a linear function of the estimated parameters, and is hence normally distributed.

For the exponential trend, equation (A.4) gives the estimate and the distribution for the logarithm of the trend. A so-called 'delta theorem' gives us the following approximate expression for the distribution of the exponential trend:

$$\hat{\mu}_T = \exp(\hat{X}_t) \approx \Phi\left(\exp(a_T \theta), \sigma^2 \exp(2 a_T \theta) a_T^T (A^T A)^{-1} a_T\right)$$

Loess and moving average trends are non-parametric and the above theory for linear models does not apply exactly. However, if we assume that the index is approximately normally distributed then the estimated expected index also becomes approximately normally distributed. This is because the estimates of these trends are linear functions of the observed indices.

A.1.1 Monte Carlo methods

Alternatively, the uncertainty around the expected index can be estimated for *any* trend using simulations as follows:

- fit the trend using N years of index data;
- using the fitted trend and a distribution fitted to the residuals, simulate – e.g. – 10,000 periods of N years of artificial data;
- fit trends to each of these periods;
- the 10,000 fitted trends will all be slightly different, over a range; this gives an indication of the range of uncertainty in our original trend estimate, and the range of expected index values derived from the detrending gives an indication of the range of uncertainty in our detrended estimate of the expected index.

Appendix B
Parameter estimation

B.1 Statistical models

A statistical model for a set of observations $x = (x_1, \ldots, x_N)$ is a specification of a probability distribution for x, typically given by a probability density f_θ that depends on a set of parameters θ. If the observations are assumed to be independent then f_θ is given as a product of the densities, f_θ^i, for each observation: $f_\theta(x) = \prod_{i=1}^N f_\theta^i(x_i)$. If the f_θ^i are assumed to be identical, the observations are said to be identically distributed and the expression for the density f_θ simplifies to

$$f_\theta(x) = \prod_{i=1}^N f_\theta(x_i)$$

Non-parametric models are models that do not have any unknown parameters θ. In the following we will describe some methods for the estimation of unknown parameters in parametric models. The methods apply to all parametric models, but for simplicity we concentrate on the estimation of a vector of parameters $\theta \in \mathbb{R}^p$ in models for independent and identically distributed observations.

B.2 Parameter estimation

After having specified a model, the first objective of a statistical analysis is to estimate the parameter vector θ. Numerous methods, both graphical and numerical, have been proposed for this purpose. Often, the basic principles for the numerical methods are based on one of two approaches: the method of moments (MoM) or maximum likelihood (ML).

B.2.1 The method of moments

MoM is probably the most simple principle for parameter estimation. The idea is to calculate theoretical expressions for some moments of the data (such as mean and variance), set these equal to their empirical equivalents and solve the equations. As an example, let us look at the model where all observations are assumed independent and gamma distributed. The parameters of the gamma distribution are the shape parameter λ and the scale parameter β, and so $\theta = (\lambda, \beta)$. The mean and the variance of the distribution are

$$EX = \beta\lambda \quad \text{and} \quad VX = \beta^2\lambda$$

The MoM equations are

$$\hat{\mu} = \beta\lambda \quad \text{and} \quad \hat{\sigma}^2 = \beta^2\lambda$$

These can be solved to give

$$\lambda = \frac{\hat{\mu}^2}{\hat{\sigma}^2} \quad \text{and} \quad \beta = \frac{\hat{\sigma}^2}{\hat{\mu}}$$

The main advantages of MoM are that it is simple and that the moments of the estimated distribution equal those of the observations (for the moments used to estimated the parameters). However, the procedure is ad hoc and the estimated parameters are, in general, not optimal in any useful sense. Furthermore, there are no general expressions for the estimation uncertainty of MoM estimators, so these have to be derived on a case-by-case basis. In many cases, such as our example above, this may not be an easy task, because the parameter estimates are complicated functions of the observations.

B.2.2 Maximum likelihood

ML estimation is, by far, the most popular method for the estimation of parameters in statistical models. The main reasons for this are that for large classes of models it can be shown that *asymptotically* the estimates are

- unbiased;
- optimal, in the sense that they give the minimum possible variance;
- multivariate normally distributed.

The likelihood function L is the density (probability mass function for discrete distributions) of the observations considered as a function of the parameter vector θ with the observations fixed:

$$L_N(\theta; x_1, \ldots, x_N) := f_\theta(x_1, \ldots, x_N)$$

The ML estimates are defined as the value of θ that maximises the likelihood function:

$$\hat{\theta} = \text{Arg Max}_\theta L_N(\theta; x_1, \ldots, x_N)$$

The intuitive argument for estimating parameters this way is that $\hat{\theta}$ is the value of the parameter vector that maximises the probability of the observations within the family f_θ of distributions. However, the main benefit of the ML estimator (MLE), apart from its asymptotic optimality, is the fact that analytical expressions exist for parameter estimation uncertainty. These expressions are still based on asymptotic arguments but they apply generally to an extremely wide range of models.

Under mild regularity conditions on the density f_θ it can be shown that the asymptotic distribution of $\hat{\theta}$ as the number of observations increases is approximately multivariate normal with mean θ (i.e. unbiased) and covariance matrix

$$\Sigma(\theta) = -\text{E}\frac{\partial^2 \log L_N(\theta)}{\partial \theta^2}$$

The quantity $I(\theta) := \Sigma(\theta)^{-1}$ is called the information matrix, and in practice it is estimated by

$$\hat{I}(\theta) = -\frac{1}{N}\frac{\partial^2 \log L(\hat{\theta})}{\partial \theta^2}$$

for identically and independent observations with likelihood function L.

Although the concept of ML estimators may seem fairly abstract, MLEs often coincide with moment estimators and simple common-sense estimators. For example, the MLE of the mean of normal, Poisson and exponential distributions is the average of the observations. An example where the MLE does not coincide with the standard estimator is the variance of the normal distribution. The MLE is $\sum_{i=1}^{N}(x_i - \hat{\mu})^2/N$, but since this is not unbiased (except asymptotically) it is common to use the standard estimator $\sum_{i=1}^{N}(x_i - \hat{\mu})^2/(N-1)$.

Appendix C

Goodness of fit tests

C.1 Goodness of fit tests

In addition to graphical methods one can also perform numerical tests of goodness of fit (GoF). The advantages of such tests are that they are objective (except for chi-square tests – see below) and provide a single number; they can thus be used in automated methods for ranking a number of distributions.

In the following discussion of the most common GoF tests we use the statistical concept of 'power' to describe the efficiency of the test. A GoF test evaluates how likely it is that the observed sample could have been generated from the distribution in question. The power of the test is the proportion of correctly rejected tests. If a test has low power it means that it is bad at rejecting distributions even if the fit is poor. Conversely, a test with high power is good at identifying distributions that do not match the sample. In practice this means that if a distribution fails a test with low power (such as, for example, chi-square or Kolmogorov–Smirnov (KS)) then this is a good indication that the distribution is not appropriate.

C.1.1 The chi-square test

The chi-square test can be used as a GoF test with any distribution, either continuous or discrete. However, if the distribution is continuous it must first be discretised by dividing the sample space into intervals and binning the observations into these intervals. For a discrete distribution the bins are simply the different outcomes in the sample. If we let n_i denote the number of observations in bin i, the chi-square test statistic is calculated as

$$\chi^2 = \sum_{i=1}^{k} \frac{(n_i - e_i)^2}{e_i}$$

Here e_i denotes the expected number of observations in bin i. The distribution of χ^2 is approximately that of a chi-square distribution with $k - p$ degrees of freedom, where p is the number of parameters in the distribution. The approximation is generally good when the expected number of observations e_i in each bin is greater than five. The approximation is generally not good if some of the e_i are less than two. For this reason, it may be necessary to combine bins to achieve a higher expected bin count.

The main drawback of the chi-square test is that it is not very specific and, as such, does not have a lot of power.

C.1.2 The Kolmogorov–Smirnov test

The KS test compares the vertical distance between the theoretical CDF and that of the observations. It is applicable to continuous distributions only and is calculated as

$$D = \max_x |F(x) - \hat{F}(x)| = \max_{x_i} |F(x_{(i)}) - i/N|$$

Here F denotes the theoretical CDF and $x_{(i)}$ denotes the i'th lowest observation. There is an exact asymptotic expression for the distribution of D in the case where all the x_i have distinct values and this distribution does not depend on the CDF F. However, the exact expression holds only if the distribution F is fully specified – i.e. no parameters are estimated. If parameters are estimated the so-called Lilliefors test can be used instead.

Because the KS test measures the maximum vertical distance between the two CDFs it is most likely to detect differences in the middle of the distributions. In the tails the two CDFs are forced to be close to 0 and 1 respectively, so the maximum difference is unlikely to appear in the tails. For this reason, the KS test has relatively little power.

C.1.3 The Anderson–Darling and Cramér–von Mises tests

The main problem with the KS test is that it is most suited for finding differences in the middle of the distributions. Several authors have proposed coping with this problem by using the integral of the difference between the theoretical and the empirical CDFs weighted by some weight function w:

$$Q = \int w(x) \left(F(x) - \hat{F}(x) \right)^2 \, \mathrm{d}x$$

Two special cases are the Cramér–von Mises test ($\frac{1}{w(x)} = n$) (CM) and the

Anderson–Darling test $(\frac{1}{w(x)} = F(x)(1 - F(x)))$ (AD). The AD and CM tests are more powerful than the KS test and can detect differences between the distributions over their entire widths. One drawback of these tests, however, is that the distributions of the test statistic depend on the distribution F, so no general expressions can be given.

C.1.4 The Shapiro–Wilk test

The Shapiro–Wilk (SW) test is a test for normality. Because it explicitly targets deviations from normal distributions it is much more powerful than the general-purpose GoF tests described above. The SW test is calculated as

$$W = \frac{\left(\sum_{i=1}^{N} w_i x_{(i)}\right)^2}{\sum_{i=1}^{N} (x_i - \bar{x})^2}$$

The w_i are constants that can be looked up in tables, such as those in Pearson and Hartley, 1962. The distributions of the test statistic can also be found in standard statistical tables.

C.1.5 Monte Carlo tests

A common feature of all the GoF tests described above is that the distributions of the test statistic are known only approximately and for relatively large samples. One way to overcome this problem is by using so-called Monte Carlo (MC) tests. An MC test is carried out by first calculating the test statistic of interest (for example, χ^2, D or Q) and then simulating samples, of the same length as the observed sample, from the theoretical distribution. For each simulated sample the test statistic can be calculated and the whole set of samples can be used to estimate the distribution of the test statistic. The difference between this approximate distribution and those described for each test above is that the approximations described above are good when the sample size is large, whereas the MC approximation is good when the number of simulations is large. In an MC test we can thus get arbitrarily accurate approximations of the test distribution just by increasing the number of simulations.

MC tests can be useful for a tailor-made GoF test that tests exactly the characteristics of a distribution that are of interest for a particular application. For example, for a weather call option one of the main properties of interest is the LEV function between the strike and the limit. Hence, a possible GoF candidate is

$$\int_S^{S+L} (L(x) - \hat{L}(x))^a \, dx$$

where L and $\hat{L}$ are the theoretical and empirical LEV functions, and a is a constant that can be used to adjust the importance of large deviations relative to small deviations.

Appendix D
Expected pay-offs for normally distributed indices

In this appendix we derive exact expressions for the pay-off distributions and the expected pay-offs of weather derivatives on a normally distributed index. Specific examples of these expressions have been given by a number of authors, such as McIntyre (1999), Jewson (2003t) and Brix et al. (2002). The derivations given below come from Jewson (2003a).

In section D.1 we define an eighth contract type in addition to the seven defined in chapter 1. This new contract type has a general piecewise linear pay-off function. In section D.2 we give the closed-form expressions for the pay-off distributions of each of these types of contracts in terms of the index distribution. In section D.3 we derive various relations that greatly simplify the subsequent algebra, and in section D.4 we derive the expected pay-offs for each of the eight contract types. Finally we give some numerical examples of each expression.

D.1 Pay-off definitions

In addition to the pay-off functions defined in chapter 1 we will also consider the general form, given below.

D.1.1 The general form

$$p(x) = \alpha_i + \beta_i x \qquad \text{if } a_i \leq x < a_{i+1} \qquad \text{(D.1)}$$

where

$$-\infty = a_1 < a_2 \ldots < a_{n-1} < a_n = \infty \qquad \text{(D.2)}$$

All the previous forms can be considered as special cases of this one general form.

D.2 Pay-off distributions

We will write the cumulative distribution function of the index by $F(x)$ and the probability density function by $f(x)$, where

$$F(x) = \int_{-\infty}^{x} f(s)ds \tag{D.3}$$

or

$$f(x) = \left(\frac{dF}{ds}\right)_x \tag{D.4}$$

D.2.1 Swaps

The distribution of the pay-off of a swap contract, $G(p)$, is given in terms of the distribution function of the index as

$$G(p) = \begin{cases} 0 & p < -L_\$ \\ F(K + \frac{p}{D}) & -L_\$ \leq p < L_\$ \\ 1 & p \geq L_\$ \end{cases} \tag{D.5}$$

The density function of the pay-off distribution $g(p)$ can be written in terms of the density of the index as

$$g(p) = \begin{cases} 0 & p < -L_\$ \\ \delta(p + L_\$)F(L_1) & p = -L_\$ \\ \frac{1}{D}f(K + \frac{p}{D}) & -L_\$ < p < L_\$ \\ \delta(p - L_\$)[1 - F(L_2)] & p = L_\$ \\ 0 & p > L_\$ \end{cases} \tag{D.6}$$

where $\delta(p)$ is the delta function of mathematical physics, which is infinite at p, zero elsewhere, and has an integral of one.

D.2.2 Call options

For a call option the CDF of the pay-off is given by

$$G(p) = \begin{cases} 0 & p < 0 \\ F(K + \frac{p}{D}) & 0 \leq p < L_\$ \\ 1 & p \geq L_\$ \end{cases} \tag{D.7}$$

and the density by

$$g(p) = \begin{cases} 0 & p < 0 \\ \delta(p)F(K) & p = 0 \\ \frac{1}{D}f(K + \frac{p}{D}) & 0 < p < L_\$ \\ \delta(p - L_\$)[1 - F(L)] & p = L_\$ \\ 0 & p > L_\$ \end{cases} \tag{D.8}$$

D.2.3 Put options

For a put option the CDF of the pay-off is given by

$$G(p) = \begin{cases} 0 & p < 0 \\ F(K - \frac{p}{D}) & 0 \le p < L_\$ \\ 1 & p \ge L_\$ \end{cases} \tag{D.9}$$

and the density by

$$g(p) = \begin{cases} 0 & p < 0 \\ \delta(p)[1 - F(K)] & p = 0 \\ \frac{1}{D}f(K - \frac{p}{D}) & 0 < p < L_\$ \\ \delta(p - L_\$)F(L) & p = L_\$ \\ 0 & p > L_\$ \end{cases} \tag{D.10}$$

D.2.4 Collars

For a collar the CDF of the pay-off is given by

$$G(p) = \begin{cases} 0 & p < L_\$ \\ F(K_1 + \frac{p}{D}) & -L_\$ \le p < 0 \\ F(K_2 + \frac{p}{D}) & 0 \le p < L_\$ \\ 1 & p \ge L_\$ \end{cases} \tag{D.11}$$

and the density by

$$g(p) = \begin{cases} 0 & p < -L_\$ \\ \delta(p + L_\$)F(L_1) & p = -L_\$ \\ \frac{1}{D}f(K_1 + \frac{p}{D}) & -L_\$ < p < 0 \\ \delta(p)[F(K_2) - F(K_1)] & p = 0 \\ \frac{1}{D}f(K_2 + \frac{p}{D}) & 0 < p < L_\$ \\ \delta(p - L_\$)[1 - F(L_2)] & p = L_\$ \\ 0 & p > L_\$ \end{cases} \tag{D.12}$$

D.2.5 Straddles

For a straddle the CDF of the pay-off is given by

$$G(p) = \begin{cases} 0 & p < 0 \\ F(K + \frac{p}{D}) + F(K - \frac{p}{D}) & 0 \leq p < L_\$ \\ 1 & p \geq L_\$ \end{cases} \qquad \text{(D.13)}$$

and the density by

$$g(p) = \begin{cases} 0 & p \leq 0 \\ \frac{1}{D}[f(K + \frac{p}{D}) + f(K - \frac{p}{D})] & 0 < p < L_\$ \\ \delta(p - L_\$)[F(-L_1) + 1 - F(L_2)] & p = L_\$ \\ 0 & p > L_\$ \end{cases} \qquad \text{(D.14)}$$

D.2.6 Strangles

For a strangle the CDF of the pay-off is given by

$$G(p) = \begin{cases} 0 & p < 0 \\ F(K_2 + \frac{p}{D}) + F(K_1 - \frac{p}{D}) & 0 \leq p < L_\$ \\ 1 & p \geq L_\$ \end{cases} \qquad \text{(D.15)}$$

and the density by

$$g(p) = \begin{cases} 0 & p < 0 \\ \delta(p)[F(K_2) - F(K_1)] & p = 0 \\ \frac{1}{D}[f(K_2 + \frac{p}{D}) + f(K_1 - \frac{p}{D})] & 0 < p < L_\$ \\ \delta(p - L_\$)[F(-L_1) + 1 - F(L_2)] & p = L_\$ \\ 0 & p > L_\$ \end{cases} \qquad \text{(D.16)}$$

D.2.7 Binary options

For a binary option the CDF of the pay-off is given by

$$G(p) = \begin{cases} 0 & p < 0 \\ F(S) & 0 \leq p < L_\$ \\ 1 & p \geq L_\$ \end{cases} \qquad \text{(D.17)}$$

and the density by

$$g(p) = \begin{cases} 0 & p < 0 \\ \delta(p)F(K) & p = 0 \\ 0 & 0 < p < L_\$ \\ \delta(p - L_\$)[1 - F(K)] & p = L_\$ \\ 0 & p > L_\$ \end{cases} \qquad (D.18)$$

D.3 Useful relations for deriving expressions for the expected pay-off

In order to derive closed-form solutions for the expected pay-off for the normal distribution we start by noting a few properties of the normal density and distribution functions. These will make the subsequent derivations much more straightforward.

The density $\phi(x)$ for a normal distribution with expectation 0 and variance 1 is given by

$$\phi(x) = \phi_x = \frac{1}{\sqrt{2\pi}} e^{-\frac{x^2}{2}} \qquad (D.19)$$

From this it is simple to show that

$$\frac{d}{dx}\phi_x = -x\phi_x \qquad (D.20)$$

Integrating this from a to b gives

$$\int_a^b x\phi_x dx = \phi_a - \phi_b \qquad (D.21)$$

This formula will prove useful later when evaluating expressions that have the same form as the left-hand side.

We now define

$$\Phi(x) = \Phi_x = \int_{-\infty}^x \phi_y dy \qquad (D.22)$$

This is the CDF for a normal distribution with expectation 0 and variance 1.

The probability density of a normal distribution with expectation μ and standard deviation σ_x is given by

$$\frac{1}{\sigma_x} n \left(\frac{x - \mu}{\sigma_x} \right) = \frac{\phi_{x'}}{\sigma_x} \qquad (D.23)$$

where we write $x' = \frac{x-\mu}{\sigma_x}$.

The cumulative density function is given by the integral of this, which is

$$\frac{1}{\sigma_x} \int_{-\infty}^{x} n\left(\frac{y-\mu}{\sigma_x}\right) dy = \int_{-\infty}^{x'} \phi(s)ds \qquad (D.24)$$

$$= \Phi(x')$$

$$= \Phi_{x'}$$

If we integrate $\phi_{x'}$ from a to b we see that

$$\int_{a}^{b} \phi_{x'} dx = \int_{-\infty}^{b} \phi_{x'} dx - \int_{-\infty}^{a} \phi_{x'} dx \qquad (D.25)$$

$$= \sigma_x(\Phi_{b'} - \Phi_{a'})$$

This will also prove useful later.

By making the substitution $x = \sigma_x s + \mu$ we find that

$$\int_{a}^{b} x\phi_{x'} dx = \sigma_x \int_{a'}^{b'} (\sigma_x s + \mu)\phi(s)ds \qquad (D.26)$$

$$= \sigma_x^2 \int_{a'}^{b'} s\phi_s ds + \sigma_x \mu \int_{a'}^{b'} \phi_s ds$$

$$= \sigma_x^2(\phi_{a'} - \phi_{b'}) + \sigma_x \mu(\Phi_{b'} - \Phi_{a'})$$

where the last step used expression (D.21).

Finally, we note that

$$\int_{a}^{b} (x-c)\phi_{x'} dx = \int_{a}^{b} x\phi_{x'} dx - c\int_{a}^{b} \phi_{x'} dx \qquad (D.27)$$

$$= \sigma_x^2(\phi_{a'} - \phi_{b'}) + \sigma_x \mu(\Phi_{b'} - \Phi_{a'}) - c\sigma_x(\Phi_{b'} - \Phi_{a'})$$

$$= \sigma_x^2(\phi_{a'} - \phi_{b'}) + \sigma_x(\mu - c)(\Phi_{b'} - \Phi_{a'})$$

Given the various expressions above it is now easy to write the expected pay-offs of all standard contract types in terms of Φ_x and ϕ_x. Φ_x and ϕ_x can be calculated using standard functions that are available in most computer languages or spreadsheets.

D.4 Closed-form expressions for the expected pay-off

We now derive expressions for the expected pay-off for our seven contract types. The expected pay-off is useful because:

- it is the usual definition for the actuarial fair price;
- it is the long-run average pay-off;
- under certain assumptions, it is the arbitrage-free price (see chapter 11).

D.4.1 Swaps

For a swap the expected pay-off is

$$\mu_p = \frac{1}{\sigma_x} \int_{-\infty}^{\infty} p(x)\phi_{x'} dx \tag{D.28}$$

Substituting in the pay-off function from equation (1.11) gives

$$\mu_p = \frac{1}{\sigma_x} \int_{-\infty}^{L1} -L_\$\phi_{x'} dx + \frac{1}{\sigma_x} \int_{L1}^{L2} D(x-K)\phi_{x'} dx + \frac{1}{\sigma_x} \int_{L2}^{\infty} L_\$\phi_{x'} dx \tag{D.29}$$

Applying the various rules derived above we see that

$$\mu_p = -\frac{L_\$}{\sigma_x}[\sigma_x \Phi_{L1'}] \tag{D.30}$$

$$+ \frac{D}{\sigma_x}[\sigma_x^2(\phi_{L1'} - \phi_{L2'}) + \sigma_x(\mu - K)(\Phi_{L2'} - \Phi_{L1'})]$$

$$+ \frac{L_\$}{\sigma_x}[\sigma_x(1 - \Phi_{L2'})]$$

Finally, rearranging to group together all terms in n and N gives

$$\mu_p = D\sigma_x(\phi_{L1'} - \phi_{L2'}) + D\Phi_{L1'}(L_1 - \mu) + D\Phi_{L2'}(\mu - L_2) + L_\$ \tag{D.31}$$

Applying the same derivation but for the uncapped case gives

$$\mu_p = \frac{1}{\sigma_x} \int_{-\infty}^{\infty} p(x)\phi_{x'} dx \tag{D.32}$$

$$= \frac{1}{\sigma_x} \int_{-\infty}^{\infty} D(x-K)\phi_{x'} dx$$

$$= \frac{D}{\sigma_x}[\sigma_x(\mu - K)]$$

$$= D(\mu - K)$$

D.4.2 Call options

For a call option the expected pay-off is

$$\mu_p = \frac{1}{\sigma_x} \int_{-\infty}^{\infty} p(x)\phi_{x'} dx \tag{D.33}$$

$$= \frac{1}{\sigma_x} \int_K^L D(x-K)\phi_{x'} dx + \frac{1}{\sigma_x} \int_L^\infty L_\$ \phi_{x'} dx$$

$$= \frac{D}{\sigma_x} [\sigma_x^2(\phi_{K'} - \phi_{L'}) + \sigma_x(\mu - K)(\Phi_{L'} - \Phi_{K'})]$$

$$+ \frac{L_\$}{\sigma_x} [\sigma_x(1 - \Phi_{L'})]$$

$$= D\sigma_x(\phi_{K'} - \phi_{L'}) + D\Phi_{L'}(\mu - L) + D\Phi_{K'}(K - \mu) + L_\$$$

For the uncapped case it is

$$\mu_p = \frac{1}{\sigma_x} \int_{-\infty}^\infty p(x)\phi_{x'} dx \tag{D.34}$$

$$= \frac{1}{\sigma_x} \int_K^\infty D(x-K)\phi_{x'} dx$$

$$= \frac{D}{\sigma_x} [\sigma_x^2 \phi_{K'} + \sigma_x(\mu - K)(1 - \Phi_{K'})]$$

$$= D\sigma_x \phi_{K'} + D(\mu - K)(1 - \Phi_{K'})$$

D.4.3 Put options

For a put option the expected pay-off is

$$\mu_p = \frac{1}{\sigma_x} \int_{-\infty}^\infty p(x)\phi_{x'} dx \tag{D.35}$$

$$= \frac{1}{\sigma_x} \int_{-\infty}^L L_\$ \phi_{x'} dx + \frac{1}{\sigma_x} \int_L^K D(K-x)\phi_{x'} dx$$

$$= \frac{L_\$}{\sigma_x} [\sigma_x \Phi_{L'}]$$

$$- \frac{D}{\sigma_x} [\sigma_x^2(\phi_{L'} - \phi_{K'}) + \sigma_x(\mu - K)(\Phi_{K'} - \Phi_{L'})]$$

$$= D\sigma_x(\phi_{K'} - \phi_{L'}) + D\Phi_{L'}(\mu - L) + D\Phi_{K'}(K - \mu)$$

For the uncapped case it is

$$\mu_p = \frac{1}{\sigma_x} \int_{-\infty}^\infty p(x)\phi_{x'} dx \tag{D.36}$$

$$= \frac{1}{\sigma_x} \int_{-\infty}^K D(K-x)\phi_{x'} dx$$

$$= -\frac{D}{\sigma_x} [\sigma_x^2(-\phi_{K'}) + \sigma_x(\mu - K)\Phi_{K'}]$$

$$= D\sigma_x \phi_{K'} + D\Phi_{K'}(K - \mu)$$

D.4.4 Collars

For a collar the expected pay-off is

$$\mu_p = \frac{1}{\sigma_x} \int_{-\infty}^{\infty} p(x)\phi_{x'}dx \tag{D.37}$$

$$= \frac{1}{\sigma_x} \int_{-\infty}^{L1} -L_\$\phi_{x'}dx + \frac{1}{\sigma_x} \int_{L1}^{K1} D(x-K_1)\phi_{x'}dx$$

$$+ \frac{1}{\sigma_x} \int_{K2}^{L2} D(x-K_2)\phi_{x'}dx + \frac{1}{\sigma_x} \int_{L2}^{\infty} L_\$\phi_{x'}dx$$

$$= D\sigma_x(\phi_{L1'} - \phi_{K1'} + \phi_{L1'} - \phi_{K2'})$$

$$- \frac{L_\$}{\sigma_x}[\sigma_x\Phi_{L'}]$$

$$+ \frac{D}{\sigma_x}[\sigma_x^2(\phi_{L1'} - \phi_{K1'}) + \sigma_x(\mu - K_1)(\Phi_{K1'} - \Phi_{L1'})]$$

$$+ \frac{D}{\sigma_x}[\sigma_x^2(\phi_{K2'} - \phi_{L2'}) + \sigma_x(\mu - K_2)(\Phi_{L2'} - \Phi_{K2'})]$$

$$+ \frac{L_\$}{\sigma_x}[\sigma_x(1 - \Phi_{L2'})]$$

$$= D\sigma_x(\phi_{L1'} + \phi_{K2'} - \phi_{K1'} - \phi_{L2'})$$

$$+ \Phi_{L1'}(L_1 - \mu) + \Phi_{L2'}(\mu - L_2) + \Phi_{K1'}(\mu - K_1) + \Phi_{K2'}(K_2 - \mu) + L_\$$$

In the uncapped case it is

$$\mu_p = \frac{1}{\sigma_x} \int_{-\infty}^{\infty} p(x)\phi_{x'}dx \tag{D.38}$$

$$= \frac{1}{\sigma_x} \int_{-\infty}^{K1} D(x-K_1)\phi_{x'}dx + \frac{1}{\sigma_x} \int_{K2}^{\infty} D(x-K_2)\phi_{x'}dx$$

$$= \frac{D}{\sigma_x}[\sigma_x^2(-\phi_{K1'}) + \sigma_x(\mu - K_1)\Phi_{K1'}]$$

$$+ \frac{D}{\sigma_x}[\sigma_x^2\phi_{K2'} + \sigma_x(\mu - K_2)(1 - \Phi_{K2'})]$$

$$= D\sigma_x(\phi_{K2'} - \phi_{K1'}) + D\Phi_{K1'}(\mu - K_1) + D(1 - \Phi_{K2'})(\mu - K_2)$$

D.4.5 Straddles

For a straddle the expected pay-off is

$$\mu_p = \frac{1}{\sigma_x} \int_{-\infty}^{\infty} p(x)\phi_{x'}dx \tag{D.39}$$

$$= \frac{1}{\sigma_x} \int_{-\infty}^{L1} L_\$ \phi_{x'} dx + \frac{1}{\sigma_x} \int_{L1}^{K} D(K - x) \phi_{x'} dx$$

$$+ \frac{1}{\sigma_x} \int_{K}^{L2} D(x - K) \phi_{x'} dx + \frac{1}{\sigma_x} \int_{L2}^{\infty} L_\$ \phi_{x'} dx$$

$$= \frac{L_\$}{\sigma_x} \Phi_{L1'}$$

$$- \frac{D}{\sigma_x} [\sigma_x^2 (\phi_{L1'} - \phi_{K'}) + \sigma_x (\mu - K)(\Phi_{K'} - \Phi_{L1'})]$$

$$+ \frac{D}{\sigma_x} [\sigma_x^2 (\phi_{K'} - \phi_{L2'}) + \sigma_x (\mu - K)(\Phi_{L2'} - \Phi_{K'})]$$

$$+ \frac{L_\$}{\sigma_x} [\sigma_x (1 - \Phi_{L2})]$$

$$= D\sigma_x (2\phi_{K'} - \phi_{L1'} - \phi_{L2'}) + D\Phi_{L1'}(\mu - L_1)$$

$$+ 2D\Phi_{K'}(K - \mu) + D\Phi_{L2'}(\mu - L_2) + L_\$$$

For the uncapped case it is

$$\mu_p = \frac{1}{\sigma_x} \int_{-\infty}^{\infty} p(x) \phi_{x'} dx \qquad (D.40)$$

$$= \frac{1}{\sigma_x} \int_{-\infty}^{K} D(K - x) \phi_{x'} dx + \frac{1}{\sigma_x} \int_{K}^{\infty} D(x - K) \phi_{x'} dx$$

$$= -\frac{D}{\sigma_x} [\sigma_x^2 (-\phi_{K'}) + \sigma_x (\mu - K) \Phi_{K'}]$$

$$+ \frac{D}{\sigma_x} [\sigma_x^2 \phi_{K'} + \sigma_x (\mu - K)(1 - \Phi_{K'})]$$

$$= 2D\sigma_x \phi_{K'} + 2D\Phi_{K'}(K - \mu) + D(\mu - K)$$

D.4.6 Strangles

For a strangle the expected pay-off is

$$\mu_p = \frac{1}{\sigma_x} \int_{-\infty}^{\infty} p(x) \phi_{x'} dx \qquad (D.41)$$

$$= \frac{1}{\sigma_x} \int_{-\infty}^{L1} L_\$ \phi_{x'} dx + \frac{1}{\sigma_x} \int_{L1}^{K1} D(K - x) \phi_{x'} dx$$

$$+ \frac{1}{\sigma_x} \int_{K2}^{L2} D(x - K) \phi_{x'} dx + \frac{1}{\sigma_x} \int_{L2}^{\infty} L_\$ \phi_{x'} dx$$

$$= \frac{L_\$}{\sigma_x} [\sigma_x \Phi_{L1'}]$$

$$-\frac{D}{\sigma_x}[\sigma_x^2(\phi_{L1'} - \phi_{K1'}) + \sigma_x(\mu - K_1)(\Phi_{K1'} - \Phi_{L1'})]$$

$$+\frac{D}{\sigma_x}[\sigma_x^2(\phi_{L1'} - \phi_{K1'}) + \sigma_x(\mu - K_1)(\Phi_{K1'} - \Phi_{L1'})]$$

$$+\frac{L_\$}{\sigma_x}[\sigma_x(1 - \Phi_{L2'})]$$

$$= D\sigma_x(\phi_{K1'} + \phi_{K2'} - \phi_{L1'} - \phi_{L2'})$$
$$+ D\Phi_{L1'}(\mu - L_1) + D\Phi_{K1'}(K_1 - \mu) + D\Phi_{K2'}(K_2 - \mu)$$
$$+ D\Phi_{L2'}(\mu - L_2) + L_\$$$

For the uncapped case it is

$$\mu_p = \frac{1}{\sigma_x}\int_{-\infty}^{\infty} p(x)\phi_{x'}\,dx \tag{D.42}$$

$$= \frac{1}{\sigma_x}\int_{-\infty}^{K1} D(K - x)\phi_{x'}\,dx + \frac{1}{\sigma_x}\int_{K2}^{\infty} D(x - K)\phi_{x'}\,dx$$

$$= \frac{D}{\sigma_x}[\sigma_x^2(-\phi_{K1'}) + \sigma_x(\mu - K)\Phi_{K1'}]$$

$$+ \frac{D}{\sigma_x}[\sigma_x^2\phi_{K2'} + \sigma_x(\mu - K)(1 - \Phi_{K2'})]$$

$$= D\sigma_x(\phi_{K1'} + \phi_{K2'}) + D\Phi_{K1'}(K_1 - \mu) + D(\mu - K_2)(1 - \Phi_{K2'})$$

D.4.7 Binary options

For a binary option the expected pay-off is

$$\mu_p = \frac{1}{\sigma_x}\int_{-\infty}^{\infty} p(x)\phi_{x'}\,dx \tag{D.43}$$

$$= \frac{1}{\sigma_x}\int_{K}^{\infty} L_\$\phi_{x'}\,dx$$

$$= L_\$(1 - \Phi_{K'})$$

D.4.8 The general form

The expected pay-off for the general form is

$$\mu_p = \frac{1}{\sigma_x}\int_{-\infty}^{\infty} p(x)\phi_{x'}\,dx \tag{D.44}$$

$$= \frac{1}{\sigma_x}\sum_{i=1}^{n}\int_{a_i}^{a_{i+1}} p(x)\phi_{x'}\,dx$$

$$= \frac{1}{\sigma_x} \sum_{i=1}^{n} \int_{a_i}^{a_{i+1}} (\alpha_i + \beta_i x) \phi_{x'} dx$$

$$= \frac{1}{\sigma_x} \sum_{i=1}^{n} [\alpha_i \int_{a_i}^{a_{i+1}} \phi_{x'} dx + \beta_i \int_{a_i}^{a_{i+1}} x \phi_{x'} dx]$$

$$= \frac{1}{\sigma_x} \sum_{i=1}^{n} [\alpha_i \sigma_x (\Phi_{a(i+1)'} - \Phi_{ai'}) + \beta_i \sigma_x^2 (\phi_{ai'} - \phi_{a(i+1)'})$$

$$+ \beta_i \sigma_x \mu (\Phi_{a(i+1)'} - \Phi_{ai'})]$$

D.5 Numerical examples

To facilitate the debugging of computer code using these expressions, we now give numerical examples.

In all these examples we assume $\mu = 1670$ and $\sigma_x = 120$.

Swap example

Strike	1680	Expected pay-off (with caps)	−45,201.8
Tick	5000	Expected pay-off (no caps)	−50,000.0
Limit	1,000,000		

Call example

Strike	1680	Expected pay-off (with caps)	205,491.7
Tick	5000	Expected pay-off (no caps)	215,196.0
Limit	1,000,000		

Put example

Strike	1650	Expected pay-off (with caps)	184,809.7
Tick	5000	Expected pay-off (no caps)	192,682.2
Limit	1,000,000		

Collar example

Strike 1	1650	Expected pay-off (with caps)	−19,353.7
Strike 2	1700	Expected pay-off (no caps)	−20,875.4
Tick	5000		
Limit	1,000,000		

Straddle example

Strike	1660	Expected pay-off (with caps)	456,185.3
Tick	5000	Expected pay-off (no caps)	480,392.0
Limit	1,000,000		

Strangle example

Strike1	1660	Expected pay-off (with caps)	421,813.1
Strike2	1675	Expected pay-off (no caps)	442,269.2
Tick	5000		
Limit	1,000,000		

Binary example

Strike	1680	Expected pay-off (with caps)	466,793.3
Limit	1,000,000		

Appendix E

Pay-off variances for normally distributed indices

We now give exact expressions for the variance of the pay-offs of weather derivatives on a normally distributed index, taken from Jewson (2003c). The expression for the variance of the pay-off of an uncapped call option was previously given by Henderson (2002).

In section E.1 we derive various useful expressions that will help us with our subsequent derivations. In section E.2 we derive the closed-form expressions for the variance and in section E.3 we give some numerical examples.

E.1 Useful relations for deriving expressions
for the pay-off variance
E.1.1 Derivation strategy

First we explain the strategy and formulae we will use for deriving expressions for the pay-off variance of weather contracts.

The variance of the pay-off function $p(x)$ is given by

$$\sigma_p^2 = \int_{-\infty}^{\infty} (p(x) - \mu_p)^2 f(x) dx \qquad (E.1)$$

where $f(x)$ is the probability density of the settlement index x and μ_p is the expected pay-off.

This can be rearranged to give

$$\sigma_p^2 = \int_{-\infty}^{\infty} p(x)^2 f(x) dx - \mu_p^2 \qquad (E.2)$$

$$= m_2 - m_1^2$$

Our strategy is to evaluate the first term on the right-hand side, m_2. Closed-form expressions for m_1 are given in appendix D.

E.1.2 Useful expressions

First

$$\int_a^b x^2 \phi_x dx = \int_a^b x.(x\phi_x)dx \tag{E.3}$$

$$= [-x\phi_x]_a^b - \int_a^b -\phi_x dx$$

$$= [x\phi_x]_b^a + \Phi_b - \Phi_a$$

$$= a\phi_a - b\phi_b + \Phi_b - \Phi_a$$

and second

$$\int_a^b (x-c)^2 \phi_{x'} dx = \sigma_x \int_{a'}^{b'} (\mu + \sigma_x s - c)^2 \phi_s ds \tag{E.4}$$

$$= \sigma_x \int_{a'}^{b'} (\nu + \sigma_x s)^2 \phi_s ds$$

$$= \sigma_x \int_{a'}^{b'} (\nu^2 + 2\nu\sigma_x s + \sigma_x^2 s^2)\phi_s ds$$

$$= \sigma_x \nu^2 \int_{a'}^{b'} \phi_s ds + 2\sigma_x^2 \nu \int_{a'}^{b'} s\phi_s ds + \sigma_x^3 \int_{a'}^{b'} s^2 \phi_s ds$$

$$= \sigma_x \nu^2 [\Phi_{b'} - \Phi_{a'}] + 2\sigma_x^2 \nu [\phi_{a'} - \phi_{b'}]$$
$$+ \sigma_x^3 [a'\phi_{a'} - b'\phi_{b'} + \Phi_{b'} - \Phi_{a'}]$$

where we have defined ν ('nu') as $\nu = \mu - c$.

Given the various expressions above, it is now easy to write the pay-off variances of all standard contract types in terms of Φ_x and ϕ_x. Φ_x and ϕ_x can be calculated using standard functions that are available in most computer languages or spreadsheets.

E.2 Closed-form expressions for the pay-off variance
E.2.1 Swaps

For a capped swap m_2 is

$$m_2 = \frac{1}{\sigma_x} \int_{-\infty}^{\infty} p(x)^2 \phi_{x'} dx \tag{E.5}$$

Applying the definition of the pay-off of a capped swap contract given in chapter 1, this gives

$$m_2 = \frac{1}{\sigma_x} \int_{-\infty}^{L1} L_{\$}^2 \phi_{x'} dx + \frac{1}{\sigma_x} \int_{L1}^{L2} D^2 (x-K)^2 \phi_{x'} dx + \frac{1}{\sigma_x} \int_{L2}^{\infty} L_{\$}^2 \phi_{x'} dx \tag{E.6}$$

Evaluating these integrals gives

$$m_2 = L_\$^2 \Phi_{L1'}$$ (E.7)

$$+ \frac{D^2}{\sigma_x} \{ \sigma_x \nu^2 [\Phi_{L2'} - \Phi_{L1'}] + 2\nu \sigma_x^2 [\phi_{L1'} - \phi_{L2'}]$$

$$+ \sigma_x^3 [L_1' \phi_{L1'} - L_2' \phi_{L2'} + \Phi_{L2'} - \Phi_{L1'}] \}$$

$$+ L_\$^2 [1 - \Phi_{L2'}]$$

Finally, grouping together terms in n and N gives

$$m_2 = \phi_{L1'} [D^2 (2\sigma_x \nu + \sigma_x^2 L_1')] - \phi_{L2'} [D^2 (2\sigma_x \nu + \sigma_x^2 L_2')]$$ (E.8)

$$+ \Phi_{L1'} [L_\$^2 - D^2 (\nu^2 + \sigma_x^2)] + \Phi_{L2'} [D^2 (\nu^2 + \sigma_x^2) - L_\$^2]$$

$$+ L_\$^2$$

For the uncapped case it is

$$m_2 = \frac{1}{\sigma_x} \int_{-\infty}^{\infty} p(x)^2 \phi_{x'} dx$$ (E.9)

$$= \frac{1}{\sigma_x} \int_{-\infty}^{\infty} D^2 (x - K)^2 \phi_{x'} dx$$

$$= \frac{D^2}{\sigma_x} \{ \sigma_x \nu^2 + \sigma_x^3 \}$$

$$= D^2 [\nu^2 + \sigma_x^2]$$

E.2.2 Call options

For a capped call option m_2 is

$$m_2 = \frac{1}{\sigma_x} \int_{-\infty}^{\infty} p(x)^2 \phi_{x'} dx$$ (E.10)

$$= \frac{1}{\sigma_x} \int_K^L D^2 (x - K)^2 \phi_{x'} dx + \frac{1}{\sigma_x} \int_L^{\infty} L_\$^2 \phi_{x'} dx$$

$$= \frac{D^2}{\sigma_x} \int_K^L (x - K)^2 \phi_{x'} dx + \frac{L_\$^2}{\sigma_x} \int_L^{\infty} \phi_{x'} dx$$

$$= \frac{D^2}{\sigma_x} \{ \sigma_x \nu^2 [\Phi_{L'} - \Phi_{K'}] + 2\nu \sigma_x^2 [\phi_{K'} - \phi_{L'}]$$

$$+ \sigma_x^3 [K' \phi_{K'} - L' \phi_{L'} + \Phi_{L'} - \Phi_{K'}] \}$$

$$+ L_\$^2 [1 - \Phi_{L'}]$$

$$= \phi_{K'} [D^2 (2\sigma_x \nu + \sigma_x^2 K')] - \phi_{L'} [D^2 (2\sigma_x \nu + \sigma_x^2 L')]$$

$$- \Phi_{K'} [D^2 (\nu^2 + \sigma_x^2)] + \Phi_{L'} [D^2 (\nu^2 + \sigma_x^2) - L_\$^2]$$

$$+ L_\$^2$$

For the uncapped case it is

$$m_2 = \frac{1}{\sigma_x} \int_{-\infty}^{\infty} p(x)^2 \phi_{x'} dx \qquad \text{(E.11)}$$

$$= \frac{1}{\sigma_x} \int_{K}^{\infty} D^2 (x-K)^2 \phi_{x'} dx$$

$$= \frac{D^2}{\sigma_x} \int_{K}^{\infty} (x-K)^2 \phi_{x'} dx$$

$$= \frac{D^2}{\sigma_x} \{ \sigma_x \nu^2 [1 - \Phi_{K'}] + 2\nu\sigma_x^2 [\phi_{K'}] + \sigma_x^3 [K' \phi_{K'} + 1 - \Phi_{K'}] \}$$

$$= \phi_{K'} [D^2 (2\sigma_x \nu + \sigma_x^2 K')] - \Phi_{K'} [D^2 (\nu^2 + \sigma_x^2)] + D^2 (\nu^2 + \sigma_x^2)$$

E.2.3 Put options

For a capped put option m_2 is

$$m_2 = \frac{1}{\sigma_x} \int_{-\infty}^{\infty} p(x)^2 \phi_{x'} dx \qquad \text{(E.12)}$$

$$= \frac{1}{\sigma_x} \int_{-\infty}^{L} L_\$^2 \phi_{x'} dx + \frac{1}{\sigma_x} \int_{L}^{K} D^2 (K-x)^2 \phi_{x'} dx$$

$$= L_\$^2 [\Phi_{L'}]$$

$$+ \frac{D^2}{\sigma_x} \{ \sigma_x \nu^2 [\Phi_{K'} - \Phi_{L'}] + 2\nu\sigma_x^2 [\phi_{L'} - \phi_{K'}]$$

$$+ \sigma_x^3 [L' \phi_{L'} - K' \phi_{K'} + \Phi_{K'} - \Phi_{L'}] \}$$

$$= \phi_{L'} [D^2 (2\nu\sigma_x + \sigma_x^2 L')] - \phi_{K'} [D^2 (2\nu\sigma_x + \sigma_x^2 K')]$$

$$+ \Phi_{K'} [D^2 (\nu^2 + \sigma_x^2)] + \Phi_{L'} [L_\$^2 - D^2 (\sigma_x^2 + \nu^2)]$$

For the uncapped case it is

$$m_2 = \frac{1}{\sigma_x} \int_{-\infty}^{\infty} p(x)^2 \phi_{x'} dx \qquad \text{(E.13)}$$

$$= \frac{1}{\sigma_x} \int_{-\infty}^{K} D^2 (K-x)^2 \phi_{x'} dx$$

$$= \frac{D^2}{\sigma_x} \{ \sigma_x \nu^2 [\Phi_{K'}] - 2\nu\sigma_x^2 [\phi_{K'}] + \sigma_x^3 [\Phi_{K'} - K' \phi_{K'}] \}$$

$$= \Phi_{K'} [D^2 (\nu^2 + \sigma_x^2)] - \phi_{K'} [D^2 (2\nu\sigma_x + \sigma_x^2 K')]$$

E.2.4 Collars

For a capped collar m_2 is

$$m_2 = \frac{1}{\sigma_x} \int_{-\infty}^{\infty} p(x)^2 \phi_{x'} dx \qquad (E.14)$$

$$= \frac{1}{\sigma_x} \int_{-\infty}^{L1} L_\$^2 \phi_{x'} dx + \frac{1}{\sigma_x} \int_{L1}^{K1} D^2(x-K_1)^2 \phi_{x'} dx$$

$$+ \frac{1}{\sigma_x} \int_{K2}^{L2} D^2(x-K_2)^2 \phi_{x'} dx + \frac{1}{\sigma_x} \int_{L2}^{\infty} L_\$^2 \phi_{x'} dx$$

$$= L_\$^2 \Phi_{L1'}$$

$$+ \frac{D^2}{\sigma_x} \{ \sigma_x \nu_1^2 [\Phi_{K1'} - \Phi_{L1'}] + 2\nu_1 \sigma_x^2 [\phi_{L1'} - \phi_{K1'}]$$

$$+ \sigma_x^3 [L_1' \phi_{L1'} - K_1' \phi_{K1'} - \Phi_{K1'} - \Phi_{L1'}] \}$$

$$+ \frac{D^2}{\sigma_x} \{ \sigma_x \nu_2^2 [\Phi_{L2'} - \Phi_{K2'}] + 2\nu_2 \sigma_x^2 [\phi_{K2'} - \phi_{L2'}]$$

$$+ \sigma_x^3 [K_2' \phi_{K2'} - L_2' \phi_{L2'} - \Phi_{L2'} - \Phi_{K2'}] \}$$

$$+ L_\$^2 [1 - \Phi_{L2'}]$$

$$= \phi_{L1'}[D^2(2\sigma_x\nu_1 + \sigma_x^2 L_1')] - \phi_{K1'}[D^2(2\sigma_x\nu_1 + \sigma_x^2 K_1')]$$

$$+ \phi_{K2'}[D^2(2\sigma_x\nu_2 + \sigma_x^2 K_2')] - \phi_{L2'}[D^2(2\sigma_x\nu_2 + \sigma_x^2 L_2')]$$

$$+ \Phi_{L1'}[L_\$^2 - D^2(\nu_1^2 + \sigma_x^2)] + \Phi_{K1'}[D^2(\nu_1^2 + \sigma_x^2)]$$

$$- \Phi_{K2'}[D^2(\nu_2^2 + \sigma_x^2)] + \Phi_{L2'}[D^2(\nu_2^2 + \sigma_x^2) - L_\$^2]$$

$$+ L_\$^2$$

where $\nu_1 = \mu - K_1$ and $\nu_2 = \mu - K_2$.

For the uncapped case it is

$$m_2 = \frac{1}{\sigma_x} \int_{-\infty}^{\infty} p(x)^2 \phi_{x'} dx \qquad (E.15)$$

$$= \frac{1}{\sigma_x} \int_{-\infty}^{K1} D^2(x-K_1)^2 \phi_{x'} dx + \frac{1}{\sigma_x} \int_{K2}^{\infty} D^2(x-K_2)^2 \phi_{x'} dx$$

$$= \frac{D^2}{\sigma_x} \{ \sigma_x \nu_1^2 [\Phi_{K1'}] + 2\nu_1 \sigma_x^2 [-\phi_{K1'}] + \sigma_x^3 [-K_1' \phi_{K1'} - \Phi_{K1'}] \}$$

$$+ \frac{D^2}{\sigma_x} \{ \sigma_x \nu_2^2 [-\Phi_{K2'}] + 2\nu_2 \sigma_x^2 [\phi_{K2'}] + \sigma_x^3 [K_2' \phi_{K2'} - \Phi_{K2'}] \}$$

$$= \phi_{K2'}[D^2(2\sigma_x\nu_2 + \sigma_x^2 K_2')] - \phi_{K1'}[D^2(2\sigma_x\nu_1 + \sigma_x^2 K_1')]$$

$$+ \Phi_{K1'}[D^2(\nu_1^2 + \sigma_x^2)] - \Phi_{K2'}[D^2(\nu_2^2 + \sigma_x^2)] + D^2(\nu_2^2 + \sigma_x^2)$$

E.2.5 Straddles

For a capped straddle m_2 is

$$m_2 = \frac{1}{\sigma_x} \int_{-\infty}^{\infty} p(x)^2 \phi_{x'} dx \tag{E.16}$$

$$= \frac{1}{\sigma_x} \int_{-\infty}^{L1} L_\$^2 \phi_{x'} dx + \frac{1}{\sigma_x} \int_{L1}^{K} D^2(K-x)^2 \phi_{x'} dx$$

$$+ \frac{1}{\sigma_x} \int_{K}^{L2} D^2(x-K)^2 \phi_{x'} dx + \frac{1}{\sigma_x} \int_{L2}^{\infty} L_\$^2 \phi_{x'} dx$$

$$= L_\$^2 \Phi_{L1'}$$

$$+ \frac{D^2}{\sigma_x} \{ \sigma_x \nu^2 [\Phi_{K'} - \Phi_{L1'}] + 2\nu \sigma_x^2 [\phi_{L1'} - \phi_{K'}]$$

$$+ \sigma_x^3 [L_1' \phi_{L1'} - K' \phi_{K'} + \Phi_{K'} - \Phi_{L1'}] \}$$

$$+ \frac{D^2}{\sigma_x} \{ \sigma_x \nu^2 [\Phi_{L2'} - \Phi_{K'}] + 2\nu \sigma_x^2 [\phi_{K'} - \phi_{L2'}]$$

$$+ \sigma_x^3 [K' \phi_{K'} - L_2' \phi_{L2'} + \Phi_{L2'} - \Phi_{K'}] \}$$

$$+ L_\$(1 - \Phi_{L2'})$$

$$= \phi_{L1'} [D^2(2\sigma_x \nu + \sigma_x^2 L_1')] - \phi_{L2'} [D^2(2\sigma_x \nu + \sigma_x^2 L_2')]$$

$$+ \Phi_{L1'} [L_\$^2 - D^2(\nu^2 + \sigma_x^2)] + \Phi_{L2'} [D^2(\nu^2 + \sigma_x^2) - L_\$^2]$$

$$+ L_\$^2$$

For the uncapped case it is

$$m_2 = \frac{1}{\sigma_x} \int_{-\infty}^{\infty} p(x)^2 \phi_{x'} dx \tag{E.17}$$

$$= \frac{1}{\sigma_x} \int_{-\infty}^{K} D^2(K-x)^2 \phi_{x'} dx + \frac{1}{\sigma_x} \int_{K}^{\infty} D^2(x-K)^2 \phi_{x'} dx$$

$$= \frac{D^2}{\sigma_x} \{ \sigma_x \nu^2 [\Phi_{K'}] + 2\nu \sigma_x^2 [-\phi_{K'}] + \sigma_x^3 [-K' \phi_{K'} + \Phi_{K'}] \}$$

$$+ \frac{D^2}{\sigma_x} \{ \sigma_x \nu^2 [1 - \Phi_{K'}] + 2\nu \sigma_x^2 [\phi_{K'}] + \sigma_x^3 [K' \phi_{K'} + 1 - \Phi_{K'}] \}$$

$$= D^2(\nu^2 + \sigma_x^2)$$

Curiously, we see that both results are independent of K.

E.2.6 Strangles

For a capped strangle m_2 is

$$m_2 = \frac{1}{\sigma_x} \int_{-\infty}^{\infty} p(x)^2 \phi_{x'} dx \tag{E.18}$$

$$= \frac{1}{\sigma_x} \int_{-\infty}^{L1} L_\$^2 \phi_{x'} dx + \frac{1}{\sigma_x} \int_{L1}^{K1} D^2 (K_1 - x)^2 \phi_{x'} dx$$

$$+ \frac{1}{\sigma_x} \int_{K2}^{L2} D^2 (x - K_2)^2 \phi_{x'} dx + \frac{1}{\sigma_x} \int_{L2}^{\infty} L_\$^2 \phi_{x'} dx$$

$$= L_\$^2 \Phi_{L1'}$$

$$+ \frac{D^2}{\sigma_x} \{ \sigma_x \nu_1^2 [\Phi_{K1'} - \Phi_{L1'}] + 2\nu_1 \sigma_x^2 [\phi_{L1'} - \phi_{K1'}]$$

$$+ \sigma_x^3 [L_1' \phi_{L1'} - K_1' \phi_{K1'} + \Phi_{K1'} - \Phi_{L1'}] \}$$

$$+ \frac{D^2}{\sigma_x} \{ \sigma_x \nu_2^2 [\Phi_{L2'} - \Phi_{K2'}] + 2\nu_2 \sigma_x^2 [\phi_{K2'} - \phi_{L2'}]$$

$$+ \sigma_x^3 [K_2' \phi_{K2'} - L_2' \phi_{L2'} + \Phi_{L2'} - \Phi_{K2'}] \}$$

$$+ L_\$^2 (1 - \Phi_{L2'})$$

$$= \phi_{L1'} [D^2 (2\nu_1 \sigma_x + \sigma_x^2 L_1')] - \phi_{K1'} [D^2 (2\nu_1 \sigma_x + \sigma_x^2 K_1')]$$

$$+ \phi_{K2'} [D^2 (2\nu_2 \sigma_x + \sigma_x^2 K_2')] - \phi_{L2'} [D^2 (2\nu_2 \sigma_x + \sigma_x^2 L_2')]$$

$$+ \Phi_{L1'} [L_\$^2 - D^2 (\nu_1^2 + \sigma_x^2)] + \Phi_{K1'} [D^2 (\nu_1^2 + \sigma_x^2)]$$

$$- \Phi_{K2'} [D^2 (\nu_2^2 + \sigma_x^2)] + \Phi_{L2'} [D^2 (\nu_2^2 + \sigma_x^2) - L_\$^2]$$

$$+ L_\$^2$$

For the uncapped case it is

$$m_2 = \frac{1}{\sigma_x} \int_{-\infty}^{\infty} p(x)^2 \phi_{x'} dx \tag{E.19}$$

$$= \frac{1}{\sigma_x} \int_{-\infty}^{K1} D^2 (K_1 - x)^2 \phi_{x'} dx + \frac{1}{\sigma_x} \int_{K2}^{\infty} D^2 (x - K_2)^2 \phi_{x'} dx$$

$$= \frac{D^2}{\sigma_x} \{ \sigma_x \nu_1^2 [\Phi_{K1'}] + 2\nu_1 \sigma_x^2 [-\phi_{K1'}] + \sigma_x^3 [-K_1' \phi_{K1'} - \Phi_{K1'}] \}$$

$$+ \frac{D^2}{\sigma_x} \{ \sigma_x \nu_1^2 [\Phi_{K2'}] + 2\nu_1 \sigma_x^2 [-\phi_{K2'}] + \sigma_x^3 [-K_2' \phi_{K2'} - \Phi_{K2'}] \}$$

$$= \phi_{K2'} [D^2 (2\nu_2 \sigma_x + \sigma_x^2 K_2')] - \phi_{K1'} [D^2 (2\nu_1 \sigma_x + \sigma_x^2 K_1')]$$

$$+ \Phi_{K1'} [D^2 (\nu_1^2 + \sigma_x^2)] - \Phi_{K2'} [D^2 (\nu_2^2 + \sigma_x^2)] + D^2 (\nu_2^2 + \sigma_x^2)$$

E.2.7 Binary options

For a binary option m_2 is

$$m_2 = \frac{1}{\sigma_x} \int_{-\infty}^{\infty} p(x)^2 \phi_{x'} dx \qquad \text{(E.20)}$$

$$= \frac{1}{\sigma_x} \int_{K}^{\infty} L_{\$}^2 \phi_{x'} dx$$

$$= L_{\$}^2 (1 - \Phi_{K'})$$

E.3 Numerical examples

To facilitate the debugging of computer code using these expressions we now give numerical examples.

In all these examples, we assume $\mu = 1670$ and $\sigma_x = 120$.

Swap example

Strike	1680	Expected pay-off (with caps)	−45,201.8
Tick	5000	Expected pay-off (no caps)	−50,000.0
Limit	1,000,000	Pay-off variance (with caps)	548,804.7
		Pay-off variance (no caps)	600,000.0

Call example

Strike	1680	Expected pay-off (with caps)	205,491.7
Tick	5000	Expected pay-off (no caps)	215,196.0
Limit	1,000,000	Pay-off variance (with caps)	302,355.0
		Pay-off variance (no caps)	333,131.2

Put example

Strike	1650	Expected pay-off (with caps)	184,809.7
Tick	5000	Expected pay-off (no caps)	192,682.2
Limit	1,000,000	Pay-off variance (with caps)	289,223.0
		Pay-off variance (no caps)	315,878.4

Collar example

Strike 1	1650	Expected pay-off (with caps)	−19,353.7
Strike 2	1700	Expected pay-off (no caps)	−20,875.4
Tick	5000	Pay-off variance (with caps)	469,868.3
Limit	1,000,000	Pay-off variance (no caps)	505,138.1

Straddle example

Strike	1660	Expected pay-off (with caps)	456,185.3
Tick	5000	Expected pay-off (no caps)	480,392.0
Limit	1,000,000	Pay-off variance (with caps)	308,423.1
		Pay-off variance (no caps)	362,937.3

Strangle example

Strike 1	1660	Expected pay-off (with caps)	421,813.1
Strike 2	1675	Expected pay-off (no caps)	442,269.2
Tick	5000	Pay-off variance (with caps)	312,751.5
Limit	1,000,000	Pay-off variance (no caps)	360,589.2

Binary example

Strike	1680	Expected pay-off (with caps)	466,793.3
Limit	1,000,000	Pay-off variance (with caps)	498,896.1

Appendix F

Greeks for normally distributed indices

We now give exact expressions for the greeks for weather derivatives on a normally distributed index. These expressions are taken from Jewson (2003b).

F.1 Useful relations for deriving expressions for the greeks

We now derive some expressions that we will use later on.

In order to calculate deltas we note that

$$\Delta = \frac{\partial \mu_p}{\partial \mu} \tag{F.1}$$

$$= \frac{\partial}{\partial \mu} \frac{1}{\sigma_x} \left(\int_{-\infty}^{\infty} p(x) \phi_{x'} dx \right)$$

$$= \frac{1}{\sigma_x} \frac{\partial}{\partial \mu} \left(\int_{-\infty}^{\infty} p(x) \phi_{x'} dx \right)$$

$$= \frac{1}{\sigma_x} \int_{-\infty}^{\infty} p(x) \frac{\partial \phi_{x'}}{\partial \mu} dx$$

For a large class of distributions, including the normal distribution, the PDF satisfies

$$\frac{\partial \phi_{x'}}{\partial \mu} = -\frac{\partial \phi_{x'}}{\partial x} \tag{F.2}$$

and so

$$\Delta = -\frac{1}{\sigma_x} \int_{-\infty}^{\infty} p(x) \frac{\partial \phi_{x'}}{\partial x} dx \tag{F.3}$$

$$= -\frac{1}{\sigma_x} \int_{-\infty}^{\infty} \frac{\partial}{\partial x} (p(x) \phi_{x'}) dx + \frac{1}{\sigma_x} \int_{-\infty}^{\infty} \frac{dp(x)}{dx} \phi_{x'} dx$$

$$= \frac{1}{\sigma_x} \int_{-\infty}^{\infty} \frac{dp}{dx} \phi_{x'} dx$$

i.e. for the normal distribution delta is the average slope of the pay-off, weighted by the probabilities of different pay-offs.

We will derive expressions for gamma by differentiating the expressions for delta. In order to do this, we note that

$$\Phi_{x'} = \int_{-\infty}^{x'} \phi_x dx \tag{F.4}$$

$$= \frac{1}{\sigma_x} \int_{-\infty}^{x} \phi_x dx$$

and hence that

$$\frac{\partial \Phi_x'}{\partial \mu} = \frac{1}{\sigma_x} \int_{-\infty}^{x} \frac{\partial \phi_{x'}}{\partial \mu} dx \tag{F.5}$$

$$= -\frac{1}{\sigma_x} \int_{-\infty}^{x} \frac{\partial \phi_{x'}}{\partial x} dx$$

$$= -\frac{\phi_x'}{\sigma_x}$$

For zeta, we note that

$$\zeta = \frac{\partial \mu_p}{\partial \sigma_x} \tag{F.6}$$

$$= \frac{\partial}{\partial \sigma_x} \left(\frac{1}{\sigma_x} \int_{-\infty}^{\infty} p(x)\phi_{x'} dx \right)$$

$$= \frac{\partial}{\partial \sigma_x} \left(\int_{-\infty}^{\infty} p(\mu + \sigma_x s)\phi_s ds \right)$$

$$= \int_{-\infty}^{\infty} \frac{\partial}{\partial \sigma_x} p(\mu + \sigma_x s)\phi_s ds$$

$$= \int_{-\infty}^{\infty} s p'(\mu + \sigma_x s)\phi_s ds$$

$$= -\int_{-\infty}^{\infty} p'(\mu + \sigma_x s) \frac{\partial \phi_s}{\partial s} ds$$

$$= -\int_{-\infty}^{\infty} \frac{\partial p}{\partial x} \frac{\partial \phi_{x'}}{\partial x} dx$$

F.2 Closed-form expressions for the greeks

We now derive closed-form expressions for delta, gamma and zeta for each contract type. Expressions for theta and vega can be derived from the expressions for zeta, and expressions for temperature delta can be derived from the expressions for delta and zeta.

F.2.1 Swaps

For the delta

$$\Delta = \frac{1}{\sigma_x} \int_{-\infty}^{\infty} \frac{dp}{dx} \phi_{x'} \, dx \tag{F.7}$$

Using the definition of the swap pay-off function given in chapter 1, this gives

$$\Delta = \frac{1}{\sigma_x} \int_{L1}^{L2} D\phi_{x'} \, dx \tag{F.8}$$

$$= D(\Phi_{L2'} - \Phi_{L1'}) \tag{F.9}$$

In the uncapped case

$$\Delta = D \tag{F.10}$$

For the gamma

$$\Gamma = \frac{D}{\sigma_x}(\phi_{L1'} - \phi_{L2'}) \tag{F.11}$$

In the uncapped case

$$\Gamma = 0 \tag{F.12}$$

For the zeta

$$\zeta = -\int_{-\infty}^{\infty} \frac{\partial p}{\partial x} \frac{\partial \phi_{x'}}{\partial x} \, dx \tag{F.13}$$

$$= -\int_{L_1}^{L_2} D \frac{\partial \phi_{x'}}{\partial x} \, dx$$

$$= D(\phi_{L1'} - \phi_{L2'})$$

In the uncapped case

$$\zeta = -\int_{-\infty}^{\infty} \frac{\partial p}{\partial x} \frac{\partial \phi_{x'}}{\partial x} \, dx \tag{F.14}$$

$$= 0$$

F.2.2 Call options

For the delta

$$\Delta = \frac{1}{\sigma_x} \int_{-\infty}^{\infty} \frac{dp}{dx} \phi_{x'} dx \qquad (F.15)$$

$$= \frac{1}{\sigma_x} \int_K^L D\phi_{x'} dx$$

$$= D(\Phi_{L'} - \Phi_{K'})$$

In the uncapped case

$$\Delta = D(1 - \Phi_{K'}) \qquad (F.16)$$

For the gamma

$$\Gamma = \frac{D}{\sigma_x}(\phi_{K'} - \phi_{L'}) \qquad (F.17)$$

In the uncapped case

$$\Gamma = \frac{D}{\sigma_x}\phi_{K'} \qquad (F.18)$$

For the zeta

$$\zeta = -\int_{-\infty}^{\infty} \frac{\partial p}{\partial x} \frac{\partial \phi_{x'}}{\partial x} dx \qquad (F.19)$$

$$= -\int_K^L D\frac{\partial \phi_{x'}}{\partial x} dx$$

$$= D(\phi_{K'} - \phi_{L'})$$

In the uncapped case

$$\zeta = -\int_{-\infty}^{\infty} \frac{\partial p}{\partial x} \frac{\partial \phi_{x'}}{\partial x} dx \qquad (F.20)$$

$$= -\int_K^{\infty} D\frac{\partial \phi_{x'}}{\partial x} dx$$

$$= D\phi_{K'}$$

F.2.3 Put options

For the delta

$$\Delta = \frac{1}{\sigma_x} \int_{-\infty}^{\infty} \frac{dp}{dx} \phi_{x'} dx \qquad (F.21)$$

$$= \frac{1}{\sigma_x} \int_L^K -D\phi_{x'} dx$$

$$= D(\Phi_{L'} - \Phi_{K'})$$

In the uncapped case

$$\Delta = -D\Phi_{K'} \tag{F.22}$$

For the gamma

$$\Gamma = \frac{D}{\sigma_x}(\phi_{K'} - \phi_{L'}) \tag{F.23}$$

In the uncapped case

$$\Gamma = \frac{D}{\sigma_x}\phi_{K'} \tag{F.24}$$

For the zeta

$$\zeta = -\int_{-\infty}^{\infty} \frac{\partial p}{\partial x}\frac{\partial \phi_{x'}}{\partial x}dx \tag{F.25}$$

$$= -\int_{L}^{K} -D\frac{\partial \phi_{x'}}{\partial x}dx$$

$$= D(\phi_{K'} - \phi_{L'})$$

In the uncapped case

$$\zeta = -\int_{-\infty}^{\infty} \frac{\partial p}{\partial x}\frac{\partial \phi_{x'}}{\partial x}dx \tag{F.26}$$

$$= -\int_{-\infty}^{K} -D\frac{\partial \phi_{x'}}{\partial x}dx$$

$$= D\phi_{K'}$$

F.2.4 Collars

For the delta

$$\Delta = \frac{1}{\sigma_x}\int_{-\infty}^{\infty} \frac{dp}{dx}\phi_{x'}dx \tag{F.27}$$

$$= \frac{1}{\sigma_x}\int_{L1}^{K1} D\phi_{x'}dx + \frac{1}{\sigma_x}\int_{K2}^{L2} D\phi_{x'}dx$$

$$= D(\Phi_{K1'} - \Phi_{L1'} + \Phi_{L2'} - \Phi_{K2'})$$

In the uncapped case

$$\Delta = D(\Phi_{K1'} - \Phi_{K2'} + 1) \tag{F.28}$$

For the gamma

$$\Gamma = \frac{1}{\sigma_x}D(\phi_{L1'} - \phi_{K1'} + \phi_{K2'} - \phi_{L2'}) \tag{F.29}$$

In the uncapped case

$$\Gamma = \frac{1}{\sigma_x} D(\phi_{K2'} - \phi_{K1'}) \tag{F.30}$$

For the zeta

$$\zeta = -\int_{-\infty}^{\infty} \frac{\partial p}{\partial x} \frac{\partial \phi_{x'}}{\partial x} dx \tag{F.31}$$

$$= -\int_{L_1}^{K_1} D \frac{\partial \phi_{x'}}{\partial x} dx$$

$$- \int_{K_2}^{L_2} D \frac{\partial \phi_{x'}}{\partial x} dx$$

$$= D(\phi_{L1'} - \phi_{K1'} + \phi_{K2'} - \phi_{L2'})$$

In the uncapped case

$$\zeta = -\int_{-\infty}^{\infty} \frac{\partial p}{\partial x} \frac{\partial \phi_{x'}}{\partial x} dx \tag{F.32}$$

$$= -\int_{-\infty}^{K_1} D \frac{\partial \phi_{x'}}{\partial x} dx - \int_{K_2}^{\infty} D \frac{\partial \phi_{x'}}{\partial x} dx$$

$$= D(\phi_{K2'} - \phi_{K1'})$$

F.2.5 Straddles

For the delta

$$\Delta = \frac{1}{\sigma_x} \int_{-\infty}^{\infty} \frac{dp}{dx} \phi_{x'} dx \tag{F.33}$$

$$= \frac{1}{\sigma_x} \int_{L1}^{K} -D\phi_{x'} dx + \frac{1}{\sigma_x} \int_{K}^{L2} D\phi_{x'} dx$$

$$= D(\Phi_{L1'} + \Phi_{L2'} - 2\Phi_{K'})$$

In the uncapped case

$$\Delta = D(1 - 2\Phi_{K'}) \tag{F.34}$$

For the gamma

$$\Gamma = \frac{1}{\sigma_x} D(2\phi_{K'} - \phi_{L1'} - \phi_{L2'}) \tag{F.35}$$

In the uncapped case

$$\Gamma = \frac{2}{\sigma_x} D\phi_{K'} \tag{F.36}$$

For the zeta

$$\zeta = -\int_{-\infty}^{\infty} \frac{\partial p}{\partial x} \frac{\partial \phi_{x'}}{\partial x} dx \tag{F.37}$$

$$= -\int_{L_1}^{K} \frac{\partial p}{\partial x} \frac{\partial \phi_{x'}}{\partial x} dx - \int_{K}^{L_2} \frac{\partial p}{\partial x} \frac{\partial \phi_{x'}}{\partial x} dx$$

$$= D(2\phi_{K'} - \phi_{L1'} - \phi_{L2'})$$

In the uncapped case

$$\zeta = -\int_{-\infty}^{\infty} \frac{\partial p}{\partial x} \frac{\partial \phi_{x'}}{\partial x} dx \tag{F.38}$$

$$= -\int_{-\infty}^{K} \frac{\partial p}{\partial x} \frac{\partial \phi_{x'}}{\partial x} dx - \int_{K}^{\infty} \frac{\partial p}{\partial x} \frac{\partial \phi_{x'}}{\partial x} dx$$

$$= 2D\phi_{K'}$$

F.2.6 Strangles

For the delta

$$\Delta = \frac{1}{\sigma_x} \int_{-\infty}^{\infty} \frac{dp}{dx} \phi_{x'} dx \tag{F.39}$$

$$= \frac{1}{\sigma_x} \int_{L1}^{K1} -D\phi_{x'} dx + \frac{1}{\sigma_x} \int_{K2}^{L2} D\phi_{x'} dx$$

$$= D(\Phi_{L1'} - \Phi_{K1'} + \Phi_{L2'} - \Phi_{K2'})$$

In the uncapped case

$$\Delta = D(1 - \Phi_{K1'} - \Phi_{K2'}) \tag{F.40}$$

For the gamma

$$\Gamma = \frac{D}{\sigma_x} (\phi_{K1'} - \phi_{L1'} + \phi_{K2'} - \phi_{L2'}) \tag{F.41}$$

In the uncapped case

$$\Gamma = \frac{D}{\sigma_x} (\phi_{K1'} + \phi_{K2'}) \tag{F.42}$$

For the zeta

$$\zeta = -\int_{-\infty}^{\infty} \frac{\partial p}{\partial x} \frac{\partial \phi_{x'}}{\partial x} dx \tag{F.43}$$

$$= -\int_{L_1}^{K_1} \frac{\partial p}{\partial x} \frac{\partial \phi_{x'}}{\partial x} dx - \int_{K_2}^{L_2} \frac{\partial p}{\partial x} \frac{\partial \phi_{x'}}{\partial x} dx$$

$$= D(\phi_{K1'} - \phi_{L1'} - \phi_{L2'} + \phi_{K2'})$$

In the uncapped case

$$\zeta = -\int_{-\infty}^{\infty} \frac{\partial p}{\partial x} \frac{\partial \phi_{x'}}{\partial x} dx \tag{F.44}$$

$$= -\int_{-\infty}^{K_1} \frac{\partial p}{\partial x} \frac{\partial \phi_{x'}}{\partial x} dx - \int_{K_2}^{\infty} \frac{\partial p}{\partial x} \frac{\partial \phi_{x'}}{\partial x} dx$$

$$= D(\phi_{K1'} + \phi_{K2'})$$

F.2.7 Binary options

For the delta

$$\Delta = -\frac{1}{\sigma_x} \int_{-\infty}^{\infty} p \frac{\partial \phi_{x'}}{\partial x} dx \tag{F.45}$$

$$= -\frac{L_\$}{\sigma_x} \int_{K}^{L} \frac{\partial \phi_{x'}}{\partial x} dx$$

$$= \frac{L_\$}{\sigma_x} \phi_{K'}$$

For the gamma

$$\Gamma = \frac{L_\$ \phi_{K'}(K - \mu)}{\sigma_x^3} \tag{F.46}$$

For the zeta

$$\zeta = \frac{L_\$ \phi_{K'}(K - \mu)}{\sigma_x^2} \tag{F.47}$$

F.2.8 The general form

For the delta

$$\Delta = \frac{1}{\sigma_x} \int_{-\infty}^{\infty} \frac{dp}{dx} \phi_{x'} dx \tag{F.48}$$

$$= \frac{1}{\sigma_x} \sum_{i=1}^{n} \int_{a_i}^{a_{i+1}} \frac{dp}{dx} \phi_{x'} dx$$

$$= \frac{1}{\sigma_x} \sum_{i=1}^{n} \int_{a_i}^{a_{i+1}} \beta_i \phi_{x'} \, dx$$

$$= \frac{1}{\sigma_x} \sum_{i=1}^{n} \beta_i \int_{a_i}^{a_{i+1}} \phi_{x'} \, dx$$

$$= \frac{1}{\sigma_x} \sum_{i=1}^{n} \beta_i (\Phi_{a(i+1)'} - \Phi_{ai'})$$

For the gamma

$$\Gamma = \frac{1}{\sigma_x} \sum_{i=1}^{n} \beta_i (\phi_{ai'} - \phi_{a(i+1)'}) \tag{F.49}$$

For the zeta

$$\zeta = - \int_{-\infty}^{\infty} \frac{\partial p}{\partial x} \frac{\partial \phi_{x'}}{\partial x} \, dx \tag{F.50}$$

$$= - \sum_{i=1}^{n} \int_{a_i}^{a_{i+1}} \frac{\partial p}{\partial x} \frac{\partial \phi_{x'}}{\partial x} \, dx$$

$$= - \sum_{i=1}^{n} \int_{a_i}^{a_{i+1}} \beta_i \frac{\partial \phi_{x'}}{\partial x} \, dx$$

$$= - \sum_{i=1}^{n} \beta_i (\phi_{a(i+1)'} - \phi_{ai'})$$

$$= \sum_{i=1}^{n} \beta_i (\phi_{ai'} - \phi_{a(i+1)'})$$

F.3 Numerical examples

To facilitate debugging we now give numerical examples of each of the above expressions. In all these examples we assume $\mu = 1670$ and $\sigma_x = 120$.

Swap example

Strike	1680	Expected pay-off (with caps)	−45,201.8
Tick	5000	Expected pay-off (no caps)	−50,000.0
Limit	1,000,000	Delta (with caps)	4516.3
		Delta (no caps)	5000.0
		Gamma (with caps)	1.151
		Gamma (no caps)	0.0

Call example

Strike	1680	Expected pay-off (with caps)	205,491.7
Tick	5000	Expected pay-off (no caps)	215,196.0
Limit	1,000,000	Delta (with caps)	2133.7
		Delta (no caps)	2334.0
		Gamma (with caps)	12.970
		Gamma (no caps)	16.565

Put example

Strike	1650	Expected pay-off (with caps)	184,809.7
Tick	5000	Expected pay-off (no caps)	192,682.2
Limit	1,000,000	Delta (with caps)	−2002.2
		Delta (no caps)	−2169.1
		Gamma (with caps)	13.297
		Gamma (no caps)	16.393

Collar example

Strike 1	1650	Expected pay-off (with caps)	−19,353.7
Strike 2	1700	Expected pay-off (no caps)	−20,875.4
Tick	5000	Delta (with caps)	3870.5
Limit	1,000,000	Delta (no caps)	4175.5
		Gamma (with caps)	0.166
		Gamma (no caps)	−0.282

Straddle example

Strike	1660	Expected pay-off (with caps)	456,185.3
Tick	5000	Expected pay-off (no caps)	480,392.0
Limit	1,000,000	Delta (with caps)	249.0
		Delta (no caps)	332.1
		Gamma (with caps)	24.789
		Gamma (no caps)	33.130

Strangle example

Strike 1	1660	Expected pay-off (with caps)	421,813.1
Strike 2	1675	Expected pay-off (no caps)	442,269.2
Tick	5000	Delta (with caps)	64.3
Limit	1,000,000	Delta (no caps)	82.9
		Gamma (with caps)	25.715
		Gamma (no caps)	33.173

Binary example

Strike	1680	Expected pay-off (with caps)	466,793.3
Limit	1,000,000	Delta (with caps)	3313

Appendix G
Exact solutions for the kernel density

We now give exact expressions for the expected pay-off, pay-off variance and greeks for weather derivatives on indices that are modelled using the kernel density with a Gaussian kernel. These are taken from Jewson (2003d).

G.1 Closed-form solutions for the expected pay-off on a kernel density

The expected pay-off V is given by

$$V = \int_{-\infty}^{\infty} p(x)f(x)dx \tag{G.1}$$

where $p(x)$ is the pay-off function.

Substituting in a kernel density for f we have

$$V = \int_{-\infty}^{\infty} p(x)\frac{1}{N\lambda} \sum_{i=1}^{N} K\left(\frac{x - x_i}{\lambda}\right) dx \tag{G.2}$$

$$= \frac{1}{N\lambda} \sum_{i=1}^{N} \int_{-\infty}^{\infty} p(x)K\left(\frac{x - x_i}{\lambda}\right) dx$$

$$= \frac{1}{N} \sum_{i=1}^{N} V_i$$

where V_i is defined as

$$V_i = \frac{1}{\lambda} \int_{-\infty}^{\infty} p(x)K\left(\frac{x - x_i}{\lambda}\right) dx \tag{G.3}$$

We can now calculate each of the V_i using the closed-form expressions in appendix D. For instance, for a call option on a normal distribution with mean μ and standard deviation σ_x the expected pay-off is given by

$$\mu_p = D\sigma_x(\phi_{K'} - \phi_{L'}) + D\Phi_{L'}(\mu - L) + D\Phi_{K'}(K - \mu) + L_\$ \qquad (G.4)$$

where

$$K' = \frac{K - \mu}{\sigma_x} \qquad (G.5)$$

$$L' = \frac{L - \mu}{\sigma_x}$$

This gives

$$V_i = D\lambda(\phi_{K'_i} - \phi_{L'_i}) + D\Phi_{L'_i}(x_i - L) + D\Phi_{K'_i}(K - x_i) + L_\$ \qquad (G.6)$$

where

$$K'_i = \frac{K - x_i}{\lambda} \qquad (G.7)$$

$$L'_i = \frac{L - x_i}{\lambda}$$

and hence

$$V = \frac{1}{N}\sum_{i=1}^{N}[D\lambda(\phi_{K'_i} - \phi_{L'_i}) + D\Phi_{L'_i}(x_i - L) + D\Phi_{K'_i}(K - x_i)] + L_\$ \qquad (G.8)$$

Similar expressions can be derived for the other option types using the appropriate closed-form solutions instead of equation (G.6).

G.2 Closed-form solutions for the delta on a kernel density

We now consider how to calculate the delta of an option on a kernel density. From equation (G.2) we have

$$V = \frac{1}{N}\sum_{i=1}^{N} V_i \qquad (G.9)$$

Applying the definition of delta gives

$$\Delta = \frac{\partial V}{\partial \mu} \qquad (G.10)$$

$$= \frac{\partial}{\partial \mu}\left(\frac{1}{N}\sum_{i=1}^{N} V_i\right)$$

$$= \frac{1}{N}\sum_{i=1}^{N}\frac{\partial V_i}{\partial \mu}$$

But

$$\mu = \frac{1}{N} \sum_{i=1}^{N} x_i \tag{G.11}$$

and so

$$\frac{\partial}{\partial \mu} = \sum_{j=1}^{N} \frac{\partial x_j}{\partial \mu} \frac{\partial}{\partial x_j} \tag{G.12}$$

$$= \sum_{j=1}^{N} N \frac{\partial}{\partial x_j}$$

This gives

$$\Delta = \frac{1}{N} \sum_{i=1}^{N} \frac{\partial V_i}{\partial \mu} \tag{G.13}$$

$$= \frac{1}{N} \sum_{i=1}^{N} N \sum_{j=1}^{N} \frac{\partial V_i}{\partial x_j}$$

$$= \sum_{i=1}^{N} \frac{\partial V_i}{\partial x_i}$$

$$= \sum_{i=1}^{N} \Delta_i$$

i.e. the delta of the whole contract is the sum of the deltas due to each individual kernel.

We can now calculate each of the Δ_i using the closed-form expressions in appendix F. For instance, for a call option on a normal distribution with mean μ and standard deviation σ_x the delta is given by

$$\Delta = D(\Phi_{L'} - \Phi_{K'}) \tag{G.14}$$

and so

$$\Delta_i = D(\Phi_{L'_i} - \Phi_{K'_i}) \tag{G.15}$$

and

$$\Delta = \sum_{i=1}^{N} D(\Phi_{L'_i} - \Phi_{K'_i}) \tag{G.16}$$

Similar expressions can be derived for the other option types using the appropriate closed-form solutions instead of equation (G.14).

G.3 Closed-form solutions for the gamma on a kernel density

Very similar arguments apply to gamma as to delta, giving

$$\Gamma = \sum_{i=1}^{N} \Gamma_i \tag{G.17}$$

where

$$\Gamma_i = \frac{\partial^2 V_i}{\partial x_i^2} \tag{G.18}$$

We can now calculate each of the Γ_i using the closed-form expressions in appendix F. For instance, for a call option on a normal distribution with mean μ and standard deviation σ_x the gamma is given by

$$\Gamma = \frac{D}{\sigma_x}(\phi_{K'} - \phi_{L'}) \tag{G.19}$$

and so

$$\Gamma_i = \frac{D}{\sigma_x}(\phi_{K_i'} - \phi_{L_i'}) \tag{G.20}$$

and

$$\Gamma = \sum_{i=1}^{N} \frac{D}{\sigma_x}(\phi_{K_i'} - \phi_{L_i'}) \tag{G.21}$$

Similar expressions can be derived for the other option types using the appropriate closed-form solutions instead of equation (G.19).

G.4 Closed-form solutions for the pay-off variance on a kernel density

We now consider how to calculate the pay-off variance of an option on a kernel density.

The pay-off variance is given by

$$\sigma_p^2 = \int_{-\infty}^{\infty} (p(x) - \mu_p)^2 f(x)dx \tag{G.22}$$

$$= \int_{-\infty}^{\infty} (p(x) - \mu_p)^2 \frac{1}{N\lambda} \sum_{i=1}^{N} K\left(\frac{x - x_i}{\lambda}\right) dx$$

$$= \frac{1}{N} \sum_{i=1}^{N} \int_{-\infty}^{\infty} (p(x) - \mu_p)^2 \frac{1}{\lambda} K\left(\frac{x - x_i}{\lambda}\right) dx$$

$$= \frac{1}{N} \sum_{i=1}^{N} (\sigma_p^i)^2$$

We can now calculate each of the σ_p^i using the closed-form expressions given in appendix E.

G.5 An example

We now give a numerical example. We consider the ten historical index values given in the second column of table G.1. These are the observed numbers of HDDs for London Heathrow November to March from 1993 to 2002.

These values have a sample mean of 1709.06 and a sample standard deviation of 114.61.

We use a bandwidth calculated using equation (4.6), which gives 76.58.

Numerical results for the expected pay-off, delta, gamma and pay-off variance are shown below.

Table G.1. *The observed*
numbers of London
Heathrow November to
March HDDs, 1993 to 2002.

	Historical index values
1993	1637.25
1994	1657.4
1995	1770.45
1996	1667.35
1997	1681.8
1998	1549.85
1999	1817.65
2000	1951.05
2001	1579.5
2002	1778.3

Expected pay-off
Normal distribution   226,564.0
Kernel   243,914.0
Adjusted kernel   214,694.2

Delta
Normal distribution   2243.8
Kernel   1872.5
Adjusted kernel   2036.4

Gamma
Normal distribution   12.37
Kernel   9.26
Adjusted kernel   12.46

Pay-off variance
Normal distribution   315,077.8
Kernel   349,096.1
Adjusted kernel   318,188.9

Appendix H

The beta for a normally distributed index

We now derive closed-form expressions for the regression coefficients between uncapped weather swaps and options and a single weather swap or weather index, taken from Jewson (2004b). The regression coefficient between a portfolio of weather swaps and options and a single weather swap is then a simple extension. This allows fast and precise calculation of the variance-minimising swap hedge for a portfolio of weather derivatives.

H.1 Useful relations

H.1.1 Derivation strategy

The regression coefficient β between a portfolio with pay-offs p and a single contract with pay-offs q is given by

$$\beta = \frac{E(pq) - E(p)E(q)}{E(qq) - E(q)E(q)} \tag{H.1}$$

Expressions for the expected pay-offs $E(p)$ and $E(q)$ are given in appendix D, and for the variance of pay-offs $E(qq) - E(q)E(q)$ in appendix E. We will now consider $E(pq)$ to complete the calculation of β.

The total pay-off of a portfolio p is the sum of the pay-offs of the contracts in the portfolio:

$$p = \sum_{i=1}^{N} p_i \tag{H.2}$$

and so

$$E(pq) = E\left(\left(\sum p_i\right)q\right) \tag{H.3}$$
$$= \sum E(p_i q)$$

340

and so we see that calculating $E(pq)$ reduces to the problem of calculating $E(p_i q)$ for each contract in the portfolio. We will derive expressions for $E(p_i q)$ for uncapped swaps, calls and puts.

We start, however, by deriving various expressions related to the normal distribution that will prove useful in our subsequent calculations.

H.1.2 Useful expressions

We will need the following relations:

$$
\begin{aligned}
I_1(a,b) &= \int_0^\infty x e^{-\frac{1}{2}(x^2 + 2ax + b)}\,dx \qquad\qquad\qquad\qquad \text{(H.4)}\\
&= \int_0^\infty x e^{-\frac{1}{2}[(x+a)^2 - a^2 + b]}\,dx \\
&= e^{-\frac{1}{2}(b-a^2)} \int_0^\infty x e^{-\frac{1}{2}(x+a)^2}\,dx \\
&= e^{-\frac{1}{2}(b-a^2)} \int_a^\infty (y-a) e^{-\frac{1}{2}y^2}\,dy \\
&= e^{-\frac{1}{2}(b-a^2)} \left(\int_a^\infty y e^{-\frac{1}{2}y^2}\,dy - a \int_a^\infty e^{-\frac{1}{2}y^2}\,dy \right) \\
&= \sqrt{2\pi}\, e^{-\frac{1}{2}(b-a^2)} \left(\int_a^\infty y \phi_y\,dy - a \int_a^\infty \phi_y\,dy \right) \\
&= \sqrt{2\pi}\, e^{-\frac{1}{2}(b-a^2)} ([-\phi_y]_a^\infty - a[\Phi_y]_a^\infty) \\
&= \sqrt{2\pi}\, e^{-\frac{1}{2}(b-a^2)} (\phi_a - a(1 - \Phi_a)) \\
&= \sqrt{2\pi}\, e^{-\frac{1}{2}(b-a^2)} [\phi_a - a(1 - \Phi_a)]
\end{aligned}
$$

$$
\begin{aligned}
\int_0^\infty x e^{-\frac{1}{2}(\alpha^2 x^2 + 2\beta x + \gamma)}\,dx &= \int_0^\infty \frac{y}{\alpha} e^{-\frac{1}{2}(y^2 + 2\frac{\beta}{\alpha}y + \gamma)}\frac{dy}{\alpha} \qquad \text{(H.5)}\\
&= \frac{1}{\alpha^2} \int_0^\infty y e^{-\frac{1}{2}(y^2 + 2\frac{\beta}{\alpha}y + \gamma)}\,dy \\
&= \frac{1}{\alpha^2} I_1\left(\frac{\beta}{\alpha}, \gamma\right)
\end{aligned}
$$

$$
I_2(a,b) = \int_{-\infty}^\infty x e^{-\frac{1}{2}(x^2 + 2ax + b)}\,dx \qquad\qquad\qquad\qquad \text{(H.6)}
$$

$$= \int_{-\infty}^{\infty} xe^{-\frac{1}{2}[(x+a)^2-a^2+b]}dx$$

$$= e^{-\frac{1}{2}(b-a^2)} \int_{-\infty}^{\infty} xe^{-\frac{1}{2}(x+a)^2} dx$$

$$= e^{-\frac{1}{2}(b-a^2)} \int_{-\infty}^{\infty} (y-a)e^{-\frac{1}{2}y^2} dy$$

$$= e^{-\frac{1}{2}(b-a^2)} \left(\int_{-\infty}^{\infty} ye^{-\frac{1}{2}y^2} dy - a \int_{-\infty}^{\infty} e^{-\frac{1}{2}y^2} dy \right)$$

$$= \sqrt{2\pi}e^{-\frac{1}{2}(b-a^2)} \left(\int_{-\infty}^{\infty} y\phi_y dy - a \int_{-\infty}^{\infty} \phi_y \right) dy$$

$$= \sqrt{2\pi}e^{-\frac{1}{2}(b-a^2)}(-a)$$

$$= -\sqrt{2\pi}ae^{-\frac{1}{2}(b-a^2)}$$

$$\int_{-\infty}^{\infty} xe^{-\frac{1}{2}(\alpha^2 x^2+2\beta x+\gamma)}dx = \int_0^{\infty} \frac{y}{\alpha}e^{-\frac{1}{2}(y^2+2\frac{\beta}{\alpha}y+\gamma)}\frac{dy}{\alpha} \qquad \text{(H.7)}$$

$$= \frac{1}{\alpha^2} \int_0^{\infty} ye^{-\frac{1}{2}(y^2+2\frac{\beta}{\alpha}y+\gamma)}dy$$

$$= \frac{1}{\alpha^2} I_2\left(\frac{\beta}{\alpha},\gamma\right)$$

$$J_1(a,b) = \int_0^{\infty} x^2 e^{-\frac{1}{2}(x^2+2ax+b)}dx \qquad \text{(H.8)}$$

$$= \int_0^{\infty} x^2 e^{-\frac{1}{2}[(x+a)^2-a^2+b]}dx$$

$$= e^{-\frac{1}{2}(b-a^2)} \int_a^{\infty} x^2 e^{-\frac{1}{2}(x+a)^2} dx$$

$$= e^{-\frac{1}{2}(b-a^2)} \int_a^{\infty} (y-a)^2 e^{-\frac{1}{2}y^2} dy$$

$$= e^{-\frac{1}{2}(b-a^2)} \int_a^{\infty} (y^2-2ay+a^2)e^{-\frac{1}{2}y^2} dy$$

$$= e^{-\frac{1}{2}(b-a^2)} \left(\int_a^{\infty} y^2 e^{-\frac{1}{2}y^2} dy + \int_a^{\infty} -2aye^{-\frac{1}{2}y^2} dy + \int_a^{\infty} a^2 e^{-\frac{1}{2}y^2} dy \right)$$

$$= e^{-\frac{1}{2}(b-a^2)} \left(\int_a^{\infty} y^2 e^{-\frac{1}{2}y^2} dy - 2a \int_a^{\infty} ye^{-\frac{1}{2}y^2} dy + a^2 \int_a^{\infty} e^{-\frac{1}{2}y^2} dy \right)$$

$$= \sqrt{2\pi}e^{-\frac{1}{2}(b-a^2)} \left(\int_a^{\infty} y^2 \phi_y dy - 2a \int_a^{\infty} y\phi_y dy + a^2 \int_a^{\infty} \phi_y dy \right)$$

$$= \sqrt{2\pi}e^{-\frac{1}{2}(b-a^2)}\left([a\phi_a + 1 - \Phi_a] - 2a[\phi_a] + a^2(1 - \Phi_a)\right)$$

$$= \sqrt{2\pi}e^{-\frac{1}{2}(b-a^2)}(1 + a^2 - a\phi_a - \Phi_a(1 + a^2))$$

$$\int_0^\infty x^2 e^{-\frac{1}{2}(\alpha^2 x^2 + 2\beta x + \gamma)}\,dx = \int_0^\infty \frac{y^2}{\alpha^2}e^{-\frac{1}{2}(y^2 + 2\frac{\beta}{\alpha}y + \gamma)}\frac{dy}{\alpha} \qquad \text{(H.9)}$$

$$= \frac{1}{\alpha^3}\int_0^\infty ye^{-\frac{1}{2}(y^2 + 2\frac{\beta}{\alpha}y + \gamma)}\,dy$$

$$= \frac{1}{\alpha^3}J_1\left(\frac{\beta}{\alpha}, \gamma\right)$$

$$J_2(a, b) = \int_{-\infty}^\infty x^2 e^{-\frac{1}{2}(x^2 + 2ax + b)}\,dx \qquad \text{(H.10)}$$

$$= \int_{-\infty}^\infty x^2 e^{-\frac{1}{2}[(x+a)^2 - a^2 + b]}\,dx$$

$$= e^{-\frac{1}{2}(b-a^2)}\int_{-\infty}^\infty x^2 e^{-\frac{1}{2}(x+a)^2}\,dx$$

$$= e^{-\frac{1}{2}(b-a^2)}\int_{-\infty}^\infty (y-a)^2 e^{-\frac{1}{2}y^2}\,dy$$

$$= e^{-\frac{1}{2}(b-a^2)}\int_{-\infty}^\infty (y^2 - 2ay + a^2)e^{-\frac{1}{2}y^2}\,dy$$

$$= e^{-\frac{1}{2}(b-a^2)}\left(\int_{-\infty}^\infty y^2 e^{-\frac{1}{2}y^2}\,dy + \int_{-\infty}^\infty -2aye^{-\frac{1}{2}y^2}\,dy + \int_{-\infty}^\infty a^2 e^{-\frac{1}{2}y^2}\,dy\right)$$

$$= e^{-\frac{1}{2}(b-a^2)}\left(\int_{-\infty}^\infty y^2 e^{-\frac{1}{2}y^2}\,dy - 2a\int_{-\infty}^\infty ye^{-\frac{1}{2}y^2}\,dy + a^2\int_{-\infty}^\infty e^{-\frac{1}{2}y^2}\,dy\right)$$

$$= \sqrt{2\pi}e^{-\frac{1}{2}(b-a^2)}\left(\int_{-\infty}^\infty y^2\phi_y\,dy - 2a\int_{-\infty}^\infty y\phi_y\,dy + a^2\int_{-\infty}^\infty \phi_y\,dy\right)$$

$$= \sqrt{2\pi}e^{-\frac{1}{2}(b-a^2)}\left([1] + [0] + [a^2]\right)$$

$$= \sqrt{2\pi}e^{-\frac{1}{2}(b-a^2)}(1 + a^2)$$

$$\int_{-\infty}^\infty x^2 e^{-\frac{1}{2}(\alpha^2 x^2 + 2\beta x + \gamma)}\,dx = \int_0^\infty \frac{y^2}{\alpha^2}e^{-\frac{1}{2}(y^2 + 2\frac{\beta}{\alpha}y + \gamma)}\frac{dy}{\alpha} \qquad \text{(H.11)}$$

$$= \frac{1}{\alpha^3}\int_0^\infty ye^{-\frac{1}{2}(y^2 + 2\frac{\beta}{\alpha}y + \gamma)}\,dy$$

$$= \frac{1}{\alpha^3}J_2\left(\frac{\beta}{\alpha}, \gamma\right)$$

H.2 Definitions
H.2.1 Swaps

The pay-off of the swaps we consider is given by

$$p(x) = D_s(x - K_s) \tag{H.12}$$

H.2.2 Calls

The pay-off of the call options we consider is given by

$$p(x) = \begin{cases} 0 & \text{if } x \leq K \\ D(x - K) & \text{if } x \geq K \end{cases} \tag{H.13}$$

H.2.3 Puts

The pay-off of the put options we consider is given by

$$p(x) = \begin{cases} D(K - x) & \text{if } x \leq K \\ 0 & \text{if } x \geq K \end{cases} \tag{H.14}$$

H.2.4 Indices

We assume that both indices we consider are normally distributed.

$$x \sim \Phi(\mu_1, \sigma_1) \tag{H.15}$$

$$y \sim \Phi(\mu_2, \sigma_2) \tag{H.16}$$

with a linear correlation given by

$$\text{correlation}(x, y) = c \tag{H.17}$$

We also define

$$\text{determinant}(x, y) = d = \sigma_1^2 \sigma_2^2 (1 - c^2) \tag{H.18}$$

H.3 Closed-form expressions for the beta

We are now in a position to derive the closed-form expressions for the beta for a swap contract.

H.3.1 Swap-swap covariance

The indices for the two swaps are x and y, and the pay-offs are p and q. We then have

$$E(pq) = \int_{-\infty}^{\infty} dy \int_{-\infty}^{\infty} dx \, D_x(y - K_y)D_y(x - K_x)\rho(x, y) \qquad (H.19)$$

$$= D_y D_x \int_{-\infty}^{\infty} dy \int_{-\infty}^{\infty} dx (y - K_y)(x - K_x)\rho(x, y)$$

where

$$\rho(x, y) = \frac{1}{2\pi} \frac{1}{\sqrt{d}} e^{-\frac{1}{2d}[\sigma_2^2(x-\mu_x)^2 - 2c\sigma_1\sigma_2(x-\mu_x)(y-\mu_y) + \sigma_1^2(y-\mu_y)^2]} \qquad (H.20)$$

We now make a number of substitutions. These are designed to suit both the calculations in this section and those in the subsequent sections for calls and puts; if all we were interested in was the swap-swap covariance, then that can be calculated much more simply in other ways.

We define

$$u = \frac{\sigma_2(x - K_x)}{d^{\frac{1}{2}}}, v = \frac{\sigma_1(y - K_y)}{d^{\frac{1}{2}}} \qquad (H.21)$$

and so

$$x = \frac{ud^{\frac{1}{2}} + K_x\sigma_2}{\sigma_2}, y = \frac{vd^{\frac{1}{2}} + K_y\sigma_1}{\sigma_1} \qquad (H.22)$$

We also define

$$t_1 = \frac{\sigma_2(K_x - \mu_x)}{d^{\frac{1}{2}}}, t_2 = \frac{\sigma_1(K_y - \mu_y)}{d^{\frac{1}{2}}} \qquad (H.23)$$

which gives

$$\frac{\sigma_2^2 x^2}{d} = (u + t_1)^2, \frac{\sigma_1^2 y^2}{d} = (v + t_2)^2 \qquad (H.24)$$

and so

$$E(pq) = \frac{D_x D_y}{2\pi} \frac{d^{\frac{3}{2}}}{\sigma_1^2 \sigma_2^2} \int_{-\infty}^{\infty} dv \int_{-\infty}^{\infty} uve^{-\frac{1}{2}[(u+t_1)^2 - 2c(u+t_1)(v+t_2) + (v+t_2)^2]} du$$
$$\qquad (H.25)$$

$$= \frac{D_x D_y}{2\pi} \frac{d^{\frac{3}{2}}}{\sigma_1^2 \sigma_2^2} \int_{-\infty}^{\infty} dv \int_{-\infty}^{\infty} uve^{-\frac{1}{2}(u^2 + 2au + b)} du$$

$$= \frac{D_x D_y}{2\pi} \frac{d^{\frac{3}{2}}}{\sigma_1^2 \sigma_2^2} \int_{-\infty}^{\infty} v \left(\int_{-\infty}^{\infty} ue^{-\frac{1}{2}(u^2 + 2au + b)} du \right) dv$$

$$= \frac{D_x D_y}{2\pi} \frac{d^{\frac{3}{2}}}{\sigma_1^2 \sigma_2^2} \int_{-\infty}^{\infty} vI_2(a, b) dv$$

where

$$a(v) = t_1 - ct_2 - cv \tag{H.26}$$

and

$$b(v) = t_1^2 - 2ct_1(v + t_2) + (v + t_2)^2 \tag{H.27}$$
$$= (t_1^2 - 2ct_1t_2 + t_2^2) + v(-2ct_1 + 2t_2) + v^2$$

and so

$$b - a^2 = (t_1^2 - 2ct_1t_2 + t_2^2) + v(-2ct_1 + 2t_2) + v^2 - (t_1 - ct_2 - cv)^2 \tag{H.28}$$
$$= (t_1^2 - 2ct_1t_2 + t_2^2) + v(-2ct_1 + 2t_2) + v^2$$
$$\quad - (t_1 - ct_2)^2 + 2(t_1 - ct_2)cv - c^2v^2$$
$$= v^2[1 - c^2] + 2v[c(t_1 - ct_2) + (t_2 - ct_1)]$$
$$\quad + [(t_1^2 - 2ct_1t_2 + t_2^2) - (t_1 - ct_2)^2]$$

Using equation (H.6)

$$I_2(a, b) = -\sqrt{(2\pi)}ae^{-\frac{1}{2}(b-a^2)} \tag{H.29}$$
$$= -\sqrt{2\pi}[(t_1 - ct_2) - cv]e^{-\frac{1}{2}[\alpha^2 v^2 + 2\beta v + \gamma]}$$

where

$$\alpha = \sqrt{1 - c^2} \tag{H.30}$$
$$\beta = t_2(1 - c^2)$$
$$\gamma = (t_1^2 - 2ct_1t_2 + t_2^2) - (t_1 - ct_2)^2$$

and so

$$\int_{-\infty}^{\infty} vI_2 dv = -\int_{-\infty}^{\infty} \sqrt{2\pi}[(t_1 - ct_2)v - cv^2]e^{-\frac{1}{2}[\alpha^2 v^2 + 2\beta v + \gamma]} dv \tag{H.31}$$

$$= -\sqrt{2\pi}(t_1 - ct_2)\frac{1}{\alpha^2}I_2\left(\frac{\beta}{\alpha}, \gamma\right) + \sqrt{2\pi}\frac{c}{\alpha^3}J_2\left(\frac{\beta}{\alpha}, \gamma\right)$$

$$= \sqrt{2\pi}\frac{c}{\alpha^3}I_2\left(\frac{\beta}{\alpha}, \gamma\right) - \sqrt{2\pi}(t_1 - ct_2)\frac{1}{\alpha^2}J_2\left(\frac{\beta}{\alpha}, \gamma\right)$$

This gives

$$E(pq) = \frac{1}{\sqrt{2\pi}}\frac{D_x D_y d^{\frac{3}{2}}}{\sigma_1^2 \sigma_2^2}\left[\frac{c}{\alpha^3}J_2\left(\frac{\beta}{\alpha}, \gamma\right) - (t_1 - ct_2)\frac{1}{\alpha^2}I_2\left(\frac{\beta}{\alpha}, \gamma\right)\right] \tag{H.32}$$

We can now evaluate $E(p_i q)$ when contract i is a swap with the following steps.

1. Calculate d using equation (H.18).
2. Calculate $t1$ and $t2$ using equation (H.23).
3. Calculate α, β and γ using equation (H.30).
4. Calculate $E(pq)$ using equation (H.32) and the definitions of I_2 and J_2 given by equations (H.4) and (H.8).

H.3.2 Swap-call covariance

We now consider the case where contract i is an uncapped call. The indices for the swap and the call are given by x and y, and the pay-offs by p and q, respectively.

$$E(pq) = \int_{K_y}^{\infty} dy \int_{-\infty}^{\infty} dx \, D_x(y - K_y) D_y(x - K_x)\rho(x,y) \qquad (H.33)$$

$$= D_y D_x \int_{K_y}^{\infty} dy \int_{-\infty}^{\infty} dx (y - K_y)(x - K_x)\rho(x,y)$$

where

$$\rho(x,y) = \frac{1}{2\pi}\frac{1}{\sqrt{d}} e^{-\frac{1}{2d}[\sigma_2^2(x-\mu_x)^2 - 2c\sigma_1\sigma_2(x-\mu_x)(y-\mu_y) + \sigma_1^2(y-\mu_y)^2]} \qquad (H.34)$$

Using the same substitutions as before

$$E(pq) = \frac{D_x D_y}{2\pi}\frac{d^{\frac{3}{2}}}{\sigma_1^2\sigma_2^2}\int_0^{\infty} dv \int_{-\infty}^{\infty} uv e^{-\frac{1}{2}[(u+t_1)^2 - 2c(u+t_1)(v+t_2) + (v+t_2)^2]} du \qquad (H.35)$$

$$= \frac{D_x D_y}{2\pi}\frac{d^{\frac{3}{2}}}{\sigma_1^2\sigma_2^2}\int_0^{\infty} dv \int_{-\infty}^{\infty} uv e^{-\frac{1}{2}(u^2+2au+b)} du$$

$$= \frac{D_x D_y}{2\pi}\frac{d^{\frac{3}{2}}}{\sigma_1^2\sigma_2^2}\int_0^{\infty} v \left(\int_{-\infty}^{\infty} ue^{-\frac{1}{2}(u^2+2au+b)} du \right) dv$$

$$= \frac{D_x D_y}{2\pi}\frac{d^{\frac{3}{2}}}{\sigma_1^2\sigma_2^2}\int_0^{\infty} vI_2(a,b)dv$$

This is exactly the same as the equivalent expression for a swap contract except for the lower limit on the integral. Using equation (H.6)

$$\int_0^{\infty} vI_2 dv = -\int_0^{\infty} \sqrt{2\pi}[(t_1 - ct_2)v - cv^2]e^{-\frac{1}{2}[\alpha^2v^2+2\beta v+\gamma]} dv \qquad (H.36)$$

$$= -\sqrt{2\pi}(t_1 - ct_2)\frac{1}{\alpha^2}I_1\left(\frac{\beta}{\alpha},\gamma\right) + \sqrt{2\pi}\frac{c}{\alpha^3}J_1\left(\frac{\beta}{\alpha},\gamma\right)$$

$$= \sqrt{2\pi}\frac{c}{\alpha^3}J_1\left(\frac{\beta}{\alpha},\gamma\right) - \sqrt{2\pi}(t_1 - ct_2)\frac{1}{\alpha^2}I_1\left(\frac{\beta}{\alpha},\gamma\right)$$

This gives

$$E(pq) = \frac{1}{\sqrt{2\pi}} \frac{D_x D_y d^{\frac{3}{2}}}{\sigma_1^2 \sigma_2^2} \left[\frac{c}{a^3} J_1\left(\frac{\beta}{\alpha}, \gamma\right) - (t_1 - ct_2)\frac{1}{a^2} I_1\left(\frac{\beta}{\alpha}, \gamma\right) \right] \quad \text{(H.37)}$$

H.3.3 Swap-put covariance

Finally, we consider the case where contract i is a put option.

The indices for the swap and the put are given by x and y, and the pay-offs by p and q, respectively.

$$E(pq) = \int_{-\infty}^{K_y} dy \int_{-\infty}^{\infty} dx\, D_y(K_y - y)D_x(x - K_x)\rho(x,y) \quad \text{(H.38)}$$

$$= D_y D_x \int_{-\infty}^{K_y} dy \int_{-\infty}^{\infty} dx (K_y - y)(x - K_x)\rho(x,y)$$

where

$$\rho(x,y) = \frac{1}{2\pi} \frac{1}{\sqrt{d}} e^{-\frac{1}{2d}[\sigma_2^2(x-\mu_x)^2 - 2c\sigma_1\sigma_2(x-\mu_x)(y-\mu_y) + \sigma_1^2(y-\mu_y)^2]} \quad \text{(H.39)}$$

Using the same substitutions as before

$$E(pq) = -\frac{D_x D_y}{2\pi} \frac{d^{\frac{3}{2}}}{\sigma_1^2 \sigma_2^2} \int_{-\infty}^{0} dv \int_{-\infty}^{\infty} uv e^{-\frac{1}{2}[(u+t_1)^2 - 2c(u+t_1)(v+t_2) + (v+t_2)^2]} du \quad \text{(H.40)}$$

$$= -\frac{D_x D_y}{2\pi} \frac{d^{\frac{3}{2}}}{\sigma_1^2 \sigma_2^2} \int_{0}^{\infty} dv \int_{-\infty}^{\infty} uv e^{-\frac{1}{2}[(u+t_1)^2 - 2c(u+t_1)(t_2-v) + (t_2-v)^2]} du$$

$$= -\frac{D_x D_y}{2\pi} \frac{d^{\frac{3}{2}}}{\sigma_1^2 \sigma_2^2} \int_{0}^{\infty} dv \int_{-\infty}^{\infty} uv e^{-\frac{1}{2}(u^2 + 2au + b)} du$$

$$= -\frac{D_x D_y}{2\pi} \frac{d^{\frac{3}{2}}}{\sigma_1^2 \sigma_2^2} \int_{0}^{\infty} v \left(\int_{-\infty}^{\infty} u e^{-\frac{1}{2}(u^2 + 2au + b)} du \right) dv$$

$$= -\frac{D_x D_y}{2\pi} \frac{d^{\frac{3}{2}}}{\sigma_1^2 \sigma_2^2} \int_{0}^{\infty} v I_2(a,b) dv$$

where now

$$a(v) = t_1 - ct_2 + cv \quad \text{(H.41)}$$

and

$$b(v) = t_1^2 - 2ct_1(t_2 - v) + (t_2 - v)^2 \quad \text{(H.42)}$$
$$= (t_1^2 - 2ct_1t_2 + t_2^2) + v(2ct_1 - 2t_2) + v^2$$

This gives

$$b - a^2 = (t_1^2 - 2ct_1t_2 + t_2^2) + v(2ct_1 - 2t_2) + v^2 - (t_1 - ct_2 + cv)^2 \quad \text{(H.43)}$$
$$= (t_1^2 - 2ct_1t_2 + t_2^2) + v(2ct_1 - 2t_2) + v^2$$
$$\quad - (t_1 - ct_2)^2 - 2(t_1 - ct_2)cv - c^2v^2$$
$$= v^2[1 - c^2] - 2v[c(t_1 - ct_2) + (t_2 - ct_1)]$$
$$\quad + [(t_1^2 - 2ct_1t_2 + t_2^2) - (t_1 - ct_2)^2]$$

Using equation (H.6)

$$I_2(a, b) = -\sqrt{(2\pi)}ae^{-\frac{1}{2}(b-a^2)} \quad \text{(H.44)}$$
$$= -\sqrt{2\pi}[(t_1 - ct_2) - cv]e^{-\frac{1}{2}[\alpha^2 v^2 + 2\beta v + \gamma]}$$

where

$$\alpha = \sqrt{1 - c^2} \quad \text{(H.45)}$$
$$\beta = t_2(c^2 - 1)$$
$$\gamma = (t_1^2 - 2ct_1t_2 + t_2^2) - (t_1 - ct_2)^2$$

(note that the only difference from the swap and call cases is the sign of β) and so

$$\int_0^\infty vI_2 dv = -\int_0^\infty \sqrt{2\pi}[(t_1 - ct_2)v + cv^2]e^{-\frac{1}{2}[\alpha^2 v^2 + 2\beta v + \gamma]} dv \quad \text{(H.46)}$$
$$= -\sqrt{2\pi}(t_1 - ct_2)\frac{1}{\alpha^2}I_1\left(\frac{\beta}{\alpha}, \gamma\right) - \sqrt{2\pi}\frac{c}{\alpha^3}J_1\left(\frac{\beta}{\alpha}, \gamma\right)$$
$$= -\sqrt{2\pi}\frac{c}{\alpha^3}I_1\left(\frac{\beta}{\alpha}, \gamma\right) - \sqrt{2\pi}(t_1 - ct_2)\frac{1}{\alpha^2}J_1\left(\frac{\beta}{\alpha}, \gamma\right)$$

This gives

$$E(pq) = \frac{1}{\sqrt{2\pi}}\frac{D_x D_y d^{\frac{3}{2}}}{\sigma_1^2 \sigma_2^2}\left[\frac{c}{\alpha^3}J_2\left(\frac{\beta}{\alpha}, \gamma\right) + (t_1 - ct_2)\frac{1}{\alpha^2}I_2\left(\frac{\beta}{\alpha}, \gamma\right)\right] \quad \text{(H.47)}$$

H.4 Discussion

We have considered how to calculate the beta for uncapped swap, call and put contracts. Other contracts, such as uncapped straddles, strangles and collars, can be made up as linear combinations of these three basic contracts, and the betas are just the sums of the betas for the contracts in the linear combination. This covers all contracts that can be traded on the CME at this point in time. However, this does not encompass many of the contracts that are traded in the OTC weather market, most of which have caps. We are not sure if it is possible to derive equivalent expressions for such contracts; the second integral becomes very hard.

Also, we are not sure if it is possible to derive closed-form solutions for the covariance between two option contracts, again because the second integral becomes very hard. If it were possible to derive closed-form solutions for the covariance between pairs of uncapped options then we could calculate the variance of the pay-offs of a portfolio of CME contracts entirely using closed-form solutions.

H.5 Numerical examples

To facilitate the debugging of computer code we now give some numerical examples of the results from these expressions.

Note that examples 4 and 5 are linked; $E(pq)$ from example 5 should be exactly half of $E(pq)$ from example 4 – and it is.

Example 1: swap-swap, correlation = 0

Mean 1	373	Mean 2	389
SD 1	48	SD 2	45
Strike 1	370	Strike 2	380
Tick 1	1	Tick 2	1
Index correlation	0		
Results			
E(pq)	27		

Example 2: swap-swap, correlation = 1

Mean 1	373	Mean 2	373
SD 1	48	SD 2	48
Strike 1	373	Strike 2	373
Tick 1	1	Tick 2	1
Index correlation	1		
Results			
E(pq)	2304		

Example 3: swap-swap, correlation = 0.5

Mean 1	373	Mean 2	389
SD 1	48	SD 2	45
Strike 1	370	Strike 2	380
Tick 1	1	Tick 2	1
Index correlation	0.5		

Results

E(pq)	1107		
E(p)	3	E(q)	9
SD(p)	48	SD(q)	45
Cov(pq)	1080	Corr(pq)	0.5

Example 4: swap-swap, correlation = 0.5

Mean 1	373	Mean 2	373
SD 1	48	SD 2	48
Strike 1	373	Strike 2	373
Tick 1	1	Tick 2	1
Index correlation	0.5		

Results

E(pq)	1152

Example 5: swap-call, correlation = 0.5

Mean 1	373	Mean 2	373
SD 1	48	SD 2	48
Strike 1	373	Strike 2	373
Tick 1	1	Tick 2	1
Index correlation	0.5		

Results

E(pq)	576		
E(p)	0	E(q)	19.15
SD(p)	48	SD(q)	28.02
Cov(pq)	576	Corr(pq)	0.482

Example 6: swap-put, correlation = 0.5

Mean 1	373	Mean 2	373
SD 1	48	SD 2	48
Strike 1	373	Strike 2	373
Tick 1	1	Tick 2	1
Index correlation	0.5		

Results

E(pq)	−576		
E(p)	0	E(q)	19.15
SD(p)	48	SD(q)	28.02
Cov(pq)	−576	Corr(pq)	−0.482

Example 7: swap-call = swap-swap/swap-put, correlation = 0.5

Mean 1	373	Mean 2	389
SD 1	48	SD 2	45
Strike 1	370	Strike 2	380
Tick 1	1	Tick 2	1
Index correlation	0.5		

Results

E(swap-swap)	1107
E(swap-call)	694.03
E(swap-put)	−412.97
E(swap-put)+E(swap-swap)	694.03

Appendix I
Simulation methods

I.1 Introduction

We now discuss some of the basic algorithms for univariate random number generation and the simulation from time series models. For more details, see textbooks such as Ripley (1987), Casella and Robert (1999) or Gentle (2003). These books also contain suggestions of specialised algorithms that may be faster than those suggested here, and they discuss methods for reducing the variability in the results (so-called variance reduction techniques).

I.1.1 Simulating independent random variables

The simplest distribution to simulate from, and the basic building block for simulating from more complex distributions, is the uniform. Most programming languages, numerical libraries and applications such as Excel, R, S-Plus and SAS have capabilities to simulate from a uniform distribution. We will assume that such functionality is available and will not discuss the details of how these simulations work.

The general approach to simulation from a given CDF

The most general approach to generate a random variable X with CDF F is by transforming a uniform random variable using the following scheme:

- simulate a random variable U with a uniform distribution;
- find the inverse F^{-1} of F, defined by $F^{-1}(u) = \min\{x | F(x) \leq u\}$;
- set $X := F^{-1}(U)$.

To see why this scheme works, consider figure I.1.

Any simulated value X on the horizontal axis is related to a value $U = F(X)$ on the vertical axis, so the probability of simulating a number less than

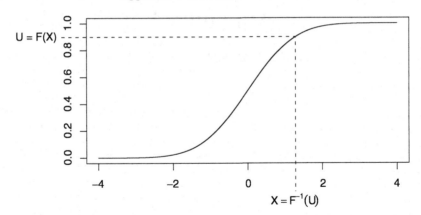

Figure I.1. The inverse of the CDF F can be used to simulate a random variable with distribution F.

or equal to X is exactly equal to U because U follows a uniform distribution. Although the CDF in the example is continuous, the method works equally well for the simulation of discrete random variables when the inverse of F is defined as described above.

Several well-known distributions can easily be simulated using this procedure:

- the exponential distribution has CDF $F(x) = 1 - \exp(-x)$, so $F^{-1}(p) = -\log(1-p)$;
- the inverse of the normal distribution CDF is often available as a mathematical function in applications (for example, it is called qnorm in R and norminv in Excel).

It may not always be possible to find an analytical expression for the inverse of F. In such cases a practical solution is to create a look-up table for the function F and use it for the evaluation of F^{-1}. This procedure may decrease the accuracy for continuous distributions and may be slow to set up, but execution can be relatively fast – in some cases even faster than direct calculation of F^{-1}. However, there are situations where simpler and faster methods for the simulation of random variables without any calculation or tabulation of the CDF exist. Below we list a few of these methods based on the recommendations in Ripley (1987).

The Polar algorithm for normal distributions

Most useful for weather derivatives is probably a fast method for the simulation of standard normal random variables – i.e. variables with density.

$$f(x) = \frac{1}{\sqrt{2\pi}} e^{-\frac{1}{2}x^2}$$

The so-called Polar method (Ripley, 1987) is such an algorithm, which generates pairs of independent standard normal variates. The steps involved are as follows.

1. Generate variables U_1, U_2, which are uniformly distributed on the interval $[-1, 1]$. Repeat this until $Y = U_1^2 + U_2^2 < 1$.
2. Let $V := \sqrt{-2Y^{-1} \log Y}$.
3. The variables $X_1 := VU_1$ and $X_2 := VU_2$ are random numbers from the standard normal distribution.

The method is a rejection-based version of the classical Box–Müller algorithm (Box and Müller, 1958) and is both simple and relatively fast. In order to obtain a sample Z from a normal distribution with mean μ and variance σ^2 from a standard normal variable X we let $Z := \sigma X + \mu$.

Algorithms for the gamma distribution

The gamma distribution is another useful distribution for weather derivatives, because of the relation between the gamma and the negative binomial (discussed below) and because it can be used as an index distribution in its own right.

The density of the standard gamma distribution with shape parameter λ is

$$f(x) = \frac{1}{\Gamma(\lambda)} \lambda^{x-1} e^{-x}$$

Because the density of a gamma distribution is unbounded at zero when the shape parameter λ is less than or equal to one, it is most efficient to treat the cases $\lambda < 1$ and $\lambda > 1$ separately. The case $\lambda = 1$ is the exponential distribution, for which the CDF can easily be inverted (as described above), and the general method from section I.1.1 can be used.

For $\lambda < 1$ Ripley (1987) recommends the algorithm by Ahrens and Dieter (1974), which proceeds as follows.

1. Generate variables U_1, U_2, which are uniformly distributed on the interval $[0, 1]$.
2. If $U_1 \leq e/(e + \lambda)$ then go to 3; else go to 4.
3. Let $X = ((\lambda + e)U_1/e)^{1/\lambda}$. If $U_2 > e^{-X}$ then go to 1; else return X.
4. Let $X = -\log((\lambda + e)(1 - U_1)/\lambda e)$. If $U_1 > X^{\lambda-1}$ then go to 1; otherwise return X.

The case $\lambda > 1$ can be treated defining the constants $c_1 := \lambda - 1$, $c_2 := (\lambda - 1/6\lambda)/c_1$, $c_3 := 2/c_1$, $c_4 := c_3 + 2$ and $c_5 := 1/\sqrt{(\lambda)}$ and using the method from Cheng and Feast, 1979.

1. Generate variables U_1, U_2, which are uniformly distributed on the interval $[0, 1]$, and set $U_1 := U_2 + c_5(1 - 1.86U_1)$. Repeat this until $0 < U_1 < 1$.
2. Let $W := c_2 U_2 / U_1$.
3. If $c_3 U_1 + W + W^{-1} \le c_4$ then go to 5.
4. If $c_3 \log U_1 - \log W + W \ge 1$ then go to 1.
5. Return $X := c_1 W$.

We can obtain a gamma distribution with a specified scale parameter β by multiplying a standard gamma variable by β.

Simulation from a Poisson distribution

The probability function for the Poisson distribution with mean λ is given by

$$p(x) = e^{-\lambda} \frac{\lambda^x}{x!}$$

For small values of the mean ($\lambda < 30$) the following simulation scheme can be used.

1. Let $p := 1$, $n := 0$ and $c := e^{-\lambda}$.
2. Generate a variable U from a uniform distribution on $[0, 1]$ and set $p := pU$, $n := n + 1$. Repeat this until $p < c$.
3. The variable $X := n - 1$ follows a Poisson distribution with mean λ.

For larger values of λ it is better to use the following scheme due to Atkinson (1979).

1. Generate U_1 from a uniform distribution on $[0, 1]$ and let $X := (\alpha - \log((1 - U_1)/U_1))/\beta$. Repeat this until $X > -0.5$.
2. Let N be the integer part of $X + 0.5$ and generate U_2 from a uniform distribution on $[0, 1]$.
3. If $\alpha - \beta X + \log \left(\frac{U_2}{(1 + \exp(\alpha - \beta X))^2} \right) > k + N \log \lambda - \log N!$ then go to 1; else return N.

Here $c = 0.767 - 3.36/\lambda$, $\beta = \pi/\sqrt{3\lambda}$ and $\alpha = \beta\lambda$.

Simulation from a negative binomial distribution

We can simulate from a negative binomial by combining the algorithms for the gamma and Poisson distributions given above. This method uses the observation that a negative binomial distribution can be constructed as a Poisson distribution where the mean parameter λ has been drawn from a gamma distribution.

The simulation of time series

How should we simulate from a time series model? The methodology we describe in this section is applicable to general stationary Gaussian processes. However, as an example, we start by considering a mean zero, stationary AR(p) process X_t with Gaussian innovations ϵ_t:

$$X_t = \phi_1 X_{t-1} + \ldots + \phi_p X_{t-p} + \epsilon_t \tag{I.1}$$

The simplest way to simulate such a process is to set the first p simulated values equal to zero and then simulate subsequent observations using equation (I.1). Because of the exponential decay of the covariance function the dependence on the initial p values will be lost very quickly, and a sample from the desired stationary distribution can be obtained by discarding the first k observations, where k depends on the covariance function.

A more sophisticated simulation procedure would sample the initial p values from the stationary distribution of the time series, in which case no simulations have to be discarded. See, for example, Brockwell and Davis (1999) for exact expressions for the stationary distribution for ARMA processes.

Another, and much more general, way of simulating observations from a Gaussian time series is by using the covariance function, for which one can often obtain explicit expressions. The covariance function can be used to construct the covariance matrix and then standard multivariate normal simulation methods can be used. However, the lengths of the time series that one would like to simulate may be very large. This results in a very large covariance matrix, which in turn can result in long computation times and computer memory exhaustion. In most cases this problem is solved by the fact that the time series is assumed stationary, so that the covariance matrix has a band structure that can be exploited to speed up the simulation routine. For more details of such simulation routines see, for example, Brockwell and Davis (1999) or Beran (1994).

Appendix J

Efficient methods for pricing against a portfolio

J.1 Efficient methods for modelling one extra contract

We now describe two numerical methods for the efficient modelling of one extra contract on a portfolio. For both these methods we make the following assumptions:

- n is the original number of indices in the portfolio;
- m is the number of years of historical data;
- k is the number of simulations;
- X_h is the original historical data in an n by m matrix;
- Z_h is the same data transformed to standard normal distributions;
- we have simulated these n indices for k years using the rank correlation method;
- Z_s is the n by k matrix of the normally distributed simulations;
- X_s are the final simulations with correct marginals;
- x_h is the 1 by m vector of the new historical data;
- z_h is the same when transformed to a standard normal distribution;
- p_h is the 1 by m vector of historical pay-offs for the portfolio;
- q_h is the same when transformed to a standard normal distribution using the empirical CDF;
- p_s is the 1 by k vector of simulated pay-offs for the portfolio;
- q_s is the same when transformed to a standard normal distribution using the empirical CDF.

J.1.1 Index regression

We model the new transformed index data as a linear combination of the old transformed index data $z_h = \alpha Z_h + e_h$, where e_h is a noise vector with variance v and α is a 1 by n vector of coefficients. This gives $\alpha = (z_h Z_h^T)(Z_h Z_h^T)^{-1}$ and $v = z_h z_h^T - \alpha Z_h Z_h^T \alpha^T$.

The method then works in two stages.

1. Given the portfolio rank correlations, convert to linear correlations and calculate the n by n matrix $A = (Z_h Z_h^T)^{-1}$.
2. Store this matrix A, the simulations Z_s and the historical data X_h.

When it is necessary to price a single contract against the portfolio, we then follow the steps below.

1. Calculate the rank correlation vector c_r between the new historical data x_h and the old historical data X_h.
2. Convert this to linear covariances $c = z_h Z_h^T$.
3. Calculate α as $\alpha = cA$.
4. Calculate v.
5. Create a new vector of normally distributed simulations z_s using linear combinations of the old simulations $z_s = \alpha Z_s + e_s$, where e_s is sampled from a normal distribution with variance v.
6. Transform z_s to the correct marginal distribution to give x_s.

J.1.2 Pay-off regression

In this method we model the new index data as a linear combination of the old portfolio pay-offs $z_h = \alpha p_h + e_h$, where e_h is a noise vector with variance v. This gives $\alpha = \frac{(z_h p_h^T)}{p_h p_h^T}$ and $v = z_h z_h^T - \alpha^2 p_h p_h^T$.

When we want to price a new contract, we follow the steps below.

1. Calculate the rank correlation between the historical pay-offs for the portfolio p_h and the historical index values for the new contract x_h.
2. Convert this rank correlation to a linear covariance $c = z_h q_h^T$, and calculate α.
3. Simulate new index values z_s: $z_s = \alpha q_s + e_s$.
4. Convert these index values to the correct distribution.
5. Convert these index values to pay-offs.

References

Ahrens, J., and U. Dieter. 1974. Computer methods for sampling from gamma, beta, Poisson and binomial distributions. *Computing*, 12: 223–246.

Akaike, H. 1974. A new look at statistical model identification. *IEEE Transactions Automatic Control*, 19: 716–723.

Alaton, P., B. Djehiche and D. Stillberger. 2002. On modelling and pricing weather derivatives. *Applied Mathematical Finance*, 9(1): 1–20.

Allcroft, D., and C. Glasbey. 2003. A latent Gaussian Markov random-field model for spatiotemporal rainfall disaggregation. *Applied Statistics*, 52: 487–498.

Allen, M. 1999. Do it yourself climate prediction. *Nature*, 401: 642.

Allen, R., and A. DeGaetano. 2000. A method to adjust long-term temperature extreme series for non-climatic inhomogeneities. *Journal of Climate*, 13: 3495–3507.

Ambaum, M., B. Hoskins and D. Stephenson. 2001. Arctic Oscillation or North Atlantic Oscillation? *Journal of Climate*, 14: 3680–3695.

Arfken, G. 1985. *Mathematical Methods for Physicists*. Academic Press.

Atkinson, A. 1979. The computer generation of Poisson random variables. *Applied Statistics*, 28: 29–35.

Baker, R. 2003. *Fragile Science*. Pan.

Banks, E. 2002. Weather fundamentals. In *Weather Risk Management*, 14–43. Palgrave.

Banks, E., and R. Henderson. 2002. Risk considerations. In *Weather Risk Management*, 262–288. Palgrave.

Barnston, A., S. Mason, L. Goddard, D. DeWitt and S. Zebiak. 2003. Multimodel ensembling in seasonal climate forecasting at IRI. *Bulletin of the American Meteorological Society*, 84: 1783–1796.

Baxter, M., and A. Rennie. 1996. *Financial Calculus*. Cambridge University Press.

Beran, J. 1994. *Statistics for Long-Memory Processes*. Chapman & Hall/CRC.

Björk, T. 1998. *Arbitrage Theory in Continuous Time*. Oxford University Press.

Black, F. 1976. The pricing of commodity contracts. *Journal of Financial Economics*, 3: 167–179.

Black, F., and M. Scholes. 1973. The pricing of options and corporate liabilities. *Journal of Political Economy*, 81: 637–654.

Boissonnade, A., L. Heitkemper and D. Whitehead. 2002. Weather data: cleaning and enhancement. In *Climate Risk and the Weather Market*, 73–98. Risk Books.

Bouchaud, J., G. Iori and D. Sornette. 1996. Real-world options: smile and residual risk. *Risk*, 9(3): 61–65.

Box, G., and D. Cox. 1964. An analysis of transformations. *Journal of the Royal Statistical Society, Series B: Methodological*, 26: 211–243.

Box, G., and G. Jenkins. 1970. *Time Series Analysis, Forecasting and Control*. Holden-Day.

Box, G., and M. Müller. 1958. A note on the generation of random normal deviates. *Annals of Mathematical Statistics*, 29: 610–611.

Boyle, P., and D. Emanuel. 1980. Discretely adjusted option hedges. *Journal of Financial Economics*, 9: 259–282.

Brier, G. 1950. Verification of forecasts expressed in terms of probabilities. *Monthly Weather Review*, 78: 1–3.

Brix, A., S. Jewson and C. Ziehmann. 2002. Weather derivative modelling and valuation: a statistical perspective. In *Climate Risk and the Weather Market*, 127–150. Risk Books.

Brockwell, P., and P. Davis. 1999. *Time Series: Theory and Methods*. Springer-Verlag, 2nd edn.

Brody, D., J. Syroka and M. Zervos. 2002. Dynamical pricing of weather derivatives. *Quantitative Finance*, 2: 189–198.

Caballero, R., S. Jewson and A. Brix. 2002. Long memory in surface air temperature: detection, modelling and application to weather derivative valuation. *Climate Research*, 21: 127–140.

Cao, M., and J. Wei. 2000. Pricing the weather. *Risk*, 13(5): 67–70.

Carmona, R., and D. Villani. 2003. Monte Carlo helps with pricing. *Environmental Finance*, June.

Casella, G., and R. L. Berger. 2002. *Statistical Inference*. Duxbury.

Casella, G., and C. Robert. 1999. *Monte Carlo Statistical Methods*. Springer-Verlag.

Chandler, R., and H. Wheater. 2002. Analysis of rainfall variability using generalized linear models: a case study from the west of Ireland. *Water Resources Research*, 38: 1192–1202.

Cheng, R., and G. Feast. 1979. Some simple gamma variate generators. *Applied Statistics*, 28: 290–295.

Cleveland, W., and S. Devlin. 1988. Locally weighted regression: an approach to regression analysis by local fitting. *Journal of the American Statistical Association*, 83: 596–610.

Coles, S. 2001. *An Introduction to Statistical Modeling of Extreme Values*. Springer-Verlag.

Coles, S., and L. Pericchi. 2003. Anticipating catastrophes through extreme value modelling. *Applied Statistics*, 52: 405–416.

Davis, M. 2001. Pricing weather derivatives by marginal value. *Quantitative Finance*, 1: 1–4.

Davison, A., and D. Hinkley. 1997. *Bootstrap Methods and Their Applications*. Cambridge University Press.

Denholm-Price, J. 2003. Can an ensemble give anything more than Gaussian probabilities? *Non-linear Processes in Geophysics*, 10: 469–475.

Dischel, R. 1998a. Black–Scholes won't do. Weather risk special report, *Energy & Power Risk Management*, October.

1998b. Seasonal forecasts and the weather risk market. *Applied Derivatives Trading*, November.

1998c. Warning – La Niña volatility. *Energy & Power Risk Management*, November.

2000. Seasonal weather forecasts and derivative valuation. Weather risk special report, *Energy & Power Risk Management*, August.

(ed.). 2002. *Climate Risk and the Weather Market*. Risk Books.

Dornier, F., and M. Querel. 2000. Caution to the wind. Weather risk special report, *Energy & Power Risk Management*, 8: 30–32.

Dowd, K. 1998. *Beyond Value at Risk*. Wiley.

Dutton, J. 2002. The weather in weather risk. In *Climate Risk and the Weather Market*, 185–214. Risk Books.

Dutton, J., and R. Dischel. 2001. Weather and climate predictions: minutes to months. Weather risk special report, *Energy & Power Risk Management*, August.

Easterling, D. 2001. Past and future changes in climate extremes. *The Climate Report*, 2(1).

Easterling, D., and T. Peterson. 1995. A new method for detecting undocumented discontinuities in climatological time series. *International Journal of Climatology*, 15: 369–377.

Economist, The. 2003. 13 February.

Element Re. 2002. *Weather Risk Management*. Palgrave.

Elton, E., and M. Gruber. 1995. *Modern Portfolio Theory and Investment Analysis*. Wiley.

Embrechts, P., C. Klüppeberg and T. Mikosch. 1997. *Modelling Extremal Events*. Springer-Verlag.

Embrechts, P., A. McNeil and D. Straumann. 2002. Correlation and dependence in risk management: properties and pitfalls. In *Risk Management: Value at Risk and Beyond*, 176–223. Cambridge University Press.

Fisher, R. 1912. On an absolute criterion for fitting frequency curves. *Messenger of Mathematics*, 41: 155–160.

1922. On the mathematical foundations of statistics. *Philosophical Transactions of the Royal Society*, A, 222: 309–368.

Frey, R., and A. Stremme. 1997. Market volatility and feedback effects from dynamic hedging. *Mathematical Finance*, 7: 351–374.

Gardiner, C. 1985. *Handbook of Stochastic Methods*. Springer.

Geman, H. 1999a. The Bermuda triangle: weather, electricity and insurance derivatives. In *Insurance and Weather Derivatives*, 197–204. Risk Books.

(ed.). 1999b. *Insurance and Weather Derivatives*. Risk Books.

Gentle, J. 2003. *Random Number Generation and Monte Carlo Methods*. Springer-Verlag, 2nd edn.

Gibbas, M. 2002. The nature of climate uncertainty and considerations for weather risk managers. In *Climate Risk and the Weather Market*, 97–114. Risk Books.

Goldman-Sachs. 1999. *Kelvin Ltd*. Offering circular.

Granger, C. W. J., and R. Joyeux. 1980. An introduction to long memory time series models and fractional differencing. *Journal of Time Series Analysis*, 1: 15–29.

Hamill, T. 1997. Reliability diagrams for multicategory probabilistic forecasts. *Weather Forecasting*, 12: 736–741.

Henderson, R. 2002. Pricing weather risk. In *Weather Risk Management*, 167–198. Palgrave.

Henderson, R., Y. Li and N. Sinha. 2002. Data. In *Weather Risk Management*, 200–223. Palgrave.

Heyer, D. 2001. Stochastic dominance: a tool for evaluating reinsurance alternatives. *Casualty Actuarial Society Forum*, summer: 95–118.

Hijikata, K. (ed.). 1999. *Tenkoo Derivatives no Subete (All about Weather Derivatives)*. Sigma Base Capital.

(ed.). 2003. *Sooron Tenkoo Derivatives (All Theories about Weather Derivatives)*. Sigma Base Capital.

Hirose, N. (ed.). 2003. *Everything about Weather Derivatives*. Tokyo Electricity University.

Hogg, R., and S. Klugman. 1984. *Loss Distributions*. Wiley.

Hoggard, T., A. E. Whalley and P. Wilmott. 1994. Hedging option portfolios in the presence of transaction costs. *Advances in Futures and Options Research*, 7: 21–35.

Hull, J. 2002. *Options, Futures and Other Derivatives*. Prentice Hall.

Iman, R., and W. Conover. 1982. A distribution-free approach to inducing rank correlation among input variables. *Communications in Statistics*, 11: 311–334.

IPCC. 2001. *Climate Change 2001 – The Scientific Basis*. Technical report, IPCC working group.

Jewson, S. 2000. Use of GCM forecasts in financial-meteorological models. In *Proceedings of the 25th Annual Climate Diagnostics and Prediction Workshop*. US Department of Commerce.

2002a. Arbitrage pricing for weather derivatives. In *Climate Risk and the Weather Market*, 314–316. Risk Books.

2002b. Weather derivative pricing and risk management: volatility and value at risk. *http://ssrn.com/abstract=405802*.

2003a. Closed-form expressions for the pricing of weather derivatives, part 1: the expected payoff. *http://ssrn.com/abstract=436262*.

2003b. Closed-form expressions for the pricing of weather derivatives, part 2: the greeks. *http://ssrn.com/abstract=436263*.

2003c. Closed-form expressions for the pricing of weather derivatives, part 3: the payoff variance. *http://ssrn.com/abstract=481902*.

2003d. Closed-form expressions for the pricing of weather derivatives, part 4: the kernel density. *http://ssrn.com/abstract=486422*.

2003e. Comparing the ensemble mean and the ensemble standard deviation as inputs for probabilistic temperature forecasts. *arXiv:physics/0310059*.

2003f. Comparing the potential accuracy of burn and index modelling for weather option valuation. *http://ssrn.com/abstract=486342*.

2003g. Convergence of the distribution of payoffs for portfolios of weather derivatives. *http://ssrn.com/abstract=531043*.

2003h. Do medium-range ensemble forecasts give useful predictions of temporal correlations? *arXiv:physics/0310079*.

2003i. Do probabilistic medium-range temperature forecasts need to allow for non-normality? *arXiv:physics/0310060*.

2003j. Estimation of uncertainty in the pricing of weather options. *http://ssrn.com/abstract=441286*.

2003k. Horizon value at risk for weather derivatives, part 1: single contracts. *http://ssrn.com/abstract=477585*.

2003l. Horizon value at risk for weather derivatives, part 2: portfolios. *http://ssrn.com/abstract=478051*.

2003m. Moment-based methods for ensemble assessment and calibration. *arXiv:physics/0309042*.

2003n. The problem with the Brier score. *arXiv:physics/0401046*.

2003o. Risk loading and implied volatility in the pricing of weather options. *http://ssrn.com/abstract=481905*.

2003p. Simple models for the daily volatility of weather derivative underlyings. *http://ssrn.com/abstract=477163*.

2003q. Use of the basic and adjusted kernel densities for weather derivative pricing. *http://ssrn.com/abstract=481923*.

2003r. Use of the likelihood for measuring the skill of probabilistic forecasts. *arXiv:physics/0308046*.

2003s. Weather forecasts, weather derivatives, Black–Scholes, Feynmann–Kac and Fokker–Planck. *arXiv:physics/0312125*.

2003t. Weather option pricing with transaction costs. *Energy & Power Risk Management*, 7(9).

2004a. The application of PCA to weather derivative portfolios. *http://ssrn.com/abstract=486503*.

2004b. Closed-form expressions for the beta of a weather derivative portfolio. *http://ssrn.com/abstract=486442*.

2004c. Four methods for the static hedging of weather derivative portfolios. *http://ssrn.com/abstract=486302*.

2004d. Improving probabilistic weather forecasts using seasonally varying calibration parameters. *arXiv:physics/0402026*.

2004e. A preliminary assessment of the utility of seasonal forecasts for the pricing of US temperature-based weather derivatives. *http://ssrn.com/abstract=531062*.

2004f. The relative importance of trends, distributions and the number of years of data in the pricing of weather options. *http://ssrn.com/abstract=516503*.

2004g. Weather derivative pricing and the normality of standard US temperature indices. *http://ssrn.com/abstract=535982*.

2004h. Weather derivative pricing and the potential accuracy of daily temperature modelling. *http://ssrn.com/abstract=535122*.

2004i. Weather derivative pricing and the year ahead forecasting of temperature, part 2: theory. *http://ssrn.com/abstract=535143*.

Jewson, S., and A. Brix. 2001. Sunny outlook for weather investors. *Environmental Finance*, February.

2004a. Weather derivative pricing and the spatial variability of US temperature trends. *http://ssrn.com/abstract=535924*.

2004b. Weather derivative pricing and the year ahead forecasting of temperature, part 1: empirical results. *http://ssrn.com/abstract=535142*.

Jewson, S., A. Brix and C. Ziehmann. 2002a. Risk modelling. In *Weather Risk Report*, 5–10. Global Reinsurance Review.

2002b. Use of meteorological forecasts in weather derivative pricing. In *Climate Risk and the Weather Market*, 169–184. Risk Books.

2003a. A new framework for the assessment and calibration of ensemble temperature forecasts. *Atmospheric Science Letters* (submitted).

Jewson, S., and R. Caballero. 2002. Multivariate long-memory modelling of daily surface air temperatures and the valuation of weather derivative portfolios. *http://ssrn.com/abstract=405800*.

2003a. Seasonality in the dynamics of surface air temperature and the pricing of weather derivatives. *Meteorological Applications*, 10(4): 367–376.

2003b. The use of weather forecasts in the pricing of weather derivatives. *Meteorological Applications*, 10(4): 377–389.

Jewson, S., F. Doblas-Reyes and R. Hagedorn. 2003b. The assessment and calibration of ensemble seasonal forecasts of equatorial Pacific Ocean temperature and the predictability of uncertainty. *arXiv:physics/0308065*.

Jewson, S., J. Hamlin and D. Whitehead. 2003c. Moving stations and making money. *Environmental Finance*, November.

Jewson, S., and D. Whitehead. 2001. Weather risk and weather data. *Environmental Finance*, November.

Jewson, S., and M. Zervos. 2003a. The Black–Scholes equation for weather derivatives. *http://ssrn.com/abstract=436282*.

2003b. No arbitrage pricing of weather derivatives in the presence of a liquid swap market. Submitted to the *International Journal of Theoretical and Applied Finance*.

Jewson, S., and C. Ziehmann. 2003. Using ensemble forecasts to predict the size of forecast changes, with application to weather swap value at risk. *Atmospheric Science Letters*, 4: 15–27.

Johnson, N., S. Kotz and N. Balakrishnan. 1994. *Continuous Univariate Distributions*. Wiley-Interscience.

1997. *Discrete Multivariate Distributions*. Wiley-Interscience.

Johnson, N., S. Kotz and A. Kemp. 1993. *Univariate Discrete Distributions*. Wiley-Interscience.

Jolliffe, I., and D. Stephenson. 2003. *Forecast Verification: A Practitioner's Guide in Atmospheric Science*. Wiley.

Jones, M. C. 1991. On correcting for variance inflation in kernel density estimation. *Computational Statistics and Data Analysis*, 11: 3–15.

Jones, P. 1999. The instrumental data record. In *Analysis of Climate Variability*, 53–76. Springer.

Karl, T., and C. Williams. 1987. An approach to adjusting climatological time series for discontinuous inhomogeneities. *Journal of Climatology and Applied Meterology*, 26: 1744–1763.

Katz, R. W. 2001. Do weather or climate variables and their impacts have heavy-tailed distributions? In *Proceedings of 13th Symposium on Global Change and Climate Variations* (American Meteorological Society).

Klugman, S., H. Panjer and G. Willmot. 1998. *Loss Models: From Data to Decisions*. Wiley-Interscience.

Kotz, S., N. Balakrishnan and N. Johnson. 1994. *Continuous Multivariate Distributions*. Wiley-Interscience.

Koutsoyiannis, D. 2003. On the appropriateness of the gumbel distribution for modelling extreme rainfall. In *Proceedings of the ESF LESC Exploratory Workshop, Bologna, Italy*.

Leadbetter, R., G. Lindgren and H. Rootzen. 1983. *Extremes and Related Properties of Random Sequences and Processes*. Springer-Verlag.

LeCam, L. 1961. A stochastic description of precipitation. In *Proceedings of the Fourth Berkeley Symposium on Mathematical Statistics and Probability*, 165–186.

Leith, C. 1974. Theoretical skill of Monte Carlo forecasts. *Monthly Weather Review*, 102: 409–418.

Leland, H. E. 1985. Option pricing and replication with transaction costs. *Journal of Finance*, 40: 1283–1301.

Livezey, R. 1999. The evaluation of forecasts. In *Analysis of Climate Variability*, 179–198. Springer.

Lloyd-Hughes, B., and M. Saunders. 2002. Seasonal prediction of European spring precipitation from ENSO and local sea surface temperatures. *International Journal of Climatology*, 22: 1–14.

Mantua, N. 2000. How does the Pacific Decadal Oscillation impact our climate? *The Climate Report*, 1(1).

Markowitz, H. 1952. Portfolio selection. *Journal of Finance*, 7: 77–91.

  (ed.). 1959. *Portfolio Selection: Efficient Diversification of Investments*. Wiley.

Marteau, D., J. Carle, S. Fourneaux, R. Holz and M. Moreno. 2004. *La Gestion du Risque Climatique*. Economica.

Mason, S., L. Goddard, N. Graham, E. Yulaeva, L. Sun and P. Arkin. 1999. The IRI seasonal climate prediction system and the 1997/1998 El Niño event. *Bulletin of the American Meteorological Society*, 80: 1853–1873.

McIntyre, R. 1999. Black–Scholes will do. *Energy & Power Risk Management*, November.

  2000. PAR for the weather course. *Environmental Finance*, April.

Mercurio, F., and T. Vorst. 1996. Option pricing with hedging at fixed trading dates. *Applied Mathematical Finance*, 3: 135–158.

Molteni, F., R. Buizza, T. Palmer and T. Petroliagis. 1996. The new ECMWF ensemble prediction system: methodology validation. *Quarterly Journal of the Royal Meteorological Society*, 122: 73–119.

Moran, P. 1947. Some theorems on time series. *Biometrika*, 34: 281–291.

Moreno, M. 2000. Riding the temp. *Futures and Options World*, November.

  2001a. Rainfall derivatives. *Derivatives Week*, 10(11): 6–7.

  2001b. Weather derivatives. *Derivatives Week*, 10(38): 7–9.

  2003. Weather derivatives hedging and swap illiquidity. *Environmental Finance*, September.

Moreno, M., and O. Roustant. 2002. Modelisation de la temperature: application aux derives climatiques. In *La reassurance, approche technique*, chap. 29. Economica.

Murphy, J., and R. Winkler. 1987. A general framework for forecast verification. *Monthly Weather Review*, 115: 1330–1338.

Mylne, K., C. Woolcock, J. Denholm-Price and R. Darvell. 2002. Operational calibrated probability forecasts from the ECMWF ensemble prediction system: implementation and verification. In *Preprints of the Symposium on Observations, Data Assimilation and Probabilistic Prediction*, 113–118. American Meteorological Society.

Ogryczak, W., and A. Ruszczynski. 1997. *On Stochastic Dominance and Mean-semideviation Models*. Working report no. 43. International Institute for Applied Systems Analysis.

Palmer, T. 2002. The economic value of ensemble forecasts as a tool for risk assessment: from days to decades. *Quarterly Journal of the Royal Meteorological Society*, 128: 747–774.

Pearson, E., and H. Hartley. 1962. *Biometrika Tables for Statisticians*. Cambridge University Press.

Penland, C., and T. Magorian. 1993. Prediction of Niño3 sea surface temperature using linear inverse modelling. *Journal of Climate*, 6: 1067–1076.

Potters, M., J. Bouchaud and D. Sestovic. 2001. Hedged Monte-Carlo: low variance derivative pricing with objective probabilities. *Physica A*, 289: 517–525.

Qian, B., and M. Saunders. 2003. Summer UK temperatures and their link to preceeding Eurasian snow cover, North Atlantic SSTs and the NAO. *Journal of Climate*, 16: 4108–4120.

Rajagopalan, B., and Y. Kushnir. 2000. Causes of year to year variability in temperature extremes in the N.E. U.S. *The Climate Report*, 1(2).

Richardson, D. 2000. Skill and relative economic value of the ECMWF ensemble prediction system. *Quarterly Journal of the Royal Meteorological Society*, 126: 649–668.

Ripley, B. 1987. *Stochastic Simulation*. Wiley.

Rodriguez-Iturbe, I., D. Cox and V. Isham. 1987. Some models for rainfall based on stochastic point processes. *Proceedings of the Royal Society London*, 410: 269–288.

1988. A point process model for rainfall: further developments. *Proceedings of the Royal Society London*, 417: 283–298.

Roulston, M., and L. Smith. 2002. Weather and seaonal forecasting. In *Climate Risk and the Weather Market*, 115–126. Risk Books.

2003. Combining dynamical and statistical ensembles. *Tellus A*, 55: 16–30.

Ruck, T. 2002. Hedging precipitation risk. In *Climate Risk and the Weather Market*, 43–54. Risk Books.

Schönbucher, P. 1993. The feedback effect of hedging in illiquid markets. Master's thesis, Oxford University.

Sharpe, W. 1964. Capital asset prices: a theory of market equilibrium under conditions of risk. *Journal of Finance*, 19: 425–442.

Shorter, J., T. Crawford and R. Boucher. 2002. The accuracy and value of operational seasonal weather forecasts in the weather risk market. In *Climate Risk and the Weather Market*, 151–168. Risk Books.

Silverman, B. 1986. *Density Estimation for Statistics and Data Analysis*. Chapman and Hall.

Smith, L., M. Roulston and J. von Hardenberg. 2001. *End to End Ensemble Forecasting: Towards Evaluating the Economic Value of the Ensemble Prediction System*. Technical report. European Centre for Medium-range Weather Forecasts.

Smith, S. 2002. Weather and climate – measurements and variability. In *Climate Risk and the Weather Market*, 55–72. Risk Books.

Stockdale, T., D. Anderson, J. Alves and M. Balmaseda. 1998. Global seasonal rainfall forecasts using a coupled ocean-atmosphere model. *Nature*, 392: 370–373.

Sutton, R., and M. Allen. 1997. Decadal predictability of North Atlantic sea surface temperature and climate. *Nature*, 388: 563–567.

Swets, J. 1988. Measuring the accuracy of diagnostic systems. *Science*, 240, June: 1285–1293.

Talagrand, O., R. Vautard and B. Strauss. 1997. Evaluation of probabilistic prediction systems. In *Proceedings, ECMWF Workshop on Predictability, 20–22 October 1997*, 1–25. European Centre for Medium-range Weather Forecasts.

Thompson, R. 1998. *Atmospheric Processes and Systems*. Routledge.

Torro, H., V. Meneu and E. Valor. 2001. *Single Factor Stochastic Models with Seasonality applied to Underlying Weather Derivatives Variables.* Technical Report no. 60. European Financial Management Association.

Toth, Z., and E. Kalnay. 1993. Ensemble forecasting at NMC: the generation of perturbations. *Bulletin of the American Meteorological Society*, 74: 2317–2330.

Tsanakas, A., and E. Desli. 2003. Risk measures and theories of choice. *British Actuarial Journal*, 9: 959–991.

Turvey, C. 2001. Weather derivatives for specific event risk in agriculture. *Review of Agricultural Economics*, 23: 333–351.

Vandermarck, P. 2003. Marking to model or to market? *Environmental Finance*, January.

Villani, D., R. Ghigliazza and R. Carmona. 2003. A discrete affair. *Energy Risk*, October.

Wang, S. 1998. Aggregation of correlated risk portfolios: models and algorithms. *Proceedings of the Casualty Actuarial Society*, 85: 848–939.

Wilks, D. 1993. Comparison of three-parameter probability distributions for representing annual extreme and partial duration precipitation series. *Water Resources Research*, 29: 3543–3549.

Wilks, D., and R. Wilby. 1999. The weather generation game: a review of stochastic weather models. *Progress in Physical Geography*, 23: 329–357.

Wilmott, P. 1994. Discrete charms. *Risk*, 7(3): 48–51.

1999. *Derivatives.* Wiley.

Wilmott, P., S. Howison and J. Dewynne. 1995. *The Mathematics of Financial Derivatives.* Cambridge University Press.

Wolfstetter, E. 2000. *Topics in Microeconomics.* Cambridge University Press.

Woo, G. 1999. *The Mathematics of Natural Catastrophes.* Imperial College Press.

Zeng, L., and K. Perry. 2002. Managing a portfolio of weather derivatives. In *Climate Risk and the Weather Market*, 241–264. Risk Books.

Index

static hedging, 117
stochastic dominance, 177, 181, 183
stochastic process
  for equity prices, 242
  for expected index, 100, 234, 255
  for weather swap price, 255
straddle
  expected pay-off example, 314
  expected pay-off for the normal, 310
  greeks example, 332
  greeks for normal, 329
  pay-off definition, 24
  pay-off distribution, 88, 305
  pay-off variance example, 322
  pay-off variance for normal, 320
strangle
  expected pay-off example, 314
  expected pay-off for the normal, 311
  greeks example, 332
  greeks for normal, 330
  pay-off definition, 24
  pay-off distribution, 88, 305
  pay-off variance example, 322
  pay-off variance for normal, 321
strike, 20–25
SVD, *see* singular value decomposition
swap
  expected pay-off example, 314
  expected pay-off for the normal, 308
  greeks example, 332
  greeks for normal, 326
  pay-off definition, 19
  pay-off distribution, 88, 303
  pay-off variance example, 322
  pay-off variance for normal, 316

temperature
  cleaning, 37
  daily modelling, 125
  detrending, 48, 56
  discontinuities, 40
  forecasts, 192
  gap filling, 38
  seasonal cycle, 126
  statistical properties, 129
  trends, 42
  value checking, 39
terminology, 27
theta
  and portfolios, 188
  definition, 95, 99
  interpretation, 107

tick, 20–25
time series modelling, 121, 163
total derivatives, 101
toy model (for the swap price process), 256
trading, 7, 66
transaction costs, 253, 264
trapezium model, 236
trends, 37
  backtesting, 54
  causes, 42
  detrending, 47, 48
  general theory, 292
  sensitivity of models, 52
  spatial structure, 45

uncertainty
  burn analysis, 68
  expected index, 68
  forecasts, 207
  index distribution, 69
  index standard deviation, 69
  option premium, 69
  trends, 52
urbanisation, 43
utility theory, 175, 179, 181, 183

value at risk, 118, 158, 171, 268, 269, 273, 275, 279
VaR, *see* value at risk
VAR (vector autoregressive), 163
VARFIMA, 164
VARMA, 163
vega
  definition, 95, 100
  interpretation, 107
volatility, 100, 233, 236, 242, 250
  and risk loading, 263
  modelling for greeks, 100
  trapezium model, 236

weather derivative (definition), 4
weather forecasts, 192, 221
Weather Risk Management Association, 1
wind farm, 10
WRMA, *see* Weather Risk Management Association

zeta
  definition, 98
  for the normal, 325
  interpretation, 106